THE LEGACY OF THE ENLIGHTENMENT

Series Editor

DARRIN MCMAHON, DARTMOUTH COLLEGE

After a period of some eclipse, the study of intellectual history has enjoyed a broad resurgence in recent years. The Life of Ideas contributes to this revitalization through the study of ideas as they are produced, disseminated, received, and practiced in different historical contexts. The series aims to embed ideas—those that endured, and those once persuasive but now forgotten—in rich and readable cultural histories. Books in this series draw on the latest methods and theories of intellectual history while being written with elegance and élan for a broad audience of readers.

THE LEGACY OF THE ENLIGHTENMENT

Ambivalences of Modernity

Antoine Lilti

Translated by C. Jon Delogu

THE UNIVERSITY OF CHICAGO PRESS
Chicago and London

The University of Chicago Press, Chicago 60637
The University of Chicago Press , London

Published 2025
Printed in the United States of America

34 33 32 31 30 29 28 27 26 25   1 2 3 4 5

ISBN-13: 978-0-226-82061-3 (cloth)
ISBN-13: 978-0-226-82062-0 (ebook)
DOI: https://doi.org/10.7208/chicago/9780226820620.001.0001

Originally published in French as *L'Héritage des Lumières. Ambivalences de la modernité*

The University of Chicago Press gratefully acknowledges the generous support of the France Chicago Center toward the translation and publication of this book.

Publication of this book was supported by translation funding from the École des hautes études en sciences sociales–Centre de Recherches Historiques.

L'ÉCOLE
DES HAUTES
ÉTUDES EN
SCIENCES
SOCIALES

www.centrenationaldulivre.fr

Library of Congress Cataloging-in-Publication Data

Names: Lilti, Antoine, author. Delogu, Christopher Jon, translator.
Title: The legacy of the Enlightenment : ambivalences of modernity / Antoine Lilti ; translated by C. Jon Delogu.
Other titles: Heritage des Lumières. English | Life of ideas.
Description: Chicago : The University of Chicago Press, 2025. | Series: The life of ideas | Includes bibliographical references and index. |
Identifiers: LCCN 2025023506 | ISBN 9780226820613 (cloth) | ISBN 9780226820620 (ebook)
Subjects: LCSH: Enlightenment—Influence. | Philosophy, French—18th century—Influence.
Classification: LCC B802 .L4813 2025 | DDC 194—dc23/eng/20250620
LC record available at https://lccn.loc.gov/2025023506

∞ This paper meets the requirements of ANSI/NISO Z39.48-1992 (Permanence of Paper).

Authorized Representative for EU General Product Safety Regulation (GPSR) queries: **Easy Access System Europe**—Mustamäe tee 50, 10621 Tallinn, Estonia, gpsr.requests @easproject.com
Any other queries: https://press.uchicago.edu/press/contact.html

CONTENTS

PREFACE

Should we abandon the Enlightenment? From a French perspective, the question may seem out of line, even blasphemous. Leading Enlightenment figures are more popular and present than ever in French political discourse and mainstream media—to the point of seemingly incarnating the official ideology of France's Fifth Republic. Of course, this phenomenon is not completely new. The French Revolution had united Voltaire and Rousseau in the Panthéon, and the Third Republic celebrated them once again. Within the national memory and the national education system, the Enlightenment is generally considered the source of all of modernity's leading values: religious tolerance, scientific progress, liberal democracy. In recent years the phenomenon has expanded, but it has also taken an unexpected turn. In a context marked by the 2015 Islamic terrorist attacks in Paris and the assassination of two schoolteachers in 2020 and 2023, and more generally by a profound crisis of political identity, the Enlightenment comes across as a national cultural totem closely linked to specific "Republican values"—notably France's version of secularism known as *laïcité*. As such, Enlightenment figures are constantly being invoked, including by French president Emmanuel Macron, who is regularly pledging his allegiance to them. And yet, even though for more than two centuries they functioned as symbols of progressivism and critical thinking, lately they have been used as part of a discourse of order and authority brandished increasingly by the Right and Far Right as a part of a bulwark against Islamism. Associated with an idea of a specifically French "republican universalism," the Enlightenment has become a political weapon against Muslim religious and cultural practices, but also against demands articulated by other minorities. The Enlightenment against "wokeism"—this is the new narrative that some are trying to impose.

In contrast, others on the left are turning away from the Enlightenment, even though open criticism of it remains discreet. In France it's no trivial pursuit to tamper with icons of the eighteenth century. In the rest of the world, however, Enlightenment figures today are subjected to heated criticism. They are accused en masse of being responsible for all the shortcomings of modernity: the cult of scientific progress that is said to have brought about today's ecological crisis, economic liberalism that is said to be responsible for the excesses of laissez-faire capitalism, and above all the Western domination of the world through colonialism and slavery. Imperialist, racist, and sexist—the Enlightenment figures now strike many as embodying the obsolete ideology of European superiority. Even the notion of universal rights, which seemed to be the Enlightenment's supreme triumph thanks to the American and French Revolutions in the late eighteenth century, is now contested. Some suspect the Enlightenment of being nothing more than a ruse of Western rationalism that sought and still seeks to impose on the entire world the rights of the white man and Western values.

Of course these accusations have, in turn, elicited passionate defenses of the Enlightenment. Harvard psychology professor Steven Pinker wrote a worldwide bestseller, *Enlightenment Now: The Case for Reason, Science, Humanism, and Progress* (2018), in which he affirms that the Enlightenment gave the world peace, prosperity, and progress, and he calls for the struggle to continue in the name of science and freedom. But what Enlightenment figures is he talking about? The scientific optimism and liberal individualism Pinker advocates make for a deformed vision of the Enlightenment, one that leaves out the irony and skepticism that are the source of the particular savor and richness of the Enlightenment as an intellectual movement. Thus, it's not surprising that the book received a cold reception from specialists.

On all sides, among the Enlightenment's adversaries and its defenders, the *Lumières*, as the Enlightenment figures are known in French, have become a sort of password, an all-encompassing concept to name Western modernity either with admiration or hostility, to sacralize it or to tear it down. These excessive and simplifying gestures invariably result in caricatures that bear little relation to the actual texts, debates, and authors of the eighteenth century. Enlightenment-age philosophers in France, Germany, England, and Scotland were not theoreticians of colonialism, nor were they naïve advocates of scientific progress. Some of them wrote vehement criticisms of slavery. Others, such as Voltaire, used irony to subvert overly easy optimism—"the rage to claim that all is well when people are really unwell." The autocritique of European pretentions and the nervousness when confronting the ambivalences of modernity are an integral part of the Enlightenment heritage.

The gap is therefore even wider between, on the one hand, the radical critics and simplistic supporters whose pronouncements are relayed in the media and, on the other, the work of historians of all genders whose writings are more nuanced and meticulous. These careful historians offer an entirely different image of Enlightenment figures and their heritage, one that is pluralist and attentive to contrasts, contradictions, and ambiguities, and sensitive to the social and political context of the eighteenth century. They are also mindful of the many interpretations the Enlightenment has undergone over the past two and half centuries. This is the research that I attempt to assess and interpret in this book in order to get beyond all the caricatures that obstruct our view. While the political debates over the Enlightenment are sometimes narrowly national, the scholarly conversation is invariably international. This book was written, therefore, to engage with the work of many colleagues on both sides of the Atlantic. For this reason, I am happy that it is now available to an English-speaking public. I am grateful to Darrin McMahon, who welcomed the volume into the prestigious collection he directs at the University of Chicago Press, as well as to Dylan Montanari, who oversaw its publication, and to C. Jon Delogu, who provided the English translation.

In the eighteenth century, the Enlightenment was a European and transatlantic phenomenon. Today, a better understanding of what we owe to the Enlightenment is once again a global matter. The Enlightenment heritage is not about the West standing against the rest of the world, as many too easily believe. In Europe and the United States, the "West" that is presumed to have inherited the Enlightenment legacy no longer takes this Enlightenment for granted at a time when it is threatened—to some extent, probably, by the excesses of identity politics and certain decolonization movements, but above all by powerful populist and nationalist movements that weaken the institutions of liberal democracies and call into question the cosmopolitan ideal of the Enlightenment. Elsewhere, whether it's in China, Iran, or Russia, great powers are displaying their deep hostility to all forms of political and intellectual freedom; and yet inside those countries, less visible currents composed of liberal intellectuals, women fighting for their rights, educated urban middle classes, artists, and activists all take inspiration from Enlightenment figures or at any rate from the projects of democratic emancipation that find in local intellectual traditions their own resources.

Defending the Enlightenment, here or there, whether as a threatened heritage or a minority hope, will not happen through transforming it into an argument founded on authority or into a new dogma, and even less by replaying a "clash of civilizations." It will come about instead by rediscovering the Enlightenment's power of invention and its mixture of emancipatory optimism and critical skepticism that remain its great achievement and lesson. To do so, a detour through history is the best path. This is the central claim and practice of this book.

Antoine Lilti (May 2024)

Introduction

Everything Regards Us

After the murderous attack against *Charlie Hebdo* journalists in January 2015, portraits of Voltaire were pasted on Paris walls proclaiming "Je suis Charlie," literally "I am Charlie"—in other words, "I stand with and support *Charlie Hebdo*." Voltaire's *Treatise on Tolerance*, first published in 1763, also sprang to the top of bestseller lists, and many were repeating his famous though doubtfully authentic maxim, "I disapprove of what you say, but I will defend to the death your right to say it." The battle lines seemed clear: freedom of speech versus religious fanaticism, Enlightenment thinkers versus abominable brutes. At the funeral for the *Charlie Hebdo* artist Tignous, the French justice minister at the time, Christiane Taubira, praised "the country of Voltaire and irreverence." After the procession of January 11, 2015, the left-leaning daily *Libération* saluted "the country of Voltaire and Cabu"[1] and the conservative daily *Figaro* entitled its editorial "Voltaire, I Shout Your Name." In truth there were plenty of ambiguities behind any direct line drawn from Voltaire to Charlie, but the gesture was all but unanimous: Voltaire was once again our contemporary. His battles were ours; our battles were his. The light of the Age of Reason was gleaming with white-hot relevance.[2]

In the years since, this mingling of intellectual and political headlines has not subsided. This fact is somewhat surprising if one considers the degree to which Enlightenment figures had dropped from the intellectual and political scene to the point of being hardly noticed at all. This apparent disregard was not out of disrespect; on the contrary: because they had been integrated so completely into the cultural and literary fabric of the country and were part of such a total consensus about national heritage, no one thought of making a formal inventory. For decades the *Persian Letters* (1721), *Candide* (1759), and other classics had served as obligatory secondary-school texts studied in a celebratory mode that made it somewhat difficult to recall that back then the Enlightenment had been a struggle. Of course it was—how could it have been otherwise?—but over time these authors became victims of their success. The oppressive power of the Church was only a distant memory, the prestige of scientific knowledge seemed uncontested, and democracy had unanimous support. The Enlightenment's traditional adversaries, the nostalgic holdouts of old counterrevolutionary thinking, emerged tarnished from the Second World War and their collusion with European fascism. As for the criticisms coming from the Communist left against the "*libertés formelles*" of liberal democracies, they never really damaged the high value accorded to the Lumières—after all, wasn't Marxism itself a direct descendant of progressive Enlightenment thinking? In any case, those criticisms became less and less audible as the red star dimmed. Even the critical theory of the 1960s and 1970s, which seemed for a while to be rattling the foundations of Western reason, appeared now to be falling into line. Michel Foucault left an intellectual testament expressing allegiance to the Lumières, and an older Jacques Derrida was signing manifestos alongside Jürgen Habermas. Indeed, by the end of the twentieth century, with the triumph of liberalism in the groves of academe and of liberal democracies on the grand geopolitical chessboard, the Enlightenment figures had no more adversaries—a new VE day had dawned.

But then the world changed before our eyes. Societies that had considered themselves secular were shocked to witness the return of religion in ways that were highly intolerant and violent. Nationalist, xenophobic Far Right movements reemerged and became politically influential even in traditional bastions of liberal democracy. Europe, forced to look squarely at its colonial past, now hesitates somewhat about declaring its universal mission. The ecological crisis casts doubt on the grand narrative of progress that was founded on the triumph of science and the mastery of nature. In addition, the digital revolution and social media have overturned conventional thinking about a shared public space founded on argued debate. In these conditions, the heritage of the Enlightenment emerges as an essential question with a lot at stake. There have been countless calls to defend that heritage, whether from the academy, in the media, or by politicians. In his election victory speech at the Louvre pyramid on May 7, 2017, President Emmanuel Macron emphatically insisted, "Europe and the world expect us to defend the spirit of the Lumières."[3]

This call to action extends beyond France's borders. In the United States, the election of Donald Trump in 2016 provoked deep concern and renewed interest in the heritage of the Enlightenment and in the traditions and norms of a republic. *New York Times* editorialist David Brooks called for new "Enlightenment heroes" to rise up and combat their reactionary adversaries.[4] Under the banner "Enlightenment Now," Harvard psychologist Steven Pinker used considerable statistical evidence to defend the idea of the continual progress of our societies, which are the direct successors of Enlightenment-era rationalism, and he called for a general extension of those efforts.[5]

Is It Still Possible to Write a History of the Enlightenment?

New Enlightenment heroes versus new villains using "dark arts"—such a simple plot would have the virtue of being clear, but it would also obscure important nuances. In truth, debates inside and outside the academy have been more complex than they appear. For a long time, the Enlightenment's successors were divided into a progressive camp that pledged allegiance to the Lumières and a conservative or even reactionary camp that kept its distance. Starting in the 1970s, several schools of thought positioning themselves on the left denounced the compromised relations between a supposedly enlightened universalism and Western imperialism. They pointed out the perilous side of scientific knowledge and the false pretenses of progress; or, more radically still, they outright rejected various figures of political or economic liberalism. The self-proclaimed inheritors of the Enlightenment thus faced a serious challenge: had their project of autonomy founded on reason degenerated into egocentric individualism? Had it caused the excesses of a cold, calculating world dominated by market fundamentalism, the industrial exploitation of nature, and the imposition of a world order by Western powers? Inversely, others more on the right of the political or intellectual spectrum enthusiastically used Enlightenment heroes to defend the European way of life, fend off all criticism of science and technology, and shunt aside Islam with either suspicions or convictions of its incompatibility with France's secularist values, enshrined as *laïcité*. No observer could deny that these debates contained lots of misunderstandings, fantasy, and some bad faith. They also gave the public conversation a binary format that was both familiar (For or against the Enlightenment—which side are you on?) and strange. Had the Enlightenment heroes who were for so long taken as avatars of emancipation now become conservative monsters?

Historians may feel thrown off-balance or out of sync with this front-page treatment of Enlightenment figures. Their teaching and research, conducted in the calm spaces of university libraries and classrooms, has been trying for thirty years to pluralize the cast of characters and complexify the stories told, and has done so to the point of rendering them almost unrecognizable. The traditional account of a small group of Parisian philosophers wielding their ironic wit and critical faculties to combat religious intolerance and absolutism has been shattered. Now, alongside the French Lumières, though retaining the metaphorical French label, there are Italian Lumières considered more reformist, German Lumières considered erudite and religious, Scottish Lumières considered speculative, conservative English Lumières, as well as Spanish, Portuguese-speaking, Greek, and American Lumières, each with their specific characteristics. More recently, historians have identified specific Lumières currents in outlying colonial territories from Calcutta to Mexico.[6] Nowadays, certain Anglophone historians refuse the term "Enlightenment" in the singular so as not to abusively unify this plural, heterogeneous movement.[7]

Yet this geographical shake-up is nothing compared to the recent radical questioning of formerly settled notions. For those who thought the Lumières were fundamentally hostile to revealed religion—remembering the deism of Voltaire or the atheism of d'Holbach—here are Catholic, Protestant, and Jewish Lumières.[8] Did you think the Enlightenment worshipped reason and science? Specialists now insist on the importance accorded to feelings—and even the presence of esoterism, hermeticism, and the irrational—at the heart of the Enlightenment.[9] What about freedom of speech? It's now reported that Enlightenment thinkers favored keeping it on a short leash, were fairly at ease with censorship, and regularly sought to have the books of their rivals banned.[10] And the rights of man and the universality of the human species? Yes, but when embracing these ideas today one must not forget that the physical anthropology of the Lumières was sometimes tainted with racism. Also, the rights of women were rarely recognized, and their intellectual aspirations were often cast aside, as though science and philosophy were necessarily male endeavors.[11] How about Enlightenment cosmopolitanism and the dreams of perpetual peace? Yes, but the Lumières also paved the way for modern nationalisms and warrior patriotism.[12] Can one at least hold on to their belief in progress, the indestructible optimism that seems to have been the core trait of the eighteenth century? But to do so would be to confuse the Lumières with the later nineteenth century, Voltaire with Monsieur Homais. The Enlightenment philosophers were really always thinking about the problem of evil and the limits of progress.[13]

In addition, the corpus of the great authors has itself changed. Alongside the figures of the scholastic pantheon, important works have been rescued from oblivion, such as the *Religious Ceremonies of the World* by Jean-François Bernard and Bernard Picart, a vast illustrated encyclopedia of religious customs that also reads like a hymn to tolerance.[14] Female authors whose work was for a long time misjudged have received more serious study. Anne Lefebvre Dacier (1645–1720), a translator of Homer, is now grouped with other savants such as the Italian Laura Bassi (1711–1778), the first woman to hold a university chair in physics, and Émilie du Châtelet (1706–1749), who explained the Newtonian system to Voltaire. Historians such as Catherine Macaulay and novelists such as Françoise de Graffigny and Louise de Kéralio have been accorded greater importance, as have uniquely unclassifiable figures such as the Marquise de Lambert and Louise d'Épinay, who both, fifty years apart, wrote about the education of women.[15] The world of the Lumières is no longer the gentlemen's parlor it used to be. In addition, faraway figures, such as the Mexican Jesuit Francisco Clavijero, have contributed to repopulating the intellectual world of the Lumières beyond the usual list of great names. This widening of perspectives, while salutary, also raises new questions. Universalist humanism has been put in question by thirty years of conversations about gender and postcolonial studies. How does one explain that so few of those philosophers, with the notable exception of Condorcet and a few others, ever defended the equality of the sexes, including their comparable intellectual capacities?[16] Can one be a feminist and still stand with the Lumières? And were they a uniquely European bunch? These and other questions challenge earlier universalist assumptions. "Who do the Lumières belong to?" asks Ecuadorian historian Jorge Cañizares-Esguerra.[17] Who today sees themselves in them and therefore claims solidarity with them?

The questions are endless, as one can tell by scrolling through the ever-lengthening bibliography. At the very moment when a certain public is calling out to the Lumières, traditionally conceived as the defenders of reason, tolerance, and freedom against religious obscurantism and political regression, historians seem only able to offer a broken mirror, a picture of the Lumières that is so pluralist as to be ungraspable.

Several prominent historians have taken up the challenge of trying to defend a reunified vision of the Lumières as part of an overtly proselytizing campaign. And yet these enterprises, despite praiseworthy efforts, propose interpretations that are mutually incompatible, thus revealing the absence of consensus and the fragility of any synthesis. Anthony Pagden, for example, praises the moderate cosmopolitanism of the Encyclopedists; Jonathan Israel identifies modernity with radical, materialist, democratic Enlightenment thinkers; John Robertson insists on the rise of political economy; Margaret Jacob on the sciences and Freemasonry; Vincenzo Ferrone on the rights of man. Each one has their leading man who is cast as the best incarnation of the Enlightenment spirit: Jean Le Rond d'Alembert, Baruch Spinoza, David Hume, John Toland, Gaetano Filangieri.[18]

And yet these historians all agree on searching for an intellectual definition of the Enlightenment conceived as a set of values, ideas, canonical texts, and major figures. However, the picture gets complicated as soon as one takes into account the essential contributions of social and cultural historians who since the 1960s have profoundly altered our understanding of the Enlightenment by emphasizing the locations of social interactions (academies, cafés, salons, Masonic lodges); the circulation of books and periodicals; new reading practices; changes in the practice of philosophy as a field of knowledge; or the social and economic changes that accompanied the rise of Enlightenment thinkers. As soon as they are inscribed within the social and political worlds from which they arose—the centuries-old monarchies that no one predicted were about to end, aristocratic societies unsettled by the emergence of capitalism and the new ideal of merit, and the tightening grip of Europe over the world—these figures cease to appear as leaders of a movement defending admirable values but rather become a bit disincarnated.[19] In other words, the historicization did not come without risks. By enlarging the historical context, is there not a chance that one may lose sight of the very nature of an intellectual movement, the consciousness the philosophers had of fighting for ideas? By identifying the Lumières with an ensemble of eighteenth-century changes, even while most of the population remained largely outside the erudite debates of this elite group, doesn't the very notion of singling out this group in the first place lose much of its effectiveness? Pioneering figures of this social and cultural history of the Enlightenment, such as Robert Darnton and Daniel Roche, faced a dilemma: how would it be possible to objectify the Lumières, inscribe them within a past that no longer exists, *and* also hold them up as the inventors of a political project that is still worth defending?[20]

One might think that this dilemma is a version of the classic debate between the history of ideas and social history, between idealism and materialism. Do ideas make history, notably the history of revolutions, or are they the products of social and cultural changes that the historian is tasked with recounting? Historians have often fallen into such chicken-and-egg debates, which are necessarily unsolvable. In the present case, however, the stakes are both more complex and more specific because the very notion of "Lumières" evokes conjointly a universalist philosophical notion and a historicist, case-sensitive approach. Is it more proper to speak of the philosophy of the Enlightenment or of the century of the Enlightenment?

For some, the Enlightenment names an ensemble of values and concepts: freedom of speech, the superiority of reason and critical thinking over faith and tradition, religious tolerance, and an optimistic attitude about the advances of sciences. Even if these values were particularly ascendant in eighteenth-century Europe, they are thought to go beyond that singular context. Their universal reach explains how calls can regularly be made to defend them, to reaffirm them, and to fight for them; whereas no one would think of fighting for the Renaissance, for Romanticism, or for the Belle Époque, despite the nostalgia that one is entitled to feel for those periods. In rather logical fashion, historians of philosophy have extended the period of the Enlightenment to well before the publication of the *Encyclopedia* as a way of marking the superiority of reason over faith. Maimonides (1138–1204), for example, is held up as the representative of the Jewish Lumières of the Middle Ages, and Averroes (1126–1198) as representing the Islamic Lumières of the twelfth century. Looking much later, some wish to develop the hypothesis of Chinese Lumières from the early twentieth century or claim the emergence of an "Islam des Lumières."[21]

For others, however, the Enlightenment cannot be reduced to a timeless struggle of reason over faith and progress over tradition. It can only be understood, they say, against the backdrop of the historical transformations of the time affecting the societies of western parts of Europe in the eighteenth century: the crisis of absolute monarchies, the advances of science and scientific method and techniques, the beginnings of the industrial revolution (and especially the increase in individual consumption), the development of print culture, and the growth of large-scale international trade. From this point of view, the Enlightenment thinkers are deeply inscribed within their time to the point that they are its main defining feature. People speak therefore of the European Enlightenment, the French Enlightenment, and the Atlantic Enlightenment.

Despite all that distinguishes and sometimes opposes them, these two conceptions cannot be totally disassociated from each other. The Enlightenment thinkers, as a philosophical category, are profoundly inscribed within their historical context. All attempts to generalize their significance and consequences have never succeeded in erasing the rootedness in eighteenth-century European history. These attempts have probably failed because the first philosophers who tried to define Enlightenment thinkers, Immanuel Kant and especially Georg Hegel, saw in them a particular moment in human history. Even Ernst Cassirer, hardly someone suspected of excessive historicism, circumscribed his masterwork *The Philosophy of the Enlightenment* around authors of the eighteenth century.[22]

Inversely, as a historical category, the Enlightenment continues to be the vehicle for a philosophical and political heritage to be defended or contested, much more so than any other period, with the possible exception of the French Revolution—which, at least in French historiography, is customarily linked to it anyway. In 1962, Alphonse Dupront began his Sorbonne University course on the Enlightenment with these words: "We are the sons of the French 'intelligentsia' of the second half of the eighteenth century. . . . The most important thing about this temporal proximity of descendance is a direct continuity which means this eighteenth century is still among us and working through us."[23] There are no better words to get across the idea that speaking of the "Lumières" to designate the eighteenth century is to recognize this persistent presence, to claim one's descendance from it, and own it as one's intellectual heritage. More recently, Tzvetan Todorov affirmed that the spirit of the Enlightenment was universal even if the Enlightenment thinkers belonged to the past: "We are all children of the Enlightenment thinkers, even when we are attacking them."[24] Anthony Pagden entitled his synthesis of the subject *The Enlightenment and Why It Still Matters*, underscoring that the heritage of the Lumières remains an essential trait of modern thinking: "If we regard ourselves as ourselves modern, if we are forward-thinking, if we are tolerant and generally open-minded . . . , then we tend to think of ourselves as *enlightened*."[25] All of these historians were open about their goal: to defend the Lumières as both a philosophical and political ideal when facing new challenges launched against them.

More explicitly still, a large exhibition organized in 2006 at France's national library was entitled "Lumières! A Heritage for Tomorrow." Its organizers stated directly that they were aiming to find in the eighteenth century a source of inspiration and hope after the terrorist attacks of September 11, 2001. The "spectacle of a world still smoke-filled after the collapse of the towers" had provoked a reemergence of the struggles of the eighteenth century and required "restoring to the Lumières their full virtue of forceful inspiration." The documents presented in the exhibition were certainly an inheritance, but they were to be an active inheritance to produce salutary political and moral effects. They were not to remain simple objects of study but were, rather, to have their spiritual power released: "The purpose of all these eighteenth century treasures assembled here is to recall the intellectual and moral foundation handed down to us, to rejuvenate our critical faculties, and to bring these prestigious documents out of the ivory tower of erudition by offering them up for examination in our times, to enlighten us and guide our actions."[26]

The entire question is there: if these eighteenth-century documents are considered to carry in themselves political and moral virtue, what is the role of historical research? It is pointless to criticize this rhetoric of "treasure" out of a preference for the rules of historic objectivity or some methodological good hygiene. To do so would be to miss the crucial issue: the Enlightenment in this construction is a philosophical and political concept; it constitutes the way we designate the origin story of European modernity, by inscribing it within the cultural transformations of the eighteenth century. From the start, the definition of the Enlightenment was a political and polemical crux—a heritage to be combatted or celebrated. Its adversaries never ceased denouncing it, whereas the revolutionaries conferred on it a retrospective coherence.[27] Later, the notion was once again at the center of twentieth-century philosophical and political debates, such as those between Ernst Cassirer and Martin Heidegger at Davos in 1929, or those found in the early work on Diderot by Franco Venturi, a militant antifascist in exile in Paris who later became one of the great historians of the Enlightenment. After World War II, the Enlightenment thinkers were both consecrated as central to the intellectual foundations of the free world and denounced, sometimes vigorously, for their supposed cult of instrumental reason or their compromising positions in relation to European colonialism.[28]

The transformation of the Enlightenment into a historiographical concept happened late and never totally.[29] One must therefore hold both ends of the string: keeping in mind the doctrinal plurality of the Enlightenment, its inscription within a specific moment of European history, but also accepting the idea that the Enlightenment does not exist as a historical object other than as successive reformulations that reactivate what's at stake in it. It is impossible to fully objectify the "Lumières" thinkers and place them at a distance, in a faraway past about which one might speak with cold detachment. One cannot easily break "these circles where the ideology of the Enlightenment repeats itself endlessly in a language that has not exhausted its virtuality," as Georges Benrekassa characterized the binds he sought to leave behind.[30] Speaking of the Enlightenment, rather than of the eighteenth century, is to seek to understand a tradition that we cannot escape, whether it be to stand with it or oppose it. This is no small paradox. The Enlightenment thinkers who wanted to break with the authority of tradition have themselves become central to an argument of authority and closely associated with a corpus of canonical works that have deeply stamped all of Western culture. More than with other objects and periods, historians must renounce any feint of objectivity and all facades of impartiality. They have no choice but to accept the hermeneutic relationship that links them to the Enlightenment, and to recognize in it a founding narrative that they may discuss and even criticize but which they cannot entirely sidestep. All history is written in the present, in a specific place. That's obvious. It is the product of the desires, worries, and questions that historians project onto it and of the numerous mediations that link them to the past.[31] This fact, however obvious, is particularly forceful in the case of those who study the Enlightenment.

Posing the question in these terms, that is, with a hermeneutic perspective, allows one to escape from a false dilemma that would force one to choose between an essentialist conception of the Enlightenment thinkers as endowed with a univocal content and a nominalist conception that sees in them only a retrospective construction open to all manner of appropriations. However, the Enlightenment is neither a coherent doctrine nor a fallacious myth but is instead the reflexive narrative gesture by which, starting in the eighteenth century, numerous authors tried to define the novelty of their time. Collectively, these authors name a conflicted intellectual space in which learned individuals both thought about the experience of modernity and fought to deepen and orient it. Whether one considers the ambivalences of individual autonomy, the potential and dangers of the exploitation of the environment, or the autonomizing of the market system, linking the Enlightenment thinkers to a single unique position is impossible. On the contrary, they distinguish themselves by the intensity of their contradictory, critical debates. One finds among them both the seeds of technology-loving and number-crunching rationalist optimism and the beginnings of a worried reflexivity, a precocious environmental awareness, and a critique of political economy.[32]

If Enlightenment thinkers have acquired and retained such importance, they have done so not only because of the persistence and resurgence of intellectual and political debates that they inaugurated but also because they present themselves from the start in a profoundly historical and reflexive form. This claim may seem surprising. Isn't the birth of history as a professional discipline generally seen as happening in the nineteenth century? And were not the eighteenth-century philosophers, on the contrary, abstract thinkers lacking any real sense of history? False. The overwhelming majority of Lumières authors, despite their differences, conceived of man as a historical being whose customs and habits, beliefs, and forms of social and political organization vary over time. From Montesquieu to Adam Smith, from Hume to Diderot, all were seeking to explore this historicity either through narrative or analytical approaches. In freeing themselves from both Christian providential history and the edifying history of the Humanists, the great Enlightenment-era historians such as William Robertson, Edward Gibbon, and Johann Christoph Gatterer were striving to grapple with the birth of the modern world and the specific role of Europe in that creation. Before it became an energized movement, the Enlightenment was first a set of narratives that took up the idea of a founding rupture with the past, notably with the so-called Dark Ages of the medieval period, but also in a more subtle way with the model handed down from antiquity. This historical and reflexive gesture takes shape in what became known as the quarrel between the ancients and the moderns, which developed a reflection on the temporality of modernity.[33] The Enlightenment thinkers added a more elaborate reflection on history as a process, and this reflection resulted in debates about "civilization"—the passage from barbarous manners to more codified societies—that became an organizing principle of historical thinking in the eighteenth century.

In this narrative, the metaphor of lights—*lumières*—became central. The word, in the plural and always spelled lowercase, did not designate a school of thought but rather all types of useful knowledge and the capacity for good judgment. The metaphor of light as meaning truth was not new; it had very old religious roots (divine light) and in philosophy as well (the natural light of reason). Using it now in the plural form marked a turning point: truth was not revealed, nor was it the fruit of individual and solitary ratiocination; it was now the result of collective efforts, the accumulation of knowledge, and the progress of critical faculties. Capacity for discernment is a properly human ability that is both individual because it derives from reason and social because it implies that each person builds on established available knowledge. In the second half of the century, especially in France, the term *lumières* becomes omnipresent and commonplace, almost a slogan.[34] The progress of these "lumières" is evaluated, their dissemination is advocated, their disappearance is worried over. The truth is no longer revealed by itself; it is incumbent on the philosophers to undo prejudices and spread "the lights." In Germany, the new term *Aufklärung* would extend the evolution of the metaphor and make clearer still the idea of a collective process and the responsibility of an enlightened elite. It would take another century before these terms became historiographical categories. But already the debates they elicited signaled the beginning of a historical consciousness: the conviction that cumulative advances are possible and that they rely on collective efforts of intellectual emancipation—the "revolution of minds," as Voltaire would often say. While one must not exaggerate the notion of a rupture nor accord too much credit to how these new philosophers were proclaiming the advent of a new "enlightened century," it remains nonetheless clear that the men and women of the Enlightenment were very often convinced that they were living in a new era. This conviction, which was accompanied by exaltation but also countervailing doubts and irony, explains the multiplication of historical diagnostics, intellectual genealogies, and philosophical prophesies that regularly occur in publications of that self-consciously special century.

"Everything Matters to Us"

If demonstrators in January 2015 naturally turned to Voltaire, they did so because the twenty-first-century fight against religious fanaticism seemed to require the author of the *Treatise on Tolerance.* But there's more to it.

Montesquieu is too moderate, Kant too abstract, Newton too scientific, Hume too much a philosopher, Smith too much an economist, Beccaria too much a judge, Rousseau too singular, Jefferson too political, Madame de Staël too literary. Voltaire is the symbol of the combat for tolerance and against injustice. His name evokes lightness, gaiety, and an infinite abundance of intellectual dexterity. He also incarnates the limitations of the Enlightenment that are often denounced: an undeniable social and political conservatism, a pronounced taste for enlightened despots, questionable positions about a hierarchy of races, and a certain superficiality, as though Voltairean irony lacked depth or any sensitivity for complexity and the tragic. And yet it is to Voltaire that people turn when the task is reaffirming the heritage of the Enlightenment. The revolutionary leaders of 1791 were already doing so when they ceremoniously transported his remains to the Panthéon. The leaders of the Third Republic also turned to Voltaire in 1878 with a grand commemoration of the centenary of his death. Public, "engaged" intellectuals turned to Voltaire throughout the twentieth century and on into recent times—including that of the bruised and shaken Republic of 2015.[35]

Voltaire is not only the slayer of fanaticism and the defender of Jean Calas. He is also the author of an important body of historical work—sadly too often neglected. *The Age of Louis XIV* is well known, even if it is rarely read today. People forget sometimes that Voltaire devoted many years to writing a universal history that was a success across Europe. His *Essay on Universal History, the Manners, and Spirit of Nations* (1756) was an ambitious story of the world that Voltaire revised and enlarged throughout his life.

As early as 1742, he was publishing short *Reflections on History* with his characteristic verve and taste for polemic when going after ancient history. In contrast to compilations of fables and unverifiable anecdotes, he offered up serious, "useful" history composed in a "philosophical spirit." And this history could only begin at "the end of the fifteenth century" when the invention of the printing press made available more and more reliable sources. The world then experienced a profound upheaval linked to the discovery and European conquest of the Americas, to the Protestant Reformation, and to the emergence of a new European political order: "We subjugate a new world and our own is completely different."[36] Of course, Voltaire was not the first to oppose modern times and medieval times, but unlike the Renaissance humanists, he was not at all interested in reconnecting with antiquity. On the contrary, he affirmed a radical and definitive break with it, and he concentrated instead on a more recent past whose effects were still being felt. History, as he saw it, was the discipline that would allow one to think about what had happened to Europe and the world since this inaugural rupture. It must not be confused with the collection of curious or edifying facts from the past. Leaving aside the pleasures of fiction, history was to propose useful knowledge about the transformations that had given rise to the modern world.

> This is the history that every man must know . . . Everything matters to us, everything is made for us: the silver on which we take our meals, our furniture, our needs, our new pleasures, everything makes us recall every day that the Americas and the Great Indies, and therefore every part of the whole world, have been united for the past two and half centuries by the industry of our ancestors. We cannot take a step without being reminded of the change that has since occurred in the world.[37]

Because this history is radically presentist, it implies the affirmation of a "we" [*nous*]. The history that must be learned is that which "matters to us." The identical quality of the views and interests that link Voltaire to his reader goes without saying. From the start it is considered obvious and directly related to a historical situation: that of enlightened Europeans with a taste for critical judgment and "serious business."

Behind Voltaire's lapidary pronouncements, we recognize, as though it were being enlarged with a magnifying glass, a conception of history that is familiar to us. We see the care given to distinguishing between serious history on the one hand and tales and legends on the other by relying on trustworthy documents; the rejection of antiquarian erudition in favor of understanding the effects of the past on the present; and the wish to understand the social, cultural, and political transformations that brought the modern world into being. History is no longer reduced to a series of proper names, kings and dynasties, and edifying tales. Instead, it seeks to nourish a total understanding of the world as it has come down to the historian. It is in this light that one can understand the primary sense of that formula with the ring of a motto: "Everything regards us." Everything makes history as soon as one knows how to integrate it within a critical and reflexive meditation on the present.

But Voltaire's confident tone here is also disconcerting. Although we recognize in his project the beginnings of a critical, ambitious, global history, it is difficult to go along with his conviction that "everything is made *for* us," if he means that the history of the world naturally converges to satisfy the needs and pleasures of Europeans. We hear in this declaration the arrogance of that time, the good conscience of the colonizer, the jubilation of the consumer—in short, that whole naïve modern attitude that we have learned to consider suspect. The heightened interdependence of various parts of the world is described as an entirely positive development for which satisfied Europeans needed only to applaud themselves, with an extra ovation for the work of their forebears. One can hear in this passage echoes of texts written a few years earlier, *Le Mondain* [The Worldly Man] and *L'Apologie du luxe* [In Praise of Luxury], where Voltaire extols the effects of "human industry" and the pleasures of abundance. One finds the same vocabulary, the same praise of commerce as having "united both hemispheres" by permitting the circulation of goods and merchandise. To the criticisms of luxury, notably from Christian sources, Voltaire was already pushing back with a celebration of happy globalism. ("The entire universe has worked for you/ So that in peace, in your happy anger/ You insulted, pious bilious one/ To the whole world, exhausted to please you.") This evocation of a world exhausted was not an invitation to rise up against European exploitation of natural resources and colonial labor, but rather to enjoy it, to profit without ingratitude from Arabian coffee, Potosí silver, and Chinese porcelain. The essential thing for Voltaire was to counter the notion of divine providence with the active role of industry and commerce. Fascinated by the English model with its alliance of science and commerce, he chose to see creature comforts as the fruits of a serious spirit. Of course, hidden behind this apology for the refined life obtained by global commerce and the accumulation of wealth are all the injustices and acts of violence that accompanied this first phase of globalization.

Does the myopia and the silence discredit Voltaire's intellectual enterprise? Must one chant the criticism of the Lumières as awful colonialists? No, because this short text from 1742 is far from being the author's last word. The desire to know and understand was the start of a more critical evaluation of the state of the world. His *Essay on Manners* offers proof. From the start, Voltaire highlights the respectful old age and grandeur of so-called oriental civilizations, especially those of China and India. His purpose is to criticize the Christian providentialist history of Bossuet, which claims universal status while "forgetting about three quarters of the globe."[38] He also aims to question Europe's place in the history of the world. Voltaire returns to this question many times. His interest in China and India, and in the grandeur and the age of their civilizations, is sincere. He enacts a new relation to the world, one emancipated from the Christian perspective and its Biblical chronology.[39]

The colonial history of Europe is also reinterpreted in a way that is increasingly critical. The discovery of America, though called "the biggest event of our world," is also described as "disastrous for its inhabitants, and sometimes for the conquerors themselves."[40] Relying on the *Short Account of the Destruction of the Indies* of Bartolomé de Las Casas published two centuries earlier, Voltaire denounces the "carnage" provoked by the conquest in terms that convey his increasing discomfort: "this mixture of grandeur and cruelty surprises and outrages. Too many horrors dishonor the great actions of those who vanquished America."[41] In the 1760s, other texts accentuate the criticism of European colonialism in America. There is no longer any ambivalence about Voltaire's judgment: the conquest was a "crime" marked by "devastation."

> In this accounting of so many horrors, let us place first the twelve million men destroyed across the vast continent of the new world. Alongside all others this banishment is like the scorching of half the earth compared to that of a few villages. Never has the globe known more horrible or more general devastation, and never has a crime been better proven.[42]

Amidst all the cruelties, one question progressively and pointedly emerged at the end of the 1750s: slavery. In a chapter added in 1761 to his *Essay on Manners*, Voltaire specifically mentions the slaves in Saint-Domingue "who abbreviate their lives to flatter our new appetites by fulfilling our new needs that our fathers did not know." Here the subject is no longer the crimes of sixteenth-century Spanish conquistadors but the situation of slaves in French colonies in Voltaire's day. While twenty years earlier he had rejoiced about benefitting from a number of exotic products thanks to "the industry of our fathers," now Voltaire denounces the needs unknown to previous generations that force his contemporaries "to make men perish." The inhuman treatment inflicted on slaves reveals the hypocrisy of the missionaries but also of the administrators and Voltaire's fellow philosophers: "After that, we dare speak of rights of man!" Was cosmopolitan humanism nothing but make-believe?

The description of cruel punishments is reminiscent of the famous chapter in *Candide* (1759) where the hero meets a slave from Suriname dressed in rags and missing a leg and an arm that were cut off by his master: "Clothing is given to us twice a year: that means a pair of blue shorts. When we're working in the sugar mills and the grinding wheel catches a finger, they cut off a hand. When we try to escape, they cut off a leg. Both things have happened to me. This is what it costs, supplying you Europeans with sugar."[43]

The irony in the last line is all the more biting with the matter-of-fact delivery and the abrupt pronoun shift from *we* and *me* to *you* that alters the perspective. The light satisfaction Voltaire expressed in earlier texts gives way here to a sharp accusation that enjoins Europeans to face their responsibilities. The sugar consumed in Europe is no longer considered a blessing of global trade but rather as the product of slave labor that comes at the cost of maiming. Instead of the formerly triumphant "we," there is the accusatory "you"; and the easy European confidence gets shaken by this sudden apostrophe. Though in a fictional mode and perhaps insufficient, this effort to conceive of the point of view of the other introduces a sliver of bad conscience, of culpability, or at least of responsibility. The gesture falls short of enlarging the "we" to include the slaves themselves, and therefore the cosmopolitanism remains incomplete, but it is an opening toward a possible reappraisal. As the receivers of the slave's tale, Europeans are constrained to see themselves from his perspective. They can no longer ignore that their prosperity has a human cost that entirely contradicts their humanist principles. The fate of slaves must also be faced and matter to them [. . . *les regarde*].

Voltaire was not the only one conscious of this culpability. Some months earlier, in his *Essays on the Mind*, Helvétius denounced slavery and commented, "One must concede that no barrel of sugar arrives in Europe that is not stained with human blood. Yet how many men, seeing the wrongs caused by the culture and exportation of this commodity, would refuse to do without it and would not renounce a pleasure bought with the tears and death of so many unfortunate souls. Let us turn our eyes from such a sorrowful spectacle that casts so much shame and horror on humanity."[44] The conclusion sheds light, though not without ambiguity, on the hypocrisy of Europeans who prefer not to see or know so that they can continue to consume in utter tranquility while flattering themselves as humane and enlightened.

Candide on the other hand does not turn away. The sight of the mutilated slave unsettles him and brings tears to his eyes:

> "O Pangloss," exclaimed Candide. "You never imagined such an abomination. If this truly happened, I have no choice but to abandon your optimism."
>
> "What's optimism?" asked Cacambo.
>
> "Lord help me," said Candide, "it's the madness of insisting that everything is good when it's bad." And he shed tears while looking at his negro.[45]

The end of this well-known tale recommends turning back toward a small, friendly community. The famous incitement that we should "cultivate our garden" does not only name a practical, minimalist wisdom in opposition to the metaphysics of Pangloss; it also invites one to renounce the world's riches (the sheep and gold of Eldorado) and to only consume simple foods produced locally.

Of course, the limitations of this critique of slavery and colonization are deafening. Voltaire is content to make the Suriname slave be one episode among many disorders of the world, and he denounces the bad treatment of slaves more than the principle of slavery itself. It's easy to find incriminating evidence to mount a case against Voltaire and his moderation, and even to attack him for holding racist prejudices.[46] But the essential point lies elsewhere, namely in the fact that his evolution demonstrates the shake-up that results mid-century as European thinking becomes conscious of a new relation to the world. One sees the first hints of that consciousness in Montesquieu's ironic tone about slavery, and this critique would widen in the following generation and become crucial by the end of the century. A similar evolution took place across all of Europe. Within the space of a few decades, Enlightenment optimism was dimmed by a veil of worry brought on by a growing consciousness of Europe's responsibility and the possible excesses of civilization. In a context marked by the Seven Years' War and colonial rivalries in the Americas and India, not even the most ardent optimists could remain carefree about the direction the world was taking. Voltaire gave a particular form to that anxiety that comes through in the writing itself. All the ironic formulas and tonal changes convey the contradictions and ambivalences working through Enlightenment thinking.[47]

Keeping this evolution in mind, we can read differently the "*tout nous regarde*" proclaimed with pride by the philosopher meditating on history. "All is made for us," he added. However, this assurance that the world is an ensemble of provisions gets upended over time. Everything matters to us because everything concerns us: we are not just the beneficiaries of this new world order; we didn't just inherit, thanks to our forefathers' industry, a unified globe; we are also the agents of this change, and we ought to look directly at the consequences of the new and superfluous "needs" we have created. Diderot and others will go further still. But that Voltaire, he who once praised without reservation the union of the two hemispheres thanks to the blessings of trade, would later introduce this scruple of bad conscience says a lot about the tensions roiling through the Enlightenment thinkers as soon as it became necessary for them to formulate their considered judgment about the benefits of conquest. *Tout nous regarde* is something that we, too, now hear a bit differently. Everything concerns us; everything makes history—fine. But we also hear in that declaration a sense that would have been foreign to Voltaire or that he could barely glimpse: namely, the idea of a great responsibility that we in turn have inherited. Everything concerns us. Everything obliges us.

What Heritage?

It is perhaps clear by now that two convictions guide the thinking pursued in this book. The first is that the Enlightenment is neither a philosophical doctrine nor a coherent ensemble of ideas and values; nor is it a reform program. Rather, it is a polyphonic and deeply reflexive intellectual movement whose tensions and cracks mark what's at stake in the emergence of the modern world. We shall examine two cruxes in particular: the relationship of Europe to the world and the new figures of the public that emerge. Examining the first crux requires questioning not only Enlightenment universalism and its contradictions but also the limits of certain "global-history" approaches that, in seeking to unburden the Enlightenment of its Eurocentric dimension, risk diluting its significance. Analyzing the second crux requires us to investigate what remains the central core of the Enlightenment, namely its intellectual activism, and thus to think about the political efficacy of Enlightenment writings. The struggle is literary as much as it is conceptual. Choices of format, style, and genre matter. And the struggle does not operate solely on a philosophical plane but in a touchy public space shaped by the press, novels, and scandals. Emotions occupy as much space as arguments. How is this new public to be addressed? How might one enlighten it?

Other choices would have been possible, and other themes will be evoked more obliquely. But these two cruxes are the foci whose sum encompasses all that's at stake in globalization and mediatization—two major sets of changes that continue to influence our situation and moment in history and about which it's best not to toss off overly simple responses. This book mainly rests on the second conviction, namely that what holds the "Lumières"—plural—together as a singular historic object, distinct from "eighteenth-century philosophy," is the need we have to constantly return to the primal scene of the hopes and fears raised by modernity. If there is no historical object outside the historiographical gesture that renews its relationship to the current moment, one might as well perform that gesture openly and thoroughly.

We are not condemned to give up the heritage of the Enlightenment. However, we ought to take it on as a heritage that is both local and plural—not as a rationalist, universalist credo to be defended against its enemies but as the inaugural intuition of a critical relation of a society with itself. Holding on to the heritage of the Enlightenment implies, therefore, a necessary reflection on the contours of who "we" are who claim this heritage, on who is affirming this filiation and the notion that "everything regards us." Enlightenment universalism today can only be a way to render it habitable for those who wish to subscribe to it. Doing so implies embracing its polyphony, not silencing the dissonances, and it requires us to allow ambivalences and contradictions to receive more attention than dogmatic proclamations. The dialogism of the Enlightenment thinkers is also what allows an expansion of the "we" to make it more hospitable or at least loosen its uncritical self-evidence. Enlightenment authors, who were for the most part European men, tried to integrate other voices, other discourses, other points of view: those of women, indigenous peoples, even slaves in the case of the most ambitious. The attempts were incomplete, sometimes dubious, and not without contradictions, but their very existence makes this heritage open to multiple appropriations. Starting at the end of the century, Olympe de Gouges and Mary Wollstonecraft would use the ideas and words of Enlightenment authors to call for equal rights. The African Olaudah Equiano, a former enslaved person, became a notable figure in the abolitionist movement and embraced the Christian humanism of the English Lumières.[48]

The chapters that follow are divided into three groups. The first opens with a reflection on the contributions and limitations of postcolonial criticism and then extends more broadly to the question of Enlightenment universalism. The latter is one of its most attractive aspects but also one of the most contested. After setting out the terms of the contemporary debate, we examine the fortunes of the notion of "civilization" that was for so long a focal point for what's at stake—from the historical and philosophical thinking of the Lumières to the social sciences of the twentieth century. For two hundred years, from Voltaire to Braudel and passing through the writings of Volney, Condorcet, Guizot, and Lucien Febvre, the idea of "civilization" has been the inescapable way to articulate the universalist horizon of the equal dignity of the human species with a more-or-less-assumed Eurocentric bias. Following a few instances of how the idea gets elaborated and the difficulties it raises will serve as an efficient introduction to the complexities of the Enlightenment that get articulated differently, case by case, around scientific ambition, philosophical theorization, and political combat.

The second group takes a wider perspective to ask about the relationship between Enlightenment thinkers and the notion of modernity. Many of the important historiographical debates of the last twenty years—about public space, the birth of a consumer society, and radical Enlightenment figures—are reexamined in these chapters. We will also consider the nature of the operations that allow one to think holistically about the sociological transformations of modernity and the theoretical heritage of the Enlightenment. The conviction at the center of these chapters and indeed throughout the whole book is that the old opposition between intellectual history and social history is obsolete.

In the third part of the book, I return to the political question of the Enlightenment as a militant pedagogical movement roiled by its own doubts as it confronts the transformations of public spaces and information spaces. The optimism so often attributed to the Enlightenment does not tell the whole story. The emancipator's ideal runs up against the challenges for expressing a discourse of truth. How does one get heard when there are so many weak books, journals, and rumors? Can one enlighten a public against their will? On what grounds can an intellectual claim to hold privileged access to the truth? How does one counteract the charlatanism that abuses the public's trust by promising illusory remedies? These questions, so familiar in our times, were already the substance of the interrogations, hopes, and occasionally the discouragement of Enlightenment philosophers.

Every historiographical project is situated in time and space, and mine is no exception. It is anchored to a particular historical moment during which the presumed certainties inherited from the Enlightenment era are the focus of bitter debates. But it is also a part of a personal intellectual journey. I felt the need to review and assess many years of work on Enlightenment figures, including reworking previously published texts to give them a new form, one sometimes significantly different because now taking into account other, previously unpublished work. My hope is that taken together the whole can be read as the product of a long-range study that offers a coherent picture of the stakes of the Enlightenment. Of course, this picture is organized around my preferred questions and objects of study. The reader will notice that even if Kant, Robertson, Swift, Hume, Franklin, Spinoza, and many others do appear in these pages, most of the examples studied belong to the French Enlightenment with which I am most familiar. Nevertheless, I will on occasion point out that the positions I advance are more widely applicable due to the centrality enjoyed by French culture at the time but also because most of the debates were unfolding on a Europe-wide scale. The Enlightenment thinkers were diverse, but that diversity was only marginally distributed according to national borders.

It should be clear by now that one will not find in this book a unified history of the Enlightenment but rather an attempt to tie together an array of recent historiographical debates. It shall be a rereading of classic and less well-known texts, and it will offer a description of social and cultural transformations. If, as I believe, historiographical reflexivity is the entryway to a properly critical approach to the past, we shall see new stakes and new questions emerging progressively in a constant back-and-forth movement between our contemporary concerns and the texts of the eighteenth century. I hope in this way to contribute to a better understanding of what the legacy and heritage of the Enlightenment can mean today.

PART I

Universalism

Europe has entered into a deep crisis. Uncertain about both its history and its destiny, frightened by masses of immigrants at its door, unsettled by its critique of its own institutions, Europe reminisces with a mixture of envy and astonishment about the days when it carried itself confidently, convinced of its grandeur and superiority. For a half century, those most enthusiastic about the European Union have searched in vain among the Enlightenment luminaries for a supplementary historical soul, a golden age of European cosmopolitanism to latch onto.[1] Nothing has fit the bill. The post-national project of a democratic Europe remains abstract and incapable of winning the allegiance of its constituent peoples. Should one blame the lack of realism of technocratic elites? The persistence of nationalisms? Or is it the new geopolitical setup that bumped Europe from its former dominant position and disrupted its sense of history?

The affirmation of Europe's destiny, its consciousness of itself, dates from the eighteenth century. Of course, the continent existed before then, and there are good arguments for claiming Europe was born in the Middle Ages.[2] And yet, the idea that Europe is the author of its own history was only able to emerge out of the ruins of Christianity. This notion was the credo of the Enlightenment intellectuals. This meditation on Europe—its history, its laws, its internal dynamics—was accompanied by much outward-facing activity, an unprecedented frenzy of global exploration and new knowledge.

Of course, Europe set out to discover the world long before the scholarly expeditions of the eighteenth century got going. In medieval times, commercial links already existed between Europe and the Muslim world and even with Asia. During the Renaissance, its reach widened further. Soon, conquistadors and missionaries had encircled the globe from Mexico to Peking.[3] However, nothing compared to the immense intellectual curiosity that would run wild in the eighteenth century. Voyages multiplied and knowledge expanded enormously in the natural sciences, geography, and ethnography.[4] Of particular note, of course, were the major expeditions of La Condamine to Peru, Bougainville and Cook in the Pacific, and Carsten Niebuhr in the Middle East. But there were also the individual journeys of Anquetil-Duperron to India, James Bruce to the source of the Nile, and Volney in Egypt and Syria. Also ever more numerous were the new books offering a wealth of knowledge to a curious public about faraway populations and cultures. Even Asia, for long so mysterious, seemed to be revealing all its secrets. Starting around 1750, the multitalented author Nicolas Lenglet-Dufresnoy marveled at the stories recounted by Jesuit missionaries: "We can now say that we know China in as much detail and as accurately as we know France or the other states of Europe."[5] In the following decades, India would also become known, especially after the conquest of Bengal by the British in 1759. The century concluded with two major events: to the west, Humboldt's expedition across the Americas (1799–1804), which would revolutionize the fields of biology and geography; and to the east, Napoleon's campaign in Egypt (1798–1801), which was both a military invasion and an intense labor of scientific discovery and inventory.

For a long time, Europeans were the ones credited with amassing all this new knowledge. Enlightenment universalism was considered justified on account of its scientific curiosity, so different from both the cruelties of the Spanish conquest in the Americas and the colonial abuses in Asia and Africa in the nineteenth and twentieth centuries. The Enlightenment appeared to be the virtuous century of a true humanism, one acknowledging human diversity while retaining a universalist horizon. Did not Montesquieu let Persians be the ones to point out the failings of European society? And did Rousseau not formulate a vast project of philosophical anthropology inviting the discovery and examination of all human ways of life on the planet?

This enchanted vision of the Enlightenment was triumphant so long as Europe was the world's dominant power and could flatter itself as being the munificent bestower of *civilization*—which was understood to mean its own. This vision was seriously questioned inside and outside Europe during the geopolitical and intellectual shake-up that intensified after 1945. With decolonization and the emergence of countries from the Global South onto the international scene, the West had to tone things down. Europe found itself under indictment. Its self-assurance, its history, its great authors were all put through the wringer. Its colonial past was vigorously contested, as were on a more general level the universalist pretensions, as they were now called, of Western thinking.

In a way, the denunciation of Eurocentrism opened a third phase in the criticism of the Enlightenment. The first, conservative and reactionary, was organized around a defense of tradition and religion. Present from the start in the eighteenth century, these criticisms were responding to the boldness and innovations of Enlightenment philosophers and were fueled by Christian apologists and later by a rejection of the Revolution and liberal modernity. Against reason, the Enlightenment's adversaries held up faith; instead of progress, they valued tradition; rather than the individual, they preferred family and a hierarchical social order. In essence, the counter-Enlightenment melded with the counter-Revolution. A second period of criticism developed at the end of World War II. It consisted of a denunciation of the abuses of reason, the coldness of technology, utopian prophesy, and the excesses of science. Its manifesto came from Marxist German intellectuals exiled in New York with the publication of *Dialectic of Enlightenment* (1944) by Max Horkheimer and Theodor Adorno. A critique of reason's excesses and the attendant forms of domination became one of the central philosophical themes of the 1950s through the 1970s, sustained by a critique of the false pretenses of humanism. One can find elements of this critique in the early Michel Foucault, from *Madness and Civilization* (1961) to *Discipline and Punish* (1975).

Postcolonial theory used this reexamination of Enlightenment rationalism to extend the critique of imperialism, but it did so with a twist. In its new form, during the decolonizing struggles, this critique often took inspiration from European thinking, whether on the rights of man, nationalism, or Marxism. Activists and intellectuals leveraged the core values of European modernity itself to oppose the colonial domination that they considered to be a military, economic, and political apparatus. They relied on the very universalist arguments of the Enlightenment that Europeans were accused of betraying or deforming. The postcolonial critique, on the contrary, attacked the ideological substratum of European domination. In this way, it claimed to offer a response not only to Western domination but also to the failures and dissatisfactions that followed independence. Decolonization is incomplete, it is said, so long as the Western model of secularized, liberal modernization remains hegemonic. One must, therefore, go back to the sources and do away with the deceiving universalism of European thinking that sprang from the Enlightenment.

Postcolonial authors were able to build on studies from the early 1970s and onwards that established links between Enlightenment-era anthropology and colonial ideology.[6] But they gave these criticisms new power, because the work was not published by European academics but by researchers from countries in the southern hemisphere who were now questioning the legitimacy of Occidentals speaking in their name. Moreover, the trial of Enlightenment philosophers was both external and internal: it was carried out by authors who claimed their life experience to be non-European, yet it took place within theoretical frameworks and often institutional spaces (American universities, notably) of Western thought. This double displacement—theoretical and geographic—explains the violence of this reexamination, which was not confined to the content of Enlightenment thinking but extended to the very possibility of continuing a universalist discourse from the position and the particular experience of European history.

Questions about the act of speaking, as we shall see, are essential for understanding the debates about Enlightenment universalism. This attention to language allows one to break free from unproductive polemics that pit the emancipating heritage of the Lumières against its racist or colonial traits, or more broadly universalism against relativism. In truth, the more interesting matters within the postcolonial debates are less about universalism as such and more about the conditions that allow one to claim a right to it or some proximity to it. In return, these questions encourage one to be particularly attentive, when considering eighteenth century authors, to the ambivalences and contradictions enfolded within their own enunciative situation, to the publics they were addressing, and to the narrative and rhetorical constraints that limit their bold undertakings.

In the historical and philosophical language of the end of the eighteenth century, the notion of *civilization* is the privileged tool of those who sought to think about the specificity of Europe but also its internal divisions, all the while affirming the universalist ambition toward an unlimited expansion of knowledge. With the Revolution, the word *civilization* takes on a new, more political ambition.[7] Then, as revolutionary enthusiasm wanes, a page is turned. The utopian optimism of the Enlightenment yielded its place to a less uncertain but also less welcoming body of knowledge, one in which Europe—without too much of a bad conscience—still occupied the dominant position. A new ordering of knowledge was installed at the end of the century that was at the same time a new geopolitics of spirit. More than a century would go by before it would be really shaken.

We should not look down on the ambiguities or contradictions of eighteenth-century authors as they tried to reconcile their projects for a universal history with their own inscription within a particular place and time. It may be that historians have never truly untangled themselves from this dilemma. The subterranean work of the notion of *civilization,* from eighteenth-century debates through to those of the social sciences in the twentieth century, is thus one way to think about the heritage of the Enlightenment, not only on a theoretical or political level but within the ordering of historical knowledge.

The position I am defending is the following: if we set aside certain rhetorical and theoretical excesses that seek to have us view the Enlightenment as the ideological apparatus of colonialism, one can nevertheless find in the postcolonial approaches productive tools that help display the tensions inherent within the Eurocentrism of leading Enlightenment figures. These approaches are not proposing an "overarching universal"; instead, they are in many respects suggestive of the "lateral universal" called for two centuries later by Maurice Merleau-Ponty, which supposes "ethnological experience, a constant test of oneself by the other and of the other by oneself."[8] They are incomplete, disrupted, and often contradictory because the detour through alterity, through the benefits of the disoriented gaze, and through linguistic pluralism is more often proclaimed or fictionalized than truly accomplished. But this type of lateral universal, as frustrating as it may be, is today the prize of this heritage. It allows one to escape from the dead end of choosing between Enlightenment universalism and the cultural relativism that would be its negation.

CHAPTER ONE

The Postcolonial Challenge

Are Enlightenment thinkers irreparably tarnished by Eurocentrism? Is their claim to defend universal values (toleration, human rights, individual liberty) just ideological makeup to cover over Europe's will to power? Was not the colonial grip imposed by Europeans on the world from the end of the eighteenth century to the middle of the twentieth century—in India, the Far East, Africa—based on an affirmation of a scientific superiority and the conviction of a moral superiority that are both directly traceable to the blithely clear conscience of leading Enlightenment figures? Even today, when those who see themselves as the inheritors of those figures defend individual rights and reason over religious dogma and customs, are they not merely the voluble continuators of Western arrogance? Such questions, though once considered the provocations of iconoclasts, have become common over the past twenty to thirty years under the aegis of postcolonial studies. These postcolonial critiques all attack, sometimes vehemently, the universalist claims undergirding Western thinking since the Enlightenment.

It is a mistake, however, to view the postcolonial challenge as merely a refutation of Enlightenment thinking—as so often happens when critics rely on reductionist, militant arguments that endlessly make use of a certain Western bad conscience. Instead, a critique of Enlightenment thinking should be understood not as a rejection but as a reflection on the conditions that made the Enlightenment possible, notably the conditions of these thinkers' linguistic performances in their written statements and speech acts. With the shift of focus it encourages, this critique allows us to take into consideration the dialogic and polyphonic character of Enlightenment thinkers, with their internal tensions and ambivalences, as we attempt to think about the historical and philosophical specificity of Europe. In so doing, this critique raises an essential question that can no longer be evaded: What does it mean to identify as an inheritor of the Enlightenment? What intellectual or political communities can recognize themselves within this heritage, and what is the cost of doing so?

The Trial of Enlightenment Thinkers

We may begin with a quick inventory and an observation. The "postcolonial critique" of Enlightenment thinkers—evoked so often it has become a cliché—is actually difficult to define. Postcolonial studies is not a homogeneous field and offers no coherent theory of itself. It is instead an intellectual constellation that has expanded since the 1978 publication of Edward Said's monumental *Orientalism*. Said believed that the intense interest in the Orient among European linguists, writers, and learned people generally during the nineteenth century was not the expression of their disinterested desire for knowledge but was above all an instrument of European domination. By reducing the "Orient" to a set of exotic stereotypes, the West, or "Occident," had produced a useful fiction, a "Western style for dominating, restructuring, and having authority over the Orient" that allowed the West to widen the gap between European superiority and Oriental stagnation.[1] In the 1980s, postcolonial studies developed within the literature departments of prestigious Anglo-Saxon universities. These studies were often conducted by intellectuals from the Global South, notably the Indian subcontinent, as part of a deliberate effort to decenter and pluralize literary, artistic, and philosophical canons. These readers were skillful at pointing out traces of ethnocentrism, racism, and contempt for the other in European literature and quick to "deconstruct" the inaccuracy of the self-evident character of rationalist discourse.[2] Then, around the year 2000, within a context that saw the rise of global studies, this critical impulse was extended in the work of historians who were keen to break with narratives that took European history as the model and measure of all history. The watchword of the day, coined by Dipesh Chakrabarty, was to "provincialize Europe"; in other words, to no longer privilege the European path to modernity.[3] Enlightenment thinkers, with their foundation narrative of European modernity, were called out in order to be removed from their pedestal and reassigned a merely local significance.

None of this happened without some misunderstanding. Beyond the questioning of Western certainties, the texts that considered themselves as part of postcolonial thinking formed a disparate and sometimes disconcerting ensemble. Their sources of inspiration were a blend of "French theory"—whether Derridean "deconstructionism" or Foucault's critique of knowledge and power—with Marxism, literary hermeneutics, subaltern studies, and even psychoanalysis.[4] This theoretical eclecticism, along with a certain esoteric quality, could give the impression of an "academic carnival" marked by theoretical or political one-upmanship in a competition of interpretive ingenuity.[5] The degree of radicality itself was quite variable, from the virulent critique of the West that often reduces Occidental thinking to a few stereotypes (abstract reasoning, the cult of performance, egocentric individualism . . .) to blanket praise for *métissage* and identity bricolage.[6] The provenance of postcolonial thinking diversified with the appearance of major contributors from Africa, South America, and China offering studies based on different historical experiences and therefore another relationship to European history.[7]

Despite the field's heterogeneity and occasional excesses, postcolonial studies was unquestionably a major impetus for the renewal of research in the human sciences—beginning with its upsetting of the established canon of authors and works. Its main contribution was to place at the center of theoretical discussions the question of the heritage of European culture in the globalized, pluralist world in which we live.

Enlightenment thinkers are curiously both very present and singularly absent from the great postcolonial texts.[8] They function as an obligatory reference point as soon as the sources of European rationalism are to be named or the monolithic conception of modernity that Europe supposedly imposed on the world is to be denounced; but they are rarely treated directly, much less studied as a period or corpus of texts and authors. They appear more as handy key words to encapsulate the theoretical apparatus of modernity (from political liberalism to philosophies of progress). Although some authors evoke, for the most part rapidly and allusively, the ties that Enlightenment thinkers are said to have had with the Atlantic slave trade and the emergence of racist theories, many more concentrate their criticism on the following period marked by the construction of second-stage colonial empires (British India, the occupation of the Middle East, the carving up of Africa), the reign of philosophies of history, and the rise of "orientalism" and colonial studies. Edward Said himself proposed only one congruent depiction of the eighteenth century in his opening definition of orientalism as "the enormously systematic discipline by which European culture was able to manage—and even produce—the Orient politically, sociologically, militarily, ideologically, scientifically, and imaginatively during the post-Enlightenment period."[9] Obviously, one can question the relation that this orientalism had with the century that preceded it. Is it a betrayal of the cosmopolitan ideals of the Enlightenment thinkers or is it the achievement produced by the slow gestation of Eurocentrism? Even if the ambiguity is maintained by Said, it would seem that Orientalism in his eyes begins only at the very end of the eighteenth century and actually marks a break with the Enlightenment thinkers who were more open to cultural diversity. After Said, postcolonial authors rarely ventured earlier than the Napoleonic era; while in the field of eighteenth-century studies proper, research in the postcolonial vein remained for a long time uninfluential.[10] The most impactful, such as the work of Srinivas Aravamudan, clearly held an open, cosmopolitan view of Enlightenment thinkers in contrast to the orientalism of the nineteenth century.[11]

This opposition produces a troubling situation for the reader who plunges into the texts of postcolonial studies. A critique of the Enlightenment is imposed as a stock gesture, a commonplace, and yet it happens at a certain remove and targets less the Enlightenment authors, texts, and ideas of the eighteenth century and more a certain fetishized cultural icon, "the Enlightenment," in French *les Lumières*, which functions like a password to designate the ideological sources of Western modernity. This gesture gives rise to a persistent ambiguity about the reproach itself. For the harshest critics, the condemnation seems focused on the compromised Enlightenment ideals when faced with colonial conquest, the slave trade, and the development of racialized thinking. Some of them harp on the existence of racial prejudice in the writings of major Enlightenment figures, on their ties with European colonialism, or the slave trade. The tone is sometimes iconoclastic and virulent as they denounce philosophers' hypocritical positions regarding slavery.[12] However, the gesture rarely goes beyond pointing to a conjunction or tendency; in other words, suggesting that these figures, *les Lumières*, are flawed from the start because their endeavors coincided with slavery and colonialism in the chronology of world history. Achille Mbembe, a strong voice within postcolonial thinking, makes the sweeping claim that far from embodying a period of humanist and cosmopolitan opening, the Enlightenment figures represent a "gregarious moment" in Western thinking. Under the influence of slavery and an "imperialist impulse," Europe, he claims, turned away from all efforts to know others and disqualified other peoples, casting them outside of history. The figure of the "negro" or "nègre" is seen as the sad symbol of this exclusion: "The expansion of the European spatial horizon, then, went hand in hand with a division and shrinking of the historical and cultural imagination and, in certain cases, a relative closing of the mind."[13]

For other authors, it is not necessary to deny Enlightenment cosmopolitanism and universalism because, in their view, it is that very universalism—even when it is used to advance abolitionism, anticolonialism, and racial equality—that is dangerous, because it serves to reinforce the European clear conscience, the belief held by European elites that it is their duty to speak in the name of other peoples and grant them access to the benefits of civilization. In this view, Enlightenment thinking takes over from Christian discourse in affirming the moral and intellectual superiority of Europe. The good conscience of nineteenth-century colonialism would therefore be the cumulative result of two conquering universalisms: first Christian missionaries and later the republican descendants of Voltaire, both operating in the service of satisfying the appetite for power of the European monarchies and their economic interests. This critique is not groundless, especially since colonial elites openly invoked Enlightenment thinkers in support of their "civilizing mission." One can see the consequences of this invocation down to the present day. Is not the human rights discourse that has occurred over the past decades in the interventions of Western powers, notably the United States, part of the inheritance from *les Lumières*—now interwoven with moral certitude, a certain condescension, and backed up by unquestioned and unquestionable technological superiority? One can note that its promoters and advocates openly affirm a connection with eighteenth-century forebears.

This postcolonial critique sometimes risks falling into a simplistic denunciation that claims to unveil, behind the West's emancipatory ideals, nefarious geopolitical and economic interests. It carries more weight when it points out the contradictions of Enlightenment universalist discourse. A certain inherent violence stems not only from its exploitation by government authorities and private interests. In truth, Enlightenment discourse is from the start contradicted by the particular position from which it speaks. This is a criticism that Hegel had already formulated about *les Lumières*. The latter's universalist pronouncements were, he claimed, unmindful of their own occurrence within a particular moment of human history and the particular conditions of their utterance. Of course, Hegel is hardly an authority favored by postcolonial theorists, who, on the contrary, take frequent aim at his philosophy of history. But this criticism of the ambivalences inherent in every universalist discourse, insofar as that discourse is situated in a particular time and place, would be relayed by others who underscored the dynamic of exclusion implicit in every instance of such discourse that is inadequately mindful of what falls outside it.

From this rapid survey of the matter, it should be clear that the postcolonial critique of the Enlightenment does not operate from an agreed-on, coherent argument. One looks in vain for a precise corpus of works among the texts and authors of the eighteenth century to prove their point. On the other hand, leading texts within the postcolonial constellation have made familiar a set of reproaches levelled at *les Lumières*. Among the most important to keep in mind: first, the direct and simplistic charges that they were complicit with colonial ideology, the development of a racist anthropology, and the Black slave trade; second, the idea that the rights of man were the rights of white men; third, that a defense of peaceful business dealings served the imperial interests of European merchants; and fourth, that the cult of Progress resulted in relegating Africa and Asia to the margins of history. A second type of reproach posits that even when European Lumières are being authentically universalist and denouncing colonialism and slavery in the name of a basic equality of all human beings, they seize on that universalism and drape themselves in it so as to insure for themselves a good conscience, claiming to emancipate others while yet reducing them to silence, eager to liberate them but without hearing them. A third type of objection is even more general when it asks: How can works, ideas, and bodies of knowledge that originated and developed within one specific part of the globe at a given moment in history have universal validity, other than by a dissembling erasure of that historical and geographical rootedness and an insidious colonization of minds?

Anticolonial Enlightenment Figures?

Several responses have been made to these criticisms. The first sought to refute all accusations of ideological collusion between Enlightenment figures and the practices of racism and colonialism by proving that *les Lumières* were essentially anticolonialists and abolitionists. Due to its extremely sensitive nature within public space, the question of slavery was the focus of debates. Against accusatory interpretations that sometimes contained misunderstandings, several researchers underscored that Enlightenment philosophers did not remain silent but indeed denounced slavery, sometimes quite vigorously. In 1781, when Condorcet published his *Reflections on the Slavery of Negros*, which is vehemently opposed to the practice, he was continuing a fifty-year tradition of criticism carried on by leading figures of the Enlightenment from Montesquieu to Diderot.[14] Economists and literary authors of the day also expressed their opposition. Olympe de Gouges, for example, wrote *Zamore et Mirza* in 1783, an openly abolitionist play that would not be performed and praised until 1789. The year before, in 1788, the *Société des amis des Noirs* was founded in Paris; however, in England a campaign to abolish slavery had been underway for several years.

Antislavery views were not limited to colonialism's leading cities.

Italy, and particularly Naples, developed a current of Enlightenment thinking using both political economy and natural rights to denounce slavery as a crime. In his colossal *Science of Legislation*, which epitomizes the Italian Enlightenment or *Illuminismo*, Gaetano Filangieri bitterly regrets that the coasts of Senegal have become "a market where Europeans are offering a pittance to buy the inviolable rights of humanity" and calls for total abolition following the Pennsylvania model.[15]

Slavery is only the most scandalous manifestation of European colonial domination. Early on, the abbot Ferdinando Galiani claimed that slavery was a consequence of colonialism. Black slavery in the Americas, he remarked with his customary incisiveness, was the sinister precondition for European prosperity, "since it is perfectly clear to anyone who gives it some thought that a people cannot enrich themselves without rendering another people poor and unhappy."[16] It was a short step from the criticism of slavery to the questioning of colonialism, and one often taken.

In a book with the explicit title *Enlightenment against Empire*, Sankar Muthu has insisted that among the Enlightenment figures there was a powerful anti-imperialist current led especially by Diderot, Raynal, Herder, and Kant. In his view, the second half of the eighteenth century is an anomalous exception within the history of European political thinking. It is the only time when a fundamentally anti-imperialist position developed and exerted significant influence. Its instigators were not content to merely denounce the abuses of colonial domination, as natural-rights theorists of the sixteenth and seventeenth centuries had done, or as would a few others in the nineteenth century. Instead they produced a radical critique of European domination by formulating a unitary conception of human nature and a recognition of the diversity of cultures and their equal dignity.[17] In contrast to the monolithic vision of *les Lumières* that often circulates among postcolonial authors (and, it's true, among some of their critics), Muthu demonstrates that philosophers as emblematic as Diderot and Kant defended a cultural and empirical definition of human beings distinct from all abstract universalism. Enlightenment universalism was not a narrow rationalism; it allowed one to conceive of an anthropological unity of the human species while acknowledging a diversity of customs, practices, and beliefs.

As soon as one abandons an a priori, monolithic, and often caricatural depiction of the Enlightenment, the rich plurality of European views of the world becomes evident. Instead of an impression of closed-mindedness denounced by Mbembe, who lamented a specular self-enclosure of European exceptionalism, numerous eighteenth-century texts display a genuine thirst for knowledge and a recognition of different cultures and knowledge that sometimes led to thorough self-criticism. The Libertine tradition, for example, which arose from heterodox thinkers who, starting in the seventeenth century, sought models outside Europe to oppose Christian thinking and question the universality of European history, would later nourish an original current of European orientalism. The Enlightenment figures who received this tradition connected it to the new discourse of global scientific exploration and thus produced an important decentering of the Christian vision of the world. They created the conditions for a hiatus, almost a hesitation, during which the diversity of the world and the plurality of mores were objects of genuine curiosity.[18] Asia was no longer just a faraway unknown land favorable for every kind of fantasy but was instead becoming a territory for exploration, a seemingly endless source of new knowledge, thoughts, and questioning. India in particular, because of its rich cultural and religious traditions, fascinated European travelers and philosophers from François Bernier during the early reign of Louis XIV to Anquetil-Duperron a century later. Others, such as Voltaire, were smitten by China, whose great age and prestige were paradoxically enhanced by Jesuit stories retold back in Europe. Even Islam was the object of scientific interest and erudition if one recalls the work of Barthélémy d'Herbelot, author of the *Bibliothèque orientale*, and his successor Antoine Galland, who became famous for his translation of the *Arabian Nights* but who was also an eminent orientalist. Manuscripts arrived in European libraries from all corners of the globe stimulating the interest of the learned and the plans of travelers.[19] Between the desire to convert souls that motivated missionaries in the early modern period and the later civilizing mission of colonial administrators of the nineteenth century, the age of the Enlightenment was a period of attentive discoveries that the Australian historian and anthropologist Greg Dening has described as a "season of observing."[20]

This curiosity was not limited to peoples and their cultures but extended to the physical environment that was foreign, exotic, and surprising—and therefore required naturalists to revise their thinking. The tropical flora and fauna fascinated travelers, specialists, and later certain writers. Individuals who served within a given colonial project were not necessarily all predators. As Richard Grove has noted, the first efforts to develop nature conservancy policies happened on tropical islands. In the 1760s, on Île de France (today Île Maurice / Mauritius), the trio of administrator Pierre Poivre, naturalist Philibert Commerson, and writer Bernardin de Saint-Pierre noted the dangers of deforestation and soil erosion and took steps to implement a policy of environmental protection. A new understanding of the pressures of economic development on natural resources blended with a new concern, both aesthetic and moral, for nature. Paradoxically, the fragility of colonial power in these far-off places, which made those involved mindful of conserving resources, also facilitated the blending of the political economy of the physiocrats, the sensitivity of Rousseauians, and the research networks of botanists.[21] One finds echoes of this early ecological consciousness in the novels of Bernardin, especially his *Paul et Virginie,* published in 1788.

Fiction was one of the leading forms among Enlightenment writings for articulating the wish to challenge the easy affirmations of European superiority. Novels from the beginning of the century with a Libertine or Spinozist tone set an example. In the *Voyages et aventures de Jacques Massé* (1710) by Simon Tyssot de Patot, the wanderings of the hero and his encounters with exotic individuals such as a Chinese freethinker become the vehicle for an acerbic critique of Christianity. Somewhat later, there is a flood of successful narratives, starting with Montesquieu's *Persian Letters* (1721), that depict the reverse scenario: of a surprised foreign traveler discovering European society. In every case the fictional detour outside one's country of origin spurs a critique, sometimes of radical proportions, regarding the impasses of European culture or abusive aspects of its civilization. In *Gulliver's Travels* (1726), Jonathan Swift borrows from earlier examples while adding satire and irony to produce his unforgettable masterpiece in the genre of the altered- or inverted-perspective narrative. Swift's text includes this biting denunciation of colonialism:

> They go on shore to rob and plunder, they see a harmless people, are entertained with kindness; they give the country a new name; they take formal possession of it for their king; they set up a rotten plank, or a stone, for a memorial; they murder two or three dozen of the natives, bring away a couple more, by force, for a sample; return home, and get their pardon. Here commences a new dominion acquired with a title by divine right. Ships are sent with the first opportunity; the natives driven out or destroyed; their princes tortured to discover their gold; a free license given to all acts of inhumanity and lust, the earth reeking with the blood of its inhabitants: and this execrable crew of butchers, employed in so pious an expedition, is a modern colony, sent to convert and civilize an idolatrous and barbarous people![22]

The notion of cultural relativism introduced by Montesquieu and Swift becomes one of the essential traits among Enlightenment thinkers.[23] The many versions of the "good savage" trope, used as a foil to expose the blemishes of European societies when set against the savage's natural virtue, attests to the link between discovery of the Other and self-critique. The idea goes back further: to Montaigne, for example, and his famous essay "On Cannibals," in which he evokes the surprise of the Tupi Indians when they encounter political and social inequality. However, the idea was only sketched there and did not receive its full development as a commonly recognized theme until the start of the eighteenth century in the *Dialogues du baron de Lahontan et d'un sauvage* (1703). There the surprise is inverted: "What sort of Men must the Europeans be? What Species of Creatures do they retain to? The Europeans, who must be forc'd to do Good, and have no other Prompter for the avoiding of Evil than the fear of Punishment."[24] The success of Lahontan's book, which continued to be widely read throughout the century, attests to a clear taste for self-critique within European public opinion. Diderot, it is well known, also uses the figure of the philosopher-savage and multiplies narrative pitfalls and ironic false pretenses in his *Supplément au Voyage de Bougainville* (1796), which concludes with a plea in favor of a prudent and pragmatic relativism: "Let's follow the good chaplain's example and be monks in France and savages in Tahiti."[25] Such is the fundamental ambivalence of the Enlightenment thinkers: an undeniable satisfaction among European writers—convinced they are living in an era of peace, prosperity, and intellectual elevation almost without precedent in human history—flows alongside a turbulent current of high anxiety about the supposed real advantages of modernity. Primitivist fiction is only one of the more striking manifestations of this phenomenon. European pride is constantly being undermined by doubt.

This rereading of Enlightenment authors is healthy. It allows one to avoid the simplistic shortcuts that are content to seize on the chronological juxtaposition of the Atlantic slave trade and Enlightenment-era publications to disqualify the latter, even if the leading representatives denounced slavery and their followers were committed abolitionists. The rediscovery of authors and texts hostile to imperialism allow one to highlight the pluralism among Enlightenment thinkers and the existence of emancipation projects that were authentically universalist and far from the caricatural image of the Lumières as all white colonialists.

And yet, despite these important contributions, the studies that insist on the presence of a cosmopolitan, critical, and self-aware current among the European Enlightenment thinkers are not enough to silence the postcolonial objection. Their protest does not present *les Lumières* as uniformly racist or colonialist, which would be absurd, but instead critiques their claim to universality (including the universality of emancipation through reason), which it considers illegitimate and dangerous because it is carried out from Europe and in the name of Europe. In other words, it's not enough to discover that Kant was hostile to colonization; one must show that the inscription of Kantian philosophy within a particular moment of European history—one marked by the crisis of monarchies of the Old Regime, the development of market capitalism, and the retreat of religion from public space—does not invalidate its aspiration toward universal validity. Moreover, in efforts to "defend" Enlightenment figures against unjust attacks and caricatures, the response itself tends to simplify the stakes, opposing anticolonial Lumières to imperialist Lumières; whereas this alternative, besides being an overly direct projection of our own ideological divisions, rarely allows one to grasp what's playing out in the texts of that time. The Enlightenment ambivalence regarding the relations between Europe and the wider world traverses practically every author with no possibility for an easy reduction into a face-off between Eurocentrists and anti-imperialists. Consider a famous example: Montesquieu's *Persian Letters*, with its sometimes-ferocious critique of Europe, does not prevent him from inventing and putting into circulation fantastical representations of the Orient based on an excessively static notion of "oriental despotism" against which he juxtaposes European liberty, guaranteed by its mores and political moderation. In his *Spirit of Laws* (1748), the criticism of slavery, which is really there behind the mask of irony, sits alongside a justification of the "laws of Europe" which guarantee the commercial exploitation of the colonies.[26] It is impossible to enlist Montesquieu in a Manichean combat. What is interesting about him and relevant today lies precisely in these two stimulating intuitions: first, that every moral judgment depends on the position of the one who utters it, and second, that the rise of commerce profoundly changes the nature of relations between Europe and rest of the world.

The ambiguity of Enlightenment anticolonialism is situated at yet another level: even the texts that appear to be the most emblematic of Europe's capacity for self-critique rarely go as far as recognizing the Other as a full-fledged subject. The philosopher remains master of the discourse. He lends his voice to the foreigner or savage, he posits fictional scenes of contact, and he has his characters speak with a level of eloquence corresponding to the verve and irony that he has also breathed into them. Whether it be Adario, Lahontan's savage interlocutor, the Persians Usbek and Rica, or the old Tahitian who casts painful insults on the Europeans at the beginning of the *Supplément au Voyage de Bougainville*, all speak with European "ideas and turns of phrase," as Diderot openly admits.[27] The ventriloquism that is often pointed out in postcolonial criticism consists in making others speak by reducing them to silence. They are not recognized as carriers of their own history and culture; they are only the spokespeople of European anxieties.

Global Enlightenment Figures?

A second type of response has come from global history. The latter shares with the postcolonial constellation of texts a criticism of Eurocentrism, but on very different grounds. Its goal is to enlarge the window of analysis of historical phenomena beyond national borders and beyond the frame of Europe. Enlightenment figures have come up for scrutiny under this global history approach, which is indissociably epistemological and political. They have been multiplied and enlarged to a global scale in order to demonstrate that the exclusively European dimension attributed to the Lumières was only a historiographical fiction that erased numerous non-European sources and permutations. The new history of the sciences, for example, has broken with the old narrative of the rise of modern science by showing that this rise, far from being a strictly European event, was nourished by vernacular non-European knowledge thanks to numerous local intermediaries. Sir Isaac Newton, an iconic figure of Enlightenment science, relied on international information networks and relays that allowed him to verify his calculations. In turn, his work was translated into Arabic by learned Indians seeking to initiate a dialogue between the new British astronomy and traditional Indian science.[28] Enlightenment science is thus relocated by such studies, and the geographic dynamics that underpin it are reevaluated and revalued.[29] Despite its claim to universal validity founded on principles of abstract reason, this science produced bodies of knowledge tied to places of contact and exchange, depending on often-distant testimonies whose credibility had to be tested. These mediating instances were largely erased starting in the eighteenth century, and then by the entire historiographical tradition that had become enclosed within a teleological and edifying narrative linking "scientific revolution," Enlightenment figures, and the technical and economic superiority of the West.[30]

This wider frame of reference initiated by the global-history approach gives rise to certain ambiguities. It can lead to a shattering of the grand narrative into a thousand tales that now privilege intermediaries, connections, local knowledge, and the processes of translations and encounters according to a circulatory storytelling model that seems to have overtaken cultural history in the last twenty years. But it rarely extends as far as fully overthrowing the idea of a general movement to elaborate modern science—a movement to which many contributed.[31]

The domination of European sciences, reinforced by their imperial domination, seems assured by the start of the nineteenth century.

Learned non-Europeans were not only informants and intermediaries; they also participated in intellectual debates and sometimes developed original currents of thinking among Enlightenment figures. Jorge Cañizares-Esguerra enlarged the geographical frame of the "New World debate" that concerns the history of America before the arrival of Christopher Columbus. Creole specialists living in Mexico developed and defended, against the views of Buffon and De Pauw, another vision of the nature and history of the American continent, one founded on a different epistemology, namely the direct observation of sources and archeological remains rather than a reliance on written testimonies only.[32]

On a political level, non-European peoples developed and deepened certain core Enlightenment values. The paradigmatic example concerns the slave revolt in Santo Domingo in 1791 that would lead to Haiti's independence in 1804. For a long time, this rebellion was played down by European historiography in favor of a narrative centered on Europe's abolitionist movement and the initiatives of French revolutionaries that led to the initial French abolition of slavery in 1794. But many historians now insist on slave autonomy and on the role enslaved people played in the widening and universalization of the notion of "rights of man."[33]

These studies—from the fields of the history of science, the history of ideas, and the political history of Atlantic revolutions—do not constitute a homogeneous body of work—quite the contrary—but they have all multiplied the known currents of modernity and widened our vision of Enlightenment figures. They are generally critical of the grand narrative of European modernity and may in that regard seem close to the postcolonial sensibility. And yet, while they do criticize an exclusively European vision of les Lumières, which they see as the fault of biased historiographies, they have nevertheless reinforced their universal dimension by loosening the bonds that associate these figures too narrowly to the geopolitical destiny of Europe. If there are Mexican or Haitian Lumières, and similar figures from Egypt and India, then their claim of universality is valid, and it would be incorrect to accuse them of being irremediably tarnished by European imperialism. In this account it is the Eurocentric historiography of the nineteenth and twentieth centuries that is to blame, not the Enlightenment figures themselves. One may provincialize Europe and universalize the Lumières. The two gestures really go together since Enlightenment figures can only be truly granted universality on condition that the bond that attaches them to Europe be loosened.

Sebastian Conrad has pushed this reasoning to the extreme by proposing a two-point argument to redefine the Enlightenment as a global phenomenon. First, he takes up and generalizes the studies that showed how non-European actors contributed to the construction of modern fields of knowledge. Second, he extends the definition of the Enlightenment to the entire ensemble of intellectual movements, be they nineteenth-century or early twentieth-century ones, that saw themselves as aligned with the values of political modernization from religious tolerance to individual liberty. Notable examples are the Japanese reformers of the Meiji era, the Young Ottomans such as Namik Kemal, figures within the Bengali Renaissance of the early nineteenth century, and the Chinese and Korean modernizers at the end of the Empire. These movements, he asserts, were not the result of a dissemination of the writings of European Enlightenment figures but instead constitute successive stages within the same global movement. The works of eighteenth-century European philosophers are just one spatially and chronologically localized episode of a long-range intellectual phenomenon that affected many regions around the world far beyond Europe and took different forms according to local circumstances.[34]

The claim has a certain attraction. It allows one to extract the Lumières thinkers from an overly rooted relationship to Europe while still preserving their ideological core: scientific progress, political liberalism, religious tolerance. In this way, even if it is part of a critique of Eurocentrism, it is far from the postcolonial kind. Instead of particularizing the Lumières to question their claims to universality, this approach further universalizes and generalizes them. Moral order is thus saved, and the principles of liberal modernity are legitimated.

However, this way of proceeding is not without risks. In the end it empties the Enlightenment of all its substance. By creating a concept broad enough to accommodate not only the eighteenth-century philosophers with all their differences and disagreements but also Muslim reformers, Japanese scholars, and Chinese modernizers, Conrad turns the Enlightenment into an empty shell and something slightly unreal—thereby reducing it to an optimistic conception of modernity. Moreover, pursuing this global historiography does not really succeed in breaking the bonds that attach the knowledge, texts, and ideas of the Enlightenment thinkers to Europe. Of course European knowledge and thinking benefited from exchanges with local sources, but they leveraged those gains by centralizing that new knowledge in European metropolitan areas, often while erasing the contributions of non-Europeans. The "sources" of modernity may well be multiple and diverse, but it was in Europe that they crystallized coherently and produced a discourse that valorized a break with tradition. The Enlightenment is not simply a collection of ideas for which one might find glimmers, traces, and precursors here and there; it is above all a narrative by means of which eighteenth-century authors analyzed and commented upon what struck them as a fundamental mutation in the history of the world.

Moreover, when the major texts of the Enlightenment were translated, circulated, and appropriated outside Europe, they were received precisely as European texts transmitting the values the local thinkers were seeking—or sometimes rejecting—*as European*, and not as particular textual manifestations of a global project. The appropriation of these values took on specific, particular forms that derived from local contexts and concerns. Rather than erasing these differences by subsuming them all under a very general concept of the Enlightenment, now reduced to a rule book of modernizing reformism, would it not be better to study the sliding senses, altering appropriations, and different ways that the Enlightenment legacy has been received, transmitted, modified, and sometimes betrayed? Approaching the question in these terms allows one to show the ambivalent relations that non-Europeans maintained with the Lumières thinkers, even when sharing an affinity with them. Non-Europeans considered the Enlightenment legacy as something both familiar and foreign—a necessary resource for working on emancipation with respect to their own traditions and societies, and yet tributary to a European conception of history that could either be attractive or, inversely, seem ill-adapted.

This is where the postcolonial approaches come in handy. Contrary to the often caricatural representations of it that circulate, aided sometimes by postcolonialists themselves, postcolonial theory is not merely a frontal attack on European culture. It seeks instead to show its contradictions and ambivalences, and the limits of its professed universalism. Its roots are in the difficulties encountered by the authors and activists originating from the colonized worlds when seeking to appropriate the emancipating values of Enlightenment thinkers. Far from being simply an anticolonial critique of the West, postcolonial theory is better seen as the outcome of heightened awareness of the political failures of post-independence nationalisms. Most postcolonial authors come from southern countries (the Indian subcontinent, the Caribbean, Africa) but have been deeply educated by Western culture. They often teach in the United States, and a few teach in Europe. Attentive to discordant experiences and to situations of exile—both real and symbolic—these writers reflect on this double heritage and its contradictions from within their own ideological, biographical, and professional positions. They are sensitive to the tensions that traverse the works produced at the point where cultures overlap. They willingly point out the limits of European anticolonialism, which is often incapable, despite its true grandeur, of conceiving of the existence of an autonomous, indigenous history outside European domination. They also point out the corresponding ambivalences of colonized intellectuals who are prisoners of a cultural heritage they neither can nor wish to extricate themselves from.[35]

It's worth noting that postcolonial theory developed alongside literary studies, especially of a postmodern sensibility. It insists on the polysemy of texts, be they canonical works or ones documenting more marginal experiences. Following the lead of Homi Bhabha, researchers have investigated the dynamics of hybridization and translation, and also how irony and simulacra perturb and impede the univocal assignment of an ideological meaning. Postcolonial studies of this sort may reject the "binary structure of opposition" between Third World and Western World, while also fighting against "the ideological discourses of modernity"—the main point being to destabilize holistic forms of identification with cultural communities.[36]

The argumentation of Dipesh Chakrabarty in *Provincializing Europe* (2000) is far more complex than the interpretation hastily made by those who only read the title. The theoretical ambition of the book is to escape from the West's hegemonic discourse once the critique of this hegemony is deployed inside this epistemological heritage—for example, starting with Marxism and more generally inside university structures inherited from European knowledge:

> As should be clear by now, provincializing Europe is not a project of rejecting or discarding European thought. Relating to a body of thought to which one largely owes one's intellectual existence cannot be a matter of exacting what Leela Gandhi has aptly called "postcolonial revenge." European thought is at once both indispensable and inadequate in helping us to think through the experiences of political modernity in non-Western nations, and provincializing Europe becomes the task of exploring how this thought—which is now everybody's heritage and which affects us all—may be renewed from and for the margins.[37]

The thesis could not be clearer: "European thought is at once both indispensable and inadequate." The goal is not to combat it or reject it but instead to force it to undergo a certain twisting, a critical turn on itself; and also to pluralize it and adapt it to the requirements of a globalized world. In the case of the Enlightenment thinkers, this exercise is all the more obviously necessary since eighteenth-century European thinking is anything but univocal. On the contrary, it is heterogeneous and dialogic, lending itself to readings that bring out its holes, tensions, and hesitations.

From Raynal to Toussaint

To better understand the stakes but also the productiveness of this approach, we may consider an emblematic text, Abbé Raynal's *Histoire philosophique du commerce et de l'établissement des Européens dans les Deux Indes* (1770–1780). This encyclopedic work was an impressive publishing success at the end of the eighteenth century though it was later neglected and even maligned. Literary historians judged it to be a "dead work," a "jumble," an indigestible compilation of materials made only slightly bearable thanks to a few eloquent passages credited to the always lively plume of Diderot.[38] After a century and a half of indifference, the republication in 1951 of an anthology of selections elicited some terse, condescending interest in this work, which had the reputation of being unreadable, and in its author, who was considered likeable enough but also loquacious and short on philosophy.[39] The pioneering work of Yves Benot and Michèle Duchet in the 1970s failed to get historians to take the work seriously. And yet, starting in the 1990s, interest in *The Philosophical History of the Two Indies* revived considerably thanks to the vogue for global history. Publication of a large critical edition was undertaken, colloquia were organized, and several monographs devoted to it soon followed.[40] And yet all this activity has produced no clear picture of Raynal's work.

There is no denying that it's a deeply puzzling text. It was published in no less than fifty different editions over the course of the eighteenth century, including three major ones in 1770, 1774, and 1780 that corresponded to different moments in the text's evolution. There were also numerous abridged editions and translations that together guaranteed its dissemination throughout Europe and the Americas. It was a collective enterprise, with Raynal mining extensively the memoirs furnished by colonial administrators, but it also incorporated contributions from his philosophy and literary friends, notably Baron d'Holbach, Jean de Pechméja, and Alexandre Deleyre. The most famous collaborator was the great Diderot, who first played the role of volunteer anonymous editor but who later intervened freely and massively, especially when it came to the last and most wordy edition, which extended to nearly a dozen volumes.[41] Given this unusual genesis and genealogy, it is not surprising that the heterogeneity of the final product would be off-putting. One finds historical accounts and reminiscences overflowing with statistics followed by impassioned tirades. Certain passages openly contradict statements that occur earlier or later, others correct statements from an earlier edition, while others offer new arguments or openly display the doubts and hesitations of the author. Should Chinese civilization be praised? In reply, Diderot adds a second, more critical response at the end of the enthusiastic chapter that appeared in the first two major editions. His text does not replace the first answer but stands as its contradictory supplement. Should slavery be abolished? Lengthy disquisitions—which get even longer with each new edition—weave across the arguments for and against, assembling remarks of reformist moderates, eloquent calls for immediate abolition, and even announcements of imminent slave revolts.

Today as in the years of the earliest editions, the book's success comes less from its mammoth synthesis of historic and economic information than from the ironic or virulent passages that call out the abuses of European colonization. For example, near the end of the first volume devoted to Portuguese colonial enterprises in Asia, one finds a thorough attack against "intrepid brigands" who have imposed their "tyranny" on the "innocent and unhappy" inhabitants. The author expresses regret at not having more forthrightly declared his indignation about their attitudes in the preceding pages, and he then proceeds to extend his criticism to encompass all colonial conquests in the following declaration:

> Oh! barbaric Europeans! I have not been dazzled by the splendour of your deeds. Their success has not obscured their injustice. . . . If I cease for one moment to see you as so many flocks of cruel and ravenous vultures, with as little morality and conscience as those birds of prey, may this work and my memory . . . become objects of the utmost contempt and execration.[42]

These virulent denunciations do not merely lay bare the injustice of the looting going on behind the apparent bravura of major discoveries. The author also breaks with the colonizers and imagines taking up arms against them. The superiority of the Europeans is shrunk to nothing as the binary pair *savage/civilized* gets reversed by revelations of European "barbarie." The stigma of animalization is no longer reserved for the indigenous peoples only but gets turned against the Europeans, who are compared to birds of prey. In another passage, the same indignation is leveled at the Dutch arrival in southern Africa. After first praising the wild ways of the Hottentots as being free and innocent, the author denounces the corruption and greed of the Europeans. He then addresses the indigenous inhabitants and exhorts them to flee or, better yet, to defend themselves:

> Hottentots! Disappear into your forests. The savage beasts which inhabit them are less fearsome than the monsters into whose power you are about to fall. The tiger may tear you apart, but it will take from you only your life. These creatures will steal your innocence and your liberty. Or if you are bold enough, take up your axes, bend your bows, let your poisoned arrows rain down on these foreigners. May not a single one of them survive to carry the news of their disaster to their countrymen.[43]

The effect of this passage was even more dramatic for eighteenth-century readers since the Hottentots were for them the very symbol of savagery and the borderline between the human and the animal. Diderot was not the first to play on the ambivalence of this liminary figure of primitive humanity and flip monstrosity into innocence.[44] But the power of his exclamation seeks above all to horrify readers by showing them, via an opposed pairing, the moral degeneracy of the civilized colonizers. Worse than wild animals, Europeans are now monsters—a retrograde descent to a lower rung on the ladder of creation. Convinced of having broken free of the state of nature thanks to the advances of civilization, they have in fact excluded themselves from the natural order by their senseless cruelty. Therefore, one can only hope for their complete disappearance.

It is hard to imagine a more caustic repudiation of European colonialism. How, then, can one accuse Enlightenment thinkers of a self-satisfied Eurocentrism if one of its leading representatives in one of the biggest bestsellers of the day calls on the colonized peoples to take up arms and exterminate the invaders? Two centuries later, Yves Benot, a militant communist and opponent of colonialism with ties to leading figures in the Pan-African movement, marvels at the contemporary relevance of these passages whose violence, even if fantasied, seems to echo the very real violence that would be a part of later movements of liberation.[45]

However, we should not jump to thinking of *The Philosophical History of the Two Indies* as an anticolonial manifesto. The diatribes added to the 1780 edition are out of sync with the rest of the text, whose main concern is instead to assemble and organize in a reformist and liberal spirit all knowledge about the history and situation of the European colonies.[46] One finds many passages with a favorable view of the role played by Europeans. The overarching idea that comes across is a defense of a model founded on free trade and in opposition to the political and religious exploitation practiced by the Spanish and Portuguese colonizers, but also the British and the Dutch—the latter being the "monsters" the

Hottentots are encouraged to flee and massacre. The virulent castigation of colonizers' behavior is not simply a European self-critique; it also seeks to explore the possibility of better alternatives. In contrast to the examples of ferocious imperialism, the text holds out the prospect of a virtuous colonization.

This positioning should be of no surprise, since the colonial rivalry between France and Great Britain was operating just below the surface. While not exactly a commissioned work, *The Philosophical History of the Two Indies* aimed to satisfy the expectations of the French government after the heavy losses suffered during the Seven Years' War (1756–1763), especially in India and North America. Protected and encouraged by the powerful Duke of Choiseul, Abbé Raynal developed the idea for his project in the months following the Treaty of Paris (1763), which put an end to military confrontation between the great powers. This period was a time of intense propaganda activity that contrasted the English "barbarians" to the "civilized" French.[47] Under the notion of civilization being deployed, Europe was not thought of as a single homogeneous bloc. Thus, the criticism of European practices would often implicitly associate two registers: on the one hand a colonial bad conscience and on the other an intra-European spirit of competition.

The disparate character of the work—a patchwork of historical narratives, descriptions of moderate reformist projects, and fiery proclamations—explains the persistent disagreements among Raynal specialists. Some, such as Yves Benot and more recently Sankar Muthu, want to see it as a thoroughly anticolonial work; while others, in keeping with Michèle Duchet, insist on Raynal's moderation and his ties with the colonial administration.[48] Kenta Ohji has shown that *The Philosophical History of the Two Indies* remains organized around the idea of the historical superiority of Europe thanks to the advances of its civilization and the contributions of its commerce.[49] *Commerce* is indeed the key word of the whole text and clearly viewed as the motor of history, the tool that guarantees prosperity and peace between the different nations of the world. Although *The Philosophical History of the Two Indies* may sometimes allow critical murmurs to echo through its pages and has no illusions about the occasionally destructive character of commercial greed, especially around the slave trade,[50] the dominant theme remains the sweet flute music of *just doing business* with occasional interjections of the thundering organ blasts of *civilizing commerce*:

> It is from thence, in a word, that, viewing those beautiful regions, in which the arts and sciences flourish, and which have been for so long a time obscured by ignorance and barbarism, I have said to

> myself: Who is it that hath digged these canals? Who is it that hath dried up these plains? Who is it that hath founded these cities? Who is it that hath collected, cloth, and civilized these people? Then I have heard the voice of all the enlightened men among them, who have answered: This is the effect of commerce [*c'est le commerce*].[51]

But what of Diderot himself? Does he not give expression to a voice authentically hostile to European expansion? Did he not transform this reformist work into an "anticolonial manifesto"?[52] His indignation against slavery and colonial violence is undeniably sincere. It eloquently expresses a critique that one also finds at the same time in the abolitionist movement. The fiery rhetoric, however, can tip into bombast. The vituperation is sometimes too theatrical, and Diderot himself takes care to note that after having called on the Hottentots to rise up, these calls to revolt hardly risk bringing about effective results: "And you, cruel Europeans, do not be angered by my harangue. It will not be heard by the Hottentots, nor by the inhabitants of those regions you have yet to lay waste. If my reproaches offend you, it is because you are no more human than your predecessors; it is because you realize that the hatred I have vowed against them is directed equally at you."[53] The "harangue" is addressed to Europeans, to Diderot's contemporaries—the goal is to make them ashamed of the behavior of their ancestors. But what does he really propose they do? Not to renounce taking up residence in far off lands but to do so without violence, without seizing and pillaging, in obedience to the powerful interests of commerce that would set an example of kindness and moderation. Reading Diderot in such contexts, one never knows if one should applaud his bold strokes, become infuriated at the moralizing poses he seems to enjoy, or oddly admire his relentless biting at the cuticles of his own discourse.

There is a long chapter at the end of book 4 of *The Philosophical History of the Two Indies* that Diderot authored alone and that deploys the program of moderate, enlightened colonization the French are encouraged to pursue in India to reestablish "their consideration and their power" after the disasters of the Seven Years' War. By taking a leading role in a revolt against the British, the French would become "the liberators of Hindustan" and "the idol of the princes and peoples of Asia"—on condition that they rule with justice and moderate their economic ambitions. Their commerce will be "extensive and flourishing" so long as they refrain from exerting direct constraints. "A wise people will never suffer that any encroachment should be made upon liberty or property. They will respect the conjugal tie; they will conform to the customs of the country; and wait for a change of manners from time. If they do not bend the knee before the gods of the country, they will at least carefully abstain from breaking their altars; let them rather fall by their antiquity."[54]

We should not minimize Diderot's enlightened humanism. It is a bit easy, two hundred years on, to judge it as too naïve or too moderate. This hope—somewhat naïve, it's true—for a type of domination founded on political exemplarity and commercial moderation is quite revealing. It supposes that the European way of life, at least when it rises to incarnate Enlightenment principles—moderation, justice, tolerance—will be sufficient to elicit the allegiance and admiration of other peoples. "If ye are just and humane, people will remain with you; they will do more; they will even quit distant countries to come and reside among you."[55] No need to fight against superstitions and religions, since they will spontaneously melt in the sun of the moral superiority of European tolerance. But his claim is not only moral; he makes an efficiency argument as well: "To ensure the affection of the inhabitants of any district, is the only circumstance that can render your settlements firm. Act in such a manner that these inhabitants shall defend you when you are attacked. If they do not defend, they will betray you."[56] In other words, ruling through terror and cupidity is a short-sighted political strategy. The indigenous population will always end up revolting and chasing off the colonizers. "What lesson shall we have learned from the massacre of so many Portuguese, Dutch, English, and French, unless it taught to keep upon good terms with the natives?"[57]

Diderot pleads for a peaceful domination, a "soft colonization"[58] that would impose itself all on its own thanks to the example of political moderation and the virtues of trade. He dreams of a liberal and liberating Europe that would become the "idol" of other peoples around the world, bringing them justice and prosperity until that day—distant but inevitable—when they would become the Europeans' equals, their friends, their brothers.[59] This humanitarian and Europe-centered cosmopolitanism can be found some years later during the Revolution, in the writings of Volney.

This superiority of Europe—so evident that it imposes itself automatically on other peoples without violence or coercion while bringing love and gratitude—is not Diderot's last word. At other moments, he lets doubts invade him and worries are revived. In those instances, one hears echoes of Rousseau's critique of civilization. The Enlightenment "lights" justify nothing as soon as one views matters from the perspective of the indigenous peoples.

> You are proud of your knowledge; but of what use is it to you? or of what service would it be to the Hottentots? Is it then of so much

> importance to know how to speak of virtue without practicing it? What obligation would the savage have to you when you have made him acquainted with arts, without which he is contented; with branches of industry, which can only serve to multiply his wants and his labours; or with laws, from which he cannot expect greater security than you yourselves enjoy?[60]

The multiple voices that traverse *The Philosophical History of the Two Indies*—with its additions and corrections, contradictions and retractions—make different points of view coexist. The Lumières, even if reduced to a coterie of Parisian philosophers who had been friends for many years, were far from articulating a unified doctrine. What stands out, though, is a high consciousness of living in new times characterized most notably by overseas expansion, the growth of trade, the horrors of slavery, and the greater interdependence of the different parts of the world. A major historical break took place at the end of the fifteenth century whose full effects were only completely felt three centuries later. "No event has been so interesting to mankind in general, and to the inhabitants of Europe in particular as the discovery of the New World, and the passage to India by the Cape of Good Hope. It gave rise to a revolution in the commerce, and in the power of nations; as well as in the manners, industry, and government of the whole world."[61]

How was one to understand this new world that Europe dominated via its commerce but where it created for itself previously unheard-of new needs? Economic and political equilibria were altered and called forth unprecedented remedies.[62] Should one denounce slavery and colonialism unrelentingly or reform them with prudence and moderation? Was civilization preferable to a "savage life"? Was commerce the solution or the problem? To these questions, Raynal's book formulated divergent—even contradictory—answers, sometimes on the very same page. His contemporaries picked up on these tensions. The abridged editions that circulated at the end of the eighteenth century were split into two big categories. One group of them presented to merchants and administrators copious statistical evidence and a comparative history of empires; in other words, a sort of how-to guide for the enlightened colonizer, one could say. A second group took the opposite tack, proposing an anthology of maxims in favor of justice and liberty—often transposable to the political situation within France itself—thus making Raynal a major figure of political radicalism in the eyes of the public.[63] Revolutionaries would soon identify him as an exemplary precursor but would then take back their praise in 1791, when he delivered to the Assembly a stinging letter denouncing the excesses of the Revolution.

This divergent reception of Raynal's text, which still goes on in contemporary historiographical debates, was made visible most strikingly by two famous interpretations of the signs of the times, which are said to have both drawn scrupulously on *The Philosophical History of the Two Indies*: one by Toussaint Louverture, the leader of the slave revolts in Santo Domingo, the other by Napoleon Bonaparte, who would reestablish slavery in the colonies and have Louverture interned at the fort of Joux in the Jura Mountains of France.

Louverture's reading of Raynal merits attention. It offers a simplified version of the Haitian revolution, with its slave insurrection and freedmen turning the ideals of the French Revolution against France itself. The events were popularized by the Haitian national historiography throughout the nineteenth century. Toussaint Louverture was made out to be a man of the Enlightenment, a self-aware revolutionary leader and originator of actions that Europeans could both recognize and fear. Positing Louverture as a "revolutionary conscience" forged by his appropriation of European writings—instead of associating the slave revolt with a millenarist movement or as the revolt of miserable masses—allowed Europeans to integrate the Haitian revolution into a larger history of the great liberation movements inspired by the Enlightenment, alongside the French and American revolutions.

The Philosophical History of the Two Indies seemed, it's true, to have anticipated the events in Haiti. A famous passage inspired by Louis-Sébastien Mercier prophesied a slave revolt and the emergence of a Black Spartacus.

> Already have two colonies of fugitive Negroes been established, to whom treaties and power give a perfect security from your attempts. These are so many indications of the impending storm, and the Negroes only want a chief, sufficiently courageous, to lead them on to vengeance and slaughter. Where is this great man, whom nature owes to her afflicted, oppressed, and tormented children? Where is he? He will undoubtedly appear, he will shew himself, he will lift up the sacred standard of liberty. This venerable signal will collect around him the companions of his misfortunes.[64]

It is tempting to imagine that Toussaint Louverture found in those lines the revelation of his destiny: to be a liberator of his people and thus become a hero, through his actions, on two continents. However, there are no testimonies from the time confirming the empirical truth of such a precocious reading of Raynal by Louverture—supposedly while he was the intendant on a plantation before the Revolution—and his biographers today are mostly skeptical about it ever happening. But it is true that Raynal was put forward as an important reference point once Louverture had gained power in the 1790s. *The Philosophical History* likely gave the Haitian revolution a more legitimate origin for its narrative than the voodoo ceremony at Bois-Caïman on August 14, 1791, that closely coincides with the actual slave uprising.

The same gesture is repeated and amplified by the Trinidadian historian C. L. R. James in a way that gives it considerable resonance in his major publication on the Haitian revolution. As its title, *The Black Jacobins*, clearly announces, James's interpretation of that revolution makes a double claim: it is the model of an anti-imperialist Black revolt *and* it is also inscribed in continuity with the French revolution. This view implies seeing Toussaint Louverture as a man of the Enlightenment, an "astute student of French politics," and one capable, thanks to his reading and a precocious understanding of his role, of leading the Black masses in revolt.[65] It was therefore necessary for James to make him out to be an assiduous reader of Raynal, discovering in *The Philosophical History of the Two Indies* the impetus and rationale for the revolt. Thus, James affirms that "Having read and re-read the long volume by the Abbé Raynal on the East and West Indies, he [Louverture] had a thorough grounding in the economics and politics, not only of San Domingo, but of all the great empires of Europe which were engaged in colonial expansion and trade."[66]

James, born in Tunapuna, Trinidad, in 1901 and a major figure within anticolonial Marxism linked to the Pan-African movement, saw no contradiction in positing Louverture in a dependent relationship to European thinking. On the contrary, having been nourished himself on Western culture from British literature to Marxism, he was resolutely seeking to place his universalist values in the service of African revolutions and decolonization. As a Caribbean author, he considered that he belonged to "a people whose literacy and aesthetic past is rooted in Western European civilization."[67] By writing the history of the Haitian revolution, he explicitly aimed to furnish a model for decolonization struggles, both in the Caribbean and Black Africa, that would not break with the universalism that he attributed to European culture—with its emancipatory potential carried on from the Enlightenment to the French Revolution and on through Marxism. The greatness of Louverture was to have revealed the universal potential of the European philosophers' humanist declarations by liberating "a backward and ignorant mass" and by taking up the mottos of Liberty and Equality that galvanized the French Revolution. For James, "that was why in the hour of danger Toussaint, uninstructed as he was, could find the language and accent of Diderot, Rousseau, and Raynal, of Mirabeau, Robespierre, and Danton."[68] Louverture was not content to merely seize on powerful texts to light the fire of revolt but instead revealed their authentic universal message by pulling them up and out beyond their rhetoric: "And in one respect he excelled them all. For even these masters of the spoken and written word, owing to the class complications of their society, too often had to pause, to hesitate, to qualify. Toussaint could defend the freedom of the blacks without reservation." Though possessing an elevated tone, says James, Louverture avoided all excess. He "had written neither bombast nor rhetoric but the simple and sober truth." Thus, the universality of the rights of man and of equality, first stated prudently by the philosophy of the Enlightenment, has its truth fully revealed when it comes in contact with anti-imperialist struggles.

It's this confidence in the universalist and emancipatory potential inherent in the Enlightenment heritage that is not so easy to go along with for the following generation of intellectuals from Global South countries who may truly be called postcolonial writers. In a fine rereading of James, Edward Said points out the difficulties the Trinidad historian encountered as soon as it came to reconciling a militant anti-imperialism and the universalist heritage that forbid all particularizing retrenchment. The solutions James hit upon for solving these problems were not theoretical or orthodox; they consisted instead of introducing fractures within the narrative line, as well as echoes and counterpoints. Thus, twenty-five years after the original publication, in a significantly altered political and intellectual context, James added an afterward to *Black Jacobins* in which he seeks to establish the continuity between Toussaint Louverture and Fidel Castro, inscribing the Haitian "Jacobins" within a broader history of Caribbean anti-imperialism. But he also interrupts this narrative to conduct a commentary of Aimé Césaire's *Cahier d'un retour au pays natal* (1939) and then turns to a poem by T. S. Eliot in which he claims to find the poetic energy that would allow him to overcome the tensions inherent to his tale. For Said, James's text did not offer a coherent doctrine nor a "memorable story," but instead invented a narrative mechanism that "can move us from the history of domination toward the actuality of liberation"; in other words, inscribe the Black Jacobins within a universal history of emancipation.[69]

These ambivalences in James's text, which were probably not entirely visible to him but become so for a reader of Said's incisive commentary, are central to the relationship that many postcolonial authors have with the Enlightenment heritage. That heritage appears to them as a common patrimony that nurtured them and about which they sense the emancipatory potential as soon as its universalism is understood in a meaningful way. But they also see it as one of the roots of European ideology and one of the cornerstones of Western imperialism. How then can one criticize this heritage while still positioning oneself as its descendant and advocate? How does one keep the critique of weak versions of Western universalism from falling into correspondingly weak relativism, racialism, or traditionalism? What would a postcolonial universalism, one fundamentally pluralist and dialogic, look like?

In truth, these questions are not exclusively the preoccupation of writers from the Global South. They invite anyone who wishes to break free of the deadly and sterile binary opposition that pits Europe or "the West" against the rest of the world—an opposition that endlessly repeats a Manichean reductionism by only lazily inverting the polarized terms. There are also European authors for whom the relationship to the Enlightenment became ambiguous, contradictory, ambivalent. The goal, as Michel Foucault put it in a memorable turn of phrase, was to break free of "Enlightenment blackmail"; in other words, from the all-or-nothing attitude of total acceptance or rejection.[70] How can one criticize the limitations of the Enlightenment thinkers, point out their contradictions, and denounce their blind spots, and yet recognize them as the precursors who are the starting point for that critique to be undertaken in the first place? At bottom, is this not the question taken up by a large swath of contemporary thinking? In a recent book, Sunil Agnani also finds it important to return to the controversy surrounding Louverture's alleged reading of Raynal, but he does so with larger aims in mind.[71] Along the way, he turns to a short text from Adorno's *Minima Moralia* (1951), ironically entitled "Savages Are Not Better Human Beings," in which the German philosopher ponders the enthusiasm that the Western cultural heritage can sometimes generate in Asian or African students. Far from being irremediably hostile to the Western tradition, these students turn out to be more ardent defenders of it than many European intellectuals. "One has to have this latter ["the force of tradition"] in oneself in order to hate it properly," Adorno surmises.[72]

Yet, if the Enlightenment thinkers can play this role of representing a tradition that one may criticize all the better if one has deeply assimilated it, or inversely that one may champion ever more effectively as one pursues a critique of it, then they can do so because that tradition does not allow for any easy reduction to a doctrine, coherent ensemble of precepts, or checklist of values. Rather, those thinkers were the originators of a collection of ambiguous, dialogical, and contradictory texts that stage a constantly renewing debate, an intellectual battle of infinite complexity. *The Philosophical History of the Two Indies* is exemplary in that regard. If its reception history is so contradictory, it's because of the internal contradictions working their way through this polyphonic text—contradictions that leave it open to multiple and sometimes incompatible appropriations. But it's also because of diverse expectations and representations that different generations of readers have projected onto the text in different social contexts. This polysemy has sometimes provoked suspicion or even disdain, as though the text lacked the decency to present itself properly dressed with a coherent doctrine—but that same polysemy is precisely what is so interesting about it, in my view. *The Two Indies* underscores that the Enlightenment was and remains a space for intellectual and political debate. This understanding is undoubtedly one of the great lessons offered by the postcolonial perspective, a lesson that far exceeds the question of the relations of Europe with the diverse other parts of the world. If this question seems so important to us today, it's simply because it constitutes the horizon of our own historical moment. Which is why, once again, we turn to the authors of the Enlightenment for clues to an answer, for reassurances of our modern convictions or, on the contrary, for confirmation of our doubts.

Raynal and his collaborators meditated on the unprecedented effects of globalization, the contours of European domination, and the future of a world where trade was playing an entirely new role. Two centuries on, we rediscover their debates at a time when a new globalization is growing by leaps and bounds. But Europe, far from being the leading beneficiary, seems instead to find itself dispossessed and thrown back on its heels, geographically and emotionally.

Enlightenment Anthropology

From the observations made thus far, we can tentatively draw this modest but essential lesson: the links between the intellectual movement known as the Enlightenment and European domination—be it commercial, military, or scientific—cannot be reduced to a slogan or equals sign. The Enlightenment is not the ideology of European imperialism, nor is it stained by silent and unanimous complicity with slavery. Inversely, it is not redeemed by a few soaring examples of humanitarianism or by its true concern for the unity of the human race. Universalism can itself be a trap, not only because of the particular speaking position from which it proceeds but also because modern universalism, if understood as humanism, implies an established definition of *the human* and thus an exclusion of all that falls outside that definition. Hence the importance in the eighteenth century of debates about human diversity and the differences (of nature, culture, and genre) that define mankind as the subject of a universal. The development of a scientific discourse inquiring into racial differences opened a new dimension challenging the theoretical unity of the human species that philosophers and naturalists were proclaiming in other quarters. Most of them tried to evade the contradiction by insisting on the role of history in the emergence of differences. Human diversity was rarely explained by fixed naturalist taxonomies like those that would become ascendant in the nineteenth century but was related instead to a plurality of factors, notably climatological and historical realities.[73] Enlightenment anthropology was founded on a new conception of time that associated geographical distance and temporal distance. The notion of civilization served the crucial role of coordinating human diversity within a historic new way of thinking about the evolution of societies. Europe, then, was in no way conceived as a coherent ensemble but rather as a mosaic of peoples more or less refined, barbaric, or wild.[74] These debates, so lively throughout the eighteenth century, strongly resonate for us today, at a time when the crisis of modern universalism forces us to rethink the status of cosmopolitanism in a way that avoids the essentialization of differences.[75]

This ambivalence regarding Enlightenment universalism is something we have inherited, not only as political and moral subjects riddled by the uncertainties of the modern world but also as self-reflexive subjects who have turned the social sciences into one of the cornerstones of our understanding of the world. Even if anthropology as a full-fledged academic discipline did not truly exist before the late nineteenth century, the demand for universally valid knowledge about the diversity of human societies and cultures took hold much earlier because of the undeniable interest that curious European Enlightenment figures had in knowing about the practices, mores, and customs of other peoples. This interest was the continuation of ethnographic curiosity that had already been sparked during the Renaissance by the discovery of new overseas populations and by travel narratives and missionary memoirs from Jean de Léry to Father Lafitau.[76] But the study of ethnic and cultural diversity became more systematic and subjected to formal scientific inquiry in the eighteenth century. In a famous footnote to his *Discourse on the Origin and the Foundations of Inequality among Men* (1755), Rousseau announced the theoretical project of a science of man that was both empirical and conceptual, one that would study the whole world "to learn to understand men by their similarities and their differences." Such disinterested inquiry would furnish "universal knowledge" about the diversity of societies and would replace the untrustworthy stories recounted by travelers or missionaries incapable of getting beyond their personal prejudices: "Although the inhabitants of Europe have for the past three or four hundred years flooded the other parts of the world and are constantly publishing new collections of travels and reports, I am convinced that the only men we know are the Europeans."[77]

A half century later the Ideologues took up and developed this program both methodologically and epistemologically, as one can see in Joseph-Marie de Gérando's *Considérations sur les diverses méthodes à suivre dans l'observation des peuples sauvages* (1800, ambiguously titled in English as *The Observation of Savage Peoples*). The *Société des observateurs de l'homme* was founded in 1799 by proud inheritors of Enlightenment thinking and is considered, despite its brief existence, as one of the "origins of French anthropology."[78] One may also recall the great expeditions in the Pacific during the 1760s and 1770s, notably those of James Cook, that display a true ethnographic ambition, as evidenced by the precise descriptions made by the German naturalist Georg Forster.[79] Land expeditions were important too, with the notable example of Göttingen researchers interested in linguistic and ethnic diversity who made use of Russian discoveries in Siberia.[80]

Contemporaries at the time had the feeling that they were witnessing unprecedented growth in knowledge of the cultural diversity of humanity, though at least to some thinkers that diversity seemed to organize itself along a graduated scale from savagery to civilization. This new era is exalted by Edmund Burke in a letter to Scottish historian William Robertson, dated June 9, 1777: "But now the Great Map of Mankind is unroll'd at once; and there is no state or Gradation of barbarism, and no mode of refinement which we have not at the same instant under our View. The very different Civility of Europe and China; The barbarism of Persia and Abyssinia. The erratick manners of Tartary, and of Arabia. The Savage State of North America, and of New Zealand."[81] It is worth noting that here China shares with Europe the privilege of "Civility." But the great innovation of the Enlightenment's ethnographic knowledge was to engage in a synthetic appreciation that allowed one to gaze over the totality of human diversity and bring into relationship societies as geographically distant from each other as Amerindians and Māori.

From this point onward, it's the comparatist project itself that gets sketched out. Although we associate it so strongly with modern anthropology, the roots of comparative studies are in the intellectual and publishing projects of Enlightenment thinkers, such as the grand enterprise *Cérémonies et coutumes religieuses de tous les peuples du monde*, published in Amsterdam between 1723 and 1737 by two French Protestants in exile, editor Jean-François Bernard and engraver Bernard Picard. The work, in seven thick volumes, republished many times during the century, familiarized readers with the religious ceremonies of Jews, Muslims, Hindus, and Buddhists, underlining the shared beliefs behind the inexhaustible diversity of customs. True, the approach involved more compilation than true comparison, and it was motivated less by a concern for erudition and more by a commercial and activist agenda seeking to satisfy public curiosity while making the case for broad tolerance. Yet, in transforming theology into comparative ethnography of religious practices, the authors unseated Christianity from its privileged place and invited readers to consider the great revealed religions as sets of geographically and culturally situated practices. Rather than knocking over the superstitions of others in the name of enlightened European advances, the authors used the critique of abuse, fanaticism, and superstition against Europe itself and made the argument all the more impactful by placing Europe's major religion alongside a multiplicity of other religious manifestations.[82]

Anthropologists who found it pleasing to seek out predecessors from the eighteenth century had plenty to choose from. However, that flattering genealogy turned into a stain when others took to vehemently denouncing the complicity between anthropology and European colonial domination. These critics did not target the directly political uses of the field (anthropology sometimes served colonial administrations) so much as they targeted the epistemological relationships inscribing the brand of Western power into the very center of anthropological knowledge.[83] Didn't anthropologists often seek to classify societies on a ladder of civilization where Europe would necessarily occupy the highest dominant position? Didn't the evolutionist thinking of the nineteenth century derive directly from the Enlightenment's new conception of historical time? Didn't universal reason, despite possible good intentions, result in the imposition of a single model of historical development and in the destruction of traditional cultures that anthropologists witnessed with a mixture of alarm, resignation, and complicity? Were not the key concepts of anthropology (religion, ritual, and so forth) the products of a specific historical experience and a specific intellectual history that happened in modern Europe? And on what grounds did European science arrogate to itself the right to transform other cultures into objects of knowledge?

A famous disagreement reveals the scale of the debate. Thirty years ago, a controversy of unprecedented intensity pitted Marshall Sahlins against Gananath Obeyesekere over their opposed interpretations of the death of Captain Cook in Hawaii in 1779. During his third expedition in the Pacific (1776–1779), James Cook discovered the archipelago of Hawaii, and his crew was given a friendly reception there that lasted several weeks. His departure provoked strong tensions among the local inhabitants. During an altercation on the beach between sailors and natives, Cook was killed somehow—the exact circumstances remain unclear.[84] For Sahlins, a major figure within contemporary anthropology, Cook's death was the result of deep cultural misunderstanding. Because his arrival coincided with a time of ritual festivities—the Makahiki—the native Hawaiians misidentified Cook as one of their gods, Lono, the god of fertility, which would explain the warm welcome he first received. However, his sudden departure in February 1779 went entirely against the ritual calendar and implied the disappearance of Lono in favor of the war god Ku. Thus Cook would have elicited the incomprehension and hostility of the Hawaiians to the point of fatal confrontation. The death of Cook, understood this way, was an "apotheosis" that conformed to an established anthropological motif, the ritual death of the king-god, a replica in the historical world of the mythic confrontation between Lono and the warrior god Ku.[85]

The analysis by Sahlins, relying as it did on extensive anthropological knowledge of Polynesia, made a strong impression because it tried to take into account the contingent history of Cook's arrival in Hawaii and inscribe that chance event within a structuralist-inspired anthropology. Nevertheless, the hypothesis that the Hawaiians had mistaken Cook as one of their gods provoked the anger of Obeyesekere, who charged Sahlins with perpetuating a condescending vision of Hawaiians that would have them trapped within a traditional and mythic culture and incapable of distinguishing a British sailor from a local god. Thus Obeyesekere completely reverses the Sahlins interpretation: the locals killed Cook because he was threatening the interests of their chief, whom he had taken to his ship. They had not mistaken Cook for a god but had, on the contrary, seen him for what he was, namely a foreign chief who had become a danger to them. His death was hardly a divine apotheosis but instead an act of war, of resistance even. If Sahlins was able to make the interpretation he did, it's because he was relying on later European sources, notably the writings of English missionaries from the early nineteenth century. Obeyesekere goes even further and claims that the myth of Cook as god, far from being a local myth, was a colonialist myth forged by the British, who were easily inclined to believe that the indigenous people would take the explorer to be a god—since at the time they themselves were transforming him into a national hero. In this view, Sahlins was therefore complicit, two centuries on, in European colonialism by replicating contempt for indigenous people and perpetuating the European cult around James Cook. In Obeyesekere's analysis, the respective positions of Polynesians and Europeans on the notion of belief gets inverted: the Polynesian myth of the "death of a god" was replaced by the colonialist myth of "the European who is a god for savages": "To put it bluntly, I doubt that the natives created their European god; the Europeans created him for them. This 'European god' is a myth of conquest, imperialism, and civilization—a triad that cannot be easily separated."[86]

Obeyesekere did not hesitate to foreground his own biography as a former colonized person born in Sri Lanka, thus further politicizing the disagreement. An epistemological conflict between two anthropology professors at prestigious American universities (Chicago and Princeton) thus became a postcolonial conflict between a Western inheritor of colonialism and a native who had himself experienced colonial violence and who felt personally insulted by the analyses of Sahlins. Despite all the geographical, historical, and cultural distance that separated him from the Hawaiians of the eighteenth century, Obeyesekere thought it legitimate to use his non-Western experience ("I as a Native") as the basis for affirming the capacity of indigenous people to tell a foreigner from a god. Against the culturalism of Sahlins, Obeyesekere proposed recognizing in the Hawaiians a "practical rationality"—a concept borrowed from Max Weber—that allowed them to behave in a rational manner and allowed "speaking of Polynesians as being people like us."

Sahlins did not take this criticism lying down. He devoted an entire book to the defense of his position and to an open attack on the errors of his adversary.[87] On the methodological and political levels, Sahlins flips the accusation back against Obeyesekere, reproaching him for turning the Hawaiians into "good nineteenth-century bourgeois Europeans" by endowing them with universal practical reason, a notion inherited from European philosophy. Despite his empathy, or perhaps because of it, Sahlins claims Obeyesekere paradoxically deprives the Hawaiians of their own culture and their own history, reducing them to passive victims of European imperialism. "Obeyesekere systematically eliminates Hawaiians from their own history."[88]

Even though the theme did not explicitly emerge during the controversy, it's clear that the heritage of the Enlightenment is the backdrop to the whole thing. In Obeyesekere's highly negative depiction of Cook—whom he compares to the notorious and terrifying character Kurtz in Conrad's *Heart of Darkness* (1899)—it's easy to recognize the stock theme of postcolonial critique. In this view, a great swath of modern anthropology is said to descend from European Enlightenment arrogance and colonial cynicism, the two being supposedly two sides of the same coin. Cook-Kurtz-Sahlins: this triple descendance posits a tripartite fusion between the Enlightenment's scientific curiosity, the most abject colonial violence, and modern anthropology. But Obeyesekere holds off from invalidating the principle of anthropological knowledge. Indeed, his claim to found it on a universalist conception of practical reason would seem to place its roots in the philosophy of the Enlightenment. His political criticism of European colonialism derives then from his personal experience in Sri Lanka but also from his clear attachment to anthropology as a learned discipline founded on the European inheritors within the social sciences who adhere to a universalist conception of human rationality. In this way, Obeyesekere performs the standard postcolonial gesture: linking intellectual resources from the Western tradition with the moral politics of indigenous utterance.

On his end, Sahlins seeks to dissociate the anthropology he practices, founded on the irreducible diversity of cultures and their equal dignity, from the rationalist universalism of the Enlightenment. It's a point he returns to many times in the years following the Cook controversy. "We are still struggling with what seemed like Enlightenment to philosophers of the eighteenth century but turned out to be a parochial self-consciousness of European expansion and the *mission civilisatrice*," he will write, in a vein that seems to place him alongside postcolonial critics.[89] More than the universalism of reason, the discipline is said to have inherited a "unilinear evolutionism"—a theory of progress according to which development in Europe becomes a valid model for all, even if it must be accompanied by the regrettable destruction of traditional societies. The oftentimes moving lamentation over the dislocation of cultures must be seen as the inverse of the optimism about progress. To save the scientific ambition of anthropology, conceived as the study of different coherent cultures, Sahlins turns to establishing a genealogy that he traces back to Herder, whom he considers as the exemplary figure representing the reaction of German thinking against the French Enlightenment thinkers. "The irony in this whole affair is that the anthropological concept of culture was, at its origin, anti-hegemonic. In German philosophy, which at the end of the eighteenth century was positioning itself in counterpoint to the French Enlightenment, culture was linked to another philosophy of history. As elaborated by Herder, it implied relations between imperialism and anthropology far removed from what the modern critique has considered them to be."[90] Far from being compromised by the civilizing project inherited from the French Enlightenment and taken up by nineteenth-century colonialism, which presupposed the superiority of Europe, anthropology according to Sahlins was the inheritor of another tradition that insisted on the diversity and singularity of different cultures (national, ethnic, and so forth).

But can one really say that Herder incarnates a hostile reaction to the French Lumières? Most contemporary specialists reject such a characterization, which rests on a restrictive and outdated equation of the French Enlightenment with Voltairean rationalism.[91] Moreover, in his anti-imperialist study of the Enlightenment, Sankar Muthu accords great importance to Herder.[92] This use does not invalidate the Sahlins genealogy, but it does modify it. The cultural anthropology defended by Muthu has its origin not in a hostile reaction to the Enlightenment but in currents of the French Enlightenment itself, notably one that valorizes diversity of cultures and rejects all forms of imposed uniformity.

In truth, the ambivalent relationship that anthropology as a discipline has had with the Enlightenment goes back further than postcolonial polemics. In certain respects, Sahlins repeats the theoretical gesture of Claude Lévi-Strauss from thirty years earlier. In the early 1960s, the Frenchman's program of comparative anthropology was divided between the intellectual inheritance within the social sciences which he saw himself a part of and a reexamination of European humanism that he would develop forcefully in *The Savage Mind* (1962). In a famous article that is more complex than it appears, Lévi-Strauss identified Jean-Jacques Rousseau as the founder of the sciences of man.[93] He did not accord him this label, as is sometimes thought, because of anything to do with Rosseau's supposed admiration for "savages"—neither Rousseau nor Lévi-Strauss were primitivists—but rather because of Rousseau's clear presentation of a scientific program for ethnographic observation that advocated, contrary to the vain curiosity of simple travelers, the systematic study of differences and variants. Above all, Lévi-Strauss contended, the author of *The Reveries of the Solitary Walker* (1782) had undertaken a critique of the rational European subject, thanks to a process of introspection that allowed him to explore the strangeness of foreign speech on its own terms. Moreover, Lévi-Strauss argued, this intimate experiment in "radical objectification," thanks to which Rousseau was able to free himself from false certainties of the Cartesian *cogito*, was the precondition for his accession to a position as truly empathic observer capable of identifying with others and of recognizing himself in the image he received from a diverse humanity. Two gestures operate together: the "total refusal of identification with oneself," which implies that the Western subject is destabilized and stripped of the position as observer and authority, and the acceptance of foreign cultures as forms equally endowed with human organization. Without going into the commentaries elicited by this interpretation, it is striking that Lévi-Strauss, being also confronted with the necessity of defending the scientific ambitions of anthropology while yet rejecting the affirmation of the moral or intellectual superiority of the Western subject, would turn to the writings of Rousseau, who was both a major Enlightenment figure and yet not entirely representative since he was such an acerbic critic, as was Herder, of the much-vaunted civilization and its prestige.[94] Both of them carried out a critique of the Enlightenment in which they indicted themselves, questioning from the inside the supposed good conscience of learned, enlightened Europeans and leaning in favor of destabilizing the certitudes of their contemporaries.[95] They therefore offer anthropologists a solid lever, that of a European knowledge, which seeks less to reassure itself but rather to welcome the affirmation of a difference. Both are exemplary figures carrying out a theoretical gesture anchored in Western culture while refusing all overarching superiority, and therefore both are able to nourish a "lateral universalism," to borrow again from the text of Merleau-Ponty quoted in my introduction, which not surprisingly focuses on Lévi-Strauss.[96] This gesture, animated by a deep desire for knowledge, both enriches and renders more delicate the universalist goal of knowledge first articulated by the Enlightenment thinkers. A major current within anthropology has used it as a source of inspiration to get beyond the sterile opposition between the universalism of Western science and the relativism of cultural particularities and particularism.

Anthropology was forced to undergo a reexamination of its status as a field of knowledge and its ties with European colonialism earlier than other social science disciplines. The two examples sketched above hardly claim to be a full account of the history of this conversation, but they do evoke the inaugural scene that for European knowledge at any rate remains central; namely the initial confrontation with a diversity of human societies during the early eighteenth-century beginnings of the Enlightenment. Modern universalism, founded on the equality of human beings as rational actors, finds there its theoretical anchor but also its limits, since it assigns as the project for the sciences of man a description of the borders, internal and external, of the human—in other words, the task of thinking about the status of natural and cultural differences. However, this inaugural scene is one of conflict that offers no coherent doctrinal program—so much so, in fact, that anthropologists, even if they are opposed to a Western rationalism that strikes them as excessively Europe-centered and exaggeratedly humanist, cannot help turning to the founding debates of the eighteenth century, which have influenced them much more than they are willing to admit.

In similar fashion, for the last twenty years or so historians have paid closer attention to the relations between Enlightenment figures and non-European worlds. This interest is not simply one of fashion but is instead the result of transformations of the intellectual space marked in particular by the emergence of researchers from formerly colonized countries. This interest takes up especially the transformations that affect our present times.[97] What does the heritage of the Enlightenment mean when Europe no longer exercises a cultural monopoly, when the globalization of trade renders the world more interdependent than ever, and when ever-more-intense instances of cultural hybridization generate in return movements that seek to essentialize differences to recreate communities of homogeneous belonging? The time has gone by when this heritage could be claimed and defended with a tranquil good conscience that nothing could perturb. But claimed by whom and defended against whom or what?

Nothing is more mistaken than to see the Enlightenment as a monolith, whether to show off one's anticolonialist and emancipatory virtues, or on the contrary to denounce an ethnocentric closed-mindedness that is incapable of seeing beyond European narcissism. In truth, on this point as with so many others, the Enlightenment was a time of intense doubts, debates, and reexaminations. Hence the great number of polysemic, fragmented, and ironic texts open to a multitude of interpretations. Nothing is less dogmatic than this period that saw the invention of both a universal concept of man outside of the Christian model as well as the idea of a destiny specific to Europe. If the Enlightenment figures were fundamentally plural and pluralist in their relations to the diversity across the globe, it is because they were responsible for the emergence of a moment of reflection stimulated by acute consciousness of the heightened interdependence between regions of the world that provoked at once hopes, worries, enthusiasm, and criticism. We must rediscover the power to question that came with that reflexivity.

It is pointless to seek to efface the local and historic inscription of Enlightenment thinkers. Postcolonial readings have the merit of putting their finger on the open wound and taking on the discomfort generated both by Enlightenment universalism and by its rejection. They are able to do so thanks to the position of postcolonial authors who are both inheritors and critics of European thinking, having been nourished by a cultural tradition whose power of exclusion they acutely perceive along with its potential to spur emancipation. This vexed relationship finds a favorable echo in the political ambivalence of eighteenth-century texts that postcolonial readings are skilled at revealing. This is probably the reason why those readings help us in our reexamination of the legacy of the Enlightenment, now that the universality of Western modernity is no longer automatic or given. They require us to ask who the "we" is claiming this heritage and to acknowledge that the legacy is something that we can only welcome by giving up all dogmatic allegiances and by remaining faithful to the hesitations it allows one to glimpse rather than to the certainties it may display.

CHAPTER TWO

Is Civilization European?

In 1934, the French historian Paul Hazard began his famous book on the crisis of the European conscience or mind [*La Crise de la conscience européenne*] with a chapter devoted to the new mobility of Europeans. The exploration of the world, the confrontation with the other, and the new interest in the great civilizations of the East are said to explain the disruptive cultural and intellectual ferment at the turn of the century in 1700. The first chapter, entitled "From Stability to Movement," concludes with these words: "the *conscience* of old Europe was troubled and, wanting to be upset, it was."[1] This diagnosis resonates strangely today, when Europe is summoned to be (morally) conscious of the limits of its universalist pretensions in part by acknowledging the existence of other histories. For postcolonial thinkers, as we have seen, the Enlightenment underscores the European conceit of having a monopoly on reason—a conceit that unfurled itself with more assurance than before as the European hold over the world increased, extending now from the Indian Ocean to the Pacific Islands. But is it true that Enlightenment thinking derived from a discovery of alterity, an opening-up to the world, and a mental shake-up and reexamination, as Hazard claimed, or are these just other names for Western hegemony?

Formulated in this way, as we saw in the last chapter, the question is unanswerable. However, it is possible to modify the terms and ask about the way Europeans in the eighteenth century exerted themselves to articulate in one historical narrative the affirmation of their specificity and their consciousness of living in a world more globalized than it had ever been before. The crisis of the European mind or conscience is perhaps better understood, then, as a heightened consciousness that came with the affirmation of a properly historic discourse on Europe. One of the specificities of the Enlightenment thinkers was to endow Europe with a history, to think of Europe as the outcome of a specific historical process, whereas until then it had been conceived as a geographic space or religious or cultural entity. The name used by thinkers of the day to designate this historic process was *civilization*. Although the word in French did not appear until 1756 in Mirabeau's *L'Ami des hommes* and in English in 1767 in Adam Ferguson's *Essay on the History of Civil Society*, the notion was in circulation already at the turn of the century and may be considered as one of the key traits of Enlightenment historical thinking. It named a gradual passage from savagery or barbarism to a civilized, polite state. At the end of the century, it began to name the result of this process: the state of a civilized society. Most often it described a movement, a history.

If the notion of civilization is complex, it's because it articulates two distinct problems. The first concerns the historicity of the passage from feudal barbarism to modern civilization, which characterizes the trajectory specific to Europe after the fall of the Roman Empire. The second is the relationship that Europe, which was then thinking of itself as now civilized, had with two sets of Others: first, the American "savages" and the "barbarians" on the steppes of Eurasia—in other words, all those who were situated before civilization; and second, the great Asian empires, China and India, whose great age and undeniable cultural richness both fascinated and troubled the Europeans.[2]

These two problems are often studied separately. The narrative of European history as a process of civilization is the focus of specialists of historiography who concentrate on the moral value, accorded or refused, to the scientific and material advances of Europe.[3] The European outlook on other societies, on the other hand, is most often pursued through the memoirs of travelers, explorers, and missionaries, through Orientalist studies, and even natural history.[4] In the first case, Europe is confronted with its own history; in the second, it is confronted with figures of alterity.

However, this dichotomy leads scholars to overlook an essential evolution in European thinking, namely that the opposition between Europe and these others is no longer a face-to-face relation between incommensurable entities—as was the case in ancient Greece or in medieval Christian times—but is instead inscribed in a history. One of the questions that leading Enlightenment authors constantly faced is the tricky matter of the integration of non-European peoples within a universal history whose narrative structures were henceforth being ordered by the process of European civilization. As the new narrative of European history is built on the ruins of the old Biblical narrative and Christian universalism, it makes possible and even necessary the construction of a truly universal history, one that includes a place for non-Europeans and non-Christians—but this place becomes in turn intrinsically contradictory, since it strives to make two incompatible points of view coexist. This unresolved contradiction between the narrative of a European exceptionality and the construction of a universal history is perhaps most evident in the book that serves as the template for the Enlightenment's great historical narrative, Voltaire's *Essay on Universal History, the Manners, and Spirit of Nations* (1756).

We will not seek to expose the "theft of history," the triumphant Eurocentrism that is said to have seized all of global history, nor are we planning to dig up proto-anticolonialist Enlightenment thinkers who would conveniently provide some reassurance about accepting the heritage of European modernity.[5] We shall instead seek to understand the specificity and the ambivalences—and perhaps certain impasses—in the historical narrative from among the numerous forms of discourse over the eighteenth century that have contributed to thinking about Europe and its relations to the world.[6]

A European History

Europe was not a new idea in the eighteenth century. As a geographic entity and as a space juxtaposed in opposition to Asia in particular, it had existed since antiquity. However, it would now take on a new meaning, as Europe came to be thought of historically, namely as the result of a long process of social, political, and cultural maturation. The first phase of this mutation of the idea of Europe occurred during the Renaissance as a consequence of colonial expansion in the Americas. The historical and no longer just mythical opposition between savages and civilized became a structuring element of representations of the world. And yet this discovery of the "historicity of alterity" was incomplete and fundamentally unstable.[7] Two elements made the binary distinction between savage and civilized reversible: first, the figure of the barbarian at the center of Europe, which was reactivated by the violence of religious wars; second, the prospect of European degeneration into savages after contact with the Other. About the barbarian figure, Jean de Léry's famous text documents the cannibalistic practices during the siege of Sancerre—practices that directly challenged the idea of a polite, civilized Europe but that were also the symptom of a wider anxiety that would affect the stability of the image of the savage.[8] The second element, the prospect of Europeans turning into savages as a result of close contact, was a fear that rippled through the entire sixteenth and seventeenth centuries.[9] The distinction between civilized Europeans and other peoples was therefore as crucial as it was fragile. The fall into savagery—either as a result of fanatical religious violence or geographic displacement—might happen very rapidly.

With this volatility in mind, one sees that the great innovation of the eighteenth century was the production of a coherent historical narrative of European history. Until then Europe had, strictly speaking, no history. It was merely the outer frame of two types of history that hardly gave it any significance of its own. One was a providential history, for which the model was Bossuet's *Discours sur l'histoire universelle* (1672); the second was the history of European states, such as one finds in Pufendorf's *Introduction to the History of the Principal Kingdoms and States of Europe* (1687). In the first kind of history, Europe is not a historical object of consideration; the important entity is Christianity. In the second kind, the history of various political entities is recounted but without the question of Europe receiving any explicit attention.[10] Over the course of the eighteenth century, however, several authors would develop a general narrative of European history, starting with the fall of the Roman Empire and the liberation from dynastic frameworks. The deliberate goal of these histories was to establish the specificity of Europe as a political and cultural entity—in other words, as a civilization. This narrative would take different forms and hesitate over the concepts it mobilized (about mores, the eras of the human spirit, the phases of development). It was above all a self-aware reflexive discourse in which eighteenth-century authors underscored the singularity of the moment that they were in the process of living, a time that they began to designate as an enlightened century.

The emergence of this history of Europe in the middle of the eighteenth century was made possible by several important changes. Even if the theme of European savagery continued sometimes as a rhetorical topos, it tended to fade against the steady affirmation of the cumulative, progressive character of European mores and of the now uncontested superiority of Europeans. The quarrel of the ancients and the moderns was especially emancipating for modern Europe, freeing it of a longstanding inferiority complex in relation to the grandeur of antiquity. The triad of ancients, moderns, and savages was replaced by the binary opposition between the barbarian and the civilized, and in this pairing Europeans always occupied the position of the civilized and therefore the modern. The theme of barbarism would then become important within discussions of the oriental margins of Europe, all those places that had not (yet) been touched by the civilization of mores.[11] Finally, the new autonomy of knowledge in its confrontation with religious dogma permitted a properly historic account of European history, one that no longer relied on theological supports but instead fully affirmed "the legitimacy of the modern age."[12]

With some differences in focus but converging results, J. G. A. Pocock and Karen O'Brien both demonstrated the existence of this new grand narrative of European history.[13] And both agreed that Voltaire's *Essay on Manners*, first published in 1756, was its founding text.[14] The importance of this treatise has often been underestimated, even though it occupied a central place in Voltaire's historiographical and philosophical project and was enormously influential throughout Europe.[15]

Voltaire's *Essai sur les mœurs* (known in its English translation as *An Essay on Universal History, the Manners, and Spirit of Nations: From the Reign of Charlemagne to the Age of Lewis XIV*) was explicitly constructed as a rejection of Bossuet's Christian history. It proposes a history of Europe starting from the time of Charlemagne (CE 748–814) with an emphasis on two essential traits: first, the progressive emergence from the barbaric and Christian Middle Ages into a system of competitive states whose rivalry assured political stability and commercial emulation; second, the evolution of manners in a progressively more civilized and refined direction. Voltaire does not use the word *civilisation*; however, the verb *to civilize*, "*civiliser*," occurs often, as does the reflexive verb "*se civiliser*." His narrative rests on the opposition between the barbarism of the High Middle Ages (CE 1000–1300)—about which he says, "the only reason to know that history is to condemn it"—and the continuous progress of manners that characterized Europe starting in the sixteenth century. Starting in late antiquity and through to the end of the Middle Ages, it seems sometimes that Voltaire can only see a long spectacle of atrocities and absurdities: "human understanding degenerated amidst the most cowardly and crazy superstitions. These superstitions were pursued to such an extent that monks became lords and princes. They had slaves and those slaves did not even dare to complain. All of Europe crawled along in this low condition until the thirteenth century and only overcame it through terrible convulsions."[16] And in another of many passages, all with more or less the same tone and tenor, he writes: "So it is that you will find in this vast tableau of human madness the feelings of theologians and the superstitions and fanaticism of different peoples in endless variety but always constantly plunging the world into stupidity and calamity—until the day arrives when a few academies, a few enlightened societies make our contemporaries blush over so many centuries of barbarism."[17]

The reference to academies and enlightened societies is no accident. Starting in the sixteenth century, and despite the convulsions of religious wars, the refinement of arts and letters—thanks to the Italian courts and afterward to great sovereigns and their academies—was one of the important motors of progress of societies and mores. With the rise of commerce, the decline of feudal society and the political role of the pope, and the establishment of a certain equilibrium of power among the great European kingdoms, the conditions were united to assure Europe's unprecedented development: "It is easy to observe from the picture we have given of Europe since the time of Charlemagne to the present day that this part of the world is incomparably more populous, more civilized, more wealthy, and more enlightened than it was before, and that it is also greatly superior to the former Roman Empire with the exception of Italy."[18] Not only is the process that leads to modern Europe cumulative from the sixteenth century onwards, but it unites in a single movement improvements in demography ("*plus peuplée*"), economics ("*plus riche*"), culture ("*plus civilisée*"), and intellect ("*plus éclairée*"). Voltaire can therefore affirm in conclusion, and with a last allusion to the Middle Ages, that the entire purpose of the *Essay on Manners* is "to see the degree to which we've gone from those barbaric and rustic times to the polite civilization of our own."[19]

In some respects, Voltaire is situating this text as the extension of *Remarks on History* and especially *The Age of Louis XIV*, which he was just finishing as he got started on the *Essay on Manners*. The book on the Sun King lays out a decidedly European perspective and claims to depict "the spirit of men in the most enlightened century there ever was." Voltaire is thrilled "to have shown that in the previous century men acquired more knowledge ["*lumières*"], from one end of Europe to the other, than in all preceding ages."[20] Going a step further, in the *Essay on Manners* Voltaire abandons the idea of the four great centuries (of Alexander, Caesar Augustus, the Medici, and Louis XIV). Antiquity is consigned to a distant past, leaving the age of Louis XIV not only as a particularly elevated summit and the focus of a history that experienced wins and losses, but as the provisional endpoint of a continuous progress. The century of Louis XIV is no longer depicted as the incarnation of perfection that invites comparisons with other glorious periods of history, but as a stage in a process of perfection within an unfinished history that extends down to the present time.

Voltaire's *Essay on Manners* became a template for the historical narrative of Europe that would serve many authors throughout the century, notably the great Scottish historian William Robertson for his *View of the Progress of Society in Europe from the Subversion of the Roman Empire to the Beginning of the Sixteenth Century*, which served as an introduction to his *History of Emperor Charles V* (1769).[21] It also influenced other, less famous authors' work, such as William Russell's *History of Modern*

Europe (1779),[22] which was republished several times, and Nicolas de Bonneville's *Histoire de l'Europe moderne* (1789).[23]

There are of course important differences between these authors. Robertson systematizes the line of progress, while Voltaire constructs a vision of history that is less coherent and more ironic and sometimes overtly sarcastic. As the leader of the presbyterian Church of Scotland, Robertson does not make the same polemical use of history against religion. For example, Voltaire denounced the Crusades as an example of absurd fanaticism, whereas Robertson draws attention to their unintended positive impact on development and intercontinental exchanges. On the other hand, Voltaire would insist on the civilizing role of cities and royal courts, and on the deeds and decisions of great sovereigns. The essential point, however, is their common framework that places the fall of the Roman Empire in the West as the starting point of European history. The latter is presented as the emergence over time of a system of competitive states of roughly equivalent power that allowed commerce to develop along with the progressive civilization of mores and respect for the rule of law. The exclusion of ancient history—in other words, of biblical history and the history of Greece and Rome—is a fundamental feature of this new conception of European history:

> It seems to me that if someone wanted to take advantage of the present moment, they would not spend their time absorbed in old fables. I would advise a young person to have only a passing knowledge of distant times, and to begin their serious study of history at the moment when it becomes truly interesting for us which I believe to be near the end of the fifteenth century. The printing press which was invented at that time makes history less uncertain. The face of Europe changes.[24]

Here two arguments intersect: first, that the reliability of sources marks a dividing line between serious written history based on printed documents as opposed to histories based on "old fables," and second, above all, that the true birth of Europe occurs at the end of the Middle Ages. The clear disqualification of ancient history as reliable signifies that continuity has been abandoned and that modern Europe takes on its own legitimacy, inscribed in a new and recent history.

The project of a philosophical history of modern Europe stands in opposition to pure fascination with antiquity—a fascination that would, however, remain important in other areas of intellectual and scholarly activity. Following Voltaire's example, Bonneville declares right from the start in his *Histoire de l'Europe* that "the history of the Greeks and

Romans will have no place in this work. Those columns of tyranny are broken and best left to the abyss of centuries gone by. The history of our modern Europe will furnish all that is necessary to know about men and empires."[25] This exclusion has major consequences. For one, it breaks with the Humanist conception that had defined Europe in relation to a Classical heritage that was considered to be in very close proximity and that had ignored the history of the intervening centuries. The historicity of modern Europe, perceived as the result of a postimperial history, rejected antiquity as its point of origin. The other essential element in this narrative of the founding historical identity of Europe is the way that the exit from feudalism is recounted as having taken place at the end of the Middle Ages and the start of the sixteenth century—without passing through the imperial stage of universal monarchy—by directly praising instead the interdependent system of a balance of powers. David Hume had earlier explained the development of knowledge in Europe as the consequence of its political divisions: "Nothing is more favorable to the rise of politeness and learning, than a number of neighboring and independent states, connected together by commerce and policy."[26] Modern Europe, he wrote, resembled ancient Greece in its fragmentation into unified rival city-states. Hence the importance for Robertson of the reign of Charles V as a founding moment whose history he would set out to write:

> It was during his reign, too, that the different kingdoms of Europe, formerly single and disjoined, became so thoroughly acquainted, and so intimately connected with each other, as to form one great political system, in which each took a station, wherein it has remained since that time with less variation, than could have been expected after the events of two active centuries.[27]

For Robertson, as for Voltaire, the historical process by which modern Europe civilizes itself is more chaotic than linear. We are not, here, in the realm of theodicies of history as they will come to be developed in Germany with Isaak Iselin.[28] Instead, both Robertson and Voltaire insist that it's the emergence of a competitive system of powerful and interdependent states that permitted the two key traits of modern Europe: the development of trade and the refinement of mores. As a result, their historical narrative definitively turns its back on political history in favor of a social and cultural history of Europe.[29] The two key words of this narrative in both its French and English versions are *commerce*, which refers in both languages to the exchange of merchandise as well as the exchange of views and attitudes through social relations, and *mœurs*, in English *mores* or *manners.*

This history of Europe is itself truly European insofar as it develops within a transnational dynamic, thanks to the already-rapid circulation of texts at the time. Robertson's thinking was nourished by his reading of Montesquieu and Voltaire, who both receive his explicit homage.[30] The *Essay on Manners* was published in France in 1754, but a British edition comes out the same year. Selected passages appear in the *Scots* magazine in 1757, and an English translation is published in Scotland in 1758.[31] William Russell refers to Voltaire many times in his *History of Modern Europe*, sometimes to criticize him—proving that the *Essay on Manners* had become the reference work for anyone wishing to write the history of Europe. In similar fashion, Robertson's works were enormously popular in Europe, as one can see from the rapid succession of editions and translations. The historiographical construction called the "Scottish Enlightenment" and presented as an idiosyncratic intellectual movement has tended to obscure this publishing success story by presenting Robertson as an important author but one situated on the margins of Europe and representing a separate tradition. It's worth recalling, however, that his *History of the Reign of Charles V* was immediately translated into French, German, and Italian.[32] In France, translator Jean-Baptiste Suard, himself already a part of the Parisian cultural milieu, was put in contact with Robertson by David Hume and Baron d'Holbach, and he later received pages of Robertson's texts piecemeal as soon as they came off the British presses.[33] Robertson did not appear to his readers as a representative of Scottish thinking but as a great European historian whom the *Correspondance littéraire* placed alongside Montesquieu and Voltaire.

From European History to Global History?

The narratives that consider Europe to be the outcome of several centuries of history have the effect of making other histories both possible and problematic. Several years later, Robertson published his famous *History of America* (1777), a major work that provoked raucous debates about the history of the new world.[34] The existence of this history of America came about after Robertson's decision to remove from his history of Charles V the passages devoted to the discovery and colonization of America—which he did in order to make them the focus of a specific study to be published later. This decision is often reported as having been purely practical: the lengthy developments would have made the Charles V history book exaggeratedly long. The truth of the matter is more complex and interesting, with Robertson himself claiming he omitted "considerable but detached articles in the reign of Charles V."[35] It's important to measure the importance of this gesture that separated out this colonial history. First, Robertson seems to hold the view that one can perfectly well write a history of Europe without saying a word about America. Secondly, one has to have first written a history of Europe in order to later write the history of America, its empires, and its colonization by Europeans.[36]

Robertson's career as a historian began with his *History of Scotland*, published in 1759. It's tempting to read a complete chronological list of his writings, which ends with reflections on the history of India, as a continuously broader evolution from national history to European history to a global history that ranges from American Indians to the venerable Indian culture. It would seem that the history of non-European civilizations becomes possible once Europe is thought of as the outcome of a historical process. Only then can other societies be graspable in their proper historicity and in comparison with the European trajectory. In this way, the history of America takes on a different status. Therefore, the way in which Father Lafitau compared the mores [*mœurs*] of American savages with the customs and habits of antiquity, trying thereby to think of Amerindian history within a universal Christian history, no longer makes any sense. Robertson, like Voltaire again in this regard, being incapable it would seem of understanding what's at stake, can only heap sarcasm on Lafitau.[37] This is why he makes assiduous efforts at historical documentation, notably by his engagement with Spanish sources, when describing the Aztec and Inca empires.[38] The result is a nuanced judgment that presents these empires as a stage on the way to civilization. They are "civilized states" compared to Indian tribes, but not yet "truly civilized" in comparison with European nations; but at any rate they have been fully integrated by Robertson within a universal history of "the progress of the species."[39]

One could imagine Voltaire following a similar evolution. Examining the line from *The Age of Louis XIV* to the *Essay on Manners* to his *Philosophy of History* and then his *Considerations on India*, it would seem his historical writings also broaden over time from national history to world history. The reality, however, is more complex. Starting in the 1730s, a recurring theme for Voltaire is the necessity of writing a truly universal history and not merely a European one. In a little-known text from 1738, he depicts the surprise of an educated Chinese merchant traveling in Amsterdam who discovers the ignorance and disinterest of Europeans when it comes to the history of China.[40] With his customary irony, Voltaire shows the limited cultural history possessed by the typical European, whose knowledge is entirely centered on history of the Church and classical antiquity. He also notes the relatively modest size of the glory of Europe's great men when placed on a world scale of grandeur. Hearing the name of Julius Caesar, the Chinese merchant exclaims, "Ah yes, I've heard of him. Wasn't he Turkish?" Voltaire is especially mocking of the European's disdain for other cultures and takes particular aim at Bossuet's *Discourse on Universal History*, a work he's constantly attacking in book after book, reproaching Bossuet for having "left the universe out of his universal history," and for giving too much attention to Greeks and Romans, and especially to "the little Jewish people."[41] His criticism of a holy history of mankind is thus paired with a criticism of Eurocentric history.

When he ventures to propose his own "general history," Voltaire tries to avoid these mistakes at all costs. Thus, the *Essay on Manners* begins with chapters on China and India and concludes with a discussion of Japan and China and India again. The "philosophy of history" that Voltaire will publish in 1766 and that will serve as an introduction to later editions of the *Essay on Manners* proposes a reflection on the origin of societies and a review of the great eastern civilizations of antiquity by means of a panoramic tableau of China, India, Persia, and Arabia.[42] Although before the eighteenth century the curiosity of European travelers and Jesuit missionaries about the refinement of the court of the great Mughal emperors or imperial China may have been more or less satisfied with an immobile and even immutable description of these great empires, Voltaire makes an effort to integrate them into a common history that would be truly universal and no longer simply have them be adjuncts within a Western Christian account conditioned by the biblical narrative.[43] The secularization of European history, freed from holy history, opens the way to writing what we would today call global or decentered history. Thus, about the inhabitants of ancient Araby, Voltaire can declare, "To my knowledge, they are not written about in our universal histories produced in our West. They bear no relation to the little Jewish nation which became the focus and foundation of our so-called universal histories wherein a certain number of authors, all copying each other, forget three-quarters of the globe."[44]

However, this bold enterprise is not really achieved. After the opening chapters, which propose a salutary decentering, two-thirds of the book are almost entirely devoted to European history and more specifically Western European history, or as Voltaire sometimes calls it, "the Catholic part of our Christian Europe." The Orient only resurfaces starting in the sixteenth century in the wake of European discoveries and conquests. The perspective that organizes the whole work above all is that of modern Europeans now assured of their superiority. For proof one need only follow the evolution of the pronoun *we* (*nous*) in Voltaire's text. It often designates the dyad author-reader, especially in the beginning, and moreover implies a female reader, since the work is openly addressed to a certain Émilie du Châtelet. Examples are "*nous avons vu*" (we have seen), "*nous verrons*" (we shall see), and so forth. More generally, *nous* names the historian and his public, in other words those directly interested in reading Voltaire's history. However, *nous* is also employed to mean "the Europeans." When Voltaire criticizes Bossuet for having "completely forgotten the ancient peoples of the Orient," he asks the following question: "If we are nourished by food from their lands, clothed in their cloth, entertained by games they invented, and even instructed by their ancient moral fables, why would we neglect the spirit of these nations where our European merchants traveled as soon as they were able to find a path to reach them?"[45] What founds and legitimates the interest in the history of the Chinese and Indians are the ties that Voltaire and his readers maintain, as Europeans, with these peoples. These ties are mostly commercial but also cultural. Opening the universal history to include the Orient is not purely speculative, nor is it motivated by a simple moral or philosophical imperative that would require, out of a sense of basic fairness or formal rigor, taking account of all human beings. It proceeds above all from an acute awareness of Europe's new situation within a globalized world: Europeans owe less now to ancient traditions that link them to a biblical heritage and to Greco-Roman antiquity than they do to the flux of commerce that has turned Europe into the point of convergence of spices, textiles, and entertainment.

This consciousness of a "we" that designates the inhabitants of modern enlightened Europe is not, however, only a matter of having this global awareness; it also implies reflecting on the specificity of Europe and the way that specific quality manifests itself historically. The last chapter of the book, entitled "Summary of This History," is entirely structured by an opposition between "us" (in French also *nous*) and "them" (*eux*). When the moment arrives for drawing lessons from his long narrative, Voltaire opposes "our Europe" (but also in these same pages "our Christian Europe," "our part of Europe," "our practices") to the rest of the world, specifically to "orientals." He makes an effort to discover "the greatest difference between us and orientals."[46] Whereas he had been constantly demonstrating both the unity of human nature and the very wide diversity of mores, even within the history of Europe, Voltaire now asserts that "Everything differs between them and us: religion, rules of politeness, government, mores, food, clothing, and ways of writing, speaking, and thinking."[47]

It would be tempting to seize on this obvious reversal to conclude that the inclusive gesture toward non-European societies was only a tactical maneuver entirely dictated by Voltaire's polemical drive against the Church and its providential history, conveniently incarnated by Bossuet. In that case, Voltaire's new history would only have produced a new form of Eurocentrism—no longer the Christian-inspired one of Bossuet but that of the Enlightenment. In the latter version, the triumph of European civilization stands out all the more, not only against the long and barbarous Middle Ages but now also in contrast to the stagnation of the once-prestigious oriental empires. The great age and grandeur of the Chinese and Indian cultures—models of civility—are indeed exalted, but they are also relegated to a distant past where they seem stuck in time and unable to evolve. And when the "orientals" reappear, it's in the context of commercial and then colonial domination by Europe, starting in the sixteenth century. At bottom, Voltaire's admiration for the venerable Chinese and Indian cultures should not fool us if in truth it is only a feint within a new form of specifically modern Eurocentrism, one that is no longer religious but historic, and its praise of the Orient merely part of kicking it upstairs and out of history. Worse still, this Eurocentrism seems to take a disturbing racialized turn with Voltaire's polygenism, evidenced by his repeated insistence on the diversity of human races and reaffirmed strongly in his "Philosophy of History," which serves as the introduction, starting in 1769, to the *Essay on Manners*.[48]

The Ambivalent Qualities of Universal History

The above analysis, however, would not do justice to the genuinely ambivalent elements that run through Voltaire's text and that may explain why he never stopped returning to it to make corrections, additions, and changes. These tensions derive from the incompatibility of two imperatives: on the one hand, to write a truly universal history that takes into account non-European peoples; on the other, to posit a genealogy of European modernity. These two goals share a desire to profoundly modify the image that Christian Europe had of itself by bringing about a double change in perspective. First, Europe is now stripped of its privileged status: its history is only one history among others, and its development, when compared to the history of civilized empires, is belated. That was already the lesson to be learned from *Interview with a Chinese Person*: viewed from the immense Chinese empire, European history is small potatoes; even Julius Caesar is practically a nobody. Second, the filiation with biblical and Greco-Roman history is broken. For Voltaire, modern Europe is explained by two phenomena: the immanent process of civilization that started in the sixteenth century and the transfer of knowledge and treasure from the Orient that resulted from the development of commerce. "In learning as a philosopher what makes the world turn, you should first look to the Orient which was the cradle of all arts and gave everything to the West," he writes in the introduction to the *Essay on Manners and the Spirit of Nations*. It is with this perspective in mind that one must understand the repeated attacks against the history of "the little Jewish people" as something more than simply Voltaire's well-known anti-Judaism. Jewish history is both reduced in significance to match Jewish people's demographic and political size on a global scale, according to a principle that one could call realist, and it is also divested of being the origin of Western history, according to a principle that one could call genealogical. Nonetheless, there is an obvious incompatibility between these two critical perspectives that may at first glance seem convergent: they follow from irreducibly different points of view. The "realist" principle, which claims to measure objectively the importance of each history on a global scale, presumes the ability to look down sagely as a distant neutral outsider and judge the various places to be occupied by ancient China, the Egypt of the pharaohs, the Roman Empire, and the Caliphate of Bagdad within that universal history. The second, genealogical principle implies a presentist point of view that organizes the history of the world as a function of the relation that the author and his public hold, or think they hold, with each particular history.[49]

By integrating the history of non-European societies into a universal history conceived as a genealogy of modern Europe, Voltaire necessarily grants them a subordinate place, no matter how sincere his admiration for them might be. But as payback, so to speak, their presence also necessarily undermines the narrative of European history. Voltaire's version of that narrative is indeed much less confident than the version produced by Scottish historians, not to mention the philosophies of history of the nineteenth century. Not only does the thousand-year narrative after the fall of the Roman Empire reduce European history to an inconsequential succession of absurdities and crimes only loosely structured around the struggle between the Empire and the Church, but the recent history itself, as presented in the *Essay on Manners*, no longer possesses the luminous self-evident quality it had in the *Remarks on History*. As he advances in the writing of this history, Voltaire increasingly emphasizes the very imperfect character of Europe's progress—imperfect because still darkened by the persistence of superstitions. This undercutting is so extensive throughout the *Essay*—with Voltaire stringing together beads of irony, criticisms of European history, and high praise for Brahmins in India, the religion of Confucius, artistic developments across the Arab world in the early Islamic age, and even the achievements of the Turco-Mongol conqueror Tamerlane—that a reader would understandably conclude that the author had serious doubts about European or Western superiority. In fact, he will be criticized for having such doubts by German historians, especially Johann Christian Gatterer and August Ludwig Schlözer, who, despite their desire to produce a global or universal history, remain attached to a providentialist conception of universal history.[50] Behind what they saw as Voltaire's dilettantism and his open disdain for erudition, it was the Frenchman's way of questioning the significance of European history that they found really dangerous.

Voltaire's irony is not solely responsible for causing trouble over the specificity of Europe. By displacing the principal object of the historical narrative—now no longer the history of kings and battles but instead one of peoples and their practices, customs, and beliefs—Voltaire foregrounds the notion of "*mœurs*" (mores, manners) so much that it becomes the watchword and program of the entire historiographic enterprise. The term does not receive a rigorous definition, but it supposes an implicit theory of historical change. For Voltaire, *mœurs* names those parts of peoples' ways of thinking and behaving that change in the course of history, as opposed to those parts that remain common and stable (which are defined as being human nature). Voltaire's insistence on the total historicity of *mœurs* is the counterpoint to his polygenism. His history is not naturalist. It does not ground differences in *mœurs* on racial or environmental distinctions but instead inscribes them in the thickness of historic time and records their variation as a function of social and political conditions and the role of religion and the state of knowledge.

This approach raises a new question: if the *mœurs* of Europeans have been constantly changing, if they are entirely unlike what they were in the Middle Ages, how does one find a fixed point in European history to explain its singular trajectory? If one can always find equivalents for European *mœurs* in non-European societies, what will serve as the opposition between "us" and "them"?[51] When Voltaire recapitulates his argument and seeks a way to characterize the opposition between Europeans and Orientals, he rejects various criteria one after another until finally retaining as his choice the place that women occupy in European societies. It's an essential point that all historians of European civilization will later insist on, and it will become a common belief on exploratory voyages and in Orientalist studies.[52] Nonetheless it is striking that the cultural specificity of Europe rests on so little at the end of such a vast historiographic undertaking. Since human nature, as Voltaire recalls, is unique and always the same, whereas *mœurs* vary over time and space, universal history could simply be an enormous cartographic project of this infinite variation. Lacking as he does a sociological theory of *mœurs* (unlike Norbert Elias two centuries later), the danger for Voltaire is that his history may dissolve in this diversity. In that case, not only would European history lose its privileged status, but the progress and advances accomplished over the previous two centuries would have their fragility revealed.

Over the course of revisions of his text, Voltaire adds skeptical remarks that undermine the grand European narrative and bring Europeans down not just a peg or two lower than the refined societies of Asia or Arabia but lower even than the most primitive peoples in the European imagination: "Considering only the customs that I've just discussed, one would think it the portrait of Negros and Hottentots; and one must confess that on more than one point we have not been superior to them."[53] Without going as far as Diderot in his *Supplément au Voyage de Bougainville* or Raynal in his supplements to the second edition of the *Histoire philosophique des deux Indes*, Voltaire introduces a growing skepticism when it comes to the colonial activities of Europeans: "While we travel the world to discover if their lands have anything to satisfy our greed, these other peoples do not inquire if there exist other types of men than themselves, and they pass their days in a happy indolence that would be considered a tragedy by us."[54] This complex statement associates European curiosity to their cupidity, in other words to an avidity that is both intellectual and economic, less a calling than a curse; whereas the "indolence" of other peoples who are less inclined to explore and conquer has its valence reversed by being named the happy aptitude to not worry about what is foreign to them.

One can now see why the *Essay on Manners* is both fundamental and disappointing and eludes all summary. It would be tempting to conclude, as has been done implicitly by those writing histories of ideas, that Voltaire lost his way and made a hash of his project by going down too many rabbit holes, thus losing the charm and alacrity of his tales while never attaining the rigor and erudition of the Scottish or German historians. In fact, the dynamism of the historical narrative is essential and subverts the philosophical intention. For this reason, it would be as reductive to see in Voltaire's *Essay* the founding gesture of a new Eurocentrism as it would be to exaggerate the importance of a few more sharply critical formulations that can be found in it. One should instead recognize that Voltaire's historiographic statement is intrinsically contradictory: conceived as the genealogy of an enlightened European modernity, it strives with only limited success to make an autonomous space for other histories, but in so doing it renders unstable its own core presupposition. The result is a display of the unresolved tensions at the heart of the Enlightenment's Eurocentrism when it seeks to present itself in the form of a historical narrative.

Authors who follow in Voltaire's footsteps are forced to confront these same tensions. If the turn from a Christian universal history to a secularized history of Europe makes space for other histories, what is the status of those histories? Are they autonomous? Are they pieces within a world history that would encompass them and subordinate them? Do they remain narratively and epistemologically dependent on European history? All the ambivalence around the notion of civilization in the second half of the eighteenth century derives from this tension between universalism and Eurocentrism. The grand narrative of European civilization proceeds from a double model: the one is a rationalist and universalist model that assures by right that every people is capable of being civilized; the other is a historicist and particularist model that insists on the specificity of European history. If the history of modern Europe is the result of a historical process that allowed it to emerge from barbarism thanks to a system of balanced diplomacy, the development of commerce, and courtly cultural flourishing, how is one to conceive of the accession of American savages or Asiatic barbarians to civil society? Hence the question that is central to debates on the "civilization" of Russia during the regimes of Peter the Great and Catherine the Great, as well as to discussions about the consequences of the colonization of America: is it possible to civilize a country through a political power's force of will, be it that of an enlightened Russian despot or a European colonizer?

Even authors who are opposed to European colonialism, such as Diderot and Raynal in certain passages of *The Philosophical History*, do not question the narrative of European exceptionality. Colonialism, and especially its abuses, is presented in that work as one of the leading stains on European history, a vestige of barbarism that the progress of civilization must erase; but at the same time, the exemplary value of European history as a process of civilization is reaffirmed in terms that resemble the language of Voltaire and Robertson. The ambiguity of the text comes through in the uses of the word "civilization," employed both to name Europe's rise out of a feudal system and the sedentarization and acculturation of the Amerindians.[55]

Although the model of European civilization was constructed in opposition to the notion of empire, civilization becomes in the colonial framework the watchword of another sort of imperial temptation. The enlargement of historic space to a global scale does not result in a de-centering of Europe; quite the contrary. It brings about the affirmation of a mission paired with a return of Eurocentrism. What has often been presented as an internal contradiction of Enlightenment universalism, as its hidden face even, its negative dialectic, can only be understood in light of the properly historical conception of Europe that emerges at that time.

Schiller, in his 1789 lesson on universal history delivered at Jena University, lays out the big division, within the same single human race, between modern Europeans and the savages or barbarians of antiquity. The division is both affirmed and finessed because the history he has in mind is one of continuous progress similar to the biological stages of life that would lead to the mature human excellence that is "the refined European of the eighteenth century." However, that European, appearances notwithstanding, is "only an advanced brother of the modern Canadian or the ancient Celt." For Schiller, universal history was to have the following mission: to understand "through which conditions did man wander until he ascended from one extreme, from the unsociable troglodyte to the ingenious thinker, the cultured man of the world?"[56] This trajectory would be the history of Europe and its successful achievements. Enlightenment Eurocentrism is a historicism.

Progress and Revolution

In the same year, 1789, Nicolas de Bonneville, a multitalented writer defended by d'Alembert, though better known during the Revolution for his role within the Society of the Friends of Truth, also known as the Social Club (Cercle Social), published the first two volumes of his *Histoire de l'Europe moderne depuis l'irruption des peuples du Nord dans l'Empire romain, jusqu'à la paix de 1783*. In many respects, this work was directly inspired by the grand narrative of European history discussed above; however, Bonneville goes even further. After the properly historical narrative, he announces a second part to be devoted to "the progress of civilization in Europe," then a third on "the history of the human spirit in Europe." But history gets the better of him and the work is never completed.

One can see in these unkept promises more than a symbol, since the French Revolution profoundly reconfigured this way of thinking about the specificity of European history and its relation to other histories. It's well known how much the end of the eighteenth century was marked by a new relation to historical time and to political experience, and by a tipping into a new "regime of historicity."[57] The direct inheritors of Enlightenment philosophy were confronted by this unsettling of the very conception of historical time. How does one articulate the Revolutionary event that thoroughly upset the present and future of Europe and with it the historical narrative of the continuous progress of civilization? How does one reconcile two so very different conceptions of historical change: one that insists on the long and secularizing time of political, social, and cultural progress in Europe, essentially the inheritance from the Enlightenment's grand narrative; and another that focuses on revolutionary action and that opened up right before their eyes a short time of upheavals marked by the freedom of those doing the heaving and by the radical enlargement of the horizon of expectations? Even if 1789 might still have appeared to many as the capstone of a long process, the unleashing of temporalities was more and more evident as the Revolution advanced and as its chaotic course seemed to defy all prediction.

Condorcet had a quite radical answer to this difficulty. He prepared his *Sketch for a Historical Picture of the Progress of the Human Mind* in the 1780s and wrote it in 1793–1794. The text is emblematic of Enlightenment optimism but remained incomplete after the arrest and death of the philosopher. Even while composing the largest part of his sketch in the fall of 1793 during his flight and in hiding, Condorcet did not deviate from his optimism about the perfectibility of the human species and about the lessons it was possible to learn, for the future, from the progress achieved by European societies since the sixteenth century, notably thanks to advances in printing and publishing. Condorcet evaded the epistemological trouble that the revolutionary upheaval and its aftershocks might have provoked by doing away with any claim to continuity between the narrative of the past nine epochs and conjectures about the future tenth epoch. The rational knowledge of human societies and a close examination of the advances of European societies over the previous three centuries allowed one to predict "with a high degree of probability" the future of the world, he felt.[58] His narrative of European history is thus rendered more coherent, being founded on the principle of infinite human perfectibility, and remains totally in line with universal history. As a result, the gap widens between enlightened, civilized Europe and the rest of the world. Here is Condorcet pausing or posing to wonder about that future:

> Must all nations one day approach the state of civilization attained by the most enlightened, the freest, the most liberated from prejudice; that is, by the French and the Anglo-Americans? The immense

> distance that separates these peoples from the slavishness of Indians, the barbarism of African tribes, and the ignorance of savages, will it little by little disappear? Are there regions of the world where nature has condemned the inhabitants to never enjoy freedom, to never exercise their reason?[59]

The answer is put forward confidently in a text written in the winter of 1794 entitled "*La propagation des lumières sur le globe*." For Condorcet, the universal path to civilization passes through the imitation of the American and French revolutions: "Soon liberty, taking flight with the wings provided by France and the United States, will subjugate all peoples and their eyes once opened will no longer be able to misrecognize them."[60] The general spread of European progress is only a matter of disseminating the benefits of reason.

One may of course be sensitive to the polysemy of the verb "subjugate" [*subjuguer*]. While naming the irresistible attraction of liberty, the fascination it exerts around the world, it also evokes the theme closely associated with the revolutionary context of liberty's despotism. Even if Condorcet believes that the European model, founded on liberty and reason, will impose itself all on its own by the sheer force of its exemplarity, unintended echoes in his formulation suggest the ambiguity of such optimism, or more precisely of his idealism. What's missing here is an argued theory of this revolutionary propagation. If civilization is a long historical process, how could peoples manage to rapidly cross "the immense distance" that separates them from Europeans? And how does one make liberty desirable?

Other ways of articulating the Enlightenment's theory of continuous progress with real-life revolutionary rupture were possible. One example was put forward by Count Volney. Although Volney shared Condorcet's optimism and the conviction that civilization would become "general," he insisted more on the effects proper to political action. There remained the matter of how to integrate, even hypothetically, non-European societies into the revolutionary effort. He imagined a general assembly of all peoples that would culminate in a unanimous rejection by the people themselves of their traditional beliefs while at the same time rallying to "legislators," that is, to French lawmakers [*constituants français*].[61] This scenario allowed Volney to represent both the physical and cultural diversity of humanity *and* the fusion toward a horizon of a common civilization. The very noticeable tension in Voltaire's text between the affirmation of the diversity of races and manners and the affirmation of humanity's common destiny is more or less smoothed over in Volney's idealistic text but at the cost of being clothed in fiction and revolutionary prophetism.

Eighteenth-century historians strived to produce a secularized narrative of the birth of Europe as a political system and cultural entity emerging gradually out of feudal barbarism. The terms *civilisation* and *lumières* were the watchwords of that narrative and essential to the idea of progress, of both manners and knowledge, that in turn was crucial for establishing the specific identity that European elites had of themselves. There remained the question of the historicity proper to *other* societies that were becoming increasingly well-known thanks to numerous testimonies: was it possible to think in terms of one time and therefore of a common history? Or alternatively, were societies outside Europe reduced to furnishing either the anthropological substrate to a natural history of man (one use of American savages, for example) or the immobile counter-model to European mobility (the case of China)? These unresolved questions explain the difficulties encountered by eighteenth-century historians, Voltaire first and foremost, when they tried to solder together a universal history and a history of European civilization. The inheritors at the end of the century had to confront these same difficulties while trying to think simultaneously in the long-term language of a process of civilization and in the short-term language of revolutionary transformation.

CHAPTER THREE

The Impossible Global History

In early 1954, Lucien Febvre published a quasi-promotional article in the journal *Annales* about a new collection he was starting with the publisher Armand Colin under the title "Destins du monde" [Destinies of the World]. The text had the air of a manifesto for a world history capable of breaking with the "old schemata fabricated by European or Western culture historians."[1] In a world experiencing major changes, notably the weakening of "old Europe" in the midst of world economic growth and decolonization movements, a new history was said to be necessary, and therefore it could not simply recycle the same old organizational rubrics and yesterday's historiographical notions. Having a combative temperament, Febvre criticized the *World History* project sponsored by UNESCO that he had tried, unsuccessfully, to steer in a less Eurocentric direction. In his conclusion, he invoked a prestigious predecessor: "It was a bold gesture on Voltaire's part to begin his history of manners with an examination of China—and that in a country where only shortly before Bossuet had begun his history with a discussion of Israelites. But it was only a gesture with no follow through. The work remained not only undone but still to be really conceived. Because more than just a change of lighting, the aim now is a total revolution in our way of thinking."[2]

Facing this new crisis of the European mind, the legacy of the Enlightenment was looked to like a ray of hope to energize an intellectual reawakening that would prevent "despair" so long as it could complete the historiographical revolution that had formerly only been sketched out. A few years earlier, at the end of the war, Febvre had modified the full title of the *Annales* journal to introduce the term "*civilisations*" in the plural: *Annales d'histoire économique et sociale* became *Annales: Économies, sociétés, civilisations*, and remained under that name until 1993.

Remembering the work performed by eighteenth-century philosophers and historians was a conscious choice toward reorganizing the historic narrative on a global scale and in response to the deep crisis of the European mind and conscience. For the next fifty years, "*civilisation*" was a key word within French historiography, especially under the direction of Fernand Braudel. Then it was gradually abandoned in the 1980s and 1990s and even disappeared from the title of the *Annales* journal, which was changed to *Annales: Histoire, Sciences sociales*. No rigorous autopsy was carried out, but the concept was clearly no longer fashionable, and one began to speak instead of cultural areas [*aires culturelles*] and to insist on *métissages*, circulations, and connections.[3]

Thus, historians were somewhat taken by surprise when at the start of the twenty-first century the term suddenly reappeared in public at the center of a controversy. Samuel Huntington had used it as the central concept in his essentialist and antagonistic account of a new geopolitics when he published *The Clash of Civilizations* in 1996. Some years later, in 2007, the French president at the time, Nicolas Sarkozy, gave a speech in Dakar that caused a stir when he affirmed that the African had not entered history. An "unfortunate speech," [*infortuné discours*] Jacques Revel called it, in his review of Jack Goody's *The Theft of History* (2006), which was published in French in 2010, and with a provocative subtitle, as *Le Vol de l'histoire: Comment l'Europe a imposé le récit de son passé au reste du monde* [How Europe Imposed the Narrative of Its Past on the Rest of the World].[4] Beyond the public polemic, historians were particularly riled up when, some weeks later, Sarkozy's right-hand man and speechwriter for the Dakar address, Henri Guaino, defended himself in the press by stating that his notion of civilization was consistent with Fernand Braudel's use of the term. The following year, a heated controversy broke out among historians around a book by Sylvain Gouguenheim, *Aristote au Mont Saint-Michel* (2008), in which the author declares Arab thinkers incapable of grasping the rationality of Greek philosophers and therefore of transmitting the knowledge of antiquity.[5] He relied on a view of civilizations as hermetic and incommensurable. European civilization, he claimed, owed nothing to the Arabs for the simple reason that they were two entirely different civilizations. In this regard he was repeating the gesture from the early nineteenth century that sided with an essentially Christian and Greek definition of Europe. Specialists were infuriated even more by the fact that the press praised the book and it became a bestseller.[6] Away from the editorial pages, however, historians found themselves faced with an embarrassing question: how could a notion like *civilization*—which for forty years had served as one of the banners of French historiography until historians themselves mostly dropped it—get twisted around and used in such ways? It should be said they were ill-prepared to answer that question because, rather than conducting a thorough assessment of the notion and its limitations, they abandoned it quietly. They gradually turned away from it, stopped using it, and privileged instead other terms, scales, coherencies, and approaches—but without ever really explaining why.

Many of those troubled by this controversy justifiably asked themselves if the notion had not been problematic from the start. With the idea of opening history to the whole world, did not the grammar of civilizations on the Braudel model end up revalidating the old Eurocentric prejudice according to which beyond a supposed plurality of *civilisations* there was really only one civilization, namely the European civilization? It is true that Braudel seemed to worsen things for himself when he decided to devote his last research project to France's identity. For all who think that national history is necessarily unhealthy, who claim that the goal of a world history is an unprecedented historiographical innovation, or who are outspoken in favoring a provincialization of Europe, the cause is clear and the matter is settled: civilization is a notion irremediably stained with Eurocentrism. Was it not forged to glorify the destiny of Europe at the very moment when European domination was expanding on a global scale? Was it not central to the West's "civilizing mission" and to the legitimation of its colonial imperialism? Civilization would then be the notion par excellence that stood guilty as charged: of universalizing Europe and contributing to the "theft of history."

As we have seen in previous chapters, these criticisms have a grain of truth but do not tell the whole story. The notion of civilization did serve to think (up and of) the cultural and political superiority of Europe. But the uses that were made of it in the nineteenth century, when its meaning stabilized as the idea of a univocal process anchored on the European model, do not do justice to the tensions and ambivalences that surrounded the term's emergence and its use in the historical writings of Enlightenment authors. In our day, the recent controversies fueled by various uses of the notion of civilization occurring in public-information spaces raise two questions that are hard to ignore. The first is epistemological. What's at stake is the circulation of a word between the vocabulary of the social sciences and everyday speech. The way that historians build their concepts, deliberately avoiding an exhaustive theoretical elaboration each time, is both a plus, because it allows them to be understood by a rather wide public, and a minus, because it maintains ambiguities, equivocal aspects, and resonances that can be suggestive or disastrous. The second question is one of intellectual history. Historians of the second half of the twentieth century believed they had found in the notion of civilization a way to escape Eurocentrism, to integrate the contributions of anthropology, to open themselves to the history of non-European societies, and to reclaim for history a central role within the human sciences. While perfectly conscious that the concept had its roots at the heart of Enlightenment thinking, these historians were unable or unwilling to give the concept its own theoretical elaboration, preferring instead to play on its echoes and connotations. They then ran into the same difficulties as their distant predecessors when their desire to speak in the plural of *civilizations* collided with the necessity of constructing a coherent narrative or at least integrating different narratives within a single historiographical framework. In other words, they ran into the genealogical character of historical discourse that blocks access to an outside onlooker position.

The Grammar of Civilizations

The twentieth-century success of the term *civilization* was much wider than the perimeter of the academic journal *Annales*. Several book collections were constructed around the notion in the 1960s and 1970s. Examples include "*Histoire générale des civilisations*," directed by Maurice Crouzet; "*Peuples et civilisations*," founded in the interwar period; and especially "*Les grandes civilisations*," a collection published by Arthaud starting in 1963 with the participation of Jacques Le Goff, Jean Delumeau, and Pierre Chaunu. At the time, the term was used plainly to designate an ensemble of social and cultural traits shared by a population in a given geographical space over a long period. People referred to the Western medieval civilization but also to the Roman civilization, the civilization of the Renaissance, the Chinese or Japanese civilization, and even to the "French civilization" about which Georges Duby and Rober Mandrou wrote a hefty two-volume history published in 1958 by Armand Colin.

Nonetheless, the notion is most commonly associated with Fernand Braudel, who gave the term the most visibility and wished to make it the watchword of historical analysis.[7] Braudel devoted several texts to the concept of civilization, but the theoretical job was left unfinished, resulting in various and to a certain extent contradictory uses of the term over the course of his work as an historian. In a first sense, *civilisation* named a level of historical reality, deriving either from cultural and religious life (what Braudel also sometimes called the intellectual civilization), or from relations to objects and techniques (what he called material civilization). In a second sense, *civilisations* are considered as geographic, social, and cultural entities of long duration and relative coherence. It was in this sense that the notion struck Braudel as the keystone of the total history he envisioned and that he deliberately called global history [*histoire globale*]. It allowed one to propose a historical reading of the cultural coherencies of societies outside Europe, and thus to preserve the status of history as a discipline central to the human sciences. For Braudel, the historian is the one best positioned to study civilizations because historians are capable of articulating the different temporalities that shape them. In this regard, the notion was a reply to the anthropologists who had made heavy use of the term in the interwar period, at the time of the creation of ethnology as an academic discipline, even if the term *culture* would later take precedence under the influence of American anthropology.

The second definition of civilization is used in a thin volume published in 1987 after Braudel's death as a testimony to his scientific legacy.[8] That book reused part of a text he wrote in 1963 with Suzanne Baille and Philippe Robert entitled *Le Monde actuel: Histoire et civilisations*. That coauthored volume was a history textbook prepared for students in the final year of high school, a context Braudel was invested in to accomplish the replacement of the chronological, political, and national narrative with an approach to the modern world organized around large geographical and cultural entities: the Muslim world, China, Africa, and so forth. Braudel's wish was to provide the keys to reading the contemporary world by presenting heritages of long duration, or more precisely by articulating the analysis of different historical temporalities within the framework of each of these civilizations.

Rereading these texts today—now that the debate launched by Huntington's *Clash of Civilizations* has rendered suspect, because accused of culturalism and essentialism, the use of the concept of civilization to mean a coherent cultural ensemble linked to a territory, language, beliefs, and a history—one is struck by the ambivalent character of Braudel's enterprise. It is true that the notion was used in rather fuzzy ways, such that the theoretical difficulties at issue were both dissimulated and more pronounced in the actual written text. Braudel's well-known fondness for metaphor and personification led him sometimes to turn civilizations into active agents of history.[9] And yet, Braudel never defended the idea of civilizations being homogeneous, coherently stable, or necessarily antagonistic. He insisted constantly on the exchanges and porousness between civilizations: "We must not believe," he wrote, "that a civilization, because it is original, is a closed and independent world, as if each one was an island in the midst of the ocean, whereas in fact it is their dialogues, the points where they meet, which are essential, especially as they are all increasingly coming to share a rich common basis."[10] In truth, the concept of civilization serves a double intellectual function in the writings of Braudel: it allows him to plead in favor of a history that is open to non-European spaces and to conceive of historic change, because civilizations live, die, and transform. Nothing was further from his thinking than the idea of hermetic and immobile civilizations with a fixed identity from time immemorial.

Adapting an old expression, we can say that the road to historiographic hell is paved with good intentions. The successive presentation of different civilizations, notably in the 1963 textbook *The World Today*, inevitably produced an impression of homogeneity reinforced by the teacherly goal of synthesis that led the authors to privilege coherencies and continuities. On a more theoretical plane, Braudel's work was characterized by a curious mixture of serious and loose behavior. Although he devoted several articles to the notion of civilization with discussions of different uses of the term by other twentieth-century authors, he almost never goes further back, such as to its origin in the eighteenth century.[11] In that regard, his work was typical of the way most historians work on their concepts by means of a kind of historiographical review that distributes good and bad grades and ends with an attempt at definition that doesn't think it important to break with the equivocations in ordinary language. In an article in which he tried to reflect on the notion of civilization and claimed to be taking inspiration from the Belgian medieval historian Henri Pirenne, Braudel states: "The historian has the advantage of using the words of living everyday language to the exclusion of all others, and therefore of resolutely distancing himself from an immobilized vocabulary such as that of philosophers."[12] This is an excellent summary of a conviction that is certainly widely held: historians use words such as *civilization* for their pragmatic value, in other words for what they allow one to do (modify the contours of the discipline and enrich the vocabulary of the historian, for example), but they would gain nothing from employing those words to accomplish a true conceptual analysis. The division of labor seems to be as follows: historians of philosophy or of language study the use of concepts by authors of the past, and historians who today use the same concepts confine themselves to studying their contemporary uses by academics with whom they are in dialogue. What's missing in this tidy setup is the relationship historians maintain with knowledge from the past and with the way that earlier knowledge continues to exert an influence over ordinary everyday language. A true analysis of concepts that historians use ought to rely on the history of the words themselves in order to historically problematize their equivocations, and to understand the ways in which they were borrowed from ordinary language and often reformulated by the social sciences or philosophy before being imported into the historiographical lexicon.[13]

The Paradoxes of a Philosophical History

As discussed above, the notion of civilization was at the heart of the Enlightenment's historiographic ambitions. It organized various reflections on Europe, from Voltaire to the Scottish historians to Condorcet. The term was particularly popular at the end of the eighteenth century during the French Revolution but takes on a rigid quality at the start of the nineteenth century. It then becomes a watchword, as Bertrand Binoche has noted, naming not only a historical process of long duration but the outcome that results from it: a society of polite manners and flourishing artistic culture for which Europe serves as the model and perhaps has the monopoly.

From the Revolutionary time onward, two sources of tension traverse the notion of civilization and perhaps explain its success. On the one hand, civilization names a process in time, a process that turns "barbarian" or "savage" societies into "polite" ones. But it takes on, and rather quickly, a rather different meaning as the name for the result of that process. In other words, as a narrative scheme organizing the story of a historic evolution of long duration, the process of civilization implies from the start that this evolution is also progress, that of becoming civilized. It is a teleological concept, and one directed toward the historian's present moment: the apogee, at least provisionally, of human history.

The second tension is the opposition between universalism and Eurocentrism. The concept of civilization was forged to understand the specificity of European history, the passage from medieval feudalism to the polite society of the Enlightenment, and at the same time it was conceived in universalist terms as a model capable of being imitated. This tension was at the very heart of the definition that Europe gave to the Enlightenment as a process of emancipation both historically situated and potentially generalizable. It was, indeed, so central that numerous debates in the eighteenth century centered on the following questions: Was it possible to civilize American Indians? Was China a civilized empire? And perhaps the most urgent question of all: Under what conditions could Russia be the object of a deliberate civilizing campaign led by its government?

Lucien Febvre, as we have said, acknowledged that Voltaire had made a bold move by starting his universal history with the great civilizations of China, India, and Japan. But in the follow-through to that opening move, he proposed a history of civilization that was mostly about European progress. For Voltaire, history is a gradual passage from medieval barbarism, marked by the omnipresence of war and the grip of religion, to a polite Europe of courts, academies, and tolerance. In short, civilization is the Enlightenment, and the Enlightenment is Europe.

Already in the eighteenth century, methodological pronouncements were not always followed by the desired effects. The geographical enlargement of the narrative is compensated or countered by the affirmation of one point of view, that of modern Europeans, now assured of their superiority, which allows Voltaire to give the starring role to the historian, the spokesperson for his enlightened contemporaries, whether in order to judge peoples in the distant past or on other distant continents. These difficulties derive from Voltaire's extreme presentism, his taste for moral judgments, and a form of arrogant self-satisfaction that constantly undermines his tolerant humanism. These shortcomings may be the price one pays for philosophical activism, which rarely possesses a historian's prudent circumspection. But Voltaire's ambivalences go even further; they follow from the desperate attempt to make two irreconcilable approaches coexist: the outsider's point of view that observes universal history from a neutral position, and a genealogical point of view that organizes this same history as a function of a "we" whom the historian addresses and who defines the intellectual and political horizon of his historiographical decisions and his judgments.

Voltaire never surmounted this contradiction. He left to conscientious historians of later times the task of enlarging the geographical and cultural horizons of the historic narrative. With the progress of history as a discipline in university spaces, these followers presented subtler, diluted versions of the narrative, but it's uncertain whether they managed any better to free themselves from the contradiction.

The Seductions of World History

Fernand Braudel knew Voltaire well. He quotes from him in the introduction to his major theoretical article on the history of civilizations.[14] However, it is Lucien Febvre who functions as the principal relay by naming Voltaire as a precursor of world history. Febvre's interest in the history of civilization and the genealogy of that notion did not begin after the war. Already in 1929, the very year *Annales* was founded, he participated in a day of lectures on civilization organized by the Centre de Synthèse alongside the major social-science figures of the day such as Marcel Mauss, but also present were French colonial functionaries, such as Paul Doumer, concerned by the work of "*civilisation*" (as a verb) in Indochina and Algeria. Febvre's contribution was a long presentation on the history of the word *civilisation*, in which he sought to retrace the genealogy of the term by making use of eighteenth-century French authors.[15] The correspondence between Febvre and the philosopher Henri Berr allows one to see the importance he gave to this question, and also the amount of rewriting he did after the conference before submitting his text for publication. In 1946, and eager as he was to restart *Annales* with the aid of Braudel, who had just returned from a German prisoner of war camp and was completing his book *The Mediterranean*, Febvre insisted on altering the journal's full title to *Annales: Économies, sociétés, civilisations*. It is reasonable to assume that this choice of name was not made haphazardly.[16]

It is customary to think of *civilization* here as designating one of the three legs of human activity, namely the one that covers the area of culture, intellectual life, and beliefs.[17] Alongside economic and social history, the directors of *Annales* supposedly decided to recognize with the new three-term subtitle the importance of intellectual and material culture, in keeping with the most recent research of its leading contributors—for example, Febvre's own *Rabelais ou le problème de l'incroyance*, which had been published four years earlier. But if Febvre proposed this name change, he did so because the connotations of *civilisation* were much wider. In his editorial for the first postwar issue of 1946, "Face au vent" [Facing the Wind], Febvre contemplates the role of the historian in a world undergoing major changes and with Europe having experienced on its soil two apocalyptic wars in the space of just thirty years. In his eyes, there could be no doubt that European civilization was dead, and that the world was on the verge of experiencing yet more major transformations. The historian's role was to help men think about this mutation of civilizations in a nonconflictual mode, by recalling the world's diversity and by not yielding to discouragement despite melancholy meditations on the decline of the West. If Febvre cites Valéry and Spengler, he does so to mark his distance from them and to reaffirm the necessity of a history of civilizations. The latter must allow one to look with optimism and lucidity toward the grand moment of historic recomposition that awaits: "The problem is not to know whether our civilization which we continue to call simply civilization will perish by assassination. It is to know which civilization will take hold tomorrow in this new world which is already forming at the bottom of the crucible."[18] Being faithful to the program of *Annales*, which for Febvre consisted in affirming the capacity of the historian to give the keys to understanding the contemporary world, required launching a full-scale reflection on the history of civilizations and the future of the world, where, he claimed, it was urgent to unite the shipwrecked survivors of the old world around a "solidarity of work, exchange, and free cooperation." In this task, the linkup with the textual tradition of the Enlightenment becomes rather ambiguous. It's clear that Febvre is operating on more than one level in this text because *civilisation* names less a domain of human activity and more the idea of a history oriented toward continuous progress. In this vein, he initiates a reflection on the place of Europe and on its historic experience in the new world to come, and part of that reflection is to ask: what remains of the long history and civilizational ideal of the Enlightenment? But Febvre never makes explicit the relation to the history of the concept and instead plays on equivocations around the notion, thus lending his text the singular mixture of verve and insistence that was his preferred style.

He had been much more explicit the year before in a Collège de France lecture devoted to the history of Europe. That lecture was for long unpublished but is now available and yet still largely unnoticed, even though as a historiographical document it is of great interest.[19] Placing Europe in the syllabus of his teaching at the Collège de France in 1944 was not a casual choice by Febvre. The goal was hardly to just restate the general history of Europe but rather to answer two questions. The first: When was Europe born? In other words, how was it constituted as a sufficiently coherent social and cultural entity, and when did it begin to be conscious of itself as that entity? Or, to put it in Febvre's language, when did Europe cease to be a mere geographical label and become a "*civilisation*" (the omnipresent term in Febvre's course)? His answer is unambiguous: the first signs of a common European civilization date from the time of Charlemagne, and it's in the eighteenth century that the notion of Europe became the prevailing way to conceive of this common civilization overlaying the ruins of the old Christianity. The point is not to discuss this diagnosis but to see what it implies, and Febvre is constantly hammering it home for his listeners: Europe is not a continent; its geographic definition is meaningless; it is instead a historical construction, the result of a history that did not begin with Greco-Roman antiquity but after the fall of the Roman Empire. This history unfolded in two domains: one, a series of political constructions—or projects of political organization—the other, a common culture, a "*civilisation*" that was forged over centuries to the point where it appeared to elites of the eighteenth and then nineteenth centuries as a specific and self-evident common identity. Using a line of reasoning that he would later apply to his history of France, Febvre relentlessly underscores that this European civilization was forged through borrowing from other cultures. He thus ends up with a Voltairean reading of European civilization, and it's no surprise that Voltaire is abundantly quoted in the crucial chapter devoted to the eighteenth century. Febvre thus completes the circle, it would seem, by positing Voltaire as both source and precursor.

The second question is more political and more urgent: What remains in 1944 of this more-than-thousand-year-old history? What remains after four years of "hellish war" ["*enfer de guerre*"] during which the promoters of barbarism were the ones laying claim to Europe? Here, surprise, Febvre states his skepticism about the political construction projects for Europe. The ideal of civilization as it was carried forward by European elites since the Enlightenment—in other words, the ideal of conjoined material and spiritual progress—can no longer be a strictly European ideal. It cannot be so firstly because of Europe's recent suicide, which betrayed its values. But even more so, and especially—and here Febvre the historian leans in—the ideal cannot be strictly European because of deep evolutions, dating from before the war, that make Europe more than ever inseparable from the rest of the world. In eighteenth-century Europe there was a notion of hope, he states, and the dream of elites at that time spread between the end of religious wars and the emergence of modern capitalism. But since the beginning of the twentieth century, it has only been a response to the crisis (a term he borrows from Marc Bloch) and a dangerous response at that, because it exposes the egocentric mindlessness of Europeans deaf to the expectations of other peoples and blind to the realities of what has not yet been called globalization.

Europe therefore is no longer the answer, Febvre concluded. Its civilizational unity no longer exists, the war revealed cracks that were too big, and the recent past showed that European unity could also be harnessed to serve the most criminal projects.[20] What's more, "the problem of Europe is bigger than Europe; the problem of Europe is of a planetary scale, the problem of Europe is the problem of the whole world." Therefore "one can no longer refer to Europe without speaking of the entire Universe"—of China and Japan that have become great powers, of the colonial empires that Europe dominated but that are not Europe, and of Latin America that is so distant and so near.[21] Febvre is much more explicit and vehement in a 1947 lecture delivered in Brussels that begins with this assertion: "Europe, this beautiful word, we have witnessed it at the end of a day of hope become the name of a battlefield, carnage, and desolation. This is where we are." He then denounces the ties Europe has with non-European peoples, condescending and authoritarian ties that he sums up with the caustic remark "*civilisation oblige*," as one used to say *noblesse oblige*.

After that, one can reread his entire course with heightened sensitivity to the ambivalences around the word *civilisation.* Febvre contrasts two senses of the word. The one he rejects, *civilisation* in the singular, names a superior and universal value. It is the fuzzy and vulgar concept of journalists, he claims with some disdain. The other sense, which he favors and describes as ethnographic, names "the ensemble of characteristics that strike an impartial, objective observer about the collective life of a group (the material life, the political and social life, the intellectual, moral, and religious life)."[22] It is a strictly descriptive notion that implies, he states, "no form of value judgment." Every human group possesses its civilization. At the outer limit, he adds, "one could speak of a civilization of the non-civilized," a paradoxical formulation that subtly reintroduces a historical value judgment at the very moment when such a thing has just been rejected. In the following pages, the tension only increases. As he continues to specify his preferred use of the term, Febvre contrasts without hesitation poor, primitive, backward civilizations and rich, brilliant civilizations that he calls "the great civilizations." The latter are characterized by the mobility of their distinctive traits. Borrowing without attribution an argument from Mauss, Febvre distinguishes two types of elements within each civilization: the sedentary elements and the mobile elements.[23] Great civilizations are those where the mobile elements dominate and the sedentary elements are few in number. This point is essential in showing Febvre's mindfulness to avoid having his view of civilizations fall into hypostasis, in other words to avoid the error of considering them as homogeneous, hermetic, and immutable entities. On the contrary, in his account their grandeur derives from their capacity to borrow, from the provisional and heterogeneous character of the configurations they take on. The history of European civilization is no longer that of a Europe said to have evolved progressively toward the fulfillment of its own nature, but rather that of an entity that constituted itself gradually by a succession of borrowings from other great civilizations. In this view, the interaction of civilizations on a planetary scale becomes essential and is the historian's proper object of study.

In the postwar period, Lucien Febvre worked to promote a world history. During the 1946–1947 school year, his course at the Collège de France was entitled "*La civilisation et les civilisations: étude sur l'évolution du monde moderne.*"[24] In 1947, he created the *Société Marc Bloch*, an "Association for the Study of Civilizations." In 1949, he got involved in debates sponsored by UNESCO on the history of humanity. His ambitious UNESCO proposal lost out to one put forward by the American Ralph Turner. But undeterred, Febvre persisted, and in 1953 he became the director of the new journal *Cahiers d'histoire mondiale.*[25]

Did Febvre understand—thanks to the lessons of the war, his experience as a historian, and the influence of anthropology, notably the work of Marcel Mauss—what was at stake in a true world history? Did he free the notion of civilization from its Eurocentrist and naïve faith-in-progress associations? Did he set the foundation for a truly rigorous global history separate from both the philosophical history of Voltaire and the nationalist history of Michelet? That would make a good story: the truth of the matter is rather more complex.

Returning to the 1945 course on Europe, one discovers that ambiguities remain. After ruling out the use of the term *civilisation* to designate an ideal form of superior society and culture, Febvre uses the word like that anyway, half furtively. Why this contradiction or at least this nonchalant incoherence? I have two explanations that are not mutually exclusive but in fact overlap. First, the word is just too charged with meaning; the connotations are too powerful, especially the echoes from eighteenth-century writers, and that's true even for a historian as self-aware and impetuous as Febvre. In the end, this troublesome word proves to still have the upper hand. Despite the combined efforts of sociologists, anthropologists, and historians stretching over half a century, the word retains its normative charge, its link to a philosophy of progress that Enlightenment thinkers conferred on it at birth, a certain high tone that rings out infallibly as soon as the specific destiny of Europe is at stake.

A second reason that explains the contradictions at work inside the notion of civilization is that, like with Voltaire, Febvre's historiographic approach in this course even more than elsewhere is radically and explicitly presentist. His history of Europe, even if studded with calls for an ethnographic analysis of civilizations of the past, aims to judge the present and to offer a diagnosis of what Europe was, what it could be, and what it ought to be. The historian may well grant an equal dignity to all civilizations, strive to adopt an ethnographic reading of cultures, and deconstruct the idea of a European nature; and yet his analysis inevitably remains oriented by the position he himself occupies, by the historic moment from which and for which he is organizing his study and his narrative, and by the cultural elements that allow him to write the history and that are the result of a particular past. The historian does not stand on a perch outside history from which he can study different civilizations, their evolution, and their contributions. He is immersed in history—in a language, commitments, hopes, and the traditions of his discipline, and these are all outgrowths of European history. These connections render the historian an interpreter: the interpreter of the history he has inherited and to which he is connected by numerous threads and a nearly unbroken series of cultural transmissions that he cannot escape.[26]

Febvre diagnosed this difficulty perfectly in a 1929 letter addressed to Henri Berr. After having distinguished the "civilization" of historians (the ensemble of societies' concrete traits) from the "civilization" of philosophers (an abstract and normative term), Febvre pauses to ask about his job: "The word civilization, having now lost its former meaning, which was so riven with Eurocentrism, due to the current practice among French historians of extending its use to refer to all human groups no matter who they be, does it necessarily follow that in the presence of the civilizations he is studying the historian has no other task than to carry out a meticulous and complete inventory?"[27] How does one not judge these civilizations with the evaluative criteria of one's own society? How does one avoid ranking them? How does one escape from the point of view of a historian inscribed in a specific time and culture? These questions, so obviously central to anthropologists, press in the same way on the historian of civilizations. And they arise all the more strongly for a historian like Febvre, who never ceased to advocate for the engagement of the historian in the struggles of the present moment.

The difficulty evoked glancingly in 1929 traverses all of Febvre's writings. The historian does not judge men of the past, but he writes history to understand the present. In so doing, his discourse about past societies is always marked by a "we" that cannot be a pure universal or cosmopolitan mind or impartial observer outside of time and culture. He belongs to a society, and he writes in his language with his narrative tools and techniques for readers who are his colleagues and often his compatriots, or who at least share with him a certain number of values and references. Logically, then, it's when this French "we"—*nous*—appears in Febvre's writing that the term "*civilisation*" is ineluctably reloaded with its normative senses. In the 1944 course, for example, we find this statement: "It's because Europe, when we try to formulate what it represents for us, French people, despite all, Europe is essentially this: collaboration on the same work [*œuvre*] of civilization, participation in the same ideal of culture, in the same ideal of life, and the participation of very different populations."[28]

The Enlightenment legacy was consciously and explicitly claimed by Febvre and then by Braudel as part of the reorganization of the historical narrative on a global scale, and against a double tradition rooted within the social sciences of the nineteenth century: national history, whether an edifying narrative of origins or a chronicle of revolutions, and universal history centered on Europe with its categories and its periodization. The instrument for this redefinition was the notion of civilization, thanks to which Febvre especially hoped to construct a synthesis of the Enlightenment's intellectual tradition and the Durkheimian social sciences. The conceptual reflection, however, was not completely accomplished. It is probably the case that the connotations of the word, its capacity to not be reduced to a piece of social-science technical vocabulary, contributed to its success. In truth, the term retained in a latent state its Eurocentrist connotations that had at the turn of the nineteenth century allowed for the affirmation of a comparative paradigm that exclusively benefitted Europe. As praiseworthy as it may have been in principle, the use of *civilisations* in the plural led to the more or less empirical identification of distinct civilizations in a sort of global cartography where the effects of coherence and homogeneity over a long period of time took precedence over discontinuities and contradictions.[29] Finally, the institutional organization of research—notably within the framework of cultural areas [*aires culturelles*] and what they clearly owe, in France at any rate, to a grammar of civilizations—tilted the idea of exchanges and circulations to favor coherent and homogeneous cultures often associated with specific linguistic or religious areas. It did so to such an extent that when professional historians turned away from the notion, it could still resurface in lighter historical language and popular commonsense discourse carrying two seemingly contradictory dangers: the evolutionist danger that would make European modernity into the model of all history, and the essentialist danger that freezes civilizations in their singularity and presumed incommensurability.

The reference to Voltaire, however, places us on another path, namely that of the specificity of historic discourse within the epistemological regime of the social sciences. Every historic investigation produces, like it or not, a genealogical discourse, or as Michel Foucault would say, a diagnosis about "our present."[30] History is not just a social science, it is also a moral and political science whose stakes and complications are never clearer than when the historian breaks into using the "we" [*nous*]. Febvre was well aware of this truth when he wrote, just after pleading for a complete decentering, that the tragic random events in European history probably represented only "one aspect in a thousand within World History, but they're the aspect that troubles us most immediately and that holds most worrisomely our present attention."[31] As he had said in his letter to Henri Berr twenty-five years earlier, the pluralization of cultures and societies can never complete itself, because the very position of the historian, being anchored in a present, a society, and a culture, organizes the diversity of the past in service of an explanation of *our* present. And yet the historian is condemned neither to silence nor to an identitarian narrative. Being anchored in a time and place lends his discourse a political weight that is more valuable than the illusory ideal of scholarly detachment. It's up to the historian to fully own that anchoring position and to recognize its limits, since the punishment for not doing so is to be forever stuck in the whirligig of the same debates.

By means of a different path we come again to the lesson I sketched at the end of the first chapter. There, the question I asked was: How does one take account of the criticisms leveled at Enlightenment universalism without repudiating the values (tolerance, autonomy, emancipation) associated with it? And the two pieces of an answer I offered were these: first, by noting that these values were affirmed, defended, and promoted at a particular moment in European history marked by Europe's increasingly powerful hold over the world, notably the rise of slavery and the triangular trade, but also by a growing consciousness of the excesses and dangers of colonial enterprises; and second, by noting that the moment when we study this history and side with or against this heritage, we do so from a particular position, the one that allows us to say "we" and to define ethical, cultural, and political communities and to make the experience of Enlightenment thinkers resonate with our own situation. Therefore, the Enlightenment heritage, as universalist as it may be or dreams to be, cannot be exactly the same for an educated white European, an African American descended from slaves, or a Māori. These identities themselves are neither univocal nor homogeneous nor constraining. They are in part chosen, claimed, denied, and blended. One can, like C. L. R. James, be a Black Marxist universalist Trinidadian nourished on European culture. The important thing is to accept that the position—social, cultural, geopolitical—of each person (and notably each historian) and the public one addresses determine the nature of the relations one holds with the past, and in particular with the Enlightenment writers whose contemporary resonances are so alive. One can also hope that historical knowledge and confronting the past may allow us, in return, to refine, complicate, and even modify these positions.

Uses of the notion of civilization confirm us in our thinking. First, one must be mindful to not project onto eighteenth-century Enlightenment authors the Eurocentric and often racist simplifications that sometimes occurred in the nineteenth century. *Civilization* is not the code name for an alleged theft of history but rather the theoretical space of a difficulty encountered when attempting to articulate a universalist ideal and a conviction, sometimes traversed by doubts, with an exceptional historic trajectory. Second, historians are never self-aware enough. Even when historians hearken to the better angels of their nature, their repeated attempts to break with the faults of Eurocentric thinking run up against the conditions of their situation as writers and probably also the very nature of history work.

The provisional conclusion that follows from this state of affairs has neither the clarity nor the incisiveness of radical positions. It permits us, above all, to put aside solutions that may be politically comfortable but intellectually indefensible—such as allegiance to a heritage where universalism is not even questioned, or, inversely, a total rejection of the Enlightenment based on a caricatured vision of its links with colonialism. Likewise, we believe that inscribing the Enlightenment within the utopia of an objectivized world history leads us only to lose track of what's at stake, even as we reproduce the same theoretical difficulties. The task that remains is scrutinizing the tensions and ambivalences of the Enlightenment from a given position (or a diverse set of positions) that we recognize as contingent in the hope of building resources to deepen our own investigations, but also to find the strength to persevere despite the discomfort of dim lighting.

PART II

Modernity

The grammar of civilizations in the work of Fernand Braudel is not a culturalist typology. Faithful to the Enlightenment legacy, he conceived of civilizations as dynamic ensembles. Nevertheless, unlike Voltaire or Volney, he did not put the accent on mores [*mœurs*]; he privileged the logics of capitalism and material civilization. Today, a whole current of global history flows from this perspective, notably with the study of the great divergence in the eighteenth century between Europe and China—the first having embraced industrialization while the second saw its economic development stalling out.[1] While certain authors persist in defending a heroic history that sees the Enlightenment as having assured the economic development of Europe by fashioning a "culture of growth," most historians today are more circumspect.[2] On a global scale today, debates over the Enlightenment's legacy inevitably question the very nature of modernity: does it follow a unique model for which Europe opened the way, or is it irremediably plural? Does it represent an unsurpassable horizon, an incomplete project, or an outdated ideal?

Theories of modernity cannot be dissociated from the social sciences. At the start, they assigned themselves the task of distinguishing modern societies from traditional societies. The answers varied and sometimes veered toward normative constraining theories of modernization. Later, the idea of modernity underwent an epistemological crisis, and many researchers attempted to junk it or bypass it before facing up to the plain fact: the notion of modernity resists being done away with.[3] Some researchers have since made it a new central concept; others use it as a heuristic to refer in a convenient way to an ensemble of historical processes that they perceive as important yet without having a consensus about the criteria that constitute breaks: the disenchantment of the world, industrialization, individualism, democracy, the communications revolution, the Anthropocene, or sociological reflexivity itself. When it comes to chronologies, the debates are just as heated. Do modern times start with the Renaissance, as humanist history long affirmed; with the Reformation, as the German tradition believes; with the scientific revolution of the seventeenth century; later, with the Enlightenment or the French Revolution; or even later still, with the Industrial Revolution? For the historian, these uncertainties are a welcome gift since they open up greater interpretive freedom.

If the Enlightenment occupies a privileged place in the history of modernity, it does so not simply because salient traits of our societies appear at that time but because these transformations, which together produce a threshold effect, were perceived by contemporaries as an important rupture that required questioning, thinking, and critiques. The Enlightenment is the name for this reflexivity that anticipates the inauguration of the social sciences.

For a long time, modernity was considered as the affirmation of the superiority of reason deployed in various domains: the fight against religious prejudices, the defense of science and knowledge, the moral autonomy of individuals. The modern project derived from the Enlightenment was thus thought of as a process of making things rational—for better and for worse. It resulted in a secularized world, efficient and rational but also disenchanted and cold, dominated by calculations and utility. In the last thirty years, this conception of modernity has been considerably enlarged. Several propositions have unsettled the field of Enlightenment studies. The first concerns the organization of social experience according to the binary pair *private/public*. These notions do not correspond to eternal categories of human interaction. They are profoundly linked in their systemic opposition to social and cultural transformations of the eighteenth century: new practices of intimacy, the development of urban sociability, the media revolution, and so forth. The thesis defended by Jürgen Habermas about the emergence of the bourgeois public sphere gained a huge following, to the point where it seemed at the end of the twentieth century to be the dominant paradigm. Though contested since, the gist of his thesis remains compelling, on condition that it be reformulated with heightened attention to the sensible, emotional, and commercial dimensions of public space during the Enlightenment.

Enlightenment public space was not a place of rational interchange only. It is difficult to dissociate it from that other facet of modernity that was the birth of consumer society. Commerce was a watchword of the Enlightenment, indicating both sociability and—increasingly, over time—the market economy. Mobility, tolerance, exchange—for most Enlightenment authors these values are intimately linked to the ideal of a commercial society that was supposed to guarantee the convergence of private interests with general public prosperity, a durable peace between nations, and the extinction of personal ties of dependence. However, this ideal did not have unanimous support. From the inaugural moment of the 1720 speculation crisis in England, and then the bankruptcy of Law's system in France, questions and criticism raised by the nascent political economy contributed to reflections about the emerging capitalist system. Credit in particular had a profoundly transformative effect on interpersonal relations. It raised the stakes about the question of confidence in modern societies, obliging a complete rethinking of the relationship between political authorities and financial mechanisms. If in recent decades cultural history sometimes departed from economic issues, today its pursuit of a more global reading of modernity has made the development of a market society into a topic of prime importance. And yet, it is important to not fall into reductive slogans that force the reading and see in the Enlightenment the distant origins of financialized capitalism or, inversely, a moderate humanist remedy to neoliberalism. Here, too, sensitivity to real complexities needs to be maintained.

Yet another conception of Enlightenment modernity redefines its philosophical content. This redefinition is what's behind the recent push that goes by the name "Radical Enlightenment," an idea that aims to trace a direct and univocal line between the subversive dimension of atheistic materialism, the democratic revolutions of the late eighteenth century, and the emancipatory aspirations that persist in our time. The proposition is undeniably seductive to all those who wish to maintain a progressive horizon and disburden the Enlightenment of all its ambivalences and ambiguities. The universalist heritage of modernity would then be preserved—but at what price? This question must be examined and understood.

These different options, which are not mutually exclusive, correspond to different conceptions of modernity (the development of public space, the autonomization of the market economy, the rejection of the religious), but they also entail methodological choices. For a long time, Enlightenment historiography resembled an orderly battlefield. On one side, the history of ideas studied canonical authors, major texts, and big ideas. Strengthened by its proximity to the history of philosophy and literary history, the history of ideas had little doubt about its legitimacy, feeling as though the Enlightenment was its domain by right. On the other side, social history studied groups within society, institutions, the careers of authors, and the composition of libraries. Counting on support from the social sciences and cultural historians, social history barged into the field with the confidence and enthusiasm of the typical newcomer. Historians' ears are still ringing from the epic scholarly battles, haughty condemnations, and scathing criticism. A few are nostalgic for those happy days when the opposing sides were well defined, and they attempt periodically to rekindle the ardor of old combatants. But it's a waste of time. Their battle cries no longer rally any more than a few backward-facing battalions, who continue to carry out to the letter the tactics of an outdated conflict. The battlefield now resembles Waterloo as viewed by Stendhal's confused Fabrice Del Dongo. Clever indeed anyone who can find their way through it.

If things have become more complicated, it is because we have acquired two certainties: ideas do not live in an ideal world, outside of time, but are inscribed within texts, evolve, and act within specific social, cultural, and political contexts; inversely, ideas possess their own logic and energy that don't easily allow for a pat reduction to the rhythms of social history and sometimes instead dictate its tempo. Once the two reefs of idealism and materialism have been resolutely avoided, better ways can be pursued for inscribing the intellectual activism of the Enlightenment in its historical contexts.

The time is long past when ideas were treated as the ideological reflection of economic and social interests. Cultural history proposed new interpretations of the French Revolution's origins—interpretations that foreground the development of printing presses, revolutions in reading, and new practices of sociability and relationships to knowledge.[4] Inversely, in the wake of these new interpretations, the Enlightenment names not only a set of debates shaped by their historical context, but also and perhaps above all a massive effort at thinking about all the dimensions and transformations of Western societies on the threshold of modernity. Thus, rather than a social history of ideas, it is an intellectual history of the social that I wish to privilege, an approach that strives to identify sites of reflexivity; in other words, the intensely debated questions thanks to which the contemporaries of the time made sense of the changes that they both witnessed and made happen. The most fruitful heritage of the Enlightenment is not to be found in loyalty to philosophical radicalism but in the capacity to illuminate the ambivalent possibilities of historical change.

CHAPTER FOUR

Private Lives, Public Space

Can one write a social history of the Enlightenment? What links should be established between the works, ideas, and authors who deeply transformed the intellectual and political landscape of France over the eighteenth century and the evolution of French society during the same period? When social history dominated historiography and divided society into slices, there was a great temptation among historiographers to relate the innovations and limits of Enlightenment thinkers to specificities of the social structure. The rise of the bourgeoisie, the role of nobles of the robe, the resistance of the landed aristocracy, even the feudal reaction—these categories seemed self-evidently important. Marxists were not the only ones to see a bourgeois ideology behind the Enlightenment. The organizing principle of social history consisted in thinking of society as an ensemble of distinct and coherent social groups, each with different, even antagonistic, values and beliefs. Proposing a social reading of the Enlightenment implies attributing to certain of these groups, more or less subtly defined, intellectual transformations.

The extensive renewal of social history since the 1980s derived from another way of thinking about the dynamics of a society. The division by social groups, defined by juridical status or by economic position, yielded to a more subtle conception of Old Regime society, one more attentive to the practices, interactions, exchanges, networks, forms, and categories of experience.[1] Take the example of written culture: rather than going through inventories of the libraries of the nobility and the commercial bourgeoisie or comparing literacy rates of workers and servants, historians became interested in reading practices: in the spaces of intimate retreat favored by books, in the types of sociability brought about by reading, in the uses of correspondence, in the dissemination of printed matter within public spaces, and in the diversity of subject matter and its use. Social groups were no longer considered as a priori givens, defined by economic and social organization, but were rather considered to be the result of intellectual and cultural practices that came to redefine social borders and their representations.

This evolution is not confined to the historiography of the Enlightenment. However, this historiography became distinctive due to the attention it paid to the organization of social and cultural practices on a private/public axis. New frames of interpretation then appeared, from figures of intimacy to the history of public space, as historians examined the variety of forms of sociability. A history of private life, of sociability, of public space—these categories became publishing projects and productive fields of research. While proceeding from often quite different historiographical projects, these new ways of articulating social experiences with cultural practices profoundly modified our understanding of the Enlightenment.

Private Life and Intimacy

In a text written in 1983 and published as the introduction to the *History of Private Life* volume devoted to the Enlightenment, Philippe Ariès put forward the hypothesis that in the eighteenth century there was an extensive privatization of ordinary frames of experience. In preceding centuries, individuals in both villages and big cities lived permanently under the eye of others, neighbors and strangers, with practically no distinction between the private and the public. Over the course of the eighteenth century, their social experience is said to have folded back onto private and family life as a result of declining ordinary conviviality and the inexorable progress of the State. The double consequence of this move toward the private, he claimed, was the autonomization of the political sphere, now emancipated from domestic forms of power, and the privatization of social life, which now lived essentially within the family unit.[2] This analysis resulted implicitly in an interpretation of the Enlightenment and modernity: the emergence of the modern individual was less an emancipation with respect to traditional communities, as the entire liberal tradition affirmed, than an impoverishment that returned the individual to the family sphere and left him in an asymmetrical relationship with the powerful Leviathan State. Beyond the critical judgment given on the value of modernity, the lesson concerning method was important and retained: Ariès invited the reader to understand the development of modern life not by studying the philosophy of autonomy of the subject but by decoding the most material forms behind the organization of daily life.

Numerous studies followed up on this intuition to scrutinize the "birth of intimacy."[3] They demonstrated that the material conditions of people's homes underwent a profound transformation during the eighteenth century. In the lodgings of urban elites, the model of the single versatile room was gradually replaced by more complex interiors that separated sleeping quarters from common areas such as living rooms and dining rooms. New rooms allowed for isolation and intimacy: the bedroom, study, and bathroom. The boudoir is the most striking example, hence its prominent place in eighteenth-century libertine literature.[4] And yet this evolution essentially concerned elites and had only a marginal influence on the homes of ordinary people, even in Paris where often the same room served as bedroom, living room, and kitchen. Intimacy in such circumstances was limited.[5]

More complex interiors that allowed for more intimacy were also more richly furnished and decorated. Objects formerly reserved for aristocratic elites—furniture, underwear, mirrors, handkerchiefs, cutlery—were now present in urban interiors of bourgeois merchants and artisans. Ordinary households were also less spare, and one can say there was a first consumer revolution that even affected certain rural milieux, such as farming communities in areas adjacent to Paris. The eighteenth-century world was not exclusively one of rare objects, especially in the city. Inventories after the death of ordinary Parisians revealed that numerous objects had become "banal things," while in the upper classes the British ideal of "comfort" became widespread.[6] The goal was no longer the ostentatious luxury of courtly nobility entirely devoted to prestige but rather a more intimate relation to objects, the décor of rooms, and the arrangement of interior spaces.

Books are one of the prominent objects that went from rare to ordinary. In western cities, a third of the inventories of a deceased's belongings mention books. The households of ordinary people were no exception. In Paris at the end of the century, 40 percent of servants and 35 percent of tradespeople owned books. The use of books also changed. Reading was no longer only a studious activity of elites conducted in designated places such as libraries. It became ordinary, familiar, and nomadic. New figures emerged, such as the female reader of novels, but new formats and new attitudes emerged as well. Silent, intimate reading became the norm, even if it is excessive to speak, as some have, of a reading revolution—because older practices, both solitary scholarly reading and collective reading out loud, persisted alongside the new ones.[7] Probably the essential point, as Roger Chartier has shown, is that the changes in reading habits were not univocal. They took two main forms that are not as different as they appear. One was a more broken-up reading practice that only required sporadic attention. This practice was linked to the multiplication of printed material—books, pamphlets, brochures, journals. Another was absorbed reading, where the reader jumped with delight into a text and—some hours or days later—emerged transformed. This was the model of sentimental reading of popular novels that elicited the streams of tears that eighteenth-century men and women so enjoyed.[8] Enlightenment culture is indissociable from these major transformations in relation to writing: increased availability of information and texts; autonomization of the ordinary reader, male and female, with respect to traditional institutions; and an affective intensity about books that would constitute communities of shared sense and sensibility—and, later, political communities.

The family was one of the major themes of eighteenth-century moral literature. It functions as the refuge of conviviality and affective life. Paternal and maternal love express themselves with new force, as does the tender friendship of the married couple. The family was depicted no longer as merely an economic unit but as the privileged place for experimenting with a way of life that considered itself liberated from the constraints of social life and offered instead a laboratory for affections and feelings. Even writers and scholars found in familial intimacy a new, valuable space that could serve their intellectual pursuits.[9]

A whole current of eighteenth-century French painting testifies to this new way of life that prominently features intimacy, comfort within one's private life, and the sweetness of the family circle. Genre painting depicting aspects of everyday life, as opposed to history painting or the representation of religious scenes, was most in sync with this new society. In *Young Girl Reading*, Fragonard represents a young woman totally absorbed in the small book she holds up with her right hand while comfortably seated with cushions for her back and an armrest for her left hand. Boucher painted a family having lunch in the soft calm of a living room adorned with a mirror, clock, and various trinkets (*Le Déjeuner*). The family is enjoying hot chocolate or coffee—two fashionable products of the time—served in porcelain cups while exchanging affectionate looks. The children, one of whom holds a doll, are clearly well cared for. As for Greuze, even if the village dwellings he painted are more austere and rustic, his major works—*A Father Explaining the Bible to His Children*, *The Village Bride*, *Filial Piety*—all aim to elicit strong emotion by showing the family as the refuge of morality and sentiment.[10]

The Age of Sociability

Ariès concluded that sociability declined in the eighteenth century and what expanded was a face-off between family life—the private space of intimacy and feeling—and public life monopolized by the State and its agents. This diagnosis was challenged by numerous studies on the history of sociability that all showed the wealth of forms of social and associative life at that time. Maurice Agulhon was the first to use the notion of sociability as a historiographic category. In a pioneering work, he described the intensity of social relations in eighteenth-century Provence, where Masonic lodges seemed to have taken over from Christian brotherhoods.[11] This Provençal sociability is said to have paved the way for the important political mobilization at the time of the Revolution and later in 1848.

Even if the hypothesis of an intrinsic link between sociability and politicization was especially helpful for extending research in the area of contemporary political history following the example of Agulhon's work, the notion of sociability also contributed to renewing the cultural and intellectual history of the Enlightenment.[12] A notable example is Daniel Roche, who used the notion to study the mutations of knowledge work, the forms of intellectual mobility, and the inscription of scholarly debates within cultural institutions. The notion of sociability became the lever of a sociology of the intellectual world that aimed to overturn the idea favored by Tocqueville, who seemed to claim that Enlightenment philosophers developed a literary and abstract body of political thought on the side of the monarchical State or even in frontal opposition to it and with no experience of the real stakes of the Old Regime society.[13] The notion of sociability allowed for greater nuance of the politically subversive character attributed to Enlightenment thinkers, and for a better account of how their intellectual struggles were inscribed within Old Regime society: "Enlightenment academics and Enlightenment Masons were not in themselves protestors. They tended in certain respects to combine old positions with new arguments."[14]

In this way, the Enlightenment thinkers lost some of the ethereal, abstract quality that a certain disincarnated history-of-ideas approach had allowed to build up around them. Many social configurations—from the most institutional, such as learned academies, to the most informal, such as correspondence between friends—were examined. These studies revealed an intense network of social interactions and intellectual exchanges in an intermediate space that was not that of the close family or of the State or of the workplace. Cafés, salons, clubs, societies for amusement, and Masonic lodges were all places that resisted the private/public dichotomy. They defined an intermediate space much more open than domestic family spaces but nevertheless founded on invitation and membership. This space, referred to in the eighteenth century by the term *la société*, was one of codified exchanges, both intellectual and earthy, that nourished various forms of conversation. This conversation had three distinct functions that were in practice indissociable. It was, first of all, a form of communication that permitted the exchange of knowledge and the circulation of opinions, thus assuring the penetration of enlightened ideas into social milieux far from scholarly spaces. Conversation was also a constantly aestheticized verbal game that appeared futile to some but to others symbolized the pure pleasure of social life, an ideal form valuing elegance and virtuosity. Thirdly, it was a social and cultural aptitude relying on codes of civility that permitted and defined a sense of belonging.

Specialized academies multiply throughout Europe in the eighteenth century. They were all modeled on the Académie Française, founded in 1635, and the Royal Society, founded in London in 1660. Academies devoted to science but also to the arts, economics, and agronomy constituted a network of knowledge institutions that extended across the continent, from Lisbon to St. Petersburg, from Naples to Trondheim. By the end of the century, they had spread to colonial outposts from Saint Domingo to Batavia. Though some were founded and sponsored by a sovereign (such as in Berlin) while others were private initiatives, all these academies had regular relations with their peer organizations and thus maintained a true institutional network of intellectual exchange.[15] In France, provincial academies also multiplied throughout the eighteenth century, thereby allowing Enlightenment ideas in more moderate versions to circulate among a community's leading citizens, who had a vested interest in both the progress of knowledge and a certain social and political stability. These academies were the instituted spaces of a successful encounter between the values advanced by the philosophers and the expectations of social elites, including certain members of the nobility and clergy, under the auspices of the monarchy and its protection. In this way, they hosted a "jumbled but real alliance of knowledges and powers."[16] Sociability became an intrinsic value in this remodeled version of the Republic of Letters, where now the point was not so much to contribute as an inventor to science's progress but instead to gather together as people of merit and goodwill to encourage and accompany the dissemination of useful knowledge. It is in this sense that one can understand the development of academic competitions that spurred intellectual life, stirred passionate debates, and occasionally revealed promising talent, the most famous case being that of Jean-Jacques Rousseau, who received a prize from the Academy of Dijon in 1750.[17]

Unlike academies, salons had no official existence. They were not monarchical institutions with statutes and stable lists of members. They relied on the hospitality practices of urban elites: the mistress of a household, sometimes the master, would open their home on certain days to an array of regulars, to more occasional visitors who had already been introduced, and to newcomers who came pre-approved via formal recommendation. These salons were part court, due to the essential role played by the high nobility and the strategies of social distinction that went on, and part cultural circle, because of the customary presence of writers and philosophers and even artists. Having more freedom than a true court, these salons were nevertheless regulated by implicit but highly constraining rules of politeness and good manners. Women played an essential role. They were the guarantors of a particular form of social play that was halfway between the gallant ideal inherited from the days of Louis XIV and intellectual exchange.[18] They could modulate between mondain and cultural aptitudes that entailed a high degree of social sensitivity. On the other hand, their own intellectual ambitions were often stymied, because the salons were socially conservative spaces where female knowledge was severely censored. These worldly women had to conform to the role that good society assigned to them: admire, encourage, protect, and always serve the ambition of males. Those who attempted to break the rules were disciplined, sometimes mercilessly. They could be mocked or broadly ridiculed since the satiric tradition inherited from Molière and Boileau was very much alive. It was therefore more in the interstices of mondain life than in the salons themselves that women such as Louise d'Épinay would develop their own activities, notably through correspondence but often through associations with men or in their shadow.[19]

This mondain sociability allowed Parisian nobility to redefine social prestige with their display of a refined, cultivated way of life that also distinguished them from both financiers and the provincial nobility. Inversely, it also allowed certain writers to have access to the lifestyle of elites and to their favors and protection, while letting these bookish types affirm themselves as authentic men of the world. This new figure of the man of letters as one who is both likeable and sociable sharply contrasted with the older image of the solitary and pedantic scholar. The pleasures of sociability were the just compensation for the intellectual ardor of the thinker and allowed the knowledge worker to escape the melancholy caused by his labor.[20] Above all, the philosopher could prove his usefulness, his capacity to address a large public of honest people instead of just the small circle of his peers. "One must be a man of the world before being a man of letters," wrote Voltaire to Madame du Deffand. This remark, which rings like a motto for philosophers, was also a piece of flattery addressed to polite society. Thus, eighteenth-century salons perpetuated those of the previous century, allowing for the continued interpenetration and mutual influence of social, political, and cultural elites.[21] Like the academies, their mode of existence, in France at least, contradicts the idea that the leading Enlightenment figures lived their lives cut off from political elites and oblivious to real-life conditions and issues. In both the salon of Julie de Lespinasse and at the Académie, knowledge workers immersed in the *Encyclopédie* project with d'Alembert and Condorcet were also actively involved in the ministerial affairs of Turgot (1774–1776).

The enthusiasm of urban elites for cultural pastimes harmonized with practices of social distinction in eighteenth-century sociability. The tradition of cabinets of curiosities or wonder rooms coexisted with the new sociability of experts that was more anchored in academic institutions, international knowledge networks, and new spaces for experimental research and teaching.[22] Art lovers, for example, could gather at the home of Claude-Henri Watelet in Moulin-Joli to present their collections, trade engravings, and do some drawing themselves. This form of sociability was in no way closed in on itself; it exerted an influence on the art world through the Royal Academy of Painting and Sculpture, where the "amateur" enjoyed an official status, but also through the system of patronage and by the production and dissemination of new knowledge.[23]

Although salons and academies were around before the eighteenth century and simply grew in significance during the Enlightenment, Freemasonry on the other hand was a new phenomenon at this time and immediately experienced remarkable growth. In France, the first Masonic lodge was founded in 1725. Sixty years later, on the eve of the Revolution, there were nine hundred lodges and roughly fifty thousand Masons. Numerous lodges were started in leading provincial capitals, parliamentary cities, and ports, but they also existed in small towns.[24] As secret societies, Masonic lodges gave rise to all sorts of phantasms, especially at the start of the nineteenth century, when certain figures associated with counterrevolutionary thinking, such as Abbé Barruel, were inclined to see the Revolution as a conspiracy against the social and political order. This idea has persisted in modern forms nourished by sociology and history, notably relayed by Augustin Cochin. The Masonic lodges are said to have developed a new form of egalitarian sociability inspired by Enlightenment thinking but preferring to work in secret. They conducted a sort of semi-isolated experimentation in democracy inside the vertically ordered society but were also said to have accustomed enlightened elites to acting in secret. This view of the organization was made popular by the work of François Furet and Reinhart Koselleck, but generally today there is a more moderate interpretation of Masonic sociability.[25] Even if it may be true that certain lodges made possible the fraternization between hotheads, notably in Holland's francophone community, the Masonic lodges were places chiefly centered on conviviality and amusement. As Pierre-Yves Beaurepaire has shown, Freemasonry was not a site of democratic sociability but instead generally reproduced the practices of social distinction, like-mindedness, and exclusion that operated in other places of sociability. In the case of large cities, one can say there was a "social Masonry" openly associated to the mondain world through their organization of concerts, shows, charitable events, and dinners. Thus, for example, the high-class lodge of "*Amis réunis*" [United Friends] hosted tax collectors [*fermiers généraux*], nobles, financiers, and wealthy foreigners, modeling itself on its idea of the English club when gathering in the summer at the Château de la Chevrette.

That it operated this way explains why Freemasonry, in pre-Revolutionary France, was never perceived by the authorities as a danger. That said, the egalitarian and cosmopolitan ideals proclaimed by the Masonic lodges probably did contribute to familiarizing Old Regime elites with the principles of a less rigidly codified sociability than the practices imposed by traditional orders of distinction. They were also a factor in building the tissue of networked sociability throughout Europe by facilitating mobility and meetings.

Writers, philosophers, and other knowledge workers engaged with preexisting forms (academies, salons, cafés) or new ones (Freemasonry, reading societies, clubs). Some were explicitly devoted to an intellectual or technical knowledge ideal (the French *lycée*, museums, agricultural societies) while others were more about offering worldly cultural pastimes (the *salons*). Together, these places and their practices accelerated the social dissemination and circulation, albeit in diluted forms in some cases, of the enlightened person's leading topics, and deeply inscribed the Enlightenment authors within the society of the Old Regime, though without being able to associate them with specific socioeconomic groups. This accelerated circulation explains how a portion of the nobility, especially in Paris and certain large cities, could be so widely affected by Enlightenment ideas. The ideal of sociability, which at first was a philosophical notion favored by defenders of natural-rights theory (the natural aptitude of mankind to live in society) but which could also be used by educated elites to defend an idea of cultivated leisure, perfectly symbolized this alliance.[26] Social life—the world of writers, lovers of art and music, Parisian nobility, and finance—appeared in the eyes of its promoters to be the incarnation of a process of civilization that made Paris into the capital of Europe. "The earthly paradise is where I am," Voltaire could write proudly in *Le Mondain.*

In France, the major Enlightenment figures did not educate themselves away from Old Regime society or in radical opposition to it. They were deeply immersed in the cultural institutions of the monarchy and associated with the social practices of elite groups. Take the case of d'Alembert, the author of the veritable Enlightenment manifesto that prefaced the *Encyclopédie* (1751), the "*Discours préliminaire.*" He was a member of the Academy of Sciences and of most European academies, the permanent secretary of the Académie Française, and a fixture at the salons of the Marquise du Deffand, Marie-Thérèse Geoffrin, and Julie de Lespinasse. Therefore, the Enlightenment Lumières, with an s, represented neither a coherent philosophical doctrine nor a clearly defined camp standing against some opposing camp (Enlightenment progressives, say, against anti-Enlightenment conservative reactionaries) but were instead a heterogeneous and polyphonic intellectual current living in association with an ensemble of social practices whose common aim was to promote the public use of reason—in other words, to foster an open discussion on an array of topics that until then had been the secret prerogative of the State or Church—and to do so without any general agreement about the contours of this new publicness [*publicité*].

What Is the Public Space?

Tocqueville's teachings, which saw the Enlightenment in contrasting opposition to the State, relied on the assumption that the word public named, above all, the action of the State and its administration. Likewise, Ariès opposed private space and family to two conceptions of the public: first, the State; and second, the collective and anonymous life of the street, public parks, and large public squares. In both conceptions, reading, intellectual exchange, and friendly conversation fell entirely within the private sphere. However, the critical conversation surrounding Jürgen Habermas's book *The Structural Transformation of the Public Sphere* (1962), which accelerated in the 1980s, completely changed the historiography on this topic.[27] The grand narrative about the emergence of a bourgeois public sphere became the leading framework for interpreting the cultural transformations of the Enlightenment for all those wishing to break from idealist readings and traditional social explanations. Habermas proposed a new definition of the public, conceived of as an ensemble of private individuals who make public use of their reason. In this conception, which took its inspiration from Kant and his famous 1784 essay "What Is Enlightenment?" and added to it the lessons of historical sociology, the bourgeois public sphere was said to be constituted outside the State and against it. It resulted from three preconditions: the emergence of private economic interests; a validation of the principle of publicness [*publicité*] that implied open, rational, and critical discussion of common affairs; and an ensemble of places and institutions (cafés, lodges, journals) where individuals, independent of their social status and political responsibilities, could participate in such discussions. This bourgeois public sphere—so radically different from the traditional forms of vertical, hierarchical, and corporatist communication—was said to have emerged at the beginning of the eighteenth century through literary and artistic debates, and it was then quickly politicized, thus making public opinion into a powerful, legitimate tribunal opposed to both the absolutist will of the king and the bureaucratic rationality of the State.

Following Habermas, the historical dynamic of relations between the private and public spheres looked quite different. It was no longer the growth of the State that was considered the primary motor, with sociability relegated to the private sphere; instead, the motor was civil society, which constructed its own autonomy and took on a political significance by attacking the State's monopoly on public affairs. Private life, as a concept, was vested with a radically new political dimension, namely the development of a new public sphere that would carry forth modern ideals of publicness.[28]

In the wake of the German philosopher's reinterpretation of eighteenth-century cultural and political history, historians reevaluated the importance of the notion of public opinion in pre-Revolutionary political culture, insisting on its normative coherence and rhetorical uses.[29] They linked the development of printed materials and the new practices of reading to the construction of this public space where all questions—from the rules of tragedy to the wheat business, from Jansenism to the American war of independence—were now debated publicly. These debates fueled the conviction, for readers, that they were participating in a public space of discussion.

The ideal of publicness, of being public, implied greater flexibility around the conditions for publishing and the circulation of information. Although censorship rules remained officially strict, the system of tacit authorizations allowed for publication without official approval. French-language books and gazettes printed in Geneva, Amsterdam, or

London generally made their way into the kingdom. In many respects, the sharp increase in pamphlets and other publications during the two years preceding the opening of the Estates General can be seen as the spectacular effect of the continuous development of this public sphere.

The focus of Habermas's conception of the public sphere was not publishing, however, but rather the cafés, Masonic lodges, and salons where texts could be read and discussed. Following his initiative, many authors considered the leading places of sociability in the eighteenth century to have formed the institutional base of public space devoted principally to the back-and-forth of rational argument and to making progress as defined by the Enlightenment.[30] These studies, in turn, became the object of much criticism.[31] For one thing, a conception of public space that concentrated on the practices of polite society and the publishing world left out other forms of participation in public debates. Women, excluded from the official institutions of the Republic of Letters, had only limited access to publication. Jeanne-Marie Phlipon, the future Manon Roland, kept her writings piled in a corner of her library with no thought of having them printed: "Never did I have the least inclination to become an author one day. I was quick to see that a woman who gains that title loses much more than she acquires. Men dislike her and her own sex criticizes her. If her writings are bad, she is mocked, and deservedly so; if they are good, they are taken away from her."[32] Some women published anonymously or through the intermediary of doing translations. It was only with the Revolution that the number of female authors would increase substantially.[33] Likewise, more ordinary sociability, such as on the street or at markets, fueled a different form of public opinion, one actively watched by the police. It often expressed itself through slander, satirical songs, or rumors, and it could sometimes turn into open revolt or rioting.[34] The strained economic conditions in the 1770s illustrate well the divisions that could arise, in this case between debates in the public spaces of the educated, which generally favored the liberalization of grain markets, versus rumors and conspiracy theories about a plot to starve the people, which circulated within a moral economy of the crowd, via an intense working-class sociability.[35]

In addition, Habermas's account of the eighteenth century projected an idyllic vision of public space as though to better denounce the degeneration that would follow. He overestimated the critical capacity of sociability practices. The dense network of various types of sociability did not amount to a public space of deliberation, nor was it a private, intimate family space. It was instead a mixed, hybrid space reflecting the life of "society." This society named an ensemble of social experiences that eluded the most traditional social sharing and instead created new forms of distinction, social prestige, and power. In salons, alongside a smiling welcome to world amusements, high-stakes methods for the social and political control of reputations were in full force and considered essential. Even London cafés, an emblem of the public sphere according to Habermas, had their habits of ostentation and strict rules of inclusion and exclusion. The case of Masonic lodges is even more striking since their prevalence and universalist ideals ran counter to their use of social cooptation as a recruitment tool.[36]

A large quantity of Enlightenment-era literature features the multitude of social experiences in which a society redefined its divisions and categories in spaces that were simultaneously open and closed—and that proclaimed their openness to make all the clearer the effects of closed borders. From the *Persian Letters* (1721) to *Dangerous Liaisons* (1782), the French epistolary novel was particularly adept at displaying the stakes adjacent to the Enlightenment's light and cruel sociability.

A Media Revolution

After two decades of sometimes excessive enthusiasm, specialists of the Enlightenment turned away from the Habermas model almost as quickly as they had embraced it. The study of sociability continued, however, with new attention to international forms of circulation. This research valorized mobility, whether of people, objects, or ideas. New digital technologies made possible a more systematic study of large bodies of documents; they also enabled the mapping of "networks of sociability" that insisted on the multiplication of links and connections. This research delivered valuable results that offered a new vision of the big picture, thanks to the exploitation of metadata derived from vast quantities of Enlightenment correspondence.[37] With the importance it accorded to epistolary exchanges and to knowledge institutions such as academies and scholarly journals, this research reactivated the venerable tradition of studying the Republic of Letters, which had always described intellectual life as an ensemble of personal ties that didn't bother about government-imposed national borders.[38]

The reference to a Republic of Letters is both the strength and limitation of these endeavors because it supposes that the intensity of interpersonal relations was the principal characteristic of Enlightenment figures. However, the main difference that affected intellectual life in the eighteenth century was neither the existence of networks of correspondence nor their expansion—which has yet to be proved—but actually the rapid development of printed material (books, pamphlets, journals, engravings) that significantly modified the forms of communication. What distinguishes Voltaire and Rousseau from Erasmus and Gassendi is that the former are addressing not simply an extensive number of correspondents or a small circle of savants but also the public and an anonymous readership. The emergence of "the public" completely changed the Enlightenment writers' forms of address, and it spurred intense reflection on the act of publication itself as a form of action that was both intellectual and political.[39] For most writers at that time, with the probable exception of those operating in scholarly spaces, the Republic of Letters was an obsolete ideal. Their principal concern was how to enlighten the public by transmitting knowledge and critical thinking beyond academic circles. This ambition, really the heart of the Enlightenment intellectual project, took two forms: first, a reflection on education that elites throughout Europe conducted in the second half of the eighteenth century, and secondly, public addresses via printed material directed to a public that was anonymous and potentially infinite in size.

The public they had in mind is not "the public sphere" imagined by Habermas, founded on the back-and-forth exchange of rational arguments between private individuals. It resulted from the development of media-driven communication—in other words, from the increased production of books, journals, brochures, and images. One must therefore turn to the historical sociology of media to understand its rise. The eighteenth-century ground floor of today's mass media saw the development of forms of communication that were markedly different from the face-to-face interactions that characterized the practices of sociability discussed above but also from epistolary communication that remained a bilateral, reciprocal exchange.[40] Media-driven communication was distinct in that it was directed to a public that was anonymous and whose reactions were therefore difficult, if not impossible, to predict or control. In this way, such communication breaks with classical forms of sociability, which were regulated by interlocutors' mutual recognition within an understood ideal of conversation. The new communication made possible a dissemination of messages, works, and information across time and space, assuring their potentially infinite availability—giving them, in other words, an acknowledged "publicity" or public status. The public, in return, was constituted in the shared experience of this communication. The reading of journals excited the public's curiosity and modified its judgment. Readers were influenced by their reading, but they mutually influenced each other by the consciousness they had of forming a public and feeling a "sense of currentness" (sociologist Gabriel Tarde would analyze this phenomenon a century later).[41] Readers maintained relations that, even though impersonal and indirect, could be very intense. Besides the two consequences of publicness contrasted by Habermas—the normative demands of rational debate and the economic reality of marketing—a third consequence of publicness concerns the messages transmitted by media.

Of course, the media revolution in the Enlightenment era was not built in a day. Its roots go back to innovations in printing that started in the fifteenth century and will only be completed with the achievements of the mass press of the nineteenth century and the audiovisual and electronic media of the twentieth century. But over this long rise in long-distance communications, the eighteenth century played an essential role that has often been underestimated.[42] The emergence of the public as a social reality, as a cultural and political player, and as a theoretical question can only be understood within this context.

While the public sphere theorized by Habermas relied on practices of sociability, media publicity threatens them. The gulf gradually widened between the forms of traditional interaction marked by mutual acquaintanceship, reciprocity, and orality, and the new written communication addressed to an anonymous and potentially infinite public. Whether people were interacting in salons, cafés, clubs, academies, or via correspondence between experts—these forms of sociability no longer fulfilled the same functions once they had to coexist alongside the new forms of publicness. Their significance was profoundly altered.

Places of sociability all depended on closed encounters of like-minded people—this dependence was particularly acute in salons and lodges, but it was also felt in academies and even cafés. With the rise of the press, these spaces were confronted with the public divulgence of private conversations. Witticisms uttered in a salon risked being quoted in newspapers. The decisions of an academy were criticized in brochures or pamphlets. Private or semi-private correspondence could be printed. The limited circulation of information that characterized high society had to adapt to these new circumstances. Caught red-handed, André Morellet was forced to explain himself to the British minister Lord Shelburne after a letter from the minister to Morellet found its way into English newspapers.[43] Voltaire was constantly complaining that his letters were being printed by "pirates"—thus breaking the pact of semi-confidentiality between him and his correspondents and the mondain circles within which his letters circulated. The success of Freemasonry probably owed much to this new context. The secretive is not the same as the clandestine, and societies with secrets are not the same as truly secret societies. The existence of lodges was known, but the practices that went on in them remained mysterious to the uninitiated outsider. The attraction of the Masonic "secret" is probably explained less by a desire to elude the control of the State or to construct an egalitarian sociability than by the wish to preserve places of conviviality that would be totally invisible to the public's gaze.

This wariness was joined by significant ambivalence about the idea of public judgement, including among the most well-disposed authors. Being accustomed to the easy affirmation received within communities of tastemakers and the monopoly of the Académie française, artists and amateurs frowned on this creation of a public forum for spectators of a new kind of salon, one where sizeable crowds could come to view works of art shown every other year in the Louvre's large square salon.[44] The development of art criticism that accompanied this growth of art's public display testified to a rational and collective use of critical thinking. But perhaps more importantly, the violent attacks that erupted were a clear symptom of the upheaval caused by the emergence of this new public of outsiders, now suddenly inside, who lacked the qualifications and competence of the select set of connoisseurs. Even Mercier, though convinced that "the paintings are made to be judged in the end by the public's eye," could not help mocking uncouth and uncultivated spectators.[45] It was a mystery to more than one as to how these unqualified people suddenly became the infallible public. Likewise, the demands of public science contributed to a destabilization of the traditional figures of authority founded on the testimony and social qualifications of participating assistants. Public courses, scientific shows, and surprising public experiments—these new practices on offer to the public's supposed curiosity reorganized relations to knowledge beyond the circles of academic sociability.[46]

Spaces of sociability lost their monopoly over the construction of reputations. As much as the production of knowledge or the use of critical reason, maintaining this monopoly had been one of the core purposes of the Republic of Letters's networks of correspondence: assuring quality control by peer review, as it would later be called, and by upholders of proper manners who would ensure the social value of individuals in accordance with a model of vetting that was used by elites but was also the purpose behind neighborhood gossip.[47] With the rise of publicness, the old ways of building reputations were confronted with a new culture of celebrity.[48] Visits, a practice so characteristic of traditional intellectual sociability, would become torturous and threatening for Jean-Jacques Rousseau when he started to suspect that his visitors were moved only by idle curiosity.[49] Some years later, in Coppet, Lord Byron was shocked to be received as though he were "a curious animal at a country fair."[50] The comparison, which may seem burlesque, was already a commonplace and so accurately captured the new situation. Mediatized public space, far from being dialogic and rational, was above all a space of spectacle in which appearances were essential and people were personages living under the public's gaze—with all that that implies about excessive curiosity, moral exhibitionism, and powerful emotions.[51]

Women were particularly sensitive to this phenomenon, and a few analyzed it with remarkable acumen. They found themselves faced with new constraints—no longer just the caustic mondain satire directed at knowledgeable women but the iron bands of public curiosity. At the end of the century, Germaine de Staël described the desperate situation of the female celebrity confronted with slander and rumor in newspapers but lacking the means to defend herself and reduced to pathetic solitude: "Like the pariahs of India, such a woman parades her peculiar existence among classes she cannot belong to, which consider her as destined to exist on her own, the object of curiosity and perhaps a little envy: what she deserves, in fact, is pity."[52] She spoke from experience. Having been early on exposed to the public's gaze because of the visibility of her parents but also by taste and temperament, she suffered the calumny that mounted in newspapers and felt "condemned to celebrity."[53] Beyond the misogynistic prejudice she was forced to put up with, Germaine de Staël identified the media mechanisms that made all literary glory practically impossible because of a fundamental mismatch: newspapers "decide almost entirely the reputation of people who can only respond as private individuals to public attacks."[54] For her, celebrity imposed on female ambition more formidable constraints than those of the old mondain sociability—which, it's true, she had totally mastered. Over the whole Revolutionary period, she would attempt to regain favor, specifically by trying to graft traditional forms of politeness onto the new democratic manners.[55]

The development of publicness did not make practices of sociability disappear, however. The latter played an essential role in the reception and social construction of public events. This point has been well-understood by sociologists of contemporary media but was less well documented by historians.[56] Readers are not in isolation, with their noses in books and newspapers, and the interpretation of news was immediately socialized in the form of conversations and letters. The latest plays at the Comédie Française, newly published books, intellectual debates, and political news were all the focus of intense discussions in salons and literary societies. Rather than studying places of sociability as the spaces where opinion was produced and manipulated—as if they were some sort of waystation en route to publication—it's better to ask how they tried to render some order out of the profusion of news that circulated in public space. Faced with the widespread concern over the exponential multiplication of sometimes unverifiable news, sociability spaces filtered, channeled, and socialized public information and judgments. They helped individuals give meaning to this new and ever-expanding media space.[57]

Sense and Sensibility of Public Space

This conception of publicness and publicity, founded more on the specific effects of new media than on an ideal of rational exchange, allows one to better understand the complex interpenetration of the private and the public. At first glance, the development, on the one hand, of private spaces as redoubts of intimacy and subjectivity, and, on the other, the emergence of a public sphere, seem to constitute two different and even opposing phenomena. This impression stems from the fact that they were studied within very different historiographical contexts. One perspective offered a social history attentive to daily practices, material culture, and intimate spaces; the other proposed a cultural and political history devoted to scrutinizing the rise of modernity and the decline of absolutism.

And yet Habermas had well understood that a more dialectic relation between the two spheres was establishing itself. In his view, the emergence of the public sphere was founded on the rise of a bourgeoisie committed to defending its private interests. However, the "private," in his analysis, essentially meant the sphere of economic exchanges, and thus it could be anchored in a form of rationality consistent with the Marxist reading of the origins of "civil society." But Habermas had intuited another anchoring of public space in the private sphere—because it is within familial intimacy, he wrote, that individuals become conscious of belonging to a common humanity beyond all professional attachments. This point is essential to his argument because it justifies the claim that the public sphere is not just the expression of the private interests of capitalists. Yet he passes over it rather quickly, with only a brief evocation of the enthusiasm for private correspondence—and, later, for the great epistolary novels of Richardson, Rousseau, and Goethe—that allowed readers to discover within the intimate confines of their reading the universal emotions of human subjectivity.[58] What crests the surface furtively in this analysis is the role played by literature, as fiction and as mediating agent, in the constitution of a fully sensed public space where emotions permit the coordination of individual sensibilities.

As their readers experienced them, sentimental novels were indissociably both an aesthetic form and a media product, not unlike the television series of recent times. These novels allowed a generation of readers to share in the same emotions, the same sentiments—and led them to experience those emotions both as a public and as private individuals each with his or her own sensibility. Indeed, one could argue that the logic is just the reverse of what Habermas claimed: the public is not constituted by people who have forged their subjectivity in familial intimacy or by reading novels from which they would then move to the exchange of considered judgments; instead it is the public space that produces individual subjectivities through collective experience, like that of a reading, which is an intensely social activity even when it's happening in the solitude of a room.

This space can be described as *sensible* because it is built from figures and fictions as much as from arguments and reasonings, and also because it relies on the *sensibility* of individuals in the eighteenth-century sense of the term, meaning the capacity to be moved and touched by the situation of others.[59] There is no question that compassion, sympathy, and an aptitude to be affected by the emotions of others was at the heart of a major current of Enlightenment moral thinking. Faced with the spectacle of suffering, the imagination stimulates empathy, which permits feeling compassion for every human being: "By the imagination we place ourselves in his situation, we conceive ourselves enduring all the same torments, we enter as it were into his body, and become in some measure the same person with him and thence form some idea of his sensations, and even feel something which, though weaker in degree, is not altogether unlike them."[60] Sentimental literature, in novels and in theater, made of this empathic disposition an essential characteristic of fictions that nourish the collective imagination. This phenomenon has been abundantly studied, even if one must not neglect the criticisms that call such sentimentalism insincere or narcissistically indulgent.[61] There remains the question of how this literary and moral sentimentalism could take on a properly political dimension capable of fueling public addresses, shaping opinions and campaigns, and inciting collective actions. Part of the answer is that sensible public space derives from the effects proper to printed matter as a mass medium that permits the synchronization of affects through the large-scale dissemination of the same texts and images—such that one could say, paraphrasing Niklas Luhmann, that "what we feel, we feel through mass media."[62]

The sentimental novel was not only a disinterested vector of the literary use of reason; it was also cultural merchandise. Its success was accompanied by advertising campaigns—in other words, by *publicity* in the most common English sense of the word—orchestrated by the publisher and extended to tie-in products such as engravings, figurines, fans, and playing cards. Public space was from the start organized for commercial gain, and Britain was the great pioneer in these endeavors.

The commercialization of pastimes developed precociously there, both in the theater world and in publishing.[63] But in the second half of the eighteenth century, France became adept at this mixture of commercial audacity and cultivated amusement that constituted the "business of Enlightenment."[64]

The Publicness of the Intimate

The new forms of publicness that developed in the eighteenth century were indissociable from the recognition of a deep interior; and they contributed, in turn, to the imposition of a new relationship to intimacy. Private and public were not antagonistic; they formed a united couple that developed conjointly throughout the eighteenth century in the area of practices and representations.

Until the seventeenth century, the term *public* named the total number of individuals living under the same sovereign authority and constituting under this sovereignty a political body. By extension, then, the public designated the State, since the latter derived from this sovereignty and guaranteed the existence of a political community. In contrast to this juridical and political public, there were individual people who exercised no particular function within the order of power.[65] In the eighteenth century, as the notion of society began to impose itself to designate both small groups founded on conviviality and association as well as a collective of individuals, the public/private couple became more and more structuring. Private life did not name a particular condition but constituted, rather, whatever fell outside public life. At first, it corresponded to the voluntary retreat of a statesman resigning from power. This sense persisted and became general in the eighteenth century and can be found in the *Encyclopédie*: private life does not exist on its own; it is defined in opposition to the sphere of power. But increasingly, it stood in contrast to the social spectacle that imposed itself as one of the essential dimensions of urban life. Gradually, all of social life became divided between a public dimension, subject to the gaze of others and therefore to collective discussion, and a private dimension, legitimately invisible to the eye and to commentary, because it concerned intimate or family life. In the nineteenth century, the juridical recognition of a private life would develop precisely along these two complementary axes: a protection vis-à-vis the power of the State and vis-à-vis one's contemporaries.[66]

So, these two notions, the public and the private, were intimately linked. Jointly, they became the framework for thinking and talking about the conditions of social life, each evolving as a function of the evolution of the other. The development of publicness—through the press, books, urban shows—rendered all the more pressing the calls for intimacy and solitude that nourished the pre-Romantic sensibility that emerged at the end of the century under the notable influence of Rousseau. The affirmation of the authenticity of the self [*moi*] did not come out of nowhere in the history of Western thinking, nor was it a mere secularized form of the Christian soul. It arose as a reaction to the increasing number and power of new mediations of public opinion: "What does it matter to me if men want to see me other than as I am? Is the essence of my being in their looks?" exclaims Rousseau.[67]

In return, the desire to benefit from a private life fueled the curiosity and scopophilia of inquisitors. Even sovereigns were subject to desires for privacy, as we know from the emblematic case of Marie-Antoinette. Royal etiquette—which implied that the king and queen live permanently under the gaze of the court and be totally and constantly public personages, in the double sense of incarnating the state and having their lives be one uninterrupted spectacle, something Louis XIV managed very well—was unacceptable to her. Therefore, she developed an intimate private life sheltered from prying eyes, and Trianon was the symbol of this privacy. But this demand for intimacy, in perfect conformity with the new values of social elites at the end of the century, provoked in response the frenzied curiosity of the public—which in this case meant journalists, writers of every genre, and authors of pamphlets but probably also the curiosity of those who avidly bought any and every text about the queen, to the point where the royal police had to intervene many times to erase supposed revelations about her private life.[68]

Literary historians first described long ago the emergence of a new genre, written in the first person, that broke from the classical model of books of reason and from narratives centered on a public, political life. These "writings from the private interior" recount the evolution of a subjectivity with its torments, hopes, and doubts. Autobiography distances itself from memoir; the diary begins a long career as the "barometer of the soul."[69] One can observe that these writings maintain an ambiguous relation to the horizon of the public. Are they even meant to be read? Who are they addressing? While deepening an intimate and immediate relation to the self, they often seek to be published, if not during the life of the author then at some future time. With the *Confessions* but also with his *Reveries of a Solitary Walker*, Rousseau made honorable a form of autobiographical narrative centered on interiority and intimate feelings that is at the same time an argued plea addressed to the reader. What's distinctive about this type of writing is both the affirmation of the sovereignty of an interior self, indulging delightfully in solitary meditation, but also the publication of this aspiration for intimacy, turning the adventures of this subjectivity into a public spectacle.[70]

In parallel, ordinary individuals caught up in legal trouble could see their private lives displayed in the public square, so to speak, when the resounding tumult of a trial inflamed the zeal and verve of opposing lawyers.[71] The "memoirs" of lawyers, though first addressed to judges, were published in thousands of copies. They abusively exploited sentimental rhetoric to make their clients into symbols of social and political injustice and to call for the verdict of public opinion. These legal affairs contributed to the forging of a new political culture that linked with the same disapproval both ministerial despotism and aristocratic corruption, contrasting those sins to the moral virtues of familial order and the simple dignity of ordinary people. But to do so, the private life of anonymous individuals had to be turned into public narratives, some of which resembled soap operas. The domestic life, marital strife, and financial difficulties of the protagonists in these affairs were encapsulated as their "private lives" even as they became entirely public and were transformed into a spectacle for the urban readership that devoured these memoirs. The clamor around these lurid "causes célèbres" united three features of publicness: public curiosity for private litigation mediatized by printed materials, the politicization of questions linked to the family and to sexuality, and the emergence of a public composed of individuals aggregated as the figure of public opinion.

Eventually the private life of public individuals became an object of investigation and even an editorial genre of its own.[72] These "private lives" relied on two presuppositions. First, the public exposure of certain famous people, writers, criminals, and actors excites "general curiosity" for anecdotes about their private and even intimate life.[73] Second, the private life of public figures, notably politicians, reveals the hidden motives of their actions. Starting in the 1770s and then during the French Revolution, narratives of the private lives of Louis XV, Mirabeau, and Marat proliferate. Once studied from an exclusively political angle, especially as illustrating the desacralization of the monarchy, these texts were now reevaluated as testifying to the transformation of the balance between private and public—a transformation that opened a new place for calumny within the repertoire of political action.

The most decisive transformation that affected social experience in the eighteenth century—and the case study of French royalty could easily be extrapolated to other Western European societies—concerns the new types of linkages between private and public. In the last thirty years, historians have deepened their understanding of these articulations through investigations into the material history of private life, the recomposition of sociability practices, and relentless study of the genesis of the public sphere. But the distribution of approaches and methods and the long shadow of Habermas's interpretation have obscured an essential point: the development of modern forms of publicness linked to the rise of publishing significantly changed the nature and function of traditional forms of sociability.

Publicness [*publicité*] is an essential element for grasping the social and cultural changes of the Enlightenment, on condition that one not understand it simply as a principle for the educated, critical discussion of literary and political questions but also as the driving force by which things designated as intimate or private are projected onto the public stage. So stands the modern individual: with a consciousness of self that is increasingly subjective and wedded to the exigencies of authenticity, but one also subjected to the increasingly strong set of hopes and constraints of public life.

And yet the critical dimension of publicness, as a normative ideal, should not be underestimated. It was one of the principles defended by Enlightenment writers, and it guided numerous reforms, notably during the French Revolution—from guaranteeing freedom of the press to making parliamentary debates public. However, this democratic face of publicness must not be used to mask the tensions that preside over its arrival and limit its flourishing. The emergence of a critical public space relies on social conditions that permit solitary reading and autonomous reflection, whereas the new ideal of a singular subjectivity takes shape in reaction to the multiple constraints imposed by publicness. The latter, in return, capture the very ideal of the private, which may exist but only under the constant threat of being turned into spectacle. These ambivalences run through the field of heterogenous forces that nourish Enlightenment culture.

CHAPTER FIVE

Enlightenment Radicals?

Since the first decade of the 2000s, discussions about the heritage and modernity of the Enlightenment have taken a new direction, fueled by debates over "Enlightenment radicals." The notion itself is not new. It was put forward by Margaret Jacob in the early 1980s to describe the heterodox and libertine currents of the early eighteenth century.[1] However, the idea of a "radical Enlightenment" was not discussed very much until it was taken up again by Jonathan Israel and placed at the center of a very large publishing venture. Part encyclopedic synthesis, part manifesto, Israel's work unquestionably marked a new chapter in Enlightenment historiography.[2] One reason is that this work, though appearing as a single volume, showcases a number of previously little-known studies that all aim to highlight the subversive character of the Enlightenment. The very success of the term *radical Enlightenment* signals a change in orientation and perhaps a paradigm shift. While for twenty years the influence of the writings of Jürgen Habermas had imposed a neo-Kantian reading on the Enlightenment, one organized around studies of the public sphere, this study of clandestine philosophy proposes a new interpretive framework that posits Spinoza as the template for the Enlightenment and a resource for contemporary social science. As we shall see, it's the interpretation of Enlightenment "modernity" that is once again at issue.

The title "Radical Enlightenment" raises as many questions as it answers, in particular because of the equivalence the author establishes between a traditional category within the history of philosophy, Spinozism, and a historiographical category designating Enlightenment radicals. On what basis can Enlightenment figures be called radical or radicals? What is Spinozism? And what is or ought to be the point of articulation between a history of philosophy and a cultural history of intellectual production and products? Israel appears largely indifferent to all the work devoted to practices of sociability, the forms of public space, and the interpenetration of private and public, and has even less interest in the economic, social, and political practices organized around credit and consumption. In his view the Enlightenment is a philosophical matter, and its modernity has entirely to do with its ideology. This claim should not be dismissed too quickly. After all, that the Enlightenment was to a great degree an ensemble of philosophical debates is readily acknowledged. And that a portion of Enlightenment historiography turned away too quickly or too much from the texts, at the risk of perhaps no longer being able to distinguish text from context—in other words, to distinguish the primary object of study from the diffuse ensemble of eighteenth-century social and cultural mutations—is an observation worth considering, perhaps even a persuasive one. But this return of intellectual history on the basis of an alleged radicality—is it a step forward or backward? It all depends on the soundness of the arguments and how they're handled. "Radical Enlightenment" is neither miracle cure nor bogeyman. We need not bow nor flee. It is above all a historiographic operation and ought to be judged by what it accomplishes.

Rereading the Enlightenment

The magnitude of the undertaking is striking first for its enormous size. After the success of the first volume, published in 2001, which received many and mostly positive reviews, Israel seemed to be overtaken by a sort of writing fever—publishing hefty volumes of roughly a thousand pages each at regular intervals—which suggested a desire to propose an exhaustive, comprehensive history of the Enlightenment.[3] To date, five volumes have appeared, totaling more than five thousand pages, with thousands of footnotes and copious bibliographies. Many historians are unsure whether it's best to remain awestruck by the undeniably massive amount of labor and erudition behind these works, or if they're allowed to vent their frustration at the repetition of the same arguments that come back over and over. It's clear that judgments have shifted over time. The two first volumes, devoted to the period 1650–1750, elicited genuine interest. They describe the development of a philosophical radicalism inspired by the writings of Spinoza, first in the United Provinces of the Netherlands during the second half of the seventeenth century and then throughout Europe. Both volumes received a lot of critical attention and undoubtedly influenced the historiographical debate on the Enlightenment.[4] The subsequent volumes received more tepid reviews, as the author branched out from his area of expertise (Holland in the late 1600s) to take up generally more well-known authors and periods, such as the French Revolution, even if sometimes he was in over his head. It did not help matters that Israel was excessively polemical in some of his collegial exchanges. In answer to criticisms that came up, he would respond systematically with reams of text, heaping condemnation on his adversaries and refusing any adjustment of his reasoning.[5] He even hardened his positions on methodology and his interpretation of Enlightenment radicalism. On the positive side, if one looks beyond these skirmishes, this gigantic tapestry can be reduced quite easily to a few propositions that constitute the foundation of this massive history of ideas. Israel has been helpful with this synthesis, in fact, by publishing summaries of his arguments.[6]

From this profuse mass, there emerges a clear thesis that gets endlessly repeated in various guises: Spinozism exerted a profound influence across all of Europe starting at the end of the seventeenth century, but on account of censorship it expressed itself in a masked or clandestine way, so much so that historians generally underestimated it and granted more importance to moderate, liberal, empirical, and deist authors, who then became the center of the intellectual history of the Enlightenment. The radical Enlightenment that derives from the Spinozist template was defined by its hostility to all compromise between philosophy and religion, an intransigent materialism, a rationalist and mathematical vision of the world, republican and democratic convictions, and by a refusal of all inequality, be it social, racial, or gender-based. The radicals are said to have been staunchly opposed to conservatives and adversaries of the Enlightenment, but also and perhaps most of all to the moderate current that sought to reconcile reason and faith and that was always politically prudent and mindful of avoiding direct confrontation with authorities.

Jonathan Israel's ambition is clearly stated: to present a new general interpretation of the Enlightenment with the radical, materialist, democratic current at its center, which means recognizing it as the true crucible of Western modernity as opposed to the moderate, reformist current centered around stock Enlightenment figures such as Locke, Voltaire, or Christian Wolff. Israel is also open about his partisanship. The Enlightenment radicals have his complete sympathy and ought to be studied, rehabilitated, and defended. This is the heritage we ought to align ourselves with, according to Israel.[7] The "moderate" Enlightenment figures, on the other hand, receive his thinly disguised contempt. Rather than forces of emancipation, for Israel they were often the allies of conservative reactionaries, or at best soft, centrist compromisers. Locke, Voltaire, Hume, and Benjamin Franklin were, he claims, "essentially conservative thinkers" politically, socially, morally, and even religiously.[8]

In Israel's account, Enlightenment radicals prepared and made possible the revolutions at the end of the century. This argument, present in the first volumes and further developed in the later ones, is articulated with a double claim: Israel affirms forcefully that revolutions in the world are caused by ideas and that those ideas are caused by a revolution "of the minds" of people—therefore, he argues, it's absurd to insist that revolutionary events have their own dynamics. Starting in the 1770s, he writes, and even somewhat earlier in France, Enlightenment moderates had disappeared, leaving the field open to the radical current. He thus reunites with the classic thesis that validates the Revolution's intellectual origins, but he does so in a form marked by a high degree of determinism, and he offers no answer to the old question of what exactly links the actions of the avant-garde intellectuals to those of political actors, whether the sans-culottes or Assembly deputies.[9] Even more problematic is Israel's determination to interpret the events of the French Revolution itself as the projection, manifested on the political landscape, of the philosophical opposition between Enlightenment moderates and radicals—a stance that gives rise to some surprises for the reader, because this privileging of metaphysics leads him to praise Brissot as the incarnation of radicality and to criticize Robespierre for his moderation.[10]

Whether one agrees with these claims, the importance of Israel's undertaking, at least in the first volumes, is undeniable. His erudition, his mastery of several European languages, and his capacity to read prodigious quantities of mostly forgotten material have clearly contributed to the success of his books. But the true allure of what he's up to lies elsewhere and is bound up with the project's narrative, historiographic, and political force.

First, Israel proposes a grand narrative of a kind that eighteenth-century historiography had not produced for quite some time. Large forces (Spinozist radicalism, Enlightenment moderates, the conservative reaction) collide, unite, and collide again throughout this period in a sort of "triangular battle of ideas."[11] This energetic narrative dimension, as we shall see, derives from a political reading of the intellectual landscape; however, it comes at the cost of simplifying the intellectual genealogies.

Next, the seduction exerted by the Radical Enlightenment thesis comes from three major displacements it provokes in the establishment Enlightenment historiography. The first is a thematic displacement, because the materialist and revolutionary radicalism is placed center stage at the expense of more classic and consensual figures of the Enlightenment pantheon, who are reduced to being the byproduct of compromise with authorities or the reaction to all the bold initiatives. The second is a displacement of chronology, as Israel has the Enlightenment begin in the 1660s—that is, even earlier than the crisis of the European mind favored in Paul Hazard's account. While certain daring interpretations had placed Europe's intellectual turning point in the 1680s, with the writings of John Locke and Pierre Bayle and the revocation of the Edict of Nantes and Britain's Glorious Revolution, Israel considers the essential moment to have been two decades earlier, in the 1660s, when Spinoza's thinking matured, was written down, and was published.[12] What's more, Israel believes that everything important had already occurred by the start of the eighteenth century and that classic authors such as Voltaire, Hume, and Montesquieu only contributed "minor additions" to the intellectual breakthroughs of the preceding period. In a carefully provocative way, Israel affirms that "in the 1740s, before Voltaire came to be widely known, the real business was already over."[13] The third displacement is geographic, since the Dutch Enlightenment figures are given the starring role as precursors, a proposition that the usual Enlightenment historiography was hardly used to considering. The new orientation of studies on radical Dutch thinking of the seventeenth century allows Spinoza to be inscribed at the center of this intellectual culture.[14] The corresponding, opposite surprise is to find Great Britain, whether the England of Locke and Newton or the Scotland of Hume and Smith, mostly cut out of the picture. Overall, Israel posits and defends a unified conception of Enlightenment radicals on a European scale. In contrast to approaches that underscore national contexts and geographical differences, he insists on the fact that the same debates, in the same formats and with the same issues at stake, took place from Berlin to Naples, from Paris to Philadelphia. This wide constellation has a center, though—Paris—the general headquarters of the Radical Enlightenment starting at mid-century, according to Israel.

The book also has a certain political attractiveness. Israel is not content to simply shed light on the omnipresence of Spinozism in the eighteenth century; he is an ostentatious advocate of the Radical Enlightenment heritage. At a time when invoking the name of Spinoza in the disciplines of the social sciences and political philosophy has become a regular occurrence to the point of signaling a massive revival of Spinoza's critical theories, Israel's demonstrative demonstration is wind in the sails for those who seek to provide contemporary critical thinking with an intellectual genealogy.[15] It is significant that the first volume was rapidly translated into French and published by the Éditions Amsterdam. The Paris-based publisher is at the center of this trend, and their name, together with a sizeable part of their catalogue, clearly signals a close connection to the heritage of Golden Age Holland and a desire to help develop a neo-Spinozist intellectual current. More recently, the Marseille-based publisher Agone, also situated at the intersection of the human sciences and leftist activism, stepped up to publish a translation of Israel's 2009 *A Revolution of the Mind* as *Une révolution des esprits* (2017).[16]

One can ask, however, if there might not be a misunderstanding behind all this activity. Neo-Spinozism owes much to Gilles Deleuze, who sees in Spinoza's writings a philosophy of affect, a kinetic theory of bodies and desires, and an ethology of human behavior on a plane of total immanence; and to Antonio Negri, who sees Spinoza as the prophet of a power politics of multitudes as opposed to contractualist theories about popular sovereignty. Israel, on the other hand, presents Spinozism as, above all, a radicalization of Cartesian rationalism disburdened of its dualism and extended to the political domain.[17] While Deleuze and Negri make a "return to Spinoza" into a platform for thinking about contemporary struggles in a way that's perfectly compatible with contributions from other currents in postmodern philosophy, Israel claims that only the Enlightenment radicals can defend the values of Western, secularized, democratic modernity against the numerous attacks that would seek to weaken it. These attacks—against which Israel's book is explicitly constructed as a riposte—emanate from the return of religion and the criticism of the rationalist heritage but also from the reexaminations of the Enlightenment by postmodernism and postcolonialism. Far from seeing in Spinozism an example of "antimodern" thinking, as Negri does, or as "theoretical antihumanism," which is the view of Yves Citton and Frédéric Lordon, for Israel it is the source of humanist modernity.[18]

Which Intellectual History?

One might have expected that a panorama of Spinozism throughout Europe, presented by a specialist in Jewish diasporas and commercial networks in modern Europe—but one who had broken with the methods of social and economic history—would be an occasion for a dialogue between intellectual history and approaches with a social and cultural orientation.[19] Any such hopes are quickly shattered. Israel's argumentation is based exclusively on certain chosen texts and their interpretation: What was the author thinking in this text? What did he really mean to say? Whom was he influenced by? How the examined works were, historically, received is largely ignored, as are the social and cultural practices going on at the time of their composition. Freemasonry, for example, is tossed aside. Even though certain Masonic lodges and libertine circles played an essential role in the genesis of Enlightenment radicals—by permitting the circulation of English ideas in the United Provinces and by serving as a crucible where different traditions could be blended—in Israel's account, they are deliberately excluded in a single peremptory sentence: "If our aim is to get to the heart of the Enlightenment as a decisively important world-historical phenomenon, arguably the less said about Freemasonry the better."[20] The whole presentation is conducted in a rather classic, not to say old-fashioned, way: with the man and his work reviewed one by one and an evaluation made about their degree of conformity to Spinozism. The saga of Radical Enlightenment thus takes on the appearance of a long string of textual commentaries. In the end, the new intellectual history that was promised turns out to be hardly distinguishable from an old-style history of ideas.

One may note that Israel offers a rather personal vision of historiographical debates. He is constantly attacking the cultural history of the Enlightenment, which he reductively calls a "history of mentalities," though without acknowledging what raises this work above such a label: notably, a reflection on forms for appropriating texts, an attention to the history of the book, and an interest in discursive practices themselves. He criticizes the cultural historians for their materialist, structuralist approach, which—he claims—neglects the role of ideas and favors cultural transformations that are so vague as to be unprovable.[21] Such claims reveal a serious misunderstanding of this work, which he reduces to a collection of anecdotal investigations into "sociabilities" whose obsession would be to contest the fact that "philosophical ideas fundamentally shaped the entire cultural 'revolution.'" This characterization of cultural history seems to be confused with a rather clumsy Marxist vision that is both reductive and dangerous, but also—in a more surprising twist—with "postmodern" methodologies that "consciously aim to destroy the grand narratives of the Enlightenment, the Revolution, and *modernity*."[22] Behind this unintended parody of a methodological debate, the real goal clearly is to denounce all the approaches that might trouble, a little or a lot, the linear, univocal narrative of progress that leads from the Enlightenment to the Revolution and from there to an irreproachable modernity.

On the methodological level, Israel stops there, with his affirmation of an intellectual change whose history is retold as the progress, resisted but inexorable and victorious, of a coherent and combative radicalism structured by Spinozism. In so doing, he ignores an entire current of intellectual history that has insisted on the limits of the interpretive gesture and the profoundly unstable character of textual meanings. That current might have led him to be more cautious when wielding massive labels such as "Spinozism," "Enlightenment radicals," or "modernity," since it has shown that it pays to be sensitive to the ambiguity of texts, to the performative aspects of philosophical utterance, and to complex interpretive gestures.[23] To take only one well-known example, "Rousseauianism" is not a coherent philosophical system articulated by Rousseau and then taken off the shelf for use by the Revolutionaries. Already in the eighteenth century, "Rousseauian" had many different meanings, because interpretations of his writings diverged even among counterrevolutionaries. It was only later that Revolutionaries looked to Rousseau's texts for elements that would allow them to legitimate their actions, understand what they were in the process of doing, and guide their thinking. And these actions were themselves fragmentary and controversial, though they were intellectually productive.[24]

Pointing out these complexities does not mean siding with a dangerous postmodernism with nebulous borders, as Israel seems to think; it is simply a reminder that the meaning of texts is never given once and for all.[25] Their meaning is the outcome of readings, those of the leading players themselves and those of the historians who come later and—moreover—rarely agree with each other. Entirely devoted to creating order, Israel is blind to the hermeneutical dimension of historical interpretation. Of course, the role of the historian is to exercise rigorous control over the interpretation process, thanks to operations of contextualization that narrow interpretive freedom and submit the reading to strong constraints of philological and historical probability, but it cannot make that process disappear entirely since that dimension is constitutive of our relation to cultural works of the past. Denying or ignoring this fact leaves one constantly sliding back and forth between historical and political frameworks.

This double refusal—the explicit rejection of work on the social history of the culture plus the implicit rejection of all intellectual history that goes beyond history of ideas—weakens his argument. Israel is permanently braiding two strands of thought: the first is a historical claim according to which the radical, Spinozist current of Enlightenment thinking was the most influential in the eighteenth century.[26] To support this claim, Israel would need to be more attentive to the circulation and appropriation of the works he evokes; he would also need to track down the appearance of Spinozist motifs in ordinary irreligious discourses. Yet he studies at length texts that were never published under the Old Regime and sometimes never circulated in manuscript form.[27] Granted, unearthing a few texts that include radical criticism of religion demonstrates that by the end of the seventeenth century, a current of thought already existed that was radically opposed to revealed religion. However, if these texts remained unknown up until the erudite research of the last two decades, can one seriously contend that they were more important than the works of Leibniz, Voltaire, Locke, Hume, or Montesquieu and that they laid powerful groundwork for the French Revolution?

The second, more philosophical claim is that the radical Enlightenment current heralds the development of modernity. This perspective is a teleological one; it can advance based solely on a reading of texts and a reformulation of what's at stake in them, but it runs up against two difficulties. First, the claim of coherence—presenting radicalism as a "package of basic ideas and values" that are indissociable—ignores the diversity of appropriations of Spinozism.[28] The second difficulty is the restrictive definition of modernity as being a complete emancipation from religion, a rationalist approach to the world and society, and at one with egalitarianism.

It is obviously the articulation of these two strands of thought, sometimes distinguished but often confused, that makes the notion of a radical Enlightenment so interesting but also very brittle. It is therefore important to question the essential pieces of this architecture: the place of Spinozism in the Enlightenment era and the definition of radical philosophical speech.

Spinoza and the Radical Enlightenment

It's a bold move to claim, as Israel does, that Spinoza's influence has been neglected. Numerous studies have been devoted to the development of Spinozism in the United Provinces and to its repercussions across Europe; see, for example, the major publication by Paul Vernière on the reception of Spinoza in France before the Revolution.[29] It's true that this interpretation was based on a fruitful misunderstanding, considering that references to Spinoza derived often from partial or false readings. Nevertheless, Vernière's work was fundamental in precisely and patiently determining the place occupied by Spinoza in Enlightenment intellectual debates and in identifying the leading intermediaries who were responsible for his success. As for the idea of an intellectual revolution produced by Spinoza around religion and "unbelief," this notion is not new and was argued notably by Silvia Berti, who considers that the author of the *Ethics* furnished the intellectual tools for a rigorous atheism distinct from the diverse forms of skepticism.[30] The very term *Radical Enlightenment* is borrowed from Jacob, who had already advocated for the rediscovery of these currents of thought by insisting on what she saw as the Anglo-Dutch trend of the years 1690–1720, the consequences of British scientific and neo-republican revolutions, the pantheism of John Toland, and the Masonic milieu in The Hague. But Israel comes along and makes a big claim, namely of Spinozism's intellectual hegemony among Enlightenment radicals. Both the method that allows him to arrive at this claim and the conclusions that follow from it need to be examined.

Taking the authors and texts one by one, Israel tracks down the Spinozist connection with as much zeal as the censors of the day; in doing so, he does not hesitate to "read between the lines" following the method of Leo Strauss—finding Spinozism even in authors who claim to be refuting Spinoza or who never even read him. In this way, the perimeter of the radical Enlightenment is significantly enlarged to the point of including authors whose radicality is questionable. Strauss's "reading-between-the-lines" technique for decrypting the thinking of authors writing under the threat of persecution encourages attentiveness to historical conditions and to the rhetorical techniques for producing philosophical texts, but it needs to be used with great caution if one is to avoid veering toward overinterpretation and an overestimation of heterodox thinking.[31] Yet Israel's approach often involves sidestepping the interpretive debates, thus emptying the works of their share of ambiguity. Take the case of Pierre Bayle, who is presented by Israel as the second greatest Enlightenment radical after Spinoza and before Diderot. It is true that the interpretation once proposed by Élisabeth Labrousse—of Bayle as a moderate aligned with fideism—was effectively challenged by more radical readings of his thinking, but it's a bit fast and loose to portray Bayle as a committed disciple of Spinoza when for half a century he incarnated the most authentic criticism of Spinozist materialism. Even Gianluca Mori, who defends the idea of a Bayle strongly influenced by Spinoza, agrees that "the monism in the *Ethics* remains for Bayle completely absurd and unacceptable," whereas for Israel it's the touchstone of Spinozist radicality.[32] Even if certain texts could be used to show a convergence between Bayle's thinking and Spinoza's, it remains the case that Bayle's collected works, a true philosophical polyphony, are generally equivocal and continue to elicit debates and disagreements among the best specialists. Reducing this ambiguity, which is consubstantial to Bayle's way of writing and to his absolutely unsystematic way of doing philosophy, to then turn him into the second great figure of radical philosophy rules out any possibility of understanding why Bayle was so admired by most of the so-called moderate authors, Voltaire especially. It's more appropriate to inscribe Bayle within the great skeptic tradition that was so active in the early part of the century.[33]

To take an even more striking example, Israel presents Giambattista Vico as representative of the Spinozist Enlightenment in Italy. To do so, he relies on a small minority within Vico studies that emphasizes Vico's secularized reading of human history. But he entirely neglects the fact that Vico, if measured by Israel's own criteria for what defines radical thinking (be it philosophical monism, republicanism, or a critique of absolutism), stands in total opposition to Spinoza. As for Vico's insistence on the importance of providence, Israel must consider it as merely some rhetorical gesture. One can wonder, though, if it's more pertinent to make Vico into a Spinozist than into, for example, an anti-modern. The force of Vico's writings and his lasting historical interest is that they elude these bloated classifying labels and reveal their limits.[34]

The hunt for Spinozism intensifies in what can be called the heart of the radical Enlightenment: the heterodox philosophy circulating in manuscript or clandestine form at the end of the seventeenth and early eighteenth centuries. Interest in these authors and texts goes back a long time, but research on them increased—starting in the 1980s in France, Italy, Germany, and Spain—to the point where it became a dynamic sector in its own right, with critical editions, conferences, essay collections, and even a specialized journal all devoted to the topic.[35] An impressive number of authors and their manuscripts have been exhumed and their sources examined.[36] It has now been established that the period 1660–1750 was the golden age of clandestine philosophical manuscripts that became a true arm of philosophical communication. Israel's writings take advantage of all this scholarly research by proposing a comprehensive vision of these specialized studies, which have sometimes been enclosed within quarrels of attribution and by the patient labor required to identify sources. To propose this vision, his readings make use of a skeleton key that opens every door: Spinoza. This key allows Israel to lift these texts out of specialists' circles and make them part of a narrative in which the influence of the Spinozian revolution is felt on every page. However, even if most of this research has highlighted the complexity of these texts with their many references and the difficulty of establishing compatibility on a strictly philosophical level, Israel sees only the orderly arrangement of Spinozism in action: "the central thrust, the main bloc of radical ideas, stems predominantly from the Dutch radical milieu, the world of Spinoza and Spinozism."[37]

An essential point is at stake: the question of the philosophical pluralism of the radical Enlightenment. Heterodox thinking, far from being completely of Spinozian derivation, was nourished by a great variety of sources that confronted each other and combined the thinking of Hobbes; the skeptic tradition; different currents of Protestantism, such as Socinianism; the writings of libertines such as Vanini, La Mothe le Vayer, and Naudé, whose importance and impact have recently been reevaluated; and—finally—Spinoza.[38] John Tolland, for example, a leading English deist whose materialism was highly influential in the eighteenth century, owed as much to the refutations of Spinoza that emerged through Spinoza's contact with Leibniz and the new natural sciences as he did to Spinoza himself.[39] Likewise, materialist conceptions of man that refused the idea of an immortal soul often developed in England out of theological debates within Protestantism itself—debates that had no link to Spinozism whatsoever but derived instead from innovations in medical knowledge.[40] In Germany, the influence of Spinoza's writings on the authors of the *Frühaufklärung* was undeniable, but it was probably less pronounced than that of the anti-Trinitarian Protestant currents.[41] Even in Holland, the radical authors of the late seventeenth century hardly presented a single homogeneous profile.

Consider the famous *Treatise of the Three Impostors*, also known by the name *The Spirit of Spinoza*, which was the most widely circulated clandestine manuscript in Europe in the first half of the eighteenth century. Its complex history remains mysterious, even though studies over the years have established a clear general outline.[42] The first version of the text was probably written in the late 1670s by Jean-Maximilien Lucas, the author of an important *Life of Spinoza*, and it already gathered together, alongside quotations from Spinoza, diverse libertine and Hobbesian references. The text was later revised in the early 1710s by several authors, Charles Levier, Jean Aymon and Jean Rousset de Missy, who belonged to the Huguenot community in The Hague and were members of a libertine group known as the "Knights of Jubilation," linked to the milieu of the Royal Library.[43] The *Treatise* became very popular at that time and was then modified again, for an edition with limited circulation published in 1719. What matters is that this manuscript played an important role in the dissemination of Spinozist themes and more importantly in identifying Spinoza with a radical critique of religion; however, the text itself is interwoven with themes from a number of different heterodox traditions. Along with passages inspired by the *Ethics* and the *Tractatus Theologico-Politicus*, one can find numerous Hobbesian themes, notably the explanation of religion as deriving from fear, and libertine themes, such as the claim of the political imposture of religions. The *Treatise of the Three Impostors* is therefore in no way a coherent synthesis of Spinoza's thinking but is rather a collage of arguments and quotations from different philosophical traditions in which the persistence of libertine themes is in evidence and extracts from Spinoza intermingle with others from Charron, Vanini, Naudé, La Mothe le Vayer, and Hobbes.

An analysis of the social milieu in which the text was produced also undermines the claim for a strictly Spinozist reading. The authors who participated in the elaboration of the definitive version were not disciples of Spinoza but instead authors who read and wrote across many genres of the freethinker tradition. Jean Aymon remains obscure. He was an adventurer with a dubious reputation within literary circles—living a bohemian life, dabbling in espionage, and later discredited when linked to the theft of ancient manuscripts from the Royal Library. Jean Rousset de Missy was a journalist and close associate of Prosper Marchand. He had translated Collins and Locke, and his role signals the influence of English deism and proto-Masonic Dutch thinking.[44]

Israel's entire approach to the clandestine philosophical manuscripts is marked by circular reasoning: because he has identified the Enlightenment radicals as being influenced by Spinoza, he only takes seriously texts that fit that description and considers all others as marginal. Thus, when he insists that the *Treatise of the Three Impostors* was by far the most widely circulated of all the clandestine manuscripts, he notes that another manuscript, the *Colloquium heptaplomeres* of Jean Bodin, was about as successful and circulated across the same area; but he leaves it out of his study on the grounds that it was written a century earlier, included signs of belief in the devil and witches, and "is replete with what the *esprits forts* of 1700 must have regarded as thoroughly antiquated and absurd indications of beliefs in supernatural forces."[45] But in that case how does one explain its success? Logically speaking, one would have to conclude either that doctrinal coherence was not considered indispensable within the radical milieux or that the diffusion of manuscripts is not a good indicator of their level of popularity and intellectual influence.[46] Here, a social and cultural history of these manuscript collections would be useful.

Among those who appear to have played an important role in the early diffusion of the *Treatise of the Three Impostors* is Peter Friedrich Arpe, a German freethinker trained in the book-loving community of Copenhagen and associated, it seems, with Baron Hohendorf, an important collector of clandestine manuscripts for himself and for Prince Eugene of Savoy, whom Hohendorf served as diplomatic representative in The Hague. Arpe was not a Spinozist author; his thinking was influenced notably by Renaissance naturalism, the work of Giordano Bruno in particular, and by the libertine tradition. His most well-known text, published around the same time as the *Treatise* in 1712–1713, is entitled *Apology for Vanini*.[47]

It is reductive, when considering the diffusion of these texts, to see only an imperious intellectual engagement in the service of philosophical radicalism. There is much we still do not know about their composition and the exact motives of their authors. Consider the case of *De impostoris religionum*, one of the atheist treatises that circulated the most in Germany, where it was often confused with the *Treatise of the Three Impostors*. The text was at first a prank, written in Hamburg by Johann Joachim Müller and addressed to his friend Johann Friedrich Mayer, an orthodox pastor obsessed by the fight against atheism. Later, the book was taken very seriously by some of its readers, with the joking, experimental atheism of Müller becoming a vector for the diffusion of freethinking.[48] More generally, one must not overestimate the doctrinal coherence and ideological engagement of Enlightenment radicals, and the texts that have come down to us should sometimes be interpreted at several levels and leave open the possibility of play, irony, provocation, and a taste for scandal.[49]

One may therefore doubt that Spinoza was the unique or even principal source for the most virulent social and political contesting of religion. The very category of Spinozism seems problematic. Of course, the history of philosophy is in the habit of applying such labels. But can one really make Spinozism into a historiographical category, and if so at what price? For many eighteenth-century authors, Spinozism covers an ensemble of notions deriving from diverse heterodox traditions. If the *Treatise of the Three Impostors*, this Harlequin costume of freethinking, can circulate under the title *The Spirit of Spinoza*, one must answer a basic question: What exactly does the name *Spinoza* name?

What Is Spinozism?

To prove the importance of Spinozism as the template for a radical Enlightenment, Israel begins by defining the Spinoza doctrine; then he searches for everything in the writings of different eighteenth-century authors that resembles it. In his concern to reduce Spinozist thinking to a system of unified ideas, a burst of lightning in the serene philosophical sky, he seems not to be aware that the very operation of stating what Spinoza's doctrine might be is not a historiographically neutral gesture that follows from mere objective description but is, rather, an interpretive decision not unlike those Spinoza's disciples and adversaries made starting in the seventeenth century.

Moreover, what Israel describes as "Spinozism" and the radical "package" looks more like seventeenth-century Dutch radical philosophy in general, and some of its traits are especially noticeable in other authors. Thus, the criticism of holy history, certainly present in Spinoza, is even more so in the writings of Louis Meyer. Similarly, the concern for teaching and democracy is much stronger in the work of the Koerbagh brothers, who paid for that concern with their lives. And revolutionary and republican activism is hardly a salient feature of Spinoza, who was rather suspicious of revolutionary movements. Given all this other radicalism, one may ask with Pierre-François Moreau if what Israel is finding is "Spinozism without Spinoza."[50]

Why, then, grant Spinoza such central importance and downplay the diversity of radical Dutch thinking in the seventeenth century?[51] Probably because this canonical figure in the history of philosophy offers Israel a clarifying narrative and a headline—"Finally Spinoza!"—that can cut through the jumble of less well-known authors. But on a deeper level, it may be that tracing the presence of the name Spinoza throughout the eighteenth century as a symbol of atheism allows one to affirm the importance of the theoretical revolution produced in Holland. The name of the Amsterdam philosopher would then serve as a bridge and equal sign between the philosophical radicality of the eighteenth century and that of the United Provinces of the 1660s.

The problem, however, is that this line of reasoning relies implicitly on a permanent stability of Spinozism for which the name Spinoza would serve as guarantor, whereas in truth his thinking was the object of a great number of divergent interpretations from the very beginning of the eighteenth century. Different personae abounded: the dogmatic atheist among the clandestine authors of the early century; the theoretician of determinism dear to Diderot; the pantheist or even mystical Spinoza rediscovered in Germany at the end of the century, who would go on to nourish European romanticism. Invocations of Spinoza have taken place within very different philosophical contexts and practices.[52] As Pierre Macherey has observed, "from the moment all his texts became public, the year following the death of its 'author,' the philosophy of Spinoza has not ceased to be, always in the present tense, an object of fascination and rumination, such that each century of modern European culture has in a way reinvented [the philosophy] to model itself after the image created out of it. . . . Thus, it's as if, for three centuries without interruption, Spinoza had accompanied at every turning point the history of thought and of society, appearing in the most contrasting set of incarnations, each one exemplary of its kind."[53] But then what is one talking about when speaking of eighteenth-century Spinozism? The persistent influence of Spinoza's texts? The set of ideas attached to the name Spinoza by those who claim some filiation, including when they fall into what specialists would call a backwards understanding? Or the connotations attached to the name and their efficacy in intellectual disputes? Because he rarely bothers to distinguish between these different levels, Israel weakens his demonstration, notably when he cites, as he does very often, the defenders of religious orthodoxy to prove the influence of Spinoza. But when a German theologian, for example, denounces Spinoza as "the chief of modern atheists,"[54] is that proof of the influence of Spinoza's writings? If "the Spinoza doctrine" is the general name for atheism among Christian controversialists, and even for the defenders of so-called moderate Enlightenment figures, it is difficult to accept their lamentations over the tenacious influence of the Spinozist sect as credible evidence of Spinoza's theoretical hegemony among heterodox thinkers. In other words, there's a danger of too easily reversing the point of view and changing a minus to a plus. In the end, the elevation of a radical tradition praised for the virtues of criticizing an established order and the denunciation of blasphemous subversion remain two inverted faces of the same intellectual operation.

If Israel is often defending his thesis by quoting from the opponents of Enlightenment radicals, it's because he adopts a "controversialist" approach to history, he says. On the face of it, this declaration of intentions is attractive, given the extent to which the analysis of intellectual controversies has renewed the practices of intellectual history, thanks notably to pioneering work on the history and anthropology of different fields of knowledge. Numerous studies have proven that a precise and contextualized analysis of controversies—one attentive to writerly and rhetorical strategies, sociopolitical conditions, and the forums in which philosophical quarrels develop—allows for a significant renewal of the methods of intellectual history by combining an internal approach (investigating the properly theoretical and scientific stakes) with an external approach (investigating the conditions for the rise or the resolution of a controversy).[55] But Israel's way of proceeding is quite different. The controversies he studies produce nothing on the intellectual plane; they simply display more publicly the already-constituted positions. They feature opposing currents that have been defined once and for all and that remain unchanged over the whole period. Radicals and moderates oppose, unite, or destroy each other. But the controversies themselves seem powerless to reconfigure intellectual currents; they only modify the relative power between the two opposing camps—which explains the multiplication of political and even military metaphors to describe these homogeneous, hostile, and "irreconcilable" blocs.[56]

Another possible approach, instead of pointing out pieces of Spinozist thinking in this or that controversy, would be to study the ways these disagreements produce Spinozism—both inventing and configuring it.[57] In point of fact, the diffusion of Spinozist statements took place largely through the refutations that quoted the author of the *Tractatus* and the *Ethics* in order to better establish what struck the critics as unacceptable or scandalous in his writings.[58] Even authors favorable to certain aspects of Spinoza's thinking maintained a relation of inventive critique toward it, such that a reference to Spinoza necessarily circulated in the mode of controversy. For example, when it comes to Bayle, what matters is not so much knowing to what extent he was authentically Spinozist as understanding how the entry he devoted to Spinoza in his *Dictionnaire historique* profoundly influenced the definition of Spinozism for the entire eighteenth century. Asking this question would allow one to better address a key point specific to Spinozism: Why do the majority of radical eighteenth-century authors—whom Israel calls "Spinozists"—make such efforts to absolutely refute Spinoza? Israel's answer is essentially to claim that they did so out of prudence or even a desire to dissimulate, which is certainly a plausible explanation considering how formidable censorship still was at that time. However, one can also remember that Spinozism, before it became an articulated doctrine, was at first an object of scandal, the symbol of an "*athéisme mis en système*" [systematized atheism], as Bayle called it. Israel is right when he says that Spinoza operated as "the great philosophical bogeyman of early Enlightenment Europe,"[59] but he's wrong to believe that only authors whom he considers conservative or moderate saw Spinoza as dangerous. It is more constructive to acknowledge that Enlightenment radicals, even when they borrowed from Spinoza, were also opposing him. A systematic and deductive line of reasoning about Spinoza is foreign to what Paul Vernière called "neo-Spinozists" and to what were sometimes called in the second half of the eighteenth century "modern Spinozists": authors, most notably Diderot, who were rethinking materialism starting out from vitalist medicine, experimental discoveries, and the life sciences to construct an evolutionist pantheism.[60] Spinoza's language—nourished by his scholasticism, his knowledge of physics, and his will to conduct geometric proofs—appeared to them as terribly archaic, even when they were willing to follow him into the "consequences" of his system.[61] In the eyes of even the most radical thinkers, Spinoza was as much a challenge as he was an inspiration.

There's nothing easy or obvious about identifying Spinozism. A radically different approach would be to accept the interpretive character of this undertaking in the manner pursued, for example, by Yves Citton in his book *L'Envers de la liberté*. Citton's approach is resolutely nonhistorical. He does not propose to trace a presumed influence of Spinoza on the authors he studies but to read in parallel their texts with his, "noticing effects of resonances, textual encounters, metaphorical overlapping, parallel narrative constructions," and from there to display the existence of a Spinozist imaginary, defined in light of recent interpretations of Spinoza.[62] And yet historians can draw useful lessons from this book, which shows effectively how eighteenth-century Spinozism is a fleeting object, a threatening specter, that one ought to think about in terms of *invention* more than *influence*. Far from sidestepping the problems posed by an identification of a Spinozist tradition, the methodological liberties taken by Citton regarding the history of ideas reveal that eighteenth-century Spinozism only becomes truly meaningful in the interpretive act of the researcher who decides to read these texts as Spinozist for the purposes of his own intellectual agenda. In Citton's case, doing so allows him, for example, to integrate within a second circle of "Spinozists" the authors whom Israel defines as moderates—such as Montesquieu, Voltaire, and Maupertuis—and even, provocatively, certain orthodoxy defenders, such as Lamy and Pluquet, who contributed to defining Spinozism through their refutations of it. From this perspective, Spinozism is no longer a group of authors united by an intellectual and political coherence and behind a common struggle; rather, it is the dissemination of an ensemble of themes, formulations, and texts associated with the name Spinoza.

More than a theoretical corpus, Spinozism is a scandal—the extreme case of heterodoxy. Spinoza is an author who is read little or not at all and who is known by dint of the refutations that have taken him as their object and whose influence often extends out indirectly. He is an author whose writings are not well-known, generally considered to be difficult to grasp, and "famous for their obscurity."[63] It's a name, therefore, that immediately evokes subversive thinking and operates unfailingly as a catalyst of controversies. The name Spinoza most likely played an essential role during the Enlightenment because even if his writings were hardly accessible, the hagiographic sketch composed by Jean-Maximilien Lucas in his *Life of Spinoza* popularized the image of a philosopher at once disbelieving, disinterested, solitary, and wise. The sketch offers Bayle a striking figure of the virtuous atheist—the keystone of Bayle's critical thinking. Apocryphal stories maintained a certain fascination around the personage of Spinoza and in particular around the circumstances of his death: did he die serenely as an atheist, or did he recant? The debate was so virulent that it pushed Johannes Colerus, more than fifteen years afterward, to investigate on site, question the last witnesses, and devote a significant portion of his *Life of B. de Spinoza* (1705) to the philosopher's final hours.[64] The success of Spinozism among the radical authors derives in large part from this construction of a Spinoza legend: that of a Jewish atheist whose life was obscure and virtuous and whose writings, though little known, retained forever a distinct scent of scandal. The way in which Spinozism operates as an active force in the intellectual debates of the Enlightenment ought not to be characterized reductively as the effect of an ensemble of propositions that traverse below the surface the entire eighteenth century; nor should it be seen as the subversive power of a coherent doctrine. The authors who discuss Spinoza were not simply influenced by him, they constituted Spinozism by interpreting him and very often by refuting him. In the end, may one not say, following Macherey, that "Spinoza's philosophy" is an "arbitrary" denomination, a "historical fiction endlessly recreated in different conditions that undo or contest its coherence at the very moment they reconstitute its illusion"?[65]

Are Enlightenment Thinkers Radical?

Although historians of clandestine philosophy have debated the exact parameters of Spinozism within that history, the labels *Lumières radicales* and "radical Enlightenment" have spread indiscriminately, and their use without question or caution provokes serious misunderstandings. The success of the term owes much to the ambiguity that persists around the nature of this radicality. Israel always defines Enlightenment radicals based on a specific philosophical content: radical thinkers are those who defend an ensemble of positions derived from philosophical monism. But it so happens that these positions are radical not only in a logical sense, meaning that it's a matter of pushing the argument to its ultimate consequences, but also in a political sense, meaning that these positions are those most directly opposed to the established order in every domain. Israel never seems to doubt that these two senses necessarily coincide. But two problems follow from this assumption.

First, this alignment supposes coherence among the radical positions, as though a monist and materialist ontology necessarily implies socially and politically radical positions: democratic republicanism, equality between the sexes, freedom of expression, and anticolonialism. This argument rests on a vision of the field of philosophy as a continuum of homogeneous positions ranging from conservatism to radicalism, with a "moderate" status existing between the two poles. This vision is reductive and does not stand up well to the investigation of particular cases. It is uncertain, for example, whether Spinoza was a committed democrat, and even less certain is his sympathy for revolution or feminism.[66] When it comes to eighteenth-century Spinozists, the argument is even more problematic. To take just one example, Boulainvilliers, who was probably one of the most authentic commentators on Spinoza, can hardly be classified as a democratic republican and revolutionary, since he is known to have favored a strong aristocratic power opposed to absolute monarchy.[67] Likewise, one may doubt whether Spinozism, or more generally a radical materialism, was the sole theoretical basis in the eighteenth century from which one could conceive of or promote the rights of women, the emancipation of Jews, or the abolition of slavery.

Secondly, even if the definition of Enlightenment radicals is explicitly philosophical, the use of the term *radical*—which does not belong to the traditional historiographical vocabulary for talking about the Enlightenment and is instead more customary for discussing English revolutions—seems to serve the purpose of rendering more plausible a direct causality between Spinozism and the French Revolution. Yet Israel never studies the reception of these authors and leaves unexplained the passage from theory to action. The burden of proof rests entirely on this adjective *radical*, a word that inevitably calls up strong political connotations. Among historians of the radical English tradition, such as Christopher Hill or Edward P. Thompson, the point was to study the political ideas of revolutionaries; however, Israel is studying a philosophical current isolated from political action and social agitation, and yet by using the term *radical* he lends his object of study a revolutionary dimension even though there is no proof it had one.

Another way to think of how the production of texts or ideas could be something radical in the eighteenth century is to consider such production as an action, and therefore to examine the practical relation these authors had to the established order; in other words, to look at their writing and publishing strategies. Put another way, how radical can you be if you write manuscripts that no one will read or that will only circulate in very small circles? This question, raised by Pim der Boer about Holland in the seventeenth century, may seem rather provocative.[68] Can one not be radical in the privacy of one's own study? Pim der Boer's question does allow one to contemplate anew the radicality of the Enlightenment thinkers, since it insists on what's in play when one has a public use of philosophy. Indeed, one could advance the hypothesis that the true innovation of the Enlightenment is not doctrinal but has more to do with Enlightenment thinkers' willingness to publicly contemplate heterodox ideas outside merely learned spaces.[69] In that case, it would not be so much the content of freethinking that's new but instead the fact of considering freethinking as combat and therefore also reflecting on the conditions of its publication. And by *publication* one must understand both the wider disclosure [*divulgation*] of this kind of thought (in the sense that a discourse once reserved to a small elite of strong, emancipated minds will now circulate more broadly) and the constitution of a public that is literally made through these new uses of criticism.

Asking the question about radicalism in these terms sheds a different light on the historical importance of the circle of Dutch authors linked to Spinoza in the 1670s. For starters, Spinoza, a philosopher who scrupulously refused to allow his writings to be translated into Dutch or to have the *Ethics* published during his lifetime, cannot from this angle be considered a radical.[70] On the other hand, some of his close associates certainly were, such as those who, as soon as the body was cold, rushed to publish his *Opera posthuma* under his name (or at least his initials) and within a particularly hostile political context. By participating in such an undertaking, which was both intellectually diligent and a stroke of genius in the art of provocation, they powerfully contributed to constructing Spinozist philosophy as scandal by boosting the dynamic of public disputation that the *Tractatus Theologico-Politicus* had already started. The radicalism of these Dutch circles, which were active until the early eighteenth century and by custom called "Spinozist," derives perhaps as much from this will to promote Spinoza's works across wider categories of the population than from an alleged philosophical coherence, given how divided they were between an extension of Cartesianism, the interest sparked by Spinoza's propositions, and the emergence of new scientific practices.

The use of the term *radical*, with its contemporary connotations, projects onto the intellectual space of the eighteenth century a political representation where one can situate authors as more or less radical: in other words, as being implicitly more or less "on the left"[71] on the grounds of a homology between philosophical positions and political positions. Similar thinking underwrites the use of terms such as *avant-garde*.[72] This anachronism is accentuated by the identification of this radicality with a scientistic materialism that is only one of the many forms of political radicality that have occurred over the last three centuries. One might instead proceed with a more controlled practice of anachronism that explicitly asks the question of what *radical* might mean as applied to the Enlightenment era, once it has been established that the term did not then exist. To do so would then be to acknowledge a form of risk taking, a way of engaging oneself politically, of taking on a responsibility (namely, that of thinking of philosophical writing as a risk). What is at stake are the strategies of writing but also the very conception of philosophical discourse as daring, as freedom of speech, as *parrêsia*, an important notion in ancient philosophy that names the irruption of frank speech and the virtue of free speaking that completely commits the one doing it in the name of truth and leads to a dramatization of philosophical discourse.[73] From this perspective, the category of "Enlightenment moderates" is hardly more solid than that of Enlightenment radicals: it confuses in the same way what derives from philosophical moderation and what corresponds to political moderation, with no discussion of a theory of moderation such as one finds, for example, in Montesquieu. One could argue that Voltaire was in certain respects more radical than certain materialist authors by his manner of dramatizing philosophical combat, notably with his outcry against the church, "*écraser l'infâme!*" variously translated into English as "crush the infamous," "crush the loathsome thing," "crush the horror," and "smash the rogues."[74] But the most interesting case in this regard is probably Jean-Jacques Rousseau.

Jonathan Israel is hardly at ease with Rousseau. In the epilogue to *Radical Enlightenment*, he adds Rousseau to the radical-philosophy tradition.[75] However, in the second volume he claims that Rousseau, though initially allied with the radical current, broke with the Enlightenment starting in 1754 to become a "moral prophet" within a "Counter-Enlightenment," a rather strange term borrowed from a rather problematic book.[76] This embarrassing leap reveals the somewhat artificial and mostly unproductive character of these sorts of classifications, especially when one is trying to apply them to an author such as Rousseau, whose writings are marked by ambivalence and demonstrate in spectacular fashion that radical thinking is not a cohesive whole. Rousseau's republicanism and his denunciation of inequality are not at all founded on Spinozist materialism. Is Rousseau radical, moderate, or conservative? When asked in terms of doctrine the question hardly makes any sense. However, if one reformulates the question of radicality as asking about the author's commitment, his manner of articulating personal experience and his writings, and about the very conception of writing as a public act, the radicality specific to Rousseau can be grasped much more clearly.

The libertine authors of the seventeenth century and most of the freethinkers of the eighteenth century practiced all types of dissimulation—first was the use of anonymity or pseudonyms, but practices of equivocal writing were also common.[77] Anonymity could be total, and historians today still debate the attribution of certain clandestine manuscripts. Baron d'Holbach, probably the greatest figure of Enlightenment materialism and atheism, never published under his own name, and with the exception of a handful of friends no one knew he was the author of *Système de la nature* and other writings.[78] There were also more playful forms of dissimulation such as those privileged by Voltaire, a master of the art of multiplying pseudonyms and feigning the disavowal of his own books. Overall, a certain art of evasion, motivated both by prudential considerations and a wish for distinction, was the norm among those who attacked the ruling orthodoxy.

Jean-Jacques Rousseau, however, made it a point of honor to sign all his books with his name. Doing so was both a social affirmation—to declare writing a vocation in contrast to aristocratic or mondain reserve—and a truly political act of taking intellectual and legal responsibility.[79] This stance was partly a daring challenge, and it brought him some judicial problems by stimulating the severity of the authorities. That Rousseau published under his own name *The Social Contract* and *Émile* itself ignited the scandal caused by their publication in the eyes of the Archbishop of Paris, Parliament, and also Voltaire. After *The Social Contract* was condemned by the Small Council of Geneva, Rousseau explained himself, demanding to be judged because he was openly the author.[80] In the almost revolutionary atmosphere of Geneva in the years 1764–1765, this demand—published in a pamphlet and addressed to the city's authorities—constituted a position that can properly be described as radical. Rousseau took full political responsibility for the texts he published, affirming more generally the indissociable character of the writing and the writer and positing that the truth value of philosophical speech was inseparable from the exemplary life of the philosopher. He summarized his position with a strong claim: "If Socrates had died in his bed, people today might suspect that he had been nothing but a clever sophist." Of course, such a stance can tip into forms of moral exhibitionism, as Rousseau's adversaries have always been quick to point out, and it led him to turn his isolation and the misunderstandings he felt his work elicited into the focus of his last writings.[81] But his standing by his words is unquestionably a form of radicality, because it breaks with the generally shared codes of heterodox writing and because it makes public uses of philosophy into one of the essential hallmarks of the Enlightenment.

This evocation of Rousseau is not a recommendation that one definition of radical Enlightenment be replaced with another; nor am I proposing an alternate list of radical authors and texts. Instead, I am saying that it would be helpful to examine the limits of a purely ideological definition of Enlightenment radicality. Rather than seeking to propose a coherent reading of works to then situate them within grand philosophical traditions and classify them along a conservative-to-moderate-to-radical spectrum, the case of Rousseau invites one to think about the horizon of some writings whose radicality does not come from their theoretical coherence but, on the contrary, from the contradictions that they put in play and the way those contradictions reveal the tensions that traverse a period. With Rousseau, the radicality comes from the fact that he invents a new figure of the writer as one who accepts the danger inherent in publication and who permanently offers his sincerity and his private life as guarantees of the value of his word, but who also discovers himself confronted with suspicions of inauthenticity. If Rousseau is radical, it is because he radically questions the foundations of the Enlightenment—in other words, he challenges a belief in the effects of philosophical speech.[82]

Numerous studies have demonstrated the importance of heterodox, materialist, and atheist ideas in the development of Enlightenment figures, as well as their circulation throughout Europe and sometimes farther. The vitality of heterodox thinking at the turn of the seventeenth to the eighteenth century, the large size and significance of the reference to Spinoza, and the important place of the United Provinces within the European geography of the early Enlightenment are now all generally acknowledged. And yet, it would be regrettable to buy into replacing one doxa with another by artificially constructing a homogeneous philosophical tradition and a teleology of philosophical radicality linking Spinoza to the French Revolution and the Left of today. In this way, the books of Jonathan Israel operate like a trap. They gave greater visibility and resonance to numerous scholarly projects that were initiated in a spirit of pluralizing the Enlightenment, restituting intellectual diversity, and bringing to light heterodox and unexpected ideas that had often been erased from the grand narrative of liberal modernity. But Israel's books encased these theoretically bold strokes, critical experiments, and literary innovations within the reductive framework of a homogeneous Spinozist movement leading in a straight line to democratic revolutions and the advent of secularized societies. Their true radicality, which is probably linked to their irreducible singularity, is thus erased and in a way papered over by a classic gesture that consists in exalting contemporary progressivism with a prestigious genealogy. This gesture is hardly radical in the end, since it amounts to claiming the heritage of the Enlightenment in a grand Manichean billboard of progress. Only the composition of the pantheon has changed: Spinoza and Bayle have replaced Hume and Voltaire.

It's worth observing that the notion of modernity also has a starring role in Israel's work, appearing not only in the title of the first two volumes but also at the center of his argument. The goal is to show that the Spinozism of Enlightenment radicals is the foundation of European "modernity," and by this he means secularized, egalitarian, democratic spaces, and so resolutely that sometimes contemporary issues end up overshadowing the historical discourse. When Israel describes one of the essential values of Enlightenment radicals as "the personal freedom to choose one's lifestyle and sexual conduct between consenting adults, safeguarding the dignity and the freedom of the unmarried and homosexuals,"[83] there's slight chance these words came from the pen of an Enlightenment philosopher, Spinozist or not. More generally, it's the definition of modernity that poses a problem. Must one really define it in such reductive terms as signifying a definitive repudiation of all forms of religion and belief systems that open the way to the creation of an egalitarian, tolerant, and pacifist society? Do we all agree that the emancipation of men and women "no matter their race, their religion, their gender, or their social class" constitutes "the essence of the history of the eighteenth and nineteenth centuries"?[84] This endorsement of a certain vision of modernity—sure of itself and of the superiority of its rationalist, universalist values—appears dated, to say the least.

In the field of intellectual history, other propositions are used to characterize differently the relationship between the Enlightenment and modernity. For some, the modernity of Enlightenment figures resides in their capacity to think about this new entity, *society*, and to accept the emergence of new items onto the philosopher's agenda, such as questions about political economy. In no small measure, a blending of Epicureanism and Augustinian thinking is at work in this intellectual renewal.[85] For others, Enlightenment modernity has less to do with a materialist critique of religion than it does with the capacity to transform theology into the history of Christianism and to make faith and reason compatible on a plane of mutual respect. The driving force of European secularization is not located outside Christian thinking but at its center.[86] Modernity is no longer the shattering event of a radical break but is instead the patient labor of tradition working on and sometimes against itself. In this spirit, it's worth noting that a vein of thinking of increasing importance today insists, contrary to traditional narratives, on the religious sources of the Enlightenment and on little-noticed or repressed continuities between ancient beliefs and the modern credo.[87] It also should be said that methodologically these different approaches are all in alignment: to write histories of philosophical and intellectual traditions and of the transmission of their contents.

As I have tried to show in the preceding chapters, there exist other ways to define Enlightenment modernity that involve focusing on changes in sociability patterns, transformations of public space, the development of a consumer society, and the emergence of a taste for luxury items, fashion, credit, and so forth. Rather than defining modernity as a function of certain contemporary ideological preferences and seeking their sources in the eighteenth century, it would be more constructive to examine the ways in which Enlightenment authors attempted to account for the transformations that were affecting the world in which they lived and that, no more then than now, were not reducible to simple formulas. Modernity is not the product of the Enlightenment; it is its object of study.

These changes affected not only the world that was before Enlightenment thinkers' eyes but also their ways of thinking and writing and the aspiration they had to change them. Herein lies the true radicality of the philosophers of the Enlightenment: an affirmation of the capacity for action through writing, a collective ambition for emancipation through knowledge, and a willingness to take risks when confronting both authorities and their readers. Enlightenment authors were, after all, fighting on two fronts: probably against censors but also against a public that was more slippery than it appeared. The risks were both real and somewhat dramatized, since genuine philosophical heroism did not exclude doses of showing off. We shall turn now to this subject: Enlightenment politics as the dramaturgy of freedom.

PART III

Politics

There is no shortage of talking points to describe modernity's emergence around political ideas: the rights of man, political economy, popular sovereignty, the rejection of traditional inequalities, constitutionalism. This diversity can be discouraging since Enlightenment figures appear reformist here and moderate there, sometimes radical, sometimes utopian. Is the Enlightenment egalitarian or elitist? Democratic or charmed by authoritarian powers?

My approach in the following chapters is different from those of many. I am not proposing a new study of the political theory of the Enlightenment. I wish instead to understand how Enlightenment philosophers thought about their historical situation; in other words, how they conceived of their capacity to act in and on a context of profound changes in forms of communication. I believe that Enlightenment unity rests not on doctrinal coherence but on their questioning of the effectiveness of critique in public space. It is worth noting that at the time the term *philosophe*—philosopher—did not correspond simply to a professional identity or place in a university system of learned disciplines. In France especially it named a certain relationship to knowledge and the wish to have it be made useful and shared broadly. At the end of the eighteenth century, the Germans would call *Aufklärer* those authors who wished to improve the critical capacity of their contemporaries.

Enlightenment writers did not reserve knowledge for a small elite of men of letters and strong minds. They wished to place it in the service of collective emancipation. They were convinced that the diffusion of knowledge was necessary for the fight against superstition and prejudices and that it was the practical role of the learned, writers, and philosophers to lead that fight. This conviction underlies the combative and almost militant dimension of the Enlightenment. And yet, it's important to not project onto these writers the heroic loftiness that would come to characterize the French intellectual in the twentieth century—a figure forged by memories of the Dreyfus Affair. Too often, people have wanted to see eighteenth-century philosophers as dissidents *avant la lettre*, relentlessly fighting against the persecutions of the Church and monarchical censorship. Some would seem almost to want to criticize them for not having let themselves be persecuted more. True, Voltaire would spend much of his life at a careful distance from Paris; Rousseau had to flee France and then Geneva in the 1760s; and Diderot spent a few months in prison, and the *Encyclopédie* and *De l'Esprit* were censored—but for the most part Enlightenment philosophers, even the most radical, were published, read, and honored. They had support even inside the government and the police, as well as at court. In Scotland, Italy, and Germany major figures such as Adam Smith, Antonio Genovesi, and Immanuel Kant were university professors. Cesare Beccaria, the great reformer of criminal law, had official duties at the court of Milan. Throughout Europe, writers and philosophers were members of academies, were received in salons, and were sometimes the friends or counsellors of rulers. While taking some precautions, they could lead more or less peaceful lives even as they worked to disseminate heterodox ideas.

This situation is explained first by changes among the authorities. The strengthening of European monarchies provoked heightened tensions between churches and states, as these two entities were no longer moving in unison against new ideas. In Frederick II's Prussia or the Austria of Joseph II, sovereigns made open use of certain currents of enlightened thinking to modernize the state in opposition to conservative religious forces. In France, the monarchical authorities were more concerned by the fight against Jansenism and by opposition to Parlements, and therefore less worried about audacious philosophers. Besides, the state itself was divided into competing institutions and rival factions. A fairly large number of elites embraced various new ideas and were convinced of the uselessness of official censors. On the other side, among the philosophers, the goal was not direct confrontation with the ruling power. To get their ideas broadly circulated, they counted on the support of the authorities or at least their silent toleration. Far from seeking out clandestine strategies, they aspired to publish new knowledge and the most audacious theories as widely as they could. Therefore they sought to convince those in charge that they weren't dangerous. To regulate public space and encourage the advancement of knowledge, they would willingly turn to political authorities. "It's in the king's interest that the number of philosophers increase, and the number of fanatics decrease. We are tranquil and all those people are troublemakers; we are citizens, they are seditious traitors; we peacefully cultivate reason, they persecute it," wrote Voltaire to Helvétius.[1]

Nothing would be more inaccurate than to imagine Enlightenment philosophers as junior revolutionaries wishing to hasten the overthrow of the established order. Despite their differences of opinion about what the ideal regime should be, all were convinced that political stability favored the advancement of knowledge's "light." In the opening pages of volume 8 of the *Encyclopédie*, Diderot reaffirmed the project's ambition: to offer a synthesis of old and new knowledge and demonstrate the superiority of "a universal morality over all particular moralities." This expansion of the "sphere of enlightenment," he explained, did not depend solely on writers and the learned. It would only be possible if general instruction progressed, and such progress required resolute action from the monarchy. Sovereigns would have to prefer governing educated citizens over ignorant subjects. "It's up to the Masters of the World to hasten this happy revolution. It is they who enlarge or shrink the sphere of enlightenment. Happy will be the day when they will have understood that their security consists in commanding educated people."[2] Beyond this call for the benevolence of authorities, and after a period of confrontations that almost caused the *Encyclopedia* project to collapse, Diderot developed the conviction that was shared by the century's intellectual and political elites: that a happy revolution is one of knowledge and morals, and it requires the alliance of enlightened sovereigns and reasonable authors. Some lines earlier in the same passage, Diderot evokes the anxious specter of another revolution capable of ruining all of civilization's accomplishments: "Imagine if a revolution were to germinate in some obscure corner or developed secretly in the very center of orderly lands, and then erupted after a time and toppled cities, scattered once more the people, and brought back ignorance and darkness—but if just one copy of this whole book survived, all would not be lost." The role of the philosopher is to fortify knowledge and reason against the chance occurrences of history. The philosopher's writings are crucial when it comes to testifying against injustice and combating fanaticism, but they are powerless if the ruling power proves itself to be intolerant or the public indifferent.

This conception of knowledge and the role philosophers could play in it were both inseparable from a certain idea of history. There is certainly no endorsement here of a theory of progress that would proudly proclaim the inexorable advance of reason. Contrary to received ideas, such a notion, while common among nineteenth-century philosophers of history, was foreign to eighteenth-century authors. However, those authors differentiated themselves from their forebears of generations past thanks to their conviction that various kinds of progress were possible and desirable, and that knowledge (both scientific and moral) could help mankind live better by dispelling superstitions and prejudices. It was nevertheless a hope of moderate proportions: progress would be partial, there would be gaps, and it would be susceptible to reversals brought on by political crises, wars, increases in censorship, or the possible return of obscurantism. Thus, political stability, the sole guarantor of progress and the diffusion of knowledge over the long term, was essential. The authorities guaranteed what Diderot called "the sphere of enlightenment"; in other words, the space within which knowledge could expand. The expansion of that sphere depended on two factors: freedom of the press and education. Knowledge could only emancipate in a society where individuals had easy access to knowledge. Therefore, debates about education became important; but the most essential matter for the philosophers was the question of their own influence and therefore the conditions for publication and publicness.

Their optimism was founded on the conviction that the printing press would permit a wider and more efficient dissemination of ideas. Benjamin Franklin, himself a printer, was joyful about the intellectual and political progress that he believed was characteristic of his time:

> The ancient Roman and Greek Orators could only speak to the Number of Citizens capable of being assembled within the Reach of their Voice: Their Writings had little Effect because the Bulk of the People could not read. Now by the Press we can speak to Nations; and good Books & well written Pamphlets have great and general Influence. The Facility with which the same Truths may be repeatedly enforc'd by placing them daily in different Lights, in Newspapers which are every where read, gives a great Chance of establishing them.[3]

This idea would become commonplace. Growing literacy, an expanding book market, and the increasing number of newspapers and journals appeared to guarantee an optimal circulation of all kinds of knowledge. Modern writers further expanded their capacity for action. They could address large publics and convince entire "nations" of useful truths. If progress was possible, it was because the very forms of communication had changed. The nature of the link between knowledge and politics was no longer the same.

This optimism often fell short. Censorship, though less ferocious, did not disappear, and it constrained writers to evaluate risks and calibrate the dose of boldness they could allow themselves. As for the public itself, did it really want to be enlightened? Wasn't it more attracted to pulp fiction and new scandals than to philosophical works? Faced with the challenges of censorship, the public's indifference, and the low quarrels that monopolized public attention, doubts emerge. A general worry takes hold: for whom should one write? The philosophers were convinced that every individual is capable of reasoning and therefore capable—if the means are provided—of thinking for themselves. But they also considered that people harbored prejudices, crowds were often unreasonable, and the public could be overly enthusiastic and gullible. Consequently, they were always mulling over their publication strategies, concerned about the proliferation of books, and mindful of the dangers of intellectual charlatanism. Even Condorcet and Kant, two paragons of enlightened optimism, were more doubtful than one might think because they were intensely conscious of the difficulties raised by a conception of emancipation that implied the "propagation of light" by means of an active role played by an intellectual elite. Everything was a question of tempo—the role of philosophers being to hasten the dissemination of the light of knowledge but without excessive speed. This dissemination was perceived, even by the most optimistic, as necessarily a long process. In this regard it was opposed to the Revolution as well as to religious models based on immediate conversion to the revealed Truth. One finds this criticism of revolutionary enterprises articulated by Germaine de Staël, who was otherwise very favorable to the "progress of enlightenment": to place government on a philosophical foundation in a country where part of the population cannot even read, she said, is to turn "the propagation of light" into a "religion."[4] Another inheritor of the philosophers, Pierre-Louis Roederer, articulated a similar reproach: "the propagation of light" is by no means impossible, he said, but it must not be confused with "the miracle of the sudden illumination of all minds."[5] Thus the question remains open: How does one enlighten the people?

This reasonable caution is not always compatible with the indignation provoked by acts of intolerance and injustice. The philosophers displayed a constant combat against fanaticism and prejudices, but they were mindful of retaining the support or at least the neutrality of important institutions. The tension caused by these competing needs took different forms. For Voltaire, it shaped the very style of his writings. One finds both rapier wit and flattery, incisiveness and elegance—polemical daring dressed in the acceptable raiment of worldliness. Diderot offers a different incarnation of the inherent difficulties of philosophical commitment. His quasi-Promethean energy collided with multiple exterior obstacles as well as with an ideal of private happiness that led him to make choices that he had trouble fully owning. It was not so easy to give up trying to be Socrates. As we shall see, Diderot passed through moments of enthusiasm and eloquence followed by moments of doubt and irony tinged with bitterness.

The figure of the philosopher working to emancipate his contemporaries through his writings, all the while attending academies and salons, never received unanimous support. From the start, it provoked hostile reactions from conservatives and ironic remarks from wags quick to point out the contradictions of the Enlightenment philosophers. Their optimism was mocked. Their wish to implement an intellectual magisterium was denounced as an illegitimate grasp at power over the intellectual space, and these denunciations came not only from their adversaries but from within their own ranks. At the end of the century, a new generation, strongly influenced by Rousseau, questioned what it believed to be hypocritical prudence; and it invented new forms of public intervention that were more virulent, more spectacular, and more emotional.[6] These polemicists, in the manner of Brissot, for example, forged links with Revolutionary journalism that would inaugurate another sort of intellectual "engagement" within a transformed political context.

Even if we agree that the modern figure of the intellectual ought not to be projected back onto the debates of Enlightenment thinkers, there's no getting around the fact that since the Revolution, those eighteenth-century figures have cropped up in every discussion of the role of knowledge in emancipation. Some lineages are well known. After having criticized Voltaire in his youth, Victor Hugo composed vivid and emphatic pages of high praise for the writer who by the sheer power of his pen led "the war of thinking against matter, the war of reason against prejudice, the war of the just against the unjust, the war in defense of the oppressed against the oppressor, the war of goodness, the war of sweetness."[7] Jean-Paul Sartre, for his part, saw in the eighteenth century "the chance, unique in history," of French writers whose "books are free calls for the freedom of readers."[8] It regularly happens that a call to reinvent the Enlightenment leads to a revival of the figure of the eighteenth-century *philosophe*, an "engaged" and mediatized personage whose criticism of prejudices accommodates proximity to the ruling power. Other trajectories and lineages, however, are more unexpected. Taking this perspective, we conclude with an examination of the last texts of Michel Foucault in order to understand how the author of *Discipline and Punish* ended up in the early 1980s articulating a kinship with Kant and the

Enlightenment. What struck some observers as an about-face—while appearing to others as the logical end point of an intellectual journey—is also the symptom, in its relation to critique, of a modern intellectual debt, whether it likes it or not, to the ambivalent legacy of Enlightenment philosophers.

CHAPTER SIX

Can One Enlighten the People?

What place does the Enlightenment occupy in the genealogy of democracy? There are two standard answers to this question. The most widespread sees in eighteenth-century philosophy the starting point of the modern democratic tradition, on account of its opposition to absolutism, its affirmation of the rights of man, its promotion of tolerance and the desire for emancipation, and—among certain authors, such as Rousseau—its encouragement of the sovereignty of the people. This positive description is contradicted by a critical tradition that posits a darker interpretation. In this view, the Enlightenment figures were afflicted with incurable elitism, had only contempt for the people, and were comfortable with despotism so long as it was the enlightened kind, namely the kind as hard on priests as on the people. Thus, the Enlightenment must have been covertly conservative or at best moderately reformist. Furthermore, the Revolution is considered the true source of democracy and therefore was not a consequence of the Enlightenment but its negation, a popular uprising overwhelming the moderate reformism preferred by elites. Indeed, were not many Enlightenment philosophers still living at the time, such as Morellet and Raynal, frightened by this brutal eruption of the people onto the stage of history? And who believes that Voltaire would have enjoyed witnessing the events of October 1789, not to mention the massacres of September 1792 or the Reign of Terror?

So, were the Enlightenment figures emancipators or conservatives? Asked in this way, the question is obviously unanswerable, due to the diversity of authors and positions that by custom and habit have been lumped together as "The Enlightenment." It also has the disadvantage of presenting the matter as one of doctrine, which inevitably leads to evaluating the thought of this or that author on a grid of large opposing schools of thought: Enlightenment radicals versus Enlightenment moderates, admirers of Spinoza versus disciples of Locke, democracy sympathizers versus friends of despots. Such classification debates only go in circles and are rarely interesting. However, it is possible to ask the question another way, not by starting with the political theories of the Enlightenment authors but by asking about the way each conceived of the efficacy of their writings. This question haunted most of them: how does one enlighten those who are not yet enlightened?

What characterizes the Enlightenment as an intellectual movement and constitutes its unity beyond theoretical differences is its militant desire to teach, its conviction that the fight against prejudice and superstition must be carried out publicly and that knowledge and critical thinking must be nurtured and spread as widely as possible. In this regard, the Enlightenment figures broke with the esoteric tradition of the libertines and freethinkers of the seventeenth century. The latter considered daring feats of thinking to be reserved for a small elite of strong minds. They thought philosophers should have the courage to oppose the "beliefs of the masses" but without seeking to convince the masses to think differently. For them, the goal was not to destroy common superstitions but to set oneself apart from them. In his *Dialogue sur la diversité des religions*, François de La Mothe Le Vayer has one of his skeptical interlocutors declare: "I always thought it was against this torrent of the multitude that we ought to direct our leading strengths, and that having tamed this monster that is the people, we would easily overcome the rest."[1]

One still finds similar remarks in the eighteenth century, notably among materialist authors, but they are rarer and aim to reassure the authorities.[2] In the main, and despite notable specific differences, Enlightenment writers shared a concern for diffusing various forms of knowledge, addressing a broad public, and making the truth known. Their goal was less to convince the public of certain things than to impart to it the tools for thinking critically; they sought to advance individual and collective emancipation, thanks to the diffusion of critical thinking. It is in this way that the Enlightenment project is universalist: it is addressed to all. It presupposes that, at least in theory, everyone is capable of reasoning. This presupposition is why its preferred vector was printed texts, whereas the heterodox thinkers of the preceding age privileged the circulation of clandestine manuscripts and small secret societies.[3]

Therefore, the question that crossed their minds was not, as is sometimes thought, "Should the people be enlightened?" but rather "How can one enlighten the people?" Put another way, Enlightenment optimism bumped up against the practical challenge of how to achieve emancipation through knowledge. The promise of the solar metaphor—according to which the beneficent rays of knowledge and reason would progressively cause dark ignorance to dissipate—was all well and good, but the Enlightenment thinkers knew that knowledge was not literally a ray of light and that the transmission of knowledge did not happen on its own. What role, then, would writers play, especially those called *les philosophes*? How would they contribute to "enlightening" their contemporaries and thereby advance the Enlightenment project? How would they make themselves heard by people not predisposed to listen to them or to let themselves be convinced? *The people*—named here with a certain semantic ambiguity—designated both the plebes and the populace, the common classes and the mass of those not yet enlightened.[4] In the political and social discourse of the eighteenth century and today, *the people* is not a sociological reality naming a well-defined social category. As Jaucourt wrote in the *Encyclopédie*, it is a "collective noun difficult to define" that one can conceive of either in opposition to elites or, more inclusively, as the mass of the population. In the latter case, as the addressee of a philosophical discourse, *the people* becomes potentially a public. And yet how does one address this undifferentiated and anonymous public?

Far from shutting themselves away within abstract controversies, the Enlightenment thinkers were constantly asking what their proper role should be toward advancing the diffusion of knowledge and critical thinking. The first obstacle they encountered and the one that comes readily to mind was censorship. How can one enlighten the people if the government in power suppresses printed texts and locks up philosophers? This question is the most well-known and has received the most attention. It is known that the philosophers were constantly seeking to skirt and slide past official censors by having books published abroad and enter France illegally, through frequent recourse to anonymous publication or the use of pseudonyms, or by making use of whatever favor and leverage they had among monarchical authorities.[5] We shall return to these matters in the next chapter and concentrate here on a less frequently discussed problem but one that has strong resonances in our own day: the nervousness felt by the Enlightenment intellectuals regarding their public.

The People and the Philosopher

Writing for the public is a difficult task because publics are heterogeneous, fragmented, and sometimes incomprehensible or disturbing. Their diversity is first social. To enlighten "the people" implied also reaching and teaching the common classes [*catégories populaires*] (peasants, ordinary workers, artisans), who were often poor and illiterate. Elites' mistrust of the people remained strong in the eighteenth century, even among intellectuals. A theoretical universalism was often accompanied by a paternalistic attitude that could even be contemptuous of the people. One finds some striking examples of this attitude in Voltaire. In his *Questions sur l'Encyclopédie* (1772), he proposes that one "always distinguish between honest people who think and the populace which is not made for thinking."[6] This contempt for the people should not be blown out of proportion, however, as has often been done by the Enlightenment's adversaries and a certain conservative historiography. Remarks like this one occur at moments of indignation regarding popular superstitions and exasperation when observing the slow progress of enlightenment. There are texts signed by the same Voltaire that defend the necessity of writing for all people so as "to be able to enlighten both the chancellor and the cobbler."[7] This belief comes up often in his correspondence: "there are philosophers even in Paris shops," he writes in 1768 to the Marquis de Villevielle.[8] In his *Dictionnaire philosophique* (1764), Voltaire constructs a dialogue between a fakir, standing for a clerical figure, who claims that one must deceive the people to make them obey, and a disciple of Confucius—clearly the spokesperson for Voltaire's position—who claims just the opposite in his retort: "Men are all similar. They are born with the same dispositions. It is fakirs who corrupt man's nature.... Our learned men are made from the same clay as our tailors, weavers, and other laborers.... Why should we not deign to instruct our workers as we instruct our learned men?"[9]

What's important to keep in mind is the contradiction between a militant and proselytizing theoretical universalism (the idea that one must enlighten *le genre humain* [mankind], an expression Voltaire was fond of) and an actual elitism with a small number of true thinkers, as compared to the mass of those governed by prejudices and superstitions, whose minds one could only hope to convince over the very long term. For this reason, references to "the people" in the second half of the century designated less the subaltern levels than the multitude, the ensemble of individuals who had not yet acceded to the autonomy of reason and who thus allowed themselves to be guided by their prejudices or by traditional authorities.[10]

How could one reconcile the ambition to enlighten all mankind with the plain fact of a mass of people unreceptive to philosophical discussions? A first solution was based on owning the elitism: the man of letters would write for a select public while waiting for future progress. This progress would come down from the top, specifically from wise reforms inspired by philosophers and put into practice by enlightened sovereigns. This attitude was most strongly incarnated by Voltaire and embraced by numerous authors. It united a militant position, in other words a strong belief in the intellectual's capacity for action, with a restrained conception—at least for the early stages—of the Enlightenment's dissemination: the idea that knowledge is first destined to an enlightened elite. Unlike the Libertines, the Enlightenment philosopher would not aim to produce an esoteric, dissimulated, clandestine knowledge. He would openly publish. His discourse was by right addressed to all. But in practice, it was destined to political and cultural elites, to members of the polite *bonne société*, to all who lived in proximity to monarchical power, in other words to the enlightened minority of traditional elites. Worldly people were judged more receptive to new ideas, and more capable of eventually aiding in their dissemination and acceptance. They were therefore the philosophers' principal allies in their fight against intolerance and fanaticism. As Voltaire said to Helvétius in a letter about their common adversary the clergy, "They can have a few books burned, but we will crush them in polite society, we will strip them of all credit within good company, and it's good company alone that governs the opinions of men."[11]

To convince this open-to-reform elite without frightening it, the philosopher had to both prove his usefulness and blend into the social identity of elites by becoming himself a man of the world. From now on, worldly societies would become the leading site for the dissemination of philosophical discourse. Philosophical writing adapted. The weighty theoretical treatise yielded to lighter, livelier forms: dialogues, fables, stories, jokes. A strong double bind imposed itself on philosophical writings. On the one hand, they were combative and rowdy when it came to fighting superstitions and "crushing the infamous thing," and on the other, they had to be reassuring so as to convincingly show that the authors were loyal subjects and good citizens. Thus, the importance of irony, taunts, and witticisms that would align the laughers on the right side, ridicule the adversary, and seal it all reassuringly for polite society. Enlightenment progress remained a universal right, but it would come over the long term through the auspices of elites and the governing power, thanks to monarchical institutions. This theory of the intellectual's role was also in conformity with Voltaire's theory of history in which progress came through the evolution of manners, the latter being carried by the beneficent role played by arts and letters radiating out from royal courts. One can readily understand why the philosophers were a regular presence within polite society. It was not simply a case of social ambition mixed with cynicism, though such prosaic motivations no doubt existed as well, but rather because the liberal aristocracy and the Enlightenment philosophers had in fact forged an alliance.[12]

Another answer to the problem raised by a working-class public came from education in the broadest sense. The latter was not only a matter of diffusing knowledge and reducing prejudice but also concerned making men self-reliant by getting them to think for themselves. It has often been said that the Enlightenment thinkers remained fairly moderate with their education projects for the people, and it's true they were sometimes prudent to a fault.[13] Nevertheless, many authors—such as Helvétius, Diderot, and, of course, Condorcet—showed themselves to be very optimistic. Ten years before the Revolution, Condorcet decried the idea that it could in any way be useful to deceive the people or keep them in error: "The stupidity of the people is the work of social institutions and superstitions. Men are not born stupid or crazy, they become so." It was therefore both possible and necessary to instruct the people on condition that one "speak reason" to them.[14]

Education was not an end in itself; it was the means to transform the people into a public and render them receptive, over the long term, to philosophers' writings. It was therefore a bet on the future, articulated around an optimistic conception of time. The entire ambition of the *Encyclopédie* was based on this hope for rapid progress in "general instruction" that would allow an enlargement of the sphere of (the) enlightenment—"*la sphère des lumières.*"[15] Moreover, the philosopher was to write as much or more for posterity than for his contemporaries: "No one who writes should fix his eyes on his own time, his actual fellow citizens, or the land he lives in. He must speak to mankind; he must foresee future races. . . . It is after his death that the true writer triumphs," said d'Holbach before adding, "the truth . . . must survive all the errors of the earth."[16] Such optimism could seem naïve were it not coordinated with a strong belief in the capacity to educate mankind. For d'Holbach and his friends, this conviction rested on a notion of good sense [*bon sens*] inherited from Bayle and the Dutch authors: every individual is capable of acceding to some simple truths and thus of being enlightened. But these truths are not to be confused with the "common sense" of the Scottish philosophers, who tend to give it a rather conservative slant.[17] Good sense, on the contrary, reverses the most entrenched prejudices and common beliefs. It underpins the theoretical and rhetorical practice that allows one to hope for the diffusion of enlightened ideas from the elites toward the multitude: "Sensible and peaceful people become enlightened; enlightenment spreads little by little and succeeds in the long run in making an impression even on the eyes of the people [*le peuple*]."[18] Good sense allows for a point of articulation between philosophical elitism, with its condescension for the prejudices of the masses, and the universalist horizon of an Enlightenment pedagogy.

Education Optimism

With the Revolution, this pedagogic optimism seemed to have found confirmation. Time accelerated, the progress of general instruction became possible, and the people would finally gain access to the discourse of the philosophers.[19] In his *Sketch for a Historical Picture of the Progress of the Human Mind,* Condorcet announced the emancipation of all through education: "The equality of instruction that we can hope to achieve and that would be sufficient is one that excludes all dependence, whether imposed or voluntary." Passionately engaged in revolutionary political action, Condorcet participated actively in debates on public instruction. Starting in 1791, he published a set of "studies on public instruction" in which he pleaded for an education to be offered to all that would permit each individual, regardless of inequalities of aptitude and talent, to know his rights and duties and above all to free himself from prejudice and unjust forms of domination.[20] After being elected to the Legislative Assembly, Condorcet drafted a decree on public education. In the *Sketch* he describes with enthusiasm the way that instruction would liberate mankind from the constraints and domination that result from ignorance:

> The equality of instruction we can hope to attain, and with which we ought to be satisfied, is that which excludes every species of dependence, whether forced or voluntary. We may exhibit, in the actual state of human knowledge, the easy means by which this end may be attained even for those who can devote to study but a few years of infancy, and, in subsequent life, only some occasional hours of leisure. We might shew, that by a happy choice of the subjects to be taught, and of the mode of inculcating them, the entire mass of a people may be instructed in everything necessary for the purposes of domestic economy; for the transaction of their affairs; for the free development of their industry and their faculties; for the knowledge, exercise and protection of their rights; for a sense of their duties, and the power of discharging them; for the capacity of judging both their own actions, and the actions of others, by their own understanding; for the acquisition of all the delicate or dignified sentiments that are an honour to humanity; for freeing themselves from a blind confidence in those to whom they may entrust the care of their interests, and the security of their rights; for choosing and

> watching over them, so as no longer to be the dupes of those popular errors that torment and way-lay the life of man with superstitious fears and chimerical hopes; for defending themselves against prejudices by the sole energy of reason; in fine, for escaping from the delusions of imposture, which would spread snares for their fortune, their health, their freedom of opinion and of conscience, under the pretext of enriching, of healing, and of saving them.[21]

This magnificent text, a true manifesto for emancipation through knowledge and instruction, may be considered the Enlightenment testament in its most progressive and universalist vein. However, this pedagogic ambition is not without its contradictions. The principal difficulty encountered by Condorcet is what Catherine Kintzler has called "the aporia of equality": instruction, which is supposed to liberate mankind by dispelling ignorance, also risks increasing inequalities by allowing those with more talents and aptitudes to develop them further.[22] But I would like to insist on another matter that has received less attention. The education program sketched here supposes a consensus about the types of knowledge to teach and the methods of instruction. Yet, if there is one thing we know today, it's that this consensus is rarely achieved because knowledge is a veritable battlefield of controversies that are easily exploited for political purposes. Condorcet encountered that battlefield himself during committee debates on public instruction, which he witnessed turn into an eruption of political debates over science and education. The paradox is that the Revolution, which made possible the Enlightenment's education dream, also marked the introduction of the democratic principle into scientific fields. On this point Condorcet was unyielding. For him there would be no submission of knowledge to loose discussion by nonspecialists, and even less to the pseudo-experts whom he had combated as an Academician before the Revolution and who had since become powerful political figures. Conversely, these same adversaries stamped the former secretary of the Academy of Sciences as a vestige of the Old Regime and an aristocrat of science.

For Condorcet, the condition that would permit emancipation through education was that science itself was not to be questioned. In the long list of authorities from which the people were supposed to free themselves, the learned [*les savants*] were obviously not mentioned. Critical thinking was to be developed, but it needed to stop at the gates of the knowledge factory. Two lines of reasoning are in tension in Condorcet's thinking: that of the professional academician who affirms the inequality of intellectual aptitudes and that of the liberal democrat fighting for equal rights. How could these two be reconciled, the acknowledgment of a hierarchy of knowledge and the refusal of any form of subjection?[23]

To prevent revolutionary egalitarianism from abolishing the very possibility of emancipation through knowledge, Condorcet was obliged to draw a line that placed the learned in a separate category invested with their own authority. In his public instruction projects, he had already proposed a system of departmental academies based on the model of the former provincial academies. In the draft of the decree presented to the Assembly in 1792, he imagined a supervisory body, the *Société nationale de savants*, to oversee the whole project. Its members would be chosen by cooptation and their duty would be the administration of public instruction. To the bitter end, Condorcet tirelessly defended his idea—which ran against the grain of revolutionary opinion—until, in 1793, after three years of virulent criticism, the academies were finally suppressed.[24] In a short parallel text to the *Sketch* entitled "*Fragments sur l'Atlantide*," Condorcet takes up the idea of the utopia once defended by Francis Bacon: that of a learned academy that would be entirely independent of the governing power and charged with regulating knowledge. In that text, he pleads for a "conspiracy of enlightened men in favor of the progress of science" and "a society of men uniquely devoted to the search for truth."[25]

Condorcet thus came to distinguish between the capacity to free oneself through reason and the aptitude to advance knowledge and therefore, in the long run, collective emancipation. Yet, if the first capacity is universal, since every human is endowed with reason, the second is clearly unequally distributed. This higher aptitude, which is the cornerstone for the legitimacy of the learned and philosophers, is disconnected from democratic equality: "The capacity for deciding the means for reaching new truths cannot be up to the people's judgment and they should not even be a consideration in its choices."[26] It was therefore essential that the learned academy that he wanted to see created be totally independent from political power—in other words, from democratic talk about majority rights and from possible jealousies among elected officials toward the learned class: "The spirit of equality often degenerates into base envy. . . . The more those who govern remain at the level of the citizens, the more their authority is ephemeral, subdivided, circumscribed, and their pride is increasingly offended by the personal superiority provided by genius and enlightenment."[27]

This need to make the production of knowledge autonomous is related to a desire to protect the people from a dangerous threat that they are not aware of, namely demagogues and charlatans who seek to profit from the people's credulity. Among the threats evoked by Condorcet in this passage of the *Sketch*, "the fascinating tricks of charlatanism" figure prominently, along with the shackles of personal dependence, prejudices, and popular errors. If the tricks of charlatanism are so strong and dangerous, it's because the people lack instruction; but it's also due to the nature of public space and the seductiveness exerted by a discourse that plays on the emotions, makes endless promises, and dangles quick and easy solutions.

The Obstacle of the Media

Here another difficulty emerges. As soon as the philosopher turns to printed materials to enlighten the public, he enters a new communication space in which he is hardly the master. The eighteenth century was marked by a rapid increase in literacy, at least in cities; a sharp rise in the publication of books, *libelles* (a genre of political pamphlet), and journals; and major changes in the uses and practices of reading.[28] It's often imagined that the Enlightenment writers maintained an idealized vision of public opinion as the true tribune of reason and saw in the book a peerless tool for the dissemination of their enlightenment. Many of them were truly convinced of the virtues of the printing press and publicness. Malesherbes, in a famous speech, linked the progress of public opinion in "an enlightened century" to the powers of the printing press and the authority of men of letters—"those who have the talent to instruct men and the gift to move them" were now able to address a "dispersed public."[29] Raynal, or rather his collaborator Alexandre Deleyre, was even more expansive: "Books enlighten the multitude, humanize powerful men, add charm to the leisure time of the wealthy, and instruct all classes of society."[30] Condorcet made a scintillating endorsement of the printing press at the start of the eighteenth century around the time his *Sketch* was published. For him, publicness was the guarantee and motor of the Enlightenment:

> The press infinitely multiplies, and at a small expense, copies any work. Those who can read are hence enabled to furnish themselves with books suitable to their taste and their wants; and this facility of exercising the talent of reading, has increased and propagated the desire of learning it.
>
> [Thanks to] these multiplied copies, spreading themselves with greater rapidity, facts and discoveries not only acquire a more extensive publicity, but acquire it also in a shorter pace of time. Knowledge has become the object of an active and universal commerce.[31]

Despite such declarations, the philosophers generally held a more nuanced position and were sometimes explicitly pessimistic about the conditions for developing public opinion. Even if innovations in and the expansion of printing and the press allowed them to disseminate their ideas, they were fully aware that these changes also allowed instances of base imitation, enthusiasm, and general credulity. The public space that was taking shape before their eyes was very different from the learned spaces of the Republic of Letters regulated by the judgment of their peers. How could one be sure readers were reading good books? How could one prevent them from being the prey of charlatans and demagogues? How were readers to find their way amidst the mass of printed materials? And were there not perhaps too many books? Were some of them catering to the public's sometimes dubious tastes? Enlightenment writers were concerned about the proliferation of discourses. They dreamed of ranking different types of knowledge, of destroying all bad books, and even of reducing the holdings of libraries to a single authentically useful book, which was in truth the fundamental ambition behind the *Encyclopédie*.[32] "The multitude of new books which teach us nothing overwhelms and disgusts us," complained Voltaire.[33] Also, how was one going to repair the negative effects of publicness? How would one limit the curiosity piqued by the press and by the brief intensity of "the news"? How would one avoid being buried beneath the infinite mass of volumes "which fall into oblivion before the last newspaper of the year has appeared" and whose sole purpose was "the momentary satisfaction of the curiosity of a few idlers"?[34]

Witnessing the rapid development of newspapers during the Revolution, Germaine de Staël firmly denounced their pernicious influence: they inflamed the passions, spread misinformation, and forbid all political stability. Far from being a tool of information and education, she argued, they ruined public debates: "Newspapers, as they exist in France, as the interests and passions of the moment have made them, have brought about and will continue to bring about the calamities of France."[35] They had to be strictly framed and supervised by the governing power. Though a committed liberal, Germaine de Staël had no trouble making a distinction between the freedom of the press, in other words the printing of books which she considered "the greatest means for halting oppression and spreading enlightenment," and the freedom of newspapers. For her, these two liberties "should not be subject to the same laws."[36]

In addition, Enlightenment writers were wary of the commercial practices that were in the process of transforming intellectual communication. When Condorcet wrote that "Enlightenment knowledge has become the object of an active universal commerce," he was using the term *commerce* in a completely positive way to designate the exchange and circulation of ideas. But the term obviously had a second, commercial meaning referring to products and profits. Many authors worried about seeing their texts and therefore their ideas become the object of a more prosaic trade in the hands of booksellers and printers who were perhaps not always entirely scrupulous. Contrary to what one might conclude from the standard account of copyright history, the development of a literary market alongside the growth of capitalism was not always experienced as a positive liberation compared to earlier aristocratic patronage. The new market was accompanied by keen awareness of the commercial constraints imposed on writers. These constraints could take the form of new, more insidious kinds of censorship implemented by the publishers themselves. They transformed the writer wishing to earn a living into a mercenary or "prostitute," a metaphor that was already beginning to take hold and that would become a commonplace in the nineteenth century, when ideas of the writer as prostitute [*fille de joie*] became a cliché.[37] For now, the philosophers looked on nervously at this emergence of a book-buying public of "consumers" of ideas. In reaction, many of them displayed their poverty as a way to affirm their desire to resist the temptations of the literary market.[38]

These questions, which may seem very much of our own time, were already sensitive matters in the eighteenth century. They were always there in the swirl of enthusiasm and anxiety over the proliferation of texts and discourses, but they were also present around the new commercial and media mechanisms that were beginning to organize public space. Here as with other matters, *The Philosophical History of the Two Indies* displayed both hesitation and ambivalence. A defense of a free exchange of ideas, where the motto "*laissez faire*" becomes "*laissez écrire*"—let them write and publish—coexists alongside a critique of abuses of freedom of the press and increasingly strong emotions and prejudices about unscrupulous authors.[39] Enlightenment writers did not jump directly from Leo Strauss and the art of writing under persecution to Jürgen Habermas and the triumph of the public sphere.

Louis-Sébastien Mercier (1740–1814) was one of the shrewdest observers of Parisian social and cultural life at the end of the eighteenth century. He was from a working-class background and enjoyed describing the many facets of lower-class Paris life. As such, he could certainly not be accused of having had an overly elitist or Olympian vision of the Enlightenment. On the contrary, he brought close attention to the pathologies of public space. He worried about the proliferation of books, fearing that he might be buried under piles of useless or mediocre volumes, and when he dreamt of his ideal Paris—which he situated seven centuries after his birth year, in 2440—he imagined a royal library reduced to just a few volumes after an auto-da-fé.[40] He also described in detail the way that attention-capturing publicity techniques were turning the public away from useful truths. In short, his observations brilliantly anticipated what today would be called the critique of the society of spectacle. For example, when Voltaire was celebrated at the Comédie Française in 1778, Mercier did not view it as the triumph of the philosopher—and therefore a mark of the progressive integration of new ideas within public opinion—but instead as a "farce," an indecent spectacle in which the writer was celebrated like an actor, as a celebrity. The public was much less interested in Voltaire's ideas and his books than they were in his personage as crafted by these newly emergent mechanisms for celebrity-making: "a viral curiosity thrust forward to contemplate his figure, as though the essence of a writer were no longer in his writings but on his body." Far from evincing an emancipation through critical thinking, according to Mercier, this type of curiosity placed Voltaire on the same plane as another celebrity of the moment, the comic actor Janot—who was triumphing at the time with a street theater farce in very poor taste.[41]

Mercier's criticisms were not only cultural; they were political. The point was not so much to denounce a confusion of values that placed a philosopher and an actor on the same plane but to ask about the mechanisms organizing the public's attention. How can one enlighten the people if their curiosity can so flexibly pass from one star to another? What efficiency can the philosopher's speech have?

> It is therefore proven that there is no need to persecute a living person, nor the dead. When a Voltaire rises up, there will always be some Janot to place opposite him. If a crowd becomes too large around a man who has climbed on a table and begins getting worked up a little more than he should, do you want to disperse this crowd without violence? Just set up another table thirty feet away and the first speaker will see his audience disperse and will speak his words to the air.[42]

Rousseau, who for a long time had considered the public an ally in his fight against the elitism of men of letters and polite society, ended up adopting a negative view. What he criticized was not the people but specifically the public; in other words, the collective of readers constituted and shaped by the media revolution of the Enlightenment. For a philosopher or other writer, the people do not exist outside of or as other than the public, which is not only tricked by opinion manipulators but takes pleasure in this masquerade, and which enjoys watching the sincere philosopher, who wants to see the public flourish, be ridiculed by his enemies. Or at least so Rousseau came to believe: "The public is deceived; I see it, I know it. But it likes being deceived, and would not want to be disabused."[43] There was nothing left for him to do but withdraw into solitude, cursing his century and writing for himself or for posterity. How, he asked, can one enlighten the people if between the philosopher and the people there stand so many intermediaries and manipulators of opinion, and especially if the public prefers spectacular lies over useful truths, ironic insulters over sensible users of reason?[44] Rousseau's meditation on the public was much more complex than the defense of transparency to which it is sometimes reduced. He was constantly thinking about the very conditions of written communication, what "addressing" a text means, targeting a public, and so forth. As Masano Yamashita observed, "Rousseau was more aware than anyone else of the impasses that arise in modern regimes of letters that are disturbed by public opinion and its parasitical noises."[45]

Rousseau's sensitivity about his public image was extreme and probably excessive. But his worry over the public's credulity and its appetite for spectacle was widely shared. Even Diderot, the editor of the *Encyclopédie* and the philosopher who most embodied the pedagogical drive of the Enlightenment, was sometimes nervous about the public's reactions, its frivolity, its lack of interest. He was wary of the "judgment of the multitude" whose voice "is one of meanness, stupidity, inhumanity, unreason, and prejudice."[46] At such moments he allowed skepticism and sometimes even discouragement to overtake him: was the philosopher then a type of "flute player" who amuses the public but remains unable to change it?[47] Diderot dreamed of an ideal public, of an "invisible church," rational and engaged.[48]

When it comes to thinking about the practical effectiveness of their writings, the Enlightenment philosophers were confronted with a difficulty much larger than that posed by official censors. One could feint with the governing power, circumvent the censors, and collaborate in clandestine circulation schemes, but how could one enlighten the people if they were imprisoned inside prejudices, if public opinion was manipulated by unscrupulous advertisers and cynical demagogues, and if the public was governed not by critical thinking and reflection but instead by curiosity, imitation, and enthusiasm with no care for tomorrow? In one way or another, all authors were forced to come up with solutions, more or less explicitly thought out, to guarantee the legitimacy of a small number of enlightened individuals whose role was to intervene in public space—whether as members of polite society, academicians, or part of the "invisible church" of philosophers. For the public to be enlightened, the philosophers would have to have a privileged status based on their knowledge and competence. It was therefore important to invent mechanisms to clearly distinguish them from demagogues, who also exerted a direct influence on this same public the philosophers were trying to emancipate. But a paradox immediately arises: if enlightening the people means leading it to think by itself and break free from all established authorities, how could one build this autonomy if one began by sheltering an intellectual elite from all criticism?

Can the Public Enlighten Itself?

Questions about the effectiveness of enlightenment discourse and the conditions for its success were not confined to the French context. In Germany they were central and intensely debated.[49] The most well-known manifestation of this debate surrounds Immanuel Kant's famous essay "*Was ist Aufklärung?*"—"What Is Enlightenment?" Kant's essay was published in December 1784 in the journal *Berlinische Monatsschrift* in response to a debate initiated with that question in an issue from the previous year by Reverend Johann Friedrich Zöllner, who was also a Prussian government official.[50] Kant's text is often read in somewhat abstract academic fashion, perhaps because of the towering reputation of its author. In truth, the origin of the debate is not a speculative matter. Zöllner raised concerns about a project to suppress the religious sanction and officiating of marriages, and he worried about what he perceived to be an excessive attack on the Church. Kant called for a better definition of *Aufklärung*, a term formed from the verb *aufklären* (to bring light or enlighten), and his intervention provoked a large number of discussions, notably among Berlin's elites. Some months earlier, in 1783, a circle of government officials, writers, and philosophers had created a friendly society that was a cross between a club and a secret society, the Society of Friends of the Enlightenment (*Gesellschaft der Freunde der Aufklärung*). Known informally as the Wednesday Club *(Mittwochgesellschaft)*, its meetings brought together roughly twenty leading intellectuals in the Prussian capital, including Zöllner himself but also the learned government official Christian Wilhelm von Dohm; the famous bookseller Friedrich Nicolaï; and a leading Jewish figure of the Enlightenment, Moses Mendelssohn, who also published a response to the question in the same journal.[51] All were staunch defenders of new types of knowledge and wished to work toward improving society. They debated how much latitude to give to freedom of the press and the unexpected resistance encountered by "healthy reason" even as it was expressing itself quite freely during the reign of Frederick II. In November 1783, the King's doctor, Johann Karl Möhsen, made a presentation on their common project: "enlightening ourselves and our fellow citizens."[52] To reach this goal, he explained, it was necessary to fight against the public's prejudices and examine the meaning of Enlightenment.

The conversation about the Enlightenment took place among Berlin elites within a small circle of intellectuals who knew and liked each other. It's possible that Zöllner's question was asked in a lighthearted manner or as a private joke among his friends in the Wednesday club: So, what is this *Aufklärung* that we say we're friends of and trying to promote? In any case, the written responses of Kant and Mendelssohn resonated among a much wider public that would provoke further responses far outside a Berlin parlor or Prussia.[53] Kant's text, so often quoted and commented upon since, was successful in part thanks to the prestige of its author in the history of serious thinking but also because of its accessible style, as it addresses a public larger than the readers of books of philosophy. His text does not bother with the origins of the question and adopts a general observer's view. It also has some characteristics of a manifesto. There are striking formulations that define in a few words the Enlightenment's optimism for emancipation. Particularly memorable are the first lines, a declaration in favor of intellectual autonomy and the courage it takes to think—two values captured in the motto borrowed from Horace, *Sapere aude!*—Dare to know! The Enlightenment thinker is defined by Kant as demonstrating "man's emergence from his self-imposed immaturity." Thanks to boldness of will, each man is capable of making autonomous use of his own reasoning faculty in order to no longer depend on traditional tutors. The Enlightenment thinkers open the way to a process of emancipation, a passage to an adult age. They designate less a particular content of thinking and more thinking's autonomous character.

Kant distinguishes two uses of reason: a public use that must be free and a private use that is not. The enlightened man learns to think and judge by himself. He is free to share his reflections with the public, but he must continue to obey the state and behave in a way that conforms to his function. As a "learned" person he is free, writing books for an unspecified public and making use of his reason. However, in the exercise of his profession, and all the more so if it is a public profession (judge, teacher, and the like), he must obey the law as it exists and until it is changed. Then comes Kant's conclusion, with praise for Frederick the Great, the exemplary enlightened sovereign, and the motto he attributes to his monarch: "Argue as much as you want and about whatever you want, but *obey.*"

Kant's politically moderate stance has often been noted and criticized. How can one begin by praising the emancipation of thought and the courage of thinking and end by affirming obedience to a king, even if that king is conceived of as the guarantor of the law? Political reasons can explain Kant's flattery of Frederick the Great. The German monarch was adept at political realism in diplomatic and military affairs, while also being known as an enlightened leader who had made considerable efforts to build a reputation as a protector of philosophers and the learned in general. His arrival on the throne in 1740 had come with great hopes which were not totally forgotten at the end of his long reign. Also, when Kant was writing his text, another sovereign, Joseph II, was energetically promoting a set of enlightened reforms in Vienna, and these reforms may have been on Kant's mind.[54]

However, neither the political context nor Kant's prudence, if that's what it is, can sufficiently account for the apparent contradiction that traverses the text. The figure of Frederick II is not incidental. His presence is the logical consequence of a difficulty Kant is trying to solve, namely that of establishing the proper relationship between the small number of enlightened learned individuals and the mass of the people. How does the people enlighten itself? How does this exit from the state of dependency [*Unmündigkeit,* literally being without a mouth] underscored by the Enlightenment thinker happen? The question is both essential and difficult because it implies finding a point of articulation that connects individual autonomy, which is the foundation of the critical use of reason, with the collective mechanisms that render *Aufklärung* a historical process. Curiously, this difficulty is not frequently discussed.

One could imagine that the emancipation is strictly individual. If man is responsible for his dependency, due to his laziness or cowardice, then all he need do is take notice of the force of his reason and find in himself the courage to think. This would be the meaning of Horace's motto: Have the courage to think for yourself. But that is not Kant's position, since he affirms that this courage to think is an overly difficult and dangerous process and that most men are incapable of it. Their incapacity does not derive from an intellectual deficit but more from the fact that men fear freedom: "It is so easy to be immature," Kant writes. It is therefore almost impossible for individuals to break free from this state of tutelage, dependency, muteness—*Unmündigkeit*—"that has all but become their nature."[55]

However, insofar as it constitutes collectively a public—in other words, an ensemble of individuals capable of enlightening one another—

the people can access Enlightenment. It is for this reason that *Aufklärung* is a collective phenomenon, one that implies the publicness of knowledge and the free discussion of knowledge. *Aufklärung* is the historical process by which a multitude constitutes itself as a public. Thus, a relationship to truth does not derive only from a classical epistemology allowing each individual to discern true from false, but as much or more from a social epistemology that must take into account the role of prejudices, imitations, and intellectual authority. A new difficulty then arises that relates to the specific role of intellectuals, philosophers, the already enlightened, and the already adult—in short, the role of the *Aufklärer*, the enlightener. If the public can enlighten itself, it is thanks to such people—it is thanks to the positive modeling, the good example that these enlightened men offer others.

> But that the public should enlighten itself is more likely; indeed, if it is only allowed freedom, enlightenment is almost inevitable. For even among the entrenched guardians of the great masses a few will always think for themselves, a few who, after having themselves thrown off the yoke of immaturity [*Unmündigkeit*], will spread the spirit of a rational appreciation for both their own worth and for each person's calling to think for himself.[56]

This passage is crucial. Kant must reconcile the tension that exists between a public that "enlightens itself," in other words an ideal of spontaneous and collective emancipation, and the decisive role played by "a few who will always think for themselves," who belong to the traditional elite (the tutors teaching the masses), and yet who have acquired intellectual autonomy and are emancipated thanks to their force alone. It is not clear how these precursors found the means within themselves to throw off the yoke of prejudices and authorities [*das Joch der Unmündigkeit selbst abgeworfen haben*] or why certain men find in themselves this courage, this will to know which does not belong to all. Yet what matters is that freedom and the publicness of intellectual debates make these *Aufklärer*, these enlighteners, into models as men not only capable of enlightening others but also adept at giving mankind a taste for freedom and for critical thinking. But then Kant raises a supplementary problem, one that arises when the public that had earlier been placed by them [the tutors] under this yoke, forces them to remain under it, once incited to insurrection [*aufgewiegelt worden*] by some of its tutors who are themselves incapable of enlightenment [*aller Aufklärung unfähig sind*]." These particular tutors, being incapable of enlightenment, exploit the credulity of the public. They are the false learned, the demagogues, those Condorcet called charlatans, individuals who claim to meet the public's expectations but who exploit its anger and profit from its credulity such that the public, once tricked by them, instead of becoming emancipated, will find its prejudices reinforced. Thus, Kant favors the Enlightenment as a slow, progressive phenomenon over Revolution, which can only replace one set of prejudices with others:

> Thus, a public can only attain enlightenment slowly. Perhaps a revolution can overthrow autocratic despotism and profiteering or power-grabbing oppression, but it can never truly reform a manner of thinking; instead, new prejudices, just like the old ones they replace, will serve as a leash for the great unthinking mass.[57]

From this perspective, the principal danger is caused by demagogues. Although freedom, notably freedom of the press, is the necessary condition for the public's enlightenment, that same freedom opens the door to charlatans of all kinds who exploit this liberty to offer the people fake knowledge and false solutions. Some years later, in his *Critique of Judgment* (1790), Kant will insist strongly on this point: *Aufklärung* is easy in theory but difficult and slow to achieve in practice because men always want to skip the "critique" part (in other words, they want to go beyond the limits of their reason and have certitudes instead of doubts) and because "there will always be individuals promising with a great deal of self-assurance to be able to satisfy that thirst to know."[58] In working toward emancipating the public, the true philosophers, the *Aufklärer*, are always in competition with charlatans who sell the public unreasonable beliefs and flatter peoples' infinite desire for knowledge in order to be all the more successful at turning their attention away from true knowledge. Charlatans push the public to believe, not to doubt or question. The development of publicness, in the sense of a public discussion, is both a precondition for the Enlightenment and its principal danger, at least so long as the public has not yet become truly enlightened. Total liberty can be as dangerous as censorship.

This conundrum is what one could call the paradox of emancipation through enlightenment: that in order to enlighten the people, it is first necessary for people as a public to be able to recognize those who are capable of enlightening them. Herein lies the role of the state: it must not only assure freedom, which allows enlightenment to be disseminated, but it must also regulate public space by assuring to the truly learned their autonomy and intellectual authority. In Kant's Germany, this autonomy has a place-name: the university. Thus, it is not surprising that Kant's last great text, published in 1797, is devoted to defending the faculty of philosophy not only against the faculty of theology but also against the public. The faculty of philosophy is the place where the philosopher can speak freely (addressing other philosophers) without running the risk of directly addressing the public, who cares little for his writings in any case; but it is also the institutional space that guarantees for him, through the state as intermediary, a privileged position vis-à-vis the public. Here the philosopher can enlighten the people, but on condition of speaking publicly while not directly addressing the people: "Enlightenment of the masses is the public instruction of the people in its duties and rights vis-à-vis the state to which they belong," Kant affirms. To do that, enlightened men must address themselves "respectfully to the state."[59]

Kant's position was only one of many German intellectual currents at the time, and despite his personal aura it hardly received unanimous support. Most authors speaking out on the matter during those years understood the point to be specifying the social and political conditions for individual autonomy; in other words, it was less a matter of giving a doctrinal or ideological content to *Aufklärung* than of understanding how some men could effectively enlighten others. Christoph Martin Wieland, for one, decried social hierarchies, declaring that "anyone—from a Socrates or Kant to the most obscure of tailors and cobblers who without exception are naturally enlightened—has the right to enlighten humanity as he can."[60] One simply had to take precautions against secret societies and sects. Freedom of the press, on the other hand, should be total, he felt, as should that of the university chair and academic speech. Not everyone shared Wieland's optimism, however. Kant himself, over time, became increasingly pessimistic, fearing that in the modern forms of public debate, easily gullible "passive reason" was being favored to the detriment of "critical reason," which seeks to know and understand its own limits.[61] After the arrival in 1786 of Frederick William II, a Prussian king hostile to the Enlightenment, and then the start of the French Revolution, the conversation in Germany would soon quickly change character. The mixture of intellectual optimism and political moderation that had marked the 1780s would no longer be the prevailing tendency.

Despite some differences in emphasis due to different contexts, such as the high importance of universities in the German debate, the questions surrounding the public dimension of the Enlightenment were quite similar in both Paris and Berlin. The common goal was to understand what *enlighten* really meant. How could one individual enlighten others? How could a people enlighten themselves collectively if the faculty of reasoning properly was in the first instance a matter of individual understanding and personal courage? Emancipation through freedom—

this program seemed to define not only the German *Aufklärung* but the whole Enlightenment. Generalized instruction and freedom of speech were to be its two pillars. As soon as the people were instructed and writers could debate freely in public space, the "sphere of Enlightenment" would steadily expand. The project was both radical—in the sense that it was not proposing a simple change of political order but instead a major transformation of the ways of thinking and of maintaining social equilibrium—and moderate, since it rested on a long process of intellectual maturation guided by thinkers and not on a rapid overthrow of relationships of domination. Today, even if this project remains central to the democratic ambitions of modern societies, we tend to look at its underlying optimism with a certain skepticism. Theories of suspicion and the experience of history have taught us that neither freedom of speech nor public instruction is sufficient to erase prejudices and make reason triumph.

What this two-hundred-year-old history has shown us is that this skepticism, or more precisely this obsessive worry about how to achieve their goals, was already tormenting the authors of the eighteenth century. All were torn between a militant optimism founded on a confident bet about the future and a pessimism fueled by an increasingly negative assessment of the conditions necessary for the diffusion of knowledge. Contrary to what is often believed, the difficulty was not of a social order but was instead media-related: the problem was not the people but the public. The obstacle that impeded emancipation through knowledge was not the social ineligibility of the people but the nature of communication in modern public spaces, the forms of written transmission. Even leading examples of Enlightenment optimism such as Condorcet and Kant were confronted with a major challenge when it came to articulating the link between individual emancipation through reason and collective emancipation through the mechanisms of making public [*publicité*]. They tried to resolve a contradiction inherent to performing the task of "enlightening" others: to be able to teach the people to think for themselves, one must begin by creating a certain verticality; one must guarantee the institutional autonomy of the discussion within the scientific community and the authority of intellectuals. Doing so carries a high risk of creating a new clergy, secular this time but one similarly invested with potentially excessive power and prestige. The challenge not only concerns the status of philosophers and the learned, the guardians of reason, but strikes at the core of the Enlightenment project and its ambivalence: either one must encourage individual autonomy, stimulating critical thinking and the rejection of all argument from authority; or one must replace old superstitions and prejudices with new principles, instituting a reasonable moral system with the philosophers as guarantors.[62]

For two centuries, thinkers who align themselves with the Enlightenment have never truly been able to overcome this tension caused by the contradiction between the emancipation of all and the intellectual authority of the *Aufklärer*. They have constantly questioned the meaning of the position of the learned person who—in the name of a certain knowledge that he claims is truer than the prejudices of the mass—proposes to enlighten his contemporaries. Such questioning leads to the center of the complex relations that necessarily pluralist democracies maintain with the very idea of truth.[63] The critical importance of the Enlightenment legacy derives more from this acute awareness of these difficulties than from any affirmation of a mission to enlighten mankind.

Sartre, Foucault, and Bourdieu, to take just three emblematic thinkers of the second half of the twentieth century, all had to wrestle with this double question: how does one make the voice of reason heard in a public space dominated by emotion, the short-term thinking induced by "the news," and the effects of imitation? How does one justify the specific authority claimed by those who would enlighten mankind and who demand a monopoly, at least provisionally, over knowledge? Sartre, who for so long incarnated the figure of the engaged intellectual intervening on every subject in the name of a universal applicability of rationality, considered the eighteenth century to be a particularly favorable time for writers. In a late interview that at times takes on the tone of a confession, he acknowledged the contradiction that plagues the notion of the intellectual: "the intellectual as someone who thinks in the place of others is doomed to disappear: to think on behalf of others is an absurdity that condemns the very notion of the intellectual."[64]

More recently, Bourdieu attempted to ground the authority of sociology on the autonomy of the scientific field—at the risk, of course, of recreating an outside-observer position that was sometimes difficult to justify. Jacques Rancière criticized him for this attempt, affirming that one cannot claim to diffuse knowledge by starting from a claim to have a monopoly over it. To better defend another vision of intellectual emancipation, Rancière turned to a forgotten figure from the nineteenth century, Joseph Jacotot, whose pedagogical method and emancipation philosophy were based on one principle: "one can teach what one does not know." It is only on this condition that one can enlighten others without claiming to impose on them a certain knowledge or lines of thinking. For Jacotot, it was absolutely necessary to avoid explaining, because the one who explains posits a difference, a distance between his knowledge and the ignorance of others. From that point on he does not enlighten, he makes others stupid: "The stultifier is not an aged obtuse master who crams his students' skulls full of poorly digested knowledge, or a malignant character mouthing half-truths in order to shore up his power and the social order. On the contrary, he is all the more efficacious because he is knowledgeable, enlightened, and of good faith," writes Rancière.[65] The figure of the ignorant master, as described by Jacotot, practically turns upside-down the Enlightenment's learned person. It destroys at the root Condorcet's conception of emancipation founded on public instruction and the authority of the learned. The entire legacy of the Enlightenment seems to wobble: "That knowledge and freedoms were linked, that school was an institution where this link was forged, that intellectuals were charged with spelling out the discourse—all that was believed for a long time; it is what was called the Enlightenment."[66]

Even Michel Foucault, who always displayed an eagerness to fend off any attempts to cast him as a universalist intellectual, was forced to face these questions in his last courses in 1983–1984, as we shall see.[67] While claiming Kant and the Enlightenment as forebears, he asks about the conditions in which a discourse of truth could lead those who receive it to change their behavior, whether it be the counsellor addressing a head of state or a philosopher addressing the people. His response, obviously, is nothing like that of Kant or Condorcet. The point is not to restore the authority of knowledge as the guarantee of the true learned person's speech. Nor is he out to revive the figure of the ignorant master. The free speaker [*parrêsiaste*], according to Foucault, uses his own work on himself and his pursuit of an effective subjective written expression to find the courage to offer a diagnosis that may call forth the subjective engagement of his readers. This solution is a seductive but obviously elitist one that risks reuniting with a form of philosophical heroism. Intellectuals are endlessly zigzagging between the figure of the learned person and that of the writer—always divided between a stubborn belief in the effectiveness of their speech and a nervous, sometimes disenchanted pessimism when faced with the games of opinion.

CHAPTER SEVEN

Farewell, Socrates

There is a memorable declaration attributed to Charles de Gaulle, who had been advised to silence Jean-Paul Sartre: "One doesn't lock up Voltaire!"[1] That the name of the author of *Candide* came spontaneously to the general's mind testifies to the longstanding influence of the Enlightenment philosopher as a model of the combative intellectual who is both irritating and untouchable. "One doesn't lock up Voltaire!" expressed a moral imperative but also a lucid acknowledgment of powerlessness when up against the symbolic prestige of the great writer. And yet, if one did not get rid of Voltaire in de Gaulle's Fifth Republic, Diderot did get censored. In the winter of 1965–1966, the announcement of a film adaptation by Jacques Rivette of *La Religieuse* provoked concern among some Catholics, who set up a campaign to have the production blocked, including an appeal to de Gaulle himself. In March 1966, the film was censored, provoking indignation in cultural circles. "So, in 1966 Diderot is still for some only to be thrown on the fire," wrote Jean de Baroncelli, an influential cinema critic at the newspaper *Le Monde*.[2] In the 1960s, the Enlightenment heritage was double-sided. It encompassed a legitimate culture and a living memory of great writers and their fight for justice, but it also brought to mind texts still judged by some to be tinged with the diabolical, especially if they concerned religion or good manners.

Two centuries earlier, under the absolute monarchy, Diderot did not take the risk of seeing *La Religieuse* censored, since he didn't even try to get it published. It was only known among a small number of friends and subscribers to the *Correspondance littéraire*, and it only appeared for the first time in 1796.[3] Should one be surprised by this philosopher's caution? Diderot, a materialist and sometimes licentious writer but also the general supervisor of the *Encyclopédie* project, incarnates certain contradictions of the Enlightenment philosopher in general: he was quick to express indignation, but he was also a writer who generally went *with* the grain inside the select world of Parisian elites. He authored audacious texts that seem, when reread today, to herald the Revolution, and yet he didn't publish them. He also sometimes worked as an official censor in the service of Antoine de Sartine, the lieutenant general of police and the director of the Royal Library. Should he be seen, then, as a representative of the "high Enlightenment" of successful, established philosophers preoccupied with managing their careers and preserving the orderly status quo that was so beneficial to them? Robert Darnton juxtaposed to these quasi-official Enlightenment figures those he called the many "*Rousseau du ruisseau*"; in other words, the many streams of literary bohemia: often-forgotten marginal writers, authors of pamphlets, satirical writings, pornographic libelles, and scandalous chronicles of political life at court, including texts that promoted atheism and materialism. This literature is said to have been truly seditious in the eyes of authorities, since it was published clandestinely outside the kingdom and was sold illegally, and to have contributed more to the desacralization of the monarchy than the serious writings of philosophers. It's against the former that the police would take action, whereas the better-established writers with their sponsors and stipends were hardly ever bothered.[4]

And yet the censors were a true threat. Despite his status as a royal tax collector and the protections that came with it, Helvétius was forced to publicly retract his book *De l'Esprit* after being convicted by the Sorbonne and Parliament in 1758. The *Encyclopédie* lost its privilege of royal sponsorship by the Librairie and was completed semi-clandestinely. Rousseau was the target of an arrest warrant after the publication of the *Contrat social* and had to flee France in 1762. Voltaire spent more than thirty years exiled from Paris. Even if it had become possible to find ways to slide through with ruses and oblique maneuvers, freedom of expression was not a right but only, in the best of cases, a question of brittle tolerance. In this context, which could be called moderate censorship—a regime where repression was both present and discreet, and where there was deep mutual distrust among authors, authorities, and publishers—how did Diderot conceive of his role as philosopher? How did he understand the publication of his ideas? Who was he writing for? What risks was he willing to take? These are serious questions that Diderot never decisively answered because he was afflicted with doubts throughout his career and remained split between incarnating the heroic figure of Socrates, the philosopher who dies for truth, and carrying out the more pragmatic, prudent role of the writer.

Diderot specialists have done extensive research into his political thinking, regretting that he did not compose a proper political treatise in the manner of Montesquieu or Rousseau. In truth, all of Diderot's writing is political, not in the sense that it examines the exercise of power but because it never ceases to question its own effectiveness and more generally the constraints and limits that impose themselves on intellectual activity. What compromises can or should a writer accept? How much prudence or daring is permissible? How much is too much? If the coherence of the Enlightenment rests less on doctrinal uniformity than on the conviction that one must work toward man's emancipation through the dissemination of knowledge and by favoring intellectual autonomy, then the question that necessarily arises is this: How does one enlighten the people without putting oneself in danger?

Vincennes

To understand Diderot's career, one has to zero in on the middle of the eighteenth century, in particular to the summer of 1749. Diderot had just turned thirty-six. He was not in touch with his family. After having married against the wishes of his father, a knife-maker in Langres, he was living in Paris, on the rue de l'Estrapade, and trying to forge a place for himself in the literary world.[5]

Diderot was at a turning point in his life. After doing various jobs to get by, notably some translations from English to French, he had just published the first volumes of his own writings. The first was his *Philosophical Thoughts*, which appeared anonymously in 1746 and was quickly condemned for its anti-religious content. Next came a libertine novel, *The Indiscreet Jewels*. Then, in 1749, Diderot published a *Letter on the Blind for the Use of Those Who Can See*, a scientific and philosophical meditation with heterodox passages that provoked the anger of official authorities. Two years earlier, Diderot had also agreed to be the general supervisor of an extended publishing project, the composition and publication of the multivolume *Encyclopedia*, for which publishers received royal subventions.

There he was, at the intersection of different worlds. In certain respects, he was in the shadows: among the clandestine authors who composed and circulated heterodox manuscripts, either deist or openly atheist, for small circles of initiated readers. Thus, he never published his daring *Skeptic's Walk* but kept it in his possession in manuscript form. At the same time, he was on the verge of being granted a place within the official world of letters alongside those published with royal sponsorship by leading bookshops. His goal was to break out of heterodox philosophy and clandestine circles and break into the first world of publishing so that he could reach a larger public.

This move entailed an important rupture with the libertine tradition, which reserved knowledge for a small number of strong minds and was hardly interested in sharing it more broadly. As we have seen, the great innovation of the Enlightenment rested on its committed, pedagogical ambition, its wish to break with esoterism and secrets in order to reach a larger public. At mid-century, the context offered Diderot favorable conditions to make his move: the monarchy was occupied with fighting Jansenists and *parlementaires*. Philosophical ideas were making progress and no longer seemed truly threatening. The public had been prepared for new, bold gestures by books such as Voltaire's *Philosophical Letters*, published in 1734, and Montesquieu's *The Spirit of Laws*, published in 1748. The official censor seemed to have backed off somewhat, and philosophers gained support at the center of monarchical power. Authors were no longer being burned alive, as they had been still at the beginning of the seventeenth century. And censors seemed so easy to work around that one could almost think they had become a boon for publicity. Diderot would joke about the matter some years later:

> I see that the stronger the prohibition is, the more it boosts book prices; the more it excites curiosity to read it, the more it's bought and read. And how many have been lifted into notoriety by an official condemnation who otherwise would have been consigned to oblivion by their own mediocrity? How many times would a bookseller and the author of an exceptional book, had they only dared, say to the police's magistrates, "Gentlemen, please, just a little arrest that punishes me with a whipping and burning at the bottom of your great staircase"? When a book's sentence is proclaimed, the workers at the printing press cry out, "Good, another new edition!"[6]

What Diderot probably did not know was that he was being closely watched by the Paris police. He had been denounced by the priest of the Saint-Médard church in Paris three years earlier, and Inspector Joseph d'Hémery of the Librairie Française had written a report on him that identified Diderot as the author of *Philosophical Thoughts* and described him as "a young man full of spirit but extremely dangerous." On July 24, 1749, Diderot was arrested and brought to the prison at Vincennes. The philosopher was dumbstruck by this unexpected event. He discovered that the threat he had been in the habit of minimizing was altogether real. Very quickly, he cracked under pressure, behavior that was a far cry from the heroism he aspired to. Less than three weeks after his arrest, he made a full confession to the police lieutenant and promised to change his ways. It was only much later, thanks to the archives at the Bastille, that historians would be able to piece together his rapid capitulation. In the middle of the nineteenth century, the historian Michelet was still imagining a heroic Diderot valiantly resisting police demands: "Diderot was a dashing figure in prison. Sworn to complete secrecy, he would never reveal the name of his publisher who would have been sent straight to Toulon. He was determined to stay where he was, and without paper or pen, he sketched out a play on the death of Socrates. The authorities yielded and backed off." During that time, so Michelet believed, Diderot was contemplating his plan for a "universal association of men of letters" to compose the *Encyclopedia*.[7]

The reality was less glorious. Diderot quickly confessed in a very deferential letter sent to Police Lieutenant Berryer.[8] This docility won him more favorable prison conditions and an earlier release, but the experience would haunt him for the rest of his life. He discovered fear and humiliation, the reality of police surveillance, and the anxiety of being locked up. He became conscious of the distance that separated dreams of heroism from the reality of what each person can bear.[9] The point is not to criticize Diderot for a lack of courage. But it is important to measure how destabilizing this experience was for him, in particular the shock of having to admit that he didn't have what it would take to be a martyr for philosophy. He would later write in the *Encyclopedia*, "O Socrates, I little resemble you, but at least you make me weep with admiration and joy."[10]

Facing the Censors

From then on, Diderot would be much more careful. How would he guarantee his safety without giving up on disseminating his boldest ideas and instructing the public? In place of the carefree attitude of his earlier years, there came a heightened awareness of the dangers that threatened the man of letters as soon as he renounced clandestine life and set out to work publicly for greater knowledge while also having a family and social life.

Of course, Diderot was not the only one to ask this question. All writers during that century were asking it as soon as their ambition became, as we've said, to enlighten their contemporaries and widely disseminate knowledge and critical thinking. A first type of answer is perfectly incarnated by Voltaire. He used over one hundred pseudonyms, so that he might have one hundred masks. He published books and pamphlets—

while carefully affirming publicly that he wasn't their author—while also dropping hints to his friends that he of course *was*. He fully exploited the ambivalences of the official censors and the tacit complacency of institutions: his writings were tolerated so long as he refrained from acknowledging them as his. Noisy denials—sometimes joking and playful, sometimes nervous—accompanied each publication, indicating fairly clearly to his followers that he was indeed the author of the texts in question.[11] In the works themselves, the play of pseudonyms and narrators was also a literary technique that served to multiply the voices, render utterances confusing, and dissimulate the author within a theater of folds and shadows.[12] The game was a serious one, and Voltaire could pull it off because he lived far from Paris, near the Swiss border, ever ready to flee. He knew the contours of the threat he faced. And even if he played with fire, he learned that he too could get burned. Like Diderot, he also experienced fear and humiliation, particularly in 1752, when Frederick II had him arrested and imprisoned in Frankfurt to teach him the cost of believing he was the equal of a sovereign.

The idea of playing with the authorities in this way displeased Rousseau, who adopted a radically different author position. He declared loudly and firmly his authorship and insisted on publishing in his name, even when he knew that doing so would cause him problems, as was the case with *Émile* and the *Contrat social.* He had a dose of bravura and braggadocio in him, his enemies said—it was courage, retorted his friends—that derived from his sense of ethical responsibility and his pride as an author. It is true that his choice to have his name on the cover of his books appeared to authorities as a provocation, and starting in the 1760s it earned him more severe treatment, an arrest warrant, and the obligation to flee France. He justified his choices on several occasions. He criticized with irony the usual games of prudence and dissimulation, which he viewed as forms of mondain hypocrisy: "Many are in the habit of confessing authorship to attain honors while using denials of the same to take cover; the same man will be or won't be the author before the same person depending on whether the two are attending an inquest or a dinner. . . . In this way safety comes at no cost to vanity."[13] But there's more: how can one both claim to practice a discourse of truth and hide oneself? The author must be accountable for his writings; agree to put himself in danger; take responsibility, personally and legally, for his writings; and thereby place the censors before their own responsibility. When the *Contrat social* was condemned in Geneva, Rousseau demanded he be put on trial.

This posture, which openly broke with the tradition of libertine precautions, inversely reactivated the ancient tradition of *parrêsia*, the

Greek philosophical notion of the courage to speak truth to power while flouting the attendant danger. It implied putting on stage the author himself as an exemplary philosopher, one ready to be held accountable for his writings and whose life bore out the truth he affirmed.[14] The books themselves no longer sufficed; they needed to be seconded by the exemplarity of the author. In return, the author embarked on an endless dynamic of publicness and publicity wherein he was required to display, justify, and explain not only his thinking but his life.[15]

Finally, in close proximity to Diderot, Baron d'Holbach was exercising a third option. Instead of Voltairean masks or Rousseauian *parrêsia*, d'Holbach chose to be anonymous and secretive when it came to publishing his materialist and atheist writings. He attributed his radical works, such as the *Système de la nature*, to authors who were already dead, and this trick kept his secret safe throughout his whole life. With the exception of a few close friends, no one made the connection between the rich German baron who enjoyed hosting social gatherings and the materialist manifestos he had authored. This radical choice had the great advantage of allowing d'Holbach to abandon cryptic writing, with its discreet allusions meant to deceive the official censors. On the contrary, he could proselytize in favor of atheism directly and openly.[16] In return, d'Holbach completely renounced all desire for fame, something that seems not to have been all that troubling for him.

Diderot would choose none of these options. Neither Voltaire's masks nor Rousseau's intransigence nor the strict anonymity of Baron d'Holbach suited him. Commitment to any of those postures implied a clear conception of one's authorial identity and the destination of one's writings. Diderot simultaneously carried out different publishing strategies while continuously questioning the pertinence of the choices he was making.

During the twenty years that followed his release from the Vincennes prison, Diderot was most noted as the general editor of the *Encyclopédie*, the project through which he sought to spread enlightenment to a large public within an authorized framework while yet pushing the boundaries of official tolerance. At first, the *Encyclopédie* obtained royal privilege in the form of official authorizations granted to publisher-booksellers. It was able to count on numerous sources of support close to the governing power; for example, Madame de Pompadour, who was painted in 1751 by Maurice Quentin de la Tour with the first volumes of the encyclopedic dictionary at her side; or Chrétien-Guillaume de Lamoignon de Malesherbes, the director general of the Royal Library, a liberal and enlightened personage who played the role of official protector of the project.

As the general supervisor, Diderot could publish his own articles. He composed over a thousand entries, and some of them—such as the one on "Political Authority"—are true manifestos defending the new philosophy with audacious proposals. In his role as editor publishing his contemporaries, he could make certain texts more visible that formerly had only circulated clandestinely. An example is the famous entry for "Philosopher," written by the grammarian César Dumarsais in 1730, a text that amounts to a stirring plea for a totally secularized conception of philosophy.

However, Diderot also had to get along with the authorities and booksellers and therefore exercise caution and a measure of self-censorship. Putting out the *Encyclopédie* volumes was no picnic. In 1752, a first crisis erupted when Abbé de Prades, one of Diderot's collaborators, was accused by the Sorbonne of supporting heretical positions and then sent into exile. The incident forced Diderot to contemplate again the prospect of imprisonment. A second, more serious crisis occurred over the years 1757–1759, during a period of expanding powers of the official censors: the *Encyclopédie* was condemned, its sponsorship was revoked, and d'Alembert abandoned the project. Finally, thanks to the intervention of Malesherbes, a solution was found that allowed the project to resume within a semi-official framework. However, in 1766, as the last ten volumes were due to be published, more persecution occurred. On April 23, Le Breton was arrested and taken to the Bastille, though he would be quickly released. The general atmosphere was horrible, since only some weeks earlier the chevalier François-Jean Lefebvre de La Barre had been condemned to death for blasphemy. Voltaire tried to convince Diderot to flee to Germany and pursue his work in exile. But the philosopher refused, all the while recognizing the danger that hung over him. In a superb letter to Voltaire, he plainly named the worries that gripped him:

> I know well that once a ferocious animal has dipped its tongue in human blood, it can no longer go without it. . . . I know that in the space of twenty-four hours an honest man can lose his fortune because there are tricky beggars; his honor because there is no law; his freedom because the tyrants lurk in the shadows; his life because for them the life of a citizen counts for nothing and because they seek to elude contempt through acts of terror. . . . I know well that they've reached the point where good people, enlightened people are and must be unbearable. I know well that we are bound by imperceptible strings of a trap called *police* and that we're surrounded by informers. . . . My soul is filled with alarms, I hear at the bottom of my heart a voice that joins yours and tells me "Flee, flee."[17]

Despite these threats, Diderot chose to remain—out of optimism, because he hoped that the fanaticism would subside and the authorities would become reasonable. He did not think of himself as a subversive figure but as an enlightened person, a useful and virtuous citizen. Also, the thought of exile displeased him because it would have meant being cut off from friends, family, and his daughter: "What would you have me do with human existence, if I can have it only by renouncing all that makes it dear to me?"

This letter can be read in two ways. It is possible to see the choice to continue to work in the center of the capital, accepting all the risks, as almost a bragging dare flung at the ruling power. But one can also detect in it a confession: Diderot was attached to a certain comfort, to his family, his friends, his bourgeois tranquility, his "little household," as he calls it. Perhaps he was thinking of the European vagabondage of his comrade and rival Rousseau. The tone of the letter was not heroic, and Diderot seemed to be under no false illusions. If he were to remain, he wrote, it would be because he had been "detained by the most stupid and inconceivable inertia." The question he asked himself was this: Can one dream of being a Socrates fighting against prejudice and a Prometheus bringing knowledge to men, and also live the life of a good family man, father, and respected member of the Republic of Letters?

In parallel, it's true, Diderot developed a second publication strategy that allowed him to combine social caution and intellectual daring more easily. In the *Encyclopédie,* he strove to push as far as possible the outer boundaries of what official institutions would tolerate. Yet his most daring texts, the ones which are the most subversive, the most personal, and that guarantee his literary glory today, were never published in the full sense. Diderot only allowed them to become public in a handwritten literary gazette that circulated to a very small number of chosen individuals and grand European aristocrats in the private *Correspondance littéraire* of his friend Grimm. This was the case for the *Rêve de d'Alembert,* the *Supplément au Voyage de Bougainville, Jacques le Fataliste,* the *Salons,* and *La Religieuse.* Certain texts were not published at all, such as *Rameau's Nephew,* a work no one read during Diderot's lifetime.

By keeping access to his most audacious texts within a small circle of confidants, was Diderot reviving the libertine conception of clandestine philosophical combat? Not really, because he was not counting on their being read by a select number of strong minds among his contemporaries, as the libertine authors did, but instead on their reaching a large public yet to come. He was making a bet, a bet on posterity, on future readers who would be able to read him once the evolution of minds that he saw on the horizon and sought to accelerate had taken place. This is why he collected and copied his manuscripts so scrupulously, keeping several copies of each in preparation for the publication of his complete works after his death. His position is clear from what he wrote at the end of his life in the *Essay on the Reigns of Claudius and Nero*: "One only thinks and speaks with force from the bottom of one's tomb—that's where one should place oneself and it's from there that one should address mankind."[18]

This choice in favor of posterity was an intellectual choice.[19] Diderot believed in the progress of knowledge and in the weakening of censors and prejudices. "If the philosopher speaks in vain for the moment, he writes and thinks usefully for the future."[20] He left to others, notably to his loyal friend Naigeon, the responsibility of editing his works. He did not renounce the idea of making his ideas and books known, but he opted to wait until minds were ready to receive them. And this belated reception is what would happen when Naigeon published Diderot's works in 1798 under the Directory.[21] It would not be until the 1950s, however, with the discovery and inventory of the Vandeul collection by Herbert Dieckmann, that the works of Diderot would be brought fully to light, so to speak.

This choice of posthumous publication was also a personal bet. Diderot did not give up on glory or the symbolic compensation attached to his work, but he placed greater significance on the future recognition of posterity than on fame in his lifetime. He explained himself at length on this question in a long discussion with the sculptor Falconet. Instead of celebrity status, he saw glory as the spur of merit: "O the inestimable value of glory!" he wrote. A desire for glory pushed him to make the most of his talent and to address posterity without worrying about the judgment of his contemporaries. Diderot believed that, as much as possible, one ought to avoid public display during one's lifetime, while yet working to merit an enduring glory that only the future could guarantee. "There is nothing sweeter than believing that you will enrich your nation with yet one more great name."[22] In this way Diderot revived a classic conception of glory in opposition to the new forms of fame of his day.

Diderot sometimes used an additional publishing strategy, which consisted in placing texts, or rather fragments of texts, inside the books of other authors, as he did with the *Philosophical History of the Two Indies* by Abbé Raynal. Diderot made major contributions to that work—including florid pieces—that were part of its ringing success. Today, those contributions are integrated into Diderot's collected works and are widely studied after having been ignored for a long time.[23] Other pieces may exist that have not been identified, such as contributions Diderot may have made to the books of Baron d'Holbach. For those texts, Diderot made no authorial claim, not even posthumously. His authorial status disappeared behind the collective work that was accomplished.

These multiple, complex publication strategies aimed to respond as best they could to contradictory demands: to enlighten the people, to guarantee his own safety, to protect his family, and to prepare his posthumous glory. But they did not come without risks. The *Encyclopédie* project was almost halted several times, and the final product did not please Diderot because he discovered along the way that his publishers were taking precautions and quietly modifying many articles prior to printing.[24] Some of his texts, such as *Rameau's Nephew*, nearly disappeared. Others were attributed to him without his objection, such as Morelly's *Code de la nature*. As a result, his image was for a long time unclear. For his contemporaries and even his friends, he was essentially the general editor of the *Encyclopédie*, a writer in the service of others whose genius was underestimated by many and who generally regretted that he had not left a more substantial body of work.

Diderot's Doubts

The specific character of Diderot's author position derives not only from his diverse set of practices but also from his hesitations and doubts. He himself questioned this penchant for hesitation. He would often put it on display in order to better ask strategic questions: How does one disseminate a disputatious line of thinking? How does one make the Enlightenment and knowledge advance? To whom should one speak? To a small circle of intimates? To a larger public? To future generations? Must the philosopher perform as the prince's counsellor? Should he rely on government power or challenge it?

In texts from his youth, he easily imagined himself in a duel with censors in which he'd have the upper hand. He made constant references to Socrates, whom he saw as the exemplary intellectual hero, sacrificing all for truth. Diderot shared the references of his time, and the trial of Socrates was one of the great myths of the Enlightenment era, a powerful symbol of philosophy's fight against fanaticism and intolerance. Major and minor authors took up the story. Voltaire devoted a play to it and David a famous painting.[25] But it wasn't so much the actual philosophy of Socrates or Plato that interested Diderot as it was the figure of the ancient philosopher going up against the injustice of the ruling power. The modern philosopher, Diderot felt, could compare himself to his ancient counterpart: "Socrates, at the time of his death, was regarded in Athens as we are regarded in Paris." But to truly identify with this glorious predecessor, one would have to have the courage of Socrates and agree to sacrifice one's life in the name of truth.

After his prison time at Vincennes, Diderot had no more illusions: whatever it took to be a martyr, he didn't have it. He therefore tried to work out a different approach, one that relied more on trickery and dissimulation than confrontation. In a late text (1774–1775), an interview between a philosopher and La Maréchale de ***, he depicts a gallant and atheist thinker who seeks to convince a lady of polite society to share his views by using a mixture of philosophical arguments and light banter, in conformity with the reinvention of philosophical dialogue since Fontenelle. Diderot's own cautious stance is in evidence in the last words of the exchange:

> LA MARÉCHALE.—By the way, if you had to explain your principles to our magistrates, would you be open about them?
>
> DIDEROT.—I would do my best to spare them such an atrocious action.
>
> LA MARÉCHALE.—Ah! Coward! If you were on the point of dying, would you submit to the ceremonies of the Church?
>
> DIDEROT.—I wouldn't fail to, no.
>
> LA MARÉCHALE.—Hah! The base hypocrite.[26]

But these levels of caution, which amount to erasing one's tracks while yet hoping to be read between the lines by talented readers—don't they risk corrupting the significance of philosophical discourse? Diderot was smart enough to see this very danger. In the *Encyclopedia* entry devoted precisely to "Encyclopédie," a text which reads like a manifesto of sorts, he worries over the strategies of self-censorship that authors are forced to adopt: "Often one does not know what someone thought on the most important matters. He folds himself within affected shadows; his contemporaries are unaware of his feelings; and one can hardly expect the *Encyclopédie* to be free of this defect." The reader has been forewarned and invited to exercise his critical faculties to guess the intentions of authors. But the observation is also a confession, a clue to a concern: Will one ever know what Diderot truly thought? By seeking to write between the lines, does one not lose sight of the immediate effectiveness of philosophical discourse and therefore of its social usefulness? If so, the practice would threaten the entire *Encyclopedia* project. Diderot is also wary of the classic use of veils of irony to circumvent the censors, a deployment that modern criticism has so often praised as marking the genius of the editor-publishers. In the same entry for "Encyclopédie" he notes: "Frequent allusions of this sort would cover a work in shadows. Generations to follow who do not know the little circumstances that were not worth handing down will not sense the finesse of the statement and will look on these words which amuse us as childish gibberish. Instead of composing a serious philosophical dictionary, one falls into the satirical pasquinade. All things considered, I would prefer the truth be told without detours."[27]

This tension traverses Diderot's entire oeuvre: on the one hand, he offers a heroic vision of the philosopher as Socrates or even Prometheus; on the other, he offers a more careful vision, but also a more nervous and disillusioned one, in which there's uncertainty about whether philosophy will be able to fulfill its task and find its public. This hesitation was linked, as for so many others in his day, to the tension between an idealized vision of the public to be enlightened and the sociological reality of the public as it existed. The *Encyclopedia* entry for "Multitude," published in 1765, expresses great distrust toward the large majority, whose voice always falls spontaneously into error, "unreason[,] and prejudice." Only the action of philosophers allows one to hope for knowledge's progress and the retreat of fanaticism "at the end of a long lapse of time."[28] Hence the discreetly elitist vision over the short term that promotes "the small number of reasonable men" to counteract the multitude. This theme can be found in all Diderot's texts of those years, notably in his correspondence with Falconet. If Diderot preferred posthumous glory, it's also because he believed the people could only become enlightened slowly. In the meantime, one had to privilege a small number of reasonable people, and this concession led him to revive the idea of an "invisible church" to counter a public incapable of judgment. "When I speak of the public voice, I'm not talking about the mixed crowd composed of all different types of people who boisterously whistle at a masterpiece from the pit, raise dust at a Salon, and look to booklets to know if they should praise or criticize. I'm talking about the little flock, the invisible church that listens, watches, meditates, speaks softly, and whose voice prevails in the long run and forms the general opinion."[29]

The two texts express the same ambivalence. One finds in them the opposition between a small elite of enlightened minds and a multitude incapable of thinking. One can also note the underlying optimism they express. Reason is not to remain the privilege of an elite. The philosopher's voice is not shouting in the desert; it will prevail in the end. But this victory, deferred to an always distant and indeterminate future ("à la longue" / "in time") is a true bet without certainty, especially since it comes with no real analysis of the conditions necessary for reasonable judgment to win out over popular prejudice. Diderot's fondness for the acoustic metaphor of echo allows for no understanding of the mechanisms of public opinion.[30] Its training and development remain mysterious. The slow but profound influence that philosophers will exert over public opinion is an indispensable article of faith without which Diderot's system would collapse, but it is also a conviction whose possibly illusory character he also glimpses.

Sometimes he had his doubts about posterity. The progress of the Enlightenment was uncertain: "I don't criticize you for working to enlighten men; it's the most important service that one can propose to give them; but it's also what one will never be able to deliver," he wrote in *The Skeptic's Walk* (1747).[31] Some years later he was still worried. The enthusiasm for new ideas, he remarked to Catherine II, is ephemeral. In time, censorship can "render a nation stupid."[32] The people can get used to not reading, and soon they lose interest in ideas. Not only does the prudent philosopher who bets on the future renounce all present fame, but it could turn out that he condemns himself to never being read at all. Was the *Encyclopédie* worth the twenty-five years of work and hassle he endured? At such moments, Diderot's thinking resembles the very pessimistic vision handed down by the clandestine tradition. Among the late additions to his *Philosophical Thoughts*, he inserts a quotation from Juste Lipse affirming that truth "is not made to please the multitude."[33] This return to the heritage of the Stoics is particularly evident in his last great text devoted to Seneca, the *Essay on the Reigns of Claudius and Nero*. Public opinion has largely disappeared from view, amounting to no more than popular judgment, a "popular ineptness" that the wise person must learn to avoid.[34] Here, the figure of the philosopher is concentrated around his face-off with the sovereign, his role as counsellor, and his moral uncertainties. This retreat is unquestionably the sign of a worried concern or perhaps even a disillusionment regarding public opinion, present or future. But it also demonstrates that political power, as both resource and danger, remains the essential question through which Diderot, nourished by his classical education and his personal experience, conceived of the philosopher's condition. His experience at the court of Catherine II during his stay in St. Petersburg in the winter of 1773–1774 may have been decisive in this regard. There, he developed a modest conception of the philosopher's role within the large scheme of political action. It's likely that Diderot had no grand illusions about Catherine II, but he got the chance to meditate on the vanity of the philosopher who would fancy himself the ruler's counsellor and on the vulnerability of his position.[35]

In Seneca, Diderot found an alter ego to meditate on the philosopher's ambivalences about power. Should one strongly criticize Seneca for his compromised position with Nero or, on the contrary, admire his courageous decision to practice philosophy in such close proximity to power and amid the discomfort of an ambiguous and equivocal situation? The book's tone tilts quickly toward self-justification. Diderot, who chose to live in polite society and accept the protection and subsidies of Catherine II, is looking to exculpate himself in the eyes of the public, but most importantly in his own, from the charge of hypocrisy. This self-exculpation was already in certain respects one of the goals of *Rameau's Nephew*, a deliberately provocative text that questions the reassuring posture of the worldly philosopher when confronted with the bad faith of the parasite and the comedian, who represent the universal "pantomime of tricky beggars." Was not *Lui* [He/Him] naming, behind cynical and histrionic appearances, a profound truth that *Moi* [I/ME], enclosed within the confines of a smug good conscience, had great difficulty refuting?

Diderot tacked back and forth, far from all certitude. As time passed, the nervousness and the bad conscience expressed themselves more and more openly. At the end of the 1760s, his correspondence testified to increasing exasperation toward his friends Grimm, d'Holbach, and Naigeon—three who had made a firm commitment to secrecy and dissimulation. In a 1769 letter to Madame de Meaux, Diderot related a conversation he had with d'Holbach and Naigeon: "Oh how they mocked me, because I so wanted to be burned."[36] He had brought up the case of Socrates once again, but he was only laughed at. In their eyes, the reference had become overly rhetorical, whereas for Diderot it remained an ideal, inaccessible perhaps, but one that ought to guide philosophers and keep them from falling into cynicism. "When one no longer has the courage to own one's statements, one should just shut up. . . . I cannot bear a man who lets himself be called a philosopher but who prefers his life, his miserable life, to the testimony he owes to truth," he tried to argue, invoking once again the figure of the philosopher ready to sacrifice all for truth.

Ten years later, in 1781, the question returned, but this time there was no laughter or teasing attached. The conversation had turned bitter, and disagreements were now out in the open. The trigger was a discussion about their friend Raynal, who had just been sentenced to exile for having placed his name and portrait on the frontispiece of a new edition of the *Philosophical History of the Two Indies*. Grimm considered there was no justification for this lack of caution: "Either you believe that those you're attacking cannot take their revenge against you, in which case it's a low blow to attack them; or you believe that they can take revenge and moreover want to do so, in which case it's madness to expose yourself to their resentment." Diderot found it very difficult to digest this criticism, which he took personally, and he attacked his friend for behaving improperly. He wrote a long letter, probably never sent, in which he declared his anger and disappointment. Had he gone astray? Had he extended his friendship to a low hypocrite? Had his friend become an accomplice of the ruling power; had his soul shrunk within the antechamber of the High and Mighty?

Diderot criticized the excessive caution of Grimm and sided with Raynal, and more generally with all authors who did not fear confronting the censors and even repression.

> How did we rise out of barbarism? Thankfully because there were certain men who loved truth more than they feared persecution. Of course, those men were not cowards. Shall we call them mad?
>
> It is impossible for a bold page not to hurt or irritate some individuals or some powerful and vindictive body. Where is the madness, where is the cowardice in neglecting both their power and their powerlessness? . . .
>
> You no longer know, my friend, how men of genius, courageous men, virtuous men, the despisers of these great idols before which so many cowards take pride in prostrating themselves, you have forgotten how they used to write their works. Without being of their class, I know, and I shall tell you. The intention to offend or please was far from their thinking. They did not run after praise; they did not fear persecution; they wanted to be useful; they wanted to state the truth; they wanted to state it strongly.[37]

When Diderot states that he does not belong to the class of heroes of great spirit, the courageous and virtuous writers, it's important to consider this declaration as not merely a gesture of modesty but rather a lucid observation nourished by his life experience. Indeed, he had just written some of the most incendiary pages of the *Philosophical History of the Two Indies*, including his famous address to Louis XVI that sparked the monarchy's outrage, but he did so without naming himself. In standing in defense of Raynal's courage, he declares his own cautiousness and perhaps exorcises his bad conscience. In truth, Grimm's dilemma placed a double bind on him. From this perspective, Raynal would have been crazy to expose himself to repression by naming himself on the frontispiece of the work, and Diderot would have been cowardly to let his criticisms appear under someone else's name. His reply is situated at the intersection of two planes. It does not merely defend the heroic sacrifice of the courageous writer but also praises the effectiveness of the careful author. "The one who names himself on the frontispiece of his work is imprudent, but not crazy; and the anonymous author is not a coward. . . . If one among these rare men were able to lose fortune, freedom, honor, or life without muttering, will I call him crazy? If he misses his country, friends, and compatriots, will I call him a coward?"

In this last sentence one can hear an echo of the letter sent to Voltaire in 1766. There is no more cowardice in choosing caution, Diderot argued, than there is madness in taking risks. What matters is to not abandon the fight for the truth, to not give up philosophizing as both an intellectual and engaged activity on behalf of truth. Philosophy's purpose is not to be a form of solitary wisdom and certainly not to be a witty seasoning within polite society, but instead to be an activity in the service of humanity's progress.

How is one to understand the apparent contradiction in this letter between the stated intransigence that comes with a certain rhetorical insistence and the persistence of a more complex and prudent position? Certain parts of the letter are puzzling. Diderot calls the *Philosophical History of the Two Indies* "a work that neither you, nor I, nor others who consider themselves and are above us would write one paragraph of"—even though Grimm was certainly aware that Diderot had composed whole pages of that work. Better still, Diderot explicitly mentions as worthy of praise certain passages (such as the address to Louis XVI and the encomium to Eliza Drapper) that modern critics have established were texts he wrote.

To resolve these puzzles, one can adopt the interpretation proposed by Georges Benrekassa, who insists on Diderot's inability to settle on a coherent position, a fact that renders the text contradictory and indeed unpublishable.[38] The advocacy for an intransigent militancy is undermined from within by rhetorical excesses that weaken it. This "overly lyrical and showy political theatricality" is said to aim at dissimulating mental disarray and "interior upheaval." The vacillation that overtook Diderot, in Benrekassa's view, was the outward sign of a complete dissolution of the figure of the individual author in favor of a type of collective author. For Benrekassa, "Enlightenment heroism" can only be taken on by a collective subject that transcends the individual Enlightenment authors and writers and is incarnated in the publications themselves—which were the pinnacle of Enlightenment dignity and esteem.

More recently, Stéphane Lojkine has taken this interpretation further by positing a reconstruction of Diderot's entire thought as a wish for the disappearance of the figure of the individual author. In this view, the erasure of the proper name would be coherent with Diderot's metaphysical thinking: a thinking favoring a dissemination of the living person, a dispersion across the flux of nature, "in the network of moving molecules, men, and ideas."[39] This interpretation may be pushing Benrekassa's intuition too far. In the name of a supposed metaphysical and theoretical coherence, Lojkine's hypothesis makes Diderot's contradictions disappear and gives no explanation of his heroic stirrings or of the importance of the Socrates theme. It is more accurate to say that Diderot constantly vacillated between two models of Enlightenment heroism. The first is that of the individual author standing up against injustice, determined to enlighten the public, and ready to sacrifice all for truth. One can see here the avatar of a modern figure, the intellectual, the *Aufklärer*; but Diderot projects onto that avatar the ancient grandeur of the persecuted philosopher. That grandeur leads him to place the philosopher's heroic behavior in opposition to an ordinary wisdom, expressed with a formulation he was fond of: "The people say, 'First live, then philosophize.' But the one who has chosen to follow Socrates's example and who loves truth and virtue more than life will say, 'Philosophize first, then live.' If one can. . . ."[40] The second model is the position of the anonymous author, of the collective enterprise, and more precisely of the book itself, whether it's the *Encyclopedia* or the *Philosophical History of the Two Indies*, those pluralistic enterprises where the diversity of authors melts within a shared commitment to a pedagogical project.[41]

Even when transported by indignation and anger, Diderot lets his irony be heard along with the doubts and hesitations that accompany his succession of publishing strategies. This polyphonic composition is what makes him so precious, because he offers us a different understanding of the Enlightenment's place in the history of writing under political constraints. In this way he helps us avoid two classic mistakes. One comes from the history of ideas and consists in only studying doctrines. Here one seeks to measure what the political and social critiques carried out by Enlightenment figures owe to the libertine tradition or to Spinozism or to natural-rights theory. Yet the specificity of the Enlightenment resides first in its dynamic conception of philosophy, an activity that is not only speculative but charged with transforming the world. It is supposed to allow men to "rise out of barbarism," as Diderot said, and this aim implies enlightening the largest public possible and therefore asking about how best to reach that public and achieve that broad enlightenment despite the persistence of censorship. The second mistake, deriving more from sociological history, is a misleading identification of the eighteenth-century "philosopher" with the modern intellectual—the figure that will emerge on the French political scene with the Dreyfus Affair—in other words, at times and in places where democratic institutions and freedom of thought and expression are more generally established. In this view, the history of Enlightenment philosophers is the story of the gradual autonomy of the literary field that allowed writers to attack religious or political authorities with full ownership of their share of responsibility.[42]

The case of Diderot shows that Enlightenment philosophers were above all preoccupied by a multitude of binds and ties of dependence that kept them within a strong heteronomy and far from whatever heroic ideal they may have entertained. Diderot had to work amidst political threats, with social obligations to polite society (including through his friend and protector d'Holbach), with the economic power of the bookseller-publishers, and also with the constraints exerted by family life. Some of these dependencies he had to submit to and endure; others were his deliberate choices. Together, they result in a configuration that the philosopher must own and play with as best he can.

If the weight of these dependencies seems so burdensome, it is because the heroic figure of the philosopher enlightening the people at the risk of his life has become an ideal—but an ideal that remains on a distant mountaintop. This contradiction between a far-off fantasy philosopher and the situated reality of a living, breathing writer with a family and powerful sponsors makes Diderot's position difficult and uncomfortable. It leads him into endless self-justification with his own unique mixture of bad faith and ironic insight.

One of the strongest of the Enlightenment's contradictions probably derives from this tension, present in so many authors, between—on the one hand—a heroic dramaturgy of the truth (in other words, an idealized and theatrical vision of a struggle for truth) and—on the other—the prosaic reality of tending to their social and cultural success and their integration within polite society. Surprisingly, this tension—despite being deeply inscribed within a particular moment in history, a time of absolute monarchy internally torn by liberal and reformist temptations—does not place them farther away from us but instead closer, because of the uncertainties it throws up about the very nature of engaged writing.

Diderot is the best example. His eloquent and indignant speeches move us less than his doubts and worries do, because we have learned to be wary of rhetoric and theatricality. Diderot wins our sympathy when he abdicates the sovereignty of the almighty author and turns to exploring the vertigo induced by an impossible position and to exorcising the specter of a solitary statement that no one can hear. Having made that move, the voices and genres multiply at the risk of Diderot sometimes getting lost among them. As Jean Starobinski once observed, to find his voice Diderot never stopped using the words of others as a translator, editor, and commenter. He was not a solitary writer who claimed to pull out from within himself a singular discourse. He conversed with friends and adversaries and also, through constant written commentaries, with the great authors who preceded him. These conversations are what gives his writings the somewhat unraveled tone that could occasionally bother his contemporaries, but that also make them so modern. Diderot is the enthusiast who doubts, the engaged philosopher who permanently questions his role, the effectiveness of his writing, and the benefits of philosophy. The polyphony, the hesitations, far from all dogmatism, are probably the most living part of what he had to say, and they stand as the legacy that invites and obliges our attention. "After having so constantly accorded a large place to weighing the words of others, Diderot ends up having his dearest desire satisfied: we who are his posterity still regard him as our interlocutor."[43]

CHAPTER EIGHT

The Diagnosis of Modernity

Some weeks after the death of Michel Foucault in 1984, a previously unpublished text entitled "Qu'est-ce que les Lumières?" [What Is Enlightenment?] appeared in *Le Magazine Littéraire*. In these five pages, the French philosopher aligned himself with Kant and the motto *Sapere aude* [Dare to know], the watchword of intellectual emancipation through a search for the truth. A few months later, another text with the same title appeared in English. Longer and more argued, this second text offered a precise analysis of Kant's two-hundred-year-old essay "*Was ist Aufklärung?*"—which Foucault designated as the origin of philosophical modernity.[1] For those who regularly attended Foucault's courses at the Collège de France, these texts were hardly a revelation since in large part they derived from lectures given in January 1983.[2] As we shall see, they were the culmination of a series of reflections Michel Foucault had been carrying out since the late 1970s, alongside a significant philosophical and political reorientation.

On the other hand, among Foucault's adversaries, the 1984 texts came as a big shock because they appeared to many as a posthumous provocation. The author of *Madness and Civilization* [*Histoire de la folie*, 1961] had often been presented as a resolute critic of the Enlightenment's rationalist tradition. After having undermined the social sciences in *The Order of Things* [*Les Mots et les Choses*, 1966], he had proposed in *Discipline and Punish* [*Surveiller et punir*, 1975] a new theory of power that rendered obsolete the democratic pretensions of modern liberal societies descended from the Enlightenment and the French Revolution. The two pillars of Enlightenment modernity—the order of knowledge (the human sciences) and the order of power (liberal reformism)—had thus been attacked at their foundations.

The publication of this text on the Enlightenment was thus inevitably surprising. Had we all been misreading and misunderstanding Foucault? Or had he changed in the last years of his life and come around to accepting himself as an inheritor of an intellectual tradition that up until then he'd been fighting against? Jürgen Habermas, long an outspoken critic of Foucault—whom he considered a resolute adversary of modernity—was astonished by the Frenchman's late commentary on Kant. He was unsure if he should applaud this rallying to the Enlightenment cause or instead express his incomprehension upon discovering this strange reversal that seemed incompatible with Foucault's entire collected works.[3]

One must try to imagine the shock felt by readers in the mid-1980s. Since that time, the text has been the focus of much commentary, notably on account of the seductive and mysterious formulation "the historic ontology of ourselves" that he posited as the proper legacy of the *Aufklärung*. The two Enlightenment texts have now been integrated into the canon of the definitive edition of Foucault's writings, and those collected works have been considerably enlarged by the publication of course lectures, conference papers, occasional pieces, and other previously unpublished texts. The commentaries and close readings are so numerous, in fact, that they risk obscuring the crucial features and cracks. Therefore, the attempt here will be to understand the intellectual event of this rallying of Foucault to the Enlightenment heritage. Despite what Habermas may have thought, Foucault's text was not a simple retraction or about-face but rather a way to reformulate the question of the Enlightenment in relation to modifications of Foucault's own philosophical program—which underwent considerable changes in the last years of his life—and with respect to the larger context of the intellectual debates that were happening in the early eighties.

To understand the impact of this text, it is important to consider three themes that it associates with the question of the Enlightenment. The first is modernity—in other words, the relation of the philosopher to his own time and to the specific knowledge that allows him to make a diagnosis of his present moment; the second is a reflection on subjectivity and the techniques of the self; and the third is the more political question of the intellectual's political engagement. My hypothesis is that this last point is decisive. By turning to the Enlightenment, Foucault hoped above all to escape the aporias of a critical discourse that refuses to be founded on universal moral norms or an intellectual magisterium. In this regard, he revives and displaces the question that was central, as we saw, for eighteenth-century philosophers: What is emancipating speech? But before going there, it is important to first consider the genesis of the 1984 text and the way that the Enlightenment legacy gradually imposed itself on Foucault.

Foucault, Antimodern?

In Foucault's first major publications, the Enlightenment is never a pertinent category—neither philosophically nor historically. The term almost never appears, neither in its French form, *les Lumières,* nor as the German term *Aufklärung* that Foucault will privilege later. There are obvious reasons for this. The Enlightenment figures themselves, also called *les Lumières,* belong to the category within the history of ideas that he rejects. Foucault proposed another periodization of Western history around the notion of "classical age," which would cover the seventeenth and eighteenth centuries and stand in opposition to the Renaissance. The notion of a "classical age" is central to the presentation in *Histoire de la folie* (1961). In this view, the evolution of reason—as it develops and excludes unreason by constituting it as its other—covers the two centuries from Descartes (1596–1650) to Pinel (1745–1826). Again in *Les Mots et les Choses,* and then more discreetly in *Surveiller et Punir,* Foucault speaks of a classical age as a single uniform period. In his last book, however, he does evoke the "end of the eighteenth century" or the "second half of the eighteenth century" as the time of "reformers" of the penal justice system who were sensitive to lightening sentences and putting an end to torture. But Foucault's goal there was to reverse the progressive sense of these reform projects by pointing out that their results were, first, an increase in discipline and control over individuals' bodies and, second, a fight against minor forms of popular illegality. And when Foucault does use the notion of "Lumières," he places the term between quotation marks to signal that he is evoking the standard history-of-ideas discourse that he opposes and whose reasoning he turns upside down. For example, he writes, "The 'Enlightenment,' which discovered the liberties, also discovered the disciplines."[4] In this view, then, the Enlightenment figures were not the leaders of an emancipation project but instead reinforced control and surveillance.

In those years, Foucault's work was largely received and understood as a critique of the intellectual heritage of the Enlightenment. In the mid-1970s, his reputation was solidly established. His books were a success, and *Les Mots et les Choses* even reached bestseller status. Likewise, his courses at the Collège de France were packed and popular. Foucault struck most commentators as at once a critic of reason (whose power to exclude he had denounced in *Histoire de la folie*), an adversary of humanism (encapsulated in the parting shot in *Les Mots et les Choses* about the death of man), and an opponent of Enlightenment reformism (whose logic of discipline he had picked apart in *Surveiller et Punir*). Insisting, as he did, on the forms of domination inscribed in modern knowledge structures seemed to be a strategy to minimize or challenge their emancipatory capacity.

This assessment of Foucault's positions was widespread in the 1970s and early 1980s, both in France and internationally—as is clear from the criticisms addressed to him by historians. In 1978, for example, a rather tense debate pitted Foucault against several of them around the history of prisons. Two years later, Maurice Agulhon criticized Foucault's critique of rationalism and the Enlightenment, arguing that "searching for the origins of totalitarianism in the Enlightenment heritage contributes to a critique of rationalism."[5] In his reply, Foucault begins by first stating his incomprehension and then denouncing a misunderstanding: the theses that Maurice Agulhon criticizes, he says, "are not mine."[6] It is well known that this type of denegation was a favorite rhetorical strategy of Foucault, who enjoyed reformulating propositions and keeping his interlocutor off balance. He seized the occasion, however, to specify his thinking about the Enlightenment at a moment when it was in the process of changing or in any case was becoming a topic in its own right. So, what does he say exactly?

First, he relates (with a measure of polemical bad faith) rationalism to Stalinism, and therefore his own critique of rationalism's abuses to a critique of Soviet totalitarianism more than to one of liberal modernity. This point is important if one recalls that Agulhon was for a long time close to the Communist party; but it is also important because, in the French intellectual context of the 1970s marked by the progress of anti-totalitarianism, Foucault seemed to be positioning himself on the side of defenders of liberal democracy.

Secondly, Foucault affirms that he had always adopted a concrete historic approach centered on the study of *rationalities*, not an abstract approach based on reason. Therefore, his writings are not to be read as a critique of reason but as a critique of certain rationalities, specifically those located in historical and institutional contexts. In addition, he rejects Enlightenment "blackmail" around reason, the idea that one must necessarily take sides for or against a set of values. His formula about blackmail, "*chantage aux Lumières,*" returns with further development in the 1984 text. Foucault did not think of himself as an adversary of the Enlightenment thinkers because he refused to consider the Enlightenment as a corpus of doctrines or as a belief in reason and progress. But in those earlier years, he gave no positive definition of what, for him, the Enlightenment would be instead.

This reply to historians was written between 1978 and 1980—an important period during which Foucault composed two other texts that reveal changes in his thinking. In May 1978, he was invited to give a lecture to the French Society of Philosophy that he had considered calling "What is Enlightenment?"; but he abandoned that idea, and the talk was later published under the title "What Is Critique?"[7] There for the first time, he publicly examined the notion of *Aufklärung* as elaborated in Kant's essay. In continuity with the lecture courses he was giving at the Collège de France on the history of governmentality and liberalism, Foucault's text insists on the claim for autonomy with respect to ruling powers. He defines critique not from an epistemological angle and the conditions of true knowledge, but as a "critical attitude," a form of resistance that would be both intellectual and political. And the meeting point of these two definitions, he argues, is to be found in Kant. At this stage, Foucault's effort consists in playing one Kant against another, opposing the Kant of the transcendental critique to the Kant of the 1784 text on *Aufklärung*, the Kant of *Sapere aude* who insists above all on the courage required for individual and collective emancipation. Foucault underscores the tension in Kant's writings between this critical attitude that is said to define the Enlightenment and the critical philosophy that sets limits on reason. The question of the present and the news [*l'actualité*], which will be so important in the texts of 1983–1984, plays no role here—it has not yet been formulated. However, Foucault has identified a link between a "critical attitude"—in other words, a subject's decision to risk embarking on emancipation with a move toward the truth—and Kant's 1784 text. This link is the lever that will allow him to thematize the question of *Aufklärung*. The notion, so important in the German tradition, was covered over in France, Foucault claims, by an epistemological tradition and also by the association of the Enlightenment with the Revolution. Yet, he writes, the time has come for French philosophers to return to this question "that is perhaps after all the entire problem of modern philosophy."[8]

The same year, Foucault wrote an introduction for the English edition of Georges Canguilhem's *Le Normal et le Pathologique* (1974) [*On the Normal and the Pathological*, 1978] in which he brings up for the first time Kant's essay on *Aufklärung*, which he defines as a specific rapport of philosophy to its present. By claiming to be supported by Canguilhem, Foucault inscribes his critique of rationalities within a much more rationalist heritage, namely that of the epistemology and history of science, and one that he will be able to use in opposition to his adversaries, especially the German tradition from the Frankfurt school.[9]

These two texts prove that the 1983 course—which prepares the way for the 1984 texts—was itself preceded by a series of adjustments that constitute a softening of Foucault's position. He clearly was seeking to reformulate his stance and place himself in a rationalist vein, though without abandoning the critical specificity of his thinking. His archives also contain the text of a lecture given in English. Although undated, it seems to be a first version of what would become the 1984 text. In the introduction, which exists as a series of notes, Foucault states that he feels obliged, almost against his will, to intervene in the debate of the moment over the Enlightenment and modernity, adding that it strikes him as both confused and unavoidable. If the debate is confused, he writes, it is because the terms *Aufklärung* and *modernity* are particularly hard to define—the first having many meanings and the second none.

Why did Foucault feel obliged to intervene in this debate? First, because for two centuries the whole philosophical enterprise had had to specify its own position regarding the Enlightenment—an event both well-known and yet enduringly enigmatic. The *Aufklärung*, he states, replaced Christianism as the normative substratum of Western societies, and no philosopher can ignore that fact. He then adds that a second, more specific reason obliges him to make his position explicit—namely, the need to respond to those who had characterized him as an adversary of the Enlightenment and as antimodern or postmodern—and state that he objects to these labels:

> Cette caractérisation comme un "anti-*Aufklärer*" ou comme un postmoderniste a été pour moi plutôt une surprise. En fait, si on m'avait demandé, il y a plusieurs années, quel était mon arrière-plan [background] philosophique et historique, ma réponse aurait été, très innocemment: la philosophie du XVIIIe siècle, l'*Aufklärung*. Mais, peut-être, le temps est-il venu pour moi de rendre un peu plus explicite cette relation à l'*Aufklärung* dans mon esprit et dans mon travail, qui était plus une présupposition qu'un thème explicite.[10]

Thus, the 1984 texts are the result of a multi-year process during which Foucault sought to make explicit or reformulate his relationship to the philosophical legacy of the Enlightenment. What mattered to him was rejecting the notion that he was an adversary of the Enlightenment and distancing himself from the postmodern movement. Inversely, by spelling out his relationship to the Enlightenment he was able to put into coherent form multiple questions at a time when his theoretical project and political position were undergoing significant changes.

The Attitude of Modernity

A discussion of modernity is at the center of the text "What Is Enlightenment?" published in 1984 as part of *The Foucault Reader*. In it, Foucault first does a quick commentary on the Kant essay, addressing in particular its definition of Enlightenment as a collective and individual emancipation, and the famous opposition between the private use of reason (as a professional practicing one's activity) and its public use (as a learned person writing for a public of readers). The principal contribution of his reading of the essay is to theorize a "modern attitude" that would be proper to *Aufklärung* and for which Kant's essay would be the first philosophical formulation. As he did in 1978, Foucault distinguishes two lines of analysis in Kant: a universalist critical philosophy that posits the conditions and limits of knowledge and a historicist philosophy that constitutes a critical mode or attitude of thinking. But this critical attitude, which until then had been defined essentially negatively as a form of resistance residing inside power relations themselves, acquires here a positive cast: it consists in judging the present, in thinking "the news," and in understanding the truth of a moment. Foucault wishes to see in Kant's text the starting point of an intellectual tradition that assigns to philosophy the task of thinking its own time, considering what is new or specific about it and how it "differs" from the past. In this way, "*Was ist Aufklärung?*" offers "the outline of what one might call the attitude of modernity."[11]

After the opening commentary on Kant, the text turns to a reflection on modernity with a rather lengthy discussion of Baudelaire. Modernity, writes Foucault, names neither a period nor an adherence to an ensemble of values or norms that would constitute a "doctrine." Instead, it names an attitude toward the present, an ethos that consists in recognizing that one belongs to a historical moment and critiquing it. It is this relation to the present that Foucault calls the "permanent critique of our historical era"—or, elsewhere, in a more obscure formulation, a "historical ontology of ourselves."[12]

To clarify this ambivalent relation to the present, Foucault makes use of the aesthetic writings of Baudelaire, notably "The Painter of Modern Life" and "On the Heroism of Modern Life." He underlines in Baudelaire's texts the mixture of a fascination with the present and a critique of progress. The search for an atemporal beauty in the most fugitive forms of modern life is what Baudelaire called the heroism of modern life; but, Foucault insists, it is an “ironic” heroism that avoids idealizing the present and certainly does not sacralize it.[13]

By passing gradually from Kant to Baudelaire, Foucault reveals that what interests him is less the Enlightenment as an intellectual current or apogee of European humanism—in fact, he refuses any link between the Enlightenment and humanism—but instead modernity as a reflexive relation to the present. Here, modernity is no longer conceived through a genealogy of progressive thinking but from the angle of a tense critical attitude, permanently mindful of examining the limits of the present moment, and this modernity can be given a positive cast.

To understand the importance of this gesture, it is important to recall that the notion of “modernity” was an important theme in intellectual debates of the day. The theme of postmodernity had begun to gain currency in France after the success of Jean-François Lyotard’s book *The Postmodern Condition* [*La Condition postmoderne*], published in 1979.[14] The central idea of postmodern discourse for which the future seemed bright was that all the “metanarratives”—and, notably, the great modern narrative of progress—were now superseded. Although more or less associated with this postmodern current despite not recognizing himself in it, Foucault made several attempts to distance himself from this label, which struck him as reductive.[15] He was thus intent on dissociating modernity from the grand progressive narrative, whether it be that of socio-economic modernization or the progress of rights.

The second piece of historical context to keep in mind is Habermas’s offensive in favor of modernity’s values and notably the Enlightenment project.[16] Habermas’s claim constituted a rupture within the Frankfurt school tradition, since he was clearly distancing his position from the thesis of Adorno and Horkheimer’s *Dialectic of Enlightenment* (1947; 1972 for the English translation). Habermas was also conducting an argued attack against several French thinkers influenced by Nietzsche, notably Bataille, Derrida, and Foucault. In a lecture delivered in Frankfurt in 1980 and published in French in the journal *Critique* in 1981, Habermas vigorously denounced what he called the current of “young conservatives” who relied on the aesthetic experience of modernity to “found a merciless antimodernism” hostile to the Enlightenment. He developed all these themes in *The Philosophical Discourse of Modernity* (1985 in German; 1987 in English), a set of “twelve lectures” adapted from talks presented at the Collège de France in March 1983, during which he met Foucault. Two critical chapters of the book are devoted to Foucault.[17]

It is often said that the debate was completely one-sided since Foucault never explicitly responded; however, one can read the 1984

English "What Is Enlightenment?" essay as a reply to Habermas, who is mentioned by name in an early paragraph.[18] The very act of firmly placing himself in descendance from Kant and the *Aufklärung* essay can be interpreted as an ironic riposte on his German interlocutor's home turf. Moreover, Foucault insists at length on the Kantian conception of a public/private distinction, which Habermas discussed at length in his most famous book, *The Structural Transformation of the Public Sphere* (1989) [*Strukturwandel der Öffentlichkeit*, 1962], which was published in French some years earlier, in 1978. Finally, if one examines closely the evolution of Foucault's two Enlightenment texts, one notices that the entire section devoted to Baudelaire and the aesthetic definition of modernity was added to the longer 1984 version and is completely absent from the shorter French text published the year before. The presence of Baudelaire has often sparked curiosity among commentators of the essay, since it is difficult to characterize the author of *The Flowers of Evil* as a direct inheritor of the Enlightenment.[19] The reason behind Foucault's use of Baudelaire becomes clearer if one knows that Habermas had used the example of Baudelaire in his 1983 Collège de France lecture, in which the French poet and critic is posited as the archetype of aesthetic modernity, marking a rupture with tradition and a wish to give to creation its own norms. In his 1981 essay, Habermas had already used Baudelaire as a starting point to distinguish the aesthetic experience of modernity from the true modern project, derived from the Enlightenment, of developing simultaneously the sciences, the arts, rights, and morals in order to effect a rational transformation of the conditions of existence. Foucault therefore articulates his reply on this terrain by proposing an alternative reading of Baudelaire's modernity with the aim of displacing the question of modernity in general. While Habermas sees in modernity a deepening of the subject's autonomy and an extension of Enlightenment rationalism, Foucault insists instead on modernity's relation to time and on its ambivalent, critical attitude toward the present.

One can see a clear distinction between these two approaches to modernity. For Habermas, modernity is an "unfinished project," a promise for the rationalization of human relations that ought to be completed, an effort that ought to be pursued. For Foucault, the modern relation to the present takes the form of a critique. Not a transcendental critique of the conditions of knowledge, but a historical critique of the contingent forms that define our present: "But if the Kantian question was that of knowing what limits knowledge has to renounce transgressing, it seems to me that the critical question today has to be turned back into a positive one: in what is given to us as universal, necessary, obligatory, what place is occupied by whatever is singular, contingent, and the product of arbitrary constraints? The point in brief is to transform the critique conducted in the form of necessary limitation into a practical critique that takes the form of a possible transgression [*franchissement*]."[20] It is clear that Foucault departs from Kant's text by displacing critique from an epistemological plane to a historical one. The critical exercise implies conducting "a series of historical investigations as precisely as possible" to understand ourselves as "beings who are historically determined." Almost without knowing it, this deliberate displacement joins up with another aspect of the Enlightenment, namely the project carried out by Voltaire, Robertson, and many others that aimed to grasp through historical investigations the possibilities for transformation in the present. Of course, the overlap is not total since Foucault's work stood apart from the progressivist schema that undergirds the idea of civilization. Nevertheless, a link subsists, which is the mark of modernity, between historical knowledge and critical reflexivity.

Subjectivity and Technologies of the Self

The controversy with Habermas over modernity is therefore one item that is at stake in Foucault's late examination of the Enlightenment, but there are others. The redefinition of modernity only makes sense within the framework of projects Foucault was carrying out on the cultivation of the self and the aesthetics of existence. As is generally known, his thinking underwent profound changes at the end of the 1970s. The most visible sign is the complete reconception of the *History of Sexuality* between the first volume, published in 1976, and the two following volumes, which appeared in 1984.

The essential feature in this reorientation is the attention Foucault brings to the question of subjectivity. The goal is not a return to the "subject" in the sense of a philosophy of consciousness, or as a legal subject, but instead a reflection on the way individuals construct their own subjectivity, their "relation to self," through an ensemble of practices that Foucault called "technologies of the self"—practices that concern, notably though not exclusively, one's relationship to one's body and to sexuality. After years devoted to the discursive series and the microphysics of power, Foucault set out to explore a new object and a new method: the hermeneutics of the self. He was thus led toward a complete reformulation of the links between the subject, truth, and power.

This major change in Foucault's thinking probably had biographical roots—including the favorable acceptance of homosexuality, the American experience, and the role of drugs—all of which modify the relationship to the body and the practice of pleasures. It also corresponds to an internal logic within his oeuvre, if one considers that the theory of power had more or less run its course. Foucault then sought to reintroduce forms of resistance by subjects to the powers imposed on them. The goal is not a freedom that precedes the state, as in the classical liberal tradition, but rather about counter-behaviors inscribed within forms of governmentalism. He sought to think of something that would be on the order of an affirmation of will: "the trenchant desire ["*volonté décisoire*"] to not be so governed."[21] In this way, he progressively arrived at the affirmation of an ethical subjectivity, a subject who constitutes itself by work on itself [*par un travail sur soi*] alongside a movement toward truth and freedom.

The theoretical crisis emerged during work on avowal that was supposed to constitute an essential part of the history of sexuality. Foucault gradually turned away from the thesis of a political production of subjectivity and toward the idea of an auto-affirmation of subjectivity as liberating possibility. As he did so, his temporal focus went back in time. Whereas originally the project was centered on avowal in the modern era, Foucault turned his attention to ancient philosophy at the risk of idealizing Greco-Roman antiquity as free autoproduction of subjectivity through technologies of the self.[22]

It is also from this perspective, beyond the polemical usage directed against Habermas, that one ought to understand the important place accorded to Baudelaire in the fuller version of the essay on enlightenment. As we saw, Baudelaire allowed Foucault to pass subtly from the Enlightenment to modernity, from Kantian optimism toward a more ambivalent attitude, one in which the heroization of the present will occur alongside a rejection of progress. But what also stimulates Foucault's interest in Baudelaire is that he was not a philosopher. Baudelaire's relationship to modernity was not situated on a theoretical or conceptual plane but on an aesthetic and above all existential level. The Baudelairean artists—in other words, the poet himself and the painters of modern life Baudelaire admired—experimented with a new type of aesthetic relation to the self, one that consisted in making one's life a work of art. It is there that the theme of the dandy and the poet meet, each maintaining a preeminently subjective and aesthetic relationship to one's existence. And it is this relation, this capacity to construct oneself as subject through art, thinking, or poetry, that allowed them to diagnose their time. The Baudelairean artist incarnates par excellence modern autonomy, which is not a political or moral autonomy but rather a creative capacity to work on oneself. "Modernity does not 'liberate man in his own being'" Foucault argues; "it compels him to face the task of producing himself."[23] And this elaboration requires a relationship to truth.[24]

The link between technologies of the self and truth is a theme that comes up often in texts from the early 1980s. Whereas earlier, for example in *The Order of Things* (1971), Foucault would denounce the *volonté de verité* [will to truth] as a form of domination exercise, true discourse is now marked very positively.[25] And yet Foucault is not rehabilitating a realist conception of truth, and so his reversal of values here is somewhat puzzling.[26] He seems instead to be seeking to unite ethics and truth—the latter being positive insofar as it is the aim of work on oneself. This truth implies a personal courage, that of a subject willing to change themselves to accede to truth. One may even recognize here a sympathetic call for a form of spirituality that surfaces in Foucault's thinking starting in 1982, one that would require a new relationship to truth and to politics.[27] In a 1983 interview, one finds him using rather unexpected language to make the following declaration: "I know that knowledge can transform us, that truth is not only a way of deciphering the world (and maybe what we call truth doesn't decipher anything), but that if I know the truth, I will be changed. And perhaps saved."[28] Despite the presence of this surprising language of salvation, the essential idea developed by Foucault in this text is the proximity of his intellectual work and aesthetic experience. The knowledge he produces does not have as its primary goal any inscription within a cumulative university framework nor the transformation of the world—indeed one hears echoes of a disillusionment with intellectual and political activism—rather, the goal is to transform himself.[29]

The detour through Baudelairean modernity thus opens some distance with respect to the rationalist heritage of the Enlightenment. The diagnosis that the philosopher makes about the present, as Foucault understands it, is not strictly an intellectual act; it is not a theoretical demonstration but rather a gesture through writing, an intervention within the space of discourse founded both on objective knowledge and an openly owned subjectivity. He advocates for a proximity with aesthetic experience, with the gesture of the painter or poet. And this diagnosis, in turn, transforms its author.[30]

Foucault had been fascinated by writers for a long time. In the 1960s, he often wrote about literature—not only the literature of objectification, such as the "new novel" of Robbe-Grillet, which he admired, but especially the literature of high *subjectivation*, such as one finds in Roussel, Sade, Bataille, or Rousseau. Then, starting in the early 1970s, he stopped writing on literature—at the precise time when he was himself developing a very personal type of writing, the writing of an artist, as is very clear in *Les Mots et les Choses* and *Surveiller et Punir*.[31]

In an interview from 1968 that was published a few years ago under the title *Le Beau Danger*, Foucault was already articulating most of these themes with a freedom of tone and frank autoanalysis that he would almost never allow himself later. He spoke at length about writing as a discipline and a technology of the self, of the effort involved in writing, which he saw as both a way to approach the truth and an existential necessity, almost a spiritual exercise. He insisted above all on the act of diagnosis, evoking his father, who was a surgeon. The surgeon is someone who carries out a diagnosis of the patient and then performs surgery. In his own case, writes Foucault, "I transformed the scalpel into a pen [*porte-plume*]." His intellectual activity would therefore be a version of the surgical act via the act of writing. "I am a physician, a diagnostician," he continues. "I want to make a diagnosis and my work consists in bringing to light by the very incision of writing something that is the truth of what is dead. . . . I think that the alternative to death isn't life but truth."[32] In writing about the past, Foucault does not seek to make it live again but to tell the truth about it in order to better understand the present. It is therefore through writing that the diagnosis gets revealed.

The unavoidable reference at that time is of course Nietzsche, the diagnostician and therapist of culture's maladies. In a famous text from 1971, Foucault placed his entire genealogical enterprise under the tutelage of Nietzsche.[33] Fifteen years later it was Kant who became the origin figure for philosophical writing as a diagnostic act. Foucault's choice was a paradoxical one, as several commentators noted at the time, because Kant is in fact not that concerned, including in the 1784 text, with the task of thinking the present.[34] But it is an understandable choice if one recalls Foucault's determination to not allow himself to be boxed into an antimodern position and his wish to "escape from Hegel."[35] The relation to the present invoked by Foucault is not the production of a total knowledge ordered by the times and founded on a philosophy of history and the speech of an outside observer, but instead a critical gesture which by associating a genealogical investigation with a openly owned subjectivity conceives of the production of knowledge as an act of risk taking, or as he put it, "a beautiful danger."[36]

If we link this theme of diagnosis to the question of the Enlightenment heritage, it can be said that Michel Foucault strove to respond to a reproachful question that he often received, from both historians and philosophers, about the normative foundations of his critical enterprise: From where, from what normative position, and based on what theories of justice does Foucault conduct his critical work?[37] Foucault's answer refuses the idea of superior transcendental norms in the name of which the critique would be conducted, and affirms instead the necessity of a historical diagnosis founded on investigations that reveal what our own present has that is singular, contingent, and arbitrary. The critique must be local and immanent, he claimed, and it must be wary of all untimely generalizations. Its role is to reunite with the Kantian tradition while also going from a critique of "necessary limits" to that of "possible transgression or crossing-over [*franchissement*]." In this way the critique "will separate out from the contingency that has made us what we are, the possibility of no longer being, doing, or thinking what we are, do, or think."[38] The diagnostic is not a simple intellectual activity. It must permit healing; it must open onto action and change. It is the moment when, in the present, an individual can act in and on history. This affirmation of a subject's freedom, of a subject capable of intervening in history, may seem very far from the anonymous history of discursive and political determinations that were for a long time considered the trademark of Foucault's work. And yet it is the center of his ethical reflection on *subjectivation*, which was also a political reflection on history.[39]

The Engaged Intellectual

We can now glimpse a third thread in what is at stake in the weave of this return to the Enlightenment heritage; namely the question of the philosopher as an intellectual capable of intervening in the public sphere. If the legacy of the *Aufklärung* is, among other things, a philosophical practice that allows one to carry out diagnoses of the present moment, for many it also relates to the classic conception of the *philosophe*, in the eighteenth-century sense, as a leader who fights against injustice. This figure was reactivated and refashioned at the time of the Dreyfus Affair. Later, for Foucault's generation, the figure of the public intellectual was incarnated by Sartre with all his excesses. Foucault always kept his distance, rejecting all pretense to be speaking in the name of a universal and preferring instead to defend in the 1970s the notion of the "specific intellectual" devoted to making known local and dominated types of knowledge.[40] But in the early 1980s, the question of the intellectual's engagement and commitment returned with a new insistence.

Foucault was politically active in the 1970s, notably as part of the "Groupe d'information sur les prisons" [Prisons Information Group]. His involvement, often alongside Far Left activists, was sometimes strongly criticized. However, it was his articles in *Corriere della Sera* in 1979 on the subject of the Islamic Revolution in Iran that provoked the most vehement disputes. Foucault was confronted with the question of the source of his legitimacy for making a diagnosis of that revolutionary movement, whose outcome was uncertain to say the least.[41] He justified his actions in an article in *Le Monde* in which he reaffirmed his status as an intellectual who is "respectful when a singularity arises and intransigent when the ruling power violates the universal."[42] The 1984 text on the Enlightenment alludes to these matters when Foucault evokes Kant's reaction to the French Revolution and "the moral enthusiasm" that revolution elicited despite its violence and even despite the Reign of Terror.[43]

The beginning of the 1980s marked a realignment of Foucault's political positions in the sense that criticism of Marxist totalitarianism was intensifying, a shift that in effect moved him closer to more moderate authors and away from his militant friends.[44] Also, the political context was changing: in France, the Left took power in 1981 with the election of François Mitterrand as president in May and a left-leaning parliamentary majority in June[45]. The debate that stirred up French intellectuals and that Foucault was regularly summoned to address was the question of the relationship that intellectuals could and should have with the new socialist governing power. For his part, less than six months later, in the fall of 1981, Foucault was denouncing the French government's complacency regarding the coup d'état in Poland. In editorials in print media and on the radio, Foucault donned the traditional role of the intellectual who speaks out with political indignation and in the name of universal values on a topic about which he possesses no particular expertise. Also, at the beginning of Foucault's 1984 text devoted to Kant and the Enlightenment—in which he recalls that the text had first appeared in a magazine and that it was a form of philosophical journalism—Foucault likely had in mind his earlier articles on Iran and his more recent interventions in the press about events in Poland. What, then, is the role of the philosopher when he writes articles in the press and not philosophy books? Foucault insists on underscoring that Kant's critical project was not only a theoretical enterprise but also a practical project addressing a larger public than readers of philosophy.

But how does one address this larger public? With what ambitions and with what results? Foucault rediscovers here the Enlightenment's big question—which, as we saw, was not just Kant's but also Diderot's and Condorcet's: What is emancipatory speech? Certainly it is not the words of an outside observer clad in all the authority of knowledge; rather, it is words that would be capable of acting on others by helping them to be freer. How can a philosopher enlighten those who are not yet enlightened? Foucault always sought to dodge this question. He always considered that the role of the intellectual could not be that of a master thinker capable of pushing others to act.

After 1980, Foucault returned to the question of a kind of truth-speaking that would transform both speaker and receiver. This question is the theme of the last two courses Foucault gave at the Collège de France in 1983 and 1984 on government of the self and of others. And one should not forget that, as the introduction to these courses, Foucault presented his analysis of Kant and *Aufklärung* as a diagnosis of the present day. This "excursus," as he called it, may seem surprising since the course lectures over the next two years were entirely devoted to ancient philosophy and the concept of *parrêsia*, which names a type of free speech and a desire to say everything, no matter the risks to the speaker. While Foucault had first conceived of *parrêsia* within an intersubjective framework—that of a directed consciousness or of a philosopher confronting a prince—he gradually enlarged the notion in the 1984 course to include the extreme case of cynical *parrêsia*. The latter, notably in the figure of Diogenes, a fourth-century BCE "cynic" in the philosophical sense of the term, names the will to align one's life with one's beliefs, to make one's own life into a philosophical model, a "scandal of the truth," as Foucault would say.[46] *Parrêsia*, whether it be a discourse that takes the risk of telling the truth or an exemplary way of living, aims always to act on others, doggedly pushing them to question themselves and to break with their customary habits. In other words, it is the practice that best articulates the government of the self and of others, the technologies that allow the construction of oneself as subject, and the taking up of speech [*prise de parole*] addressed to an interlocutor. Cut short by death, Foucault was not able to complete this work on *parrêsia* and its modern reformulations. But by placing praise for the Enlightenment at the beginning of this course, he clearly announced his intention to reunite with the question of a speech that helps others to become more autonomous. The *Aufklärung*, in his eyes, was the modern philosophical form of *parrêsia*.[47] The horizon of his thinking was thus the question of the emancipatory potential of a discourse of truth profoundly incarnated, but he was also concerned with that discourse's limits and dangers, as one witnesses in the figure of the cynic whose "philosophical militancy" has a detachment and derision that can flip into "overt, universal, aggressive militancy."[48]

Thus, the return to the Enlightenment takes the form of a pragmatic approach to truth and intellectual engagement. Whereas in the 1970s Foucault had constantly denounced "the will to truth" as a dogmatic form of power, including in its expression in the practice of modern science, he now accepts the will to hold forth a discourse of truth—and is willing to own the name "intellectual"—on the condition that the term designate a capacity to circulate knowledge outside university settings so that it can act on oneself and on others: "This work at modifying one's own thinking and that of others strikes me as the intellectual's reason for being."[49]

But such efforts were not without their dangers. By reuniting with a certain figure of the intellectual, Foucault ran the risk of reviving a form of moral heroism. It was probably the specter of such questionable heroism that the less directly political figure of Baudelaire was meant to conjure in the 1984 text. The heroism of everyday life would be an "ironic heroization." But there remained the question of the source of authority. What is the legitimacy of the philosopher's speaking up [*la prise de parole du philosophe*]? Foucault takes care to not reactivate the Hegelian idea of philosophy's privileged relation to truth that would found an absolute knowledge. And yet he is just as wary of the sort of scholar's authority demanded by Althusser for philosophy or Bourdieu for sociology—an authority that would be based on an epistemological break. "Do not use thought to give a political action the imprimatur of truth [*une valeur de verité*]," he liked to say. And he refused to base his activist commitments on knowledge, stating that they were based above all on his "subjectivity" and on a capacity for personal indignation: "When it's unbearable, we no longer bear it [*on ne supporte plus*]."[50]

The authority of a discourse of truth can reside neither in a scientific corpus nor in some presumed absolute knowledge. It is therefore based on "courage"—the courage to construct oneself as an autonomous individual, the courage to hold a discourse of truth even at the risk of destroying one's relationships with others. Courage is precisely at the heart of the motto that defines *Aufklärung—Sapere aude*, dare to know, have the courage to think. Foucault then comments on this courage: "The Enlightenment must be considered both as a process in which men participate collectively and as an act of courage to be accomplished personally."[51] "The Courage of Truth," moreover, will be the title of his last course; and these words must be understood in their double sense: not only as signaling the intellectual heroism of the person who risks their life in formulating a dangerous truth, but also as naming the courage to seek the truth and to accept transforming oneself. This courage does not only concern the act of speaking. It concerns above all the cultivation of self, the process of constructing a subjectivity—without which no diagnosis of the present moment is possible. Commenting on Baudelaire, Foucault had insisted as much: "To be modern is not to accept oneself as one is in the flux of the passing moments; it is to take oneself as object of a complex and difficult elaboration." The modern attitude implies "an indispensable asceticism."[52] This demanding construction of self, whether grasped as intellectual courage or aesthetic asceticism, maintains at the heart of modernity a "quasi-aristocratic" dimension built on a foundation of egalitarian exigency.[53]

In his rereading of *Aufklärung*, Foucault rediscovered one of the essential questions of Enlightenment thinkers—namely the courage required to practice a language of truth once it is directed at enlightening others and changing them. The death of Socrates—which so fascinated Enlightenment philosophers, Diderot most of all—receives considerable attention in *Le Courage de la vérité* as a major episode in the history of *parrêsia*.[54] However, Foucault adds a facet to this question that was absent from all except Rousseau, namely the necessity of self-transformation as both a cause and consequence of a discourse of truth. In this vein, he took the risk of encouraging an individualist and aestheticizing position closer to Baudelaire's dandyism than to Kant's *Aufklärer*.

In this pragmatic approach to truth—an approach that is the foundation of the intellectual's role—one question remains unaccounted for; namely the conditions to guarantee the effectiveness of a true discourse in public space. How does one make sure that the diagnosis of the present day is received and produces the desired effects? Concentrated as he was on the articulation of the courage of truth and the technologies of the self, Foucault paid little attention to the question of the receiver. Yet a key feature of modernity, on the sociological level this time, is that the philosopher is no longer addressing a tyrant (as Plato did) or Alexander (as was the case for Diogenes) but instead a public of readers of books, newspapers, and magazines. Thus, as he is defending the Enlightenment legacy within his own rethinking of the courage of truth, Foucault halts before formulating one of the important questions for Enlightenment writers; namely the conditions of communication in the public media space, especially the conditions for the possibility of a cynical posture in a world shot through with so many mediations.[55] And yet Foucault had good reasons to be sensitive to this question, starting with his own celebrity status as an intellectual and the attendant constraints that he had come to know well.[56] These matters may very well have contributed to his long-distance debate with Jürgen Habermas. However, he never addressed the question head on, and as a result he seems to have had difficulty understanding Kant's appeal to Frederick II, in other words to a regulating authority who acts as guarantor of the political order without which the freedom of public debate is meaningless.[57] In the end, the result he arrives at remains very different from that of the Enlightenment philosophers. Diderot, as we saw, hesitated constantly between

Socratic heroism and dissolution within a collective. Foucault, for his part, looked for touchstones that could aid in the construction of a singularity that would be both philosophical and artistic.

This blind spot has another consequence. Because at bottom Foucault had little interest in the receivers of his discourse, he did not really seek to define the community (political, intellectual, moral) he belonged to and that he was addressing. Yet if the Enlightenment is both a personal and collective process, what form does or ought that collective take? In Foucault's text on *Aufklärung*, the pronoun *nous* [we, us] occurs often: the modern attitude implies an "ontology of ourselves [*nous-même*]"; "a permanent critique of ourselves [*nous-même*]" and so forth. But who is this *nous*? The text does not say and seems to only define *nous* implicitly, in terms of a contemporaneity in relation to the present. However, the sociological or cultural limits of this *nous* are not evoked, even though they were important for Baudelaire and more broadly for the entire tradition, from Montesquieu to Durkheimian sociology, which was concerned with the question of manners [*mœurs*].[58] That tradition remained forever foreign to Michel Foucault. In similar fashion, it was often remarked that he seemed indifferent to the set of questions raised by postcolonialism. At no moment does he pause to wonder if the diagnosis of the present carried out by the philosopher is valid across all societies or for all communities within the same society. The question of collective identities, whether social or cultural, is evaded. The courage of truth as a hermeneutics of the self encompasses individual enterprises, but these enterprises only marginally extend to a political community.

The last text Foucault worked on before his death was an article that he had promised to write in honor of Georges Canguilhem for a special issue of the *Revue de métaphysique et de morale*. Being seriously ill and pressed for time, he had to make do with returning to the preface he had written in 1978 and rewriting certain passages. A comparison of the two versions reveals, among various changes, a small but significant modification to a passage about the current relevance of the Enlightenment. Six years earlier, Foucault had written, "Two centuries later, *Aufklärung* is back: not as a way for the West to become conscious of its present possibilities and the freedoms it could have access to, but as a way for asking about the limits and the powers it abused. Reason as a despotic light." In 1984, this passage becomes, "Two centuries later, *Aufklärung* is back: both as a way for the West to become conscious of its present possibilities and the freedoms it could have access to, and as a way for asking about the limits and the powers it used. Reason both as despotism and as light."[59]

The change may seem minor but in fact it is crucial: light/enlightenment is no longer described as despotic; it is placed in opposition to despotism. The *Aufklärung* did not abuse powers, it used them. Reason is no longer condemned, it becomes ambivalent: it can lead to the worst, to despotism, or to the best, to light. There is no better testimony to the evolution of Foucault's thinking and his changed relationship to the Enlightenment tradition than this search for a position of equilibrium at the very moment when "Enlightenment blackmail" [*chantage aux Lumières*] seemed to be gaining new strength.

After the radicalism of the 1970s, the Enlightenment did indeed make a comeback in intellectual circles in the 1980s. This return was associated with a revival of a current of liberal thought attached to human rights and a critique of the abuses of May '68 thinking. In this context, it is striking to see that one of the most emblematic figures of 1970s philosophical radicalism, a man who seemed to have little in common with the Enlightenment heritage and its universalist optimism, was a promoter of this return of Enlightenment thinkers.

There are two possible interpretations of these changes. One can insist on the malleable character of the Enlightenment heritage and underscore that this heritage is above all an instrument of legitimation in the intellectual sphere. Thus, one can make the heritage say what one wants, bending it this way or that way.[60] Indeed, one can admire the philosophical dexterity of Foucault, his capacity to place his own philosophical evolution under the banner of *Aufklärung*, when he might just as well have presented that evolution as a critique of rationality and the myth of progress. Nevertheless, I consider a second interpretation to be more accurate. No modern thinker can elude for long the question of the Enlightenment and its leading figures. Considered in their diversity or collectively, they are the source of all aspirations for emancipation, whether in the form of universalist progressivism and rationalism or by way of a more romantic subjectivism. No stance of social or political critique can for long elude their influence or escape a confrontation with the heritage they represent. Moreover, the intellectual work that consists in coming to grips with that heritage, reformulating it, adapting it, placing it before the demands of the present day—this work is no mere rhetorical exercise, it is what keeps that heritage alive and recharges its political effectiveness. Foucault's intervention is the best example of such work. In turn, his work elicited many commentaries, along the way raising interest in Kant's text, which up until then had often been considered of minor importance. In many ways, Foucault made extreme use of the 1784 text, pulling it in an excessively historicist direction. To do so, he had to add Baudelaire's aesthetic theory to make the whole into a starting point of the "attitude of modernity." But in doing so he gave it a new theoretical currency—by associating the courage of truth, which is one of the major stakes of the text, with the diagnosis of the present day as a modern form of critique.

The Enlightenment—"Les Lumières"—is not a doctrine that was set in stone for all time in the eighteenth century but is instead a legacy that must be constantly reformulated, redefined, and brought up to date. Foucault said as much himself in 1980 in his reply to Maurice Agulhon: "For nearly two centuries now, Europe has maintained an extremely rich and complex relationship to this event called *Aufklärung* that Kant and Mendelssohn were already carefully examining in 1784. This relationship has undergone constant transformation but has never disappeared. *Aufklärung* is, to use Canguilhem's expression, our most 'present past.'"[61] Foucault also proposed initiating a historical-philosophical investigation into "the way *Aufklärung* was perceived, thought, lived, imagined, ejected, anathemized, or reactivated in Europe in the nineteenth and twentieth centuries."[62] The history of the Enlightenment is not the history of a legacy that imposes itself on us in some self-evident way. It is the history of a long transmission made of reinterpretations, contradictions, and redefinitions. Studying these historical mediations is the precondition for the present capacity of the Enlightenment to be something other than the name of an ideology.

CONCLUSION

Problematizing Modernity

What should be done with the Enlightenment legacy today? One temptation—which historians have not always resisted and which gets broadly expressed in public debates—is to brandish it like a flag or trophy. With all rough edges and contradictions carefully airbrushed away, the Enlightenment can be reduced to a few simple ideas: the power of reason, freedom of speech, tolerance, optimism about progress, the prestige of science, and cosmopolitan humanism. In short, it serves as a sort of modern credo, the foundation of liberal progressivism that is to be defended against its adversaries: religious fanatics, reactionaries of every stripe, obtuse nationalists.

This attitude is not necessarily without its virtues on a political level, when the goal is to promote tolerance over fanaticism or the power of persuasive argument over fascination with brute force. On an intellectual level, however, this reductive, sanitizing, edifying vision of the Enlightenment is of little use. It only serves to confirm the convictions of those already convinced and offers them a feeling of moral superiority sealed by arguments backed up by illustrious authorities—crushing the infamous as a never-ending battle. But the same Voltaire who originated that battle cry mixed into his combative ardor a skeptical irony that did not spare his own self-assurance, though similar circumspection is often lacking among his vehement inheritors. For two centuries, Enlightenment figures have been enlisted to serve in colonial or neocolonial enterprises that seek to impose, by force, the values of first European civilization and then Western civilization, in the name of universal reason, progress, and the rights of man. Within Europe, the prestige of science and reason has sometimes served to silence all protest in the name of a Manichean combat between knowledge and obscurantism. In France, republican universalism's denial of cultural identities has contributed to rendering invisible or inaudible real situations of discrimination. Today, it is difficult to act as if none of this were true and sweep these objections under the carpet. Let us acknowledge that despite all their emancipatory ambitions, Enlightenment thinkers sometimes helped legitimate forms of domination and exclusion. This acknowledgment does not overturn the Enlightenment's underlying values or its successes, but it does entail, at the very least, a more modest and self-aware attitude going forward.

The role of historians should not be to monumentalize Enlightenment figures, but to give them their present-day critique. The point is not to separate the wheat from the chaff, what's to be kept from what would be dated and discardable. The goal should be to demonstrate the complexity of that moment of thinking, restitute the controversies and debates, and insist on the tensions and ambivalences. Whatever the question is—the virtues of commerce, the dangers of religion, the benefits of publicness—one rarely finds two authors who share the same opinion. Most of them, as we saw, hesitate, change their minds, and let the reader decide. It's no accident that the dialogue was one of the favorite genres of Enlightenment philosophers and that recourse to fiction and irony was a frequent and fruitful occurrence. Bringing a pluralist sensibility to the Enlightenment and being mindful of doubts, debates, and even contradictions does not imply dissolving the notion in an open diversity of eighteenth-century texts. The point is not to pose as the gloomy historian, indifferent to the issues of the present, eager to complicate the past to great lengths until it becomes unrecognizable and, consequently, unavailable. On the contrary. I am convinced that the current relevance of Enlightenment figures, their contemporary critical potential, resides precisely in this pluralism. The mistake is to think that one must reduce the Enlightenment to a simple intellectual formula that can serve as infallible guide. Such an idea is doomed to failure because the Enlightenment figures had no doctrinal unity. Theirs was a pluralist scene of many debates and questions raised by the upheaval of traditional societies. The service of Enlightenment authors was not to justify modernity but to problematize it.

We know today that liberal modernity is fraught with ambivalences. Its undeniable contributions were accompanied by less positive aspects that were not always exactly foreseen but that were often felt as possibilities. The globalization of commerce did not always bring "peace through trade." It was also the origin of colonialism, of the destruction of ancient societies and cultures, and of trade inequality between the Global North and Global South. The industrial revolution and the rise of mass-consumption societies made possible the fulfillment of many material needs and the massive improvement of living conditions, but they also provoked new inequalities and encouraged the general transformation of human relations into commodities and transactions. Also, the guarantee of a constantly increasing number of individual rights can lead to the fragmentation of a society. Finally, if the development of media favored the implementation of a democratic public space, it also brought with it new forms of surveillance, propaganda, and attention capture. On none of these points, however, did Enlightenment authors defend a single uniform position. Within the same texts, such as *The Philosophical History of the Two Indies*, arguments favoring colonial trade precede or follow pages of vehement anticolonial declarations. The *Encyclopédie* is no less polyphonic. Individually authored texts also make room for doubt, uncertainty, and tough questions. Far from being the founders of a coherent ideology that would have transformed the world, the Enlightenment philosophers were observers—sometimes optimistic, sometimes pessimistic—of the many changes underway within the societies of their time. Confronted with the premises of modernity, eighteenth-century authors debated them, trying to give them a meaning [*sens*], anticipate evolutions, and prepare for the consequences. Though inclined to consider favorably changes that would reduce prejudices and root out superstitions, they were nevertheless conscious of the dangers of modernity and scrutinized nervously its excesses and even the vices in its foundation. Thus, authors such as Rousseau and Herder, who developed an autocritique of *les Lumières* and *Aufklärung* that was at times radical, are no less than full members of the Enlightenment for doing so—quite the opposite. Moreover, their questionings can be found in more moderate forms among many other Enlightenment authors, from Diderot to the Scottish historians.

In this book I have insisted on several of these ambivalences, in particular the problematic coordination of a universalist project with high confidence in European superiority. I also showed the importance of debates raised by economic modernity and by the new effects of publicness. The remaining essential question that traverses Enlightenment authors relates to their emancipatory ambitions. How should the power of reason be used to improve the conditions of human life and assure collective and individual happiness? A first response considers that knowledge founded on rational principles must determine modes of existence and the organization of societies. The objective is to identify those principles, produce knowledge, and then implement reformist policies. There is a great temptation, in that case, to rely on a powerful government capable of imposing such reforms. One must win over political elites to the Enlightenment ideas, for those elites will be in charge of translating theories into practices. The art of persuasion is what philosophers and economists practiced in France. That's why they were so enthusiastic when Turgot took power. But both popular resistances and those of conservative elites carried the day, leaving the philosophers to dream of becoming counsellors to a powerful and enlightened prince. Thus one can understand their admiration, mixed with second thoughts and ambiguities, for autocrats such as Frederick II and Catherine II. This reformist vein of Enlightenment thinking predicated on the close association of philosophers and the ruling power has had a long posterity. Traces of it can be seen today in the power wielded by technocrats and experts.

A second conception of emancipation through knowledge insists more on the powers of critique. As a historic process, the Enlightenment implies that each individual must learn to reason and judge for themselves and become responsible for their choices and decisions, without resorting to traditional authorities. This conception, which was given a canonical formulation by Kant but is not limited to *Aufklärung*, runs into several difficulties related to the organization of public space and the specific authority that philosophers must exert. How does one enlighten those who are not yet enlightened? Even if intellectual emancipation is an individual endeavor that derives from the free exercise of one's reason, it is only possible within a collective framework that is necessarily social. These two conceptions of the Enlightenment combat—the one operating through reform, the other through critique—do not correspond to two distinct camps, but to two foci of an ellipse, as it were. From Voltaire to Diderot and Condorcet, we have seen that Enlightenment authors navigated endlessly between these two tempting conceptions.

The Enlightenment dilemma that we highlighted through the notion of emancipation was, for the philosophers, the problem of the "propagation of lights," the diffusion of useful knowledge and critical autonomy, or, in the words of Diderot, "the extension of the sphere of lights." Enlightenment thinkers also encountered it on the scale of European societies, when it came to articulating freedom of speech and the regulation of sensible public space; they encountered it on the global level as well, because the acute consciousness of a world that had become interdependent, one in which "everything regards us," forced them to think through the conditions that would allow civilization to spread to the rest of the world. Here too, as we saw, they vacillated between the virtues of imitation and the possibilities of a more immediate emancipation. These hesitations took forms that were the most apt for dissimulating the aporias: historical narration, fiction, dialogue.

The Enlightenment is less a project than a complex dramaturgy involving individual aspiration and collective progress that collide with the resistance of prejudices, the public's indifference, and the persistence of evil. This drama gets endlessly replayed, criticized, adapted, glorified—we know this all too well, we cannot escape it, and we return to it for reassurance. We must always remain vigilant that it not be transformed into a cudgeling argument of authority or a tool of exclusion. What's in play, what ought to be in play, is not the easy reassurance of an already-constituted "we" that's well established and sure of its rights—"we moderns," "we Westerners"—but instead a "we" demanding the chance to constitute itself in the very dynamic of confrontation with a legacy and a heritage free of preordained rights that are more equivocal than they appear. Here as elsewhere, the work of the historian is a permanent endeavor of critical rereading. The historian's goal is not to impose this or that interpretation or denounce or defend the Enlightenment; it is instead to restitute the Enlightenment's power to call out and question, that singular mixture of skepticism and optimism, combativity and gaiety, irony and enthusiasm. It's necessary to leave behind all edifying legends and lazy caricatures and reopen spaces for new appropriations and interpretations. If the Enlightenment is both a legacy and a heritage, it's vital that it be neither confiscated nor travestied but instead handed over to collective intelligence and critical imagination.

NOTES

INTRODUCTION

1. Translator's note: The caricaturist Jean Maurice Jules Cabut, known as Cabu, was another of the *Charlie Hebdo* journalists killed on January 7, 2015.

2. Laurent Joffrin, "Un élan magnifique," *Libération*, January 11, 2015; Mohammed Aïssaoui, "Voltaire, je crie ton nom," *Le Figaro*, January 13, 2015. See also Christiane Taubira, "En France, on peut tout dessiner, y compris un prophète," *Dailymotion*, November 14, 2017, https://www.dailymotion.com/video/x2esfsv; Benoît Melançon, "Voltaire, Paris, 2015," in *Les Neveux de Voltaire: À André Magnan*, eds. Stéphanie Géhanne-Gavoty and Alain Sandrier (Ferney-Voltaire: Société Voltaire, 2016); Benoît Melançon, "Du Fanatisme," *L'Oreille Tendue* (blog), January 8, 2015, https://oreilletendue.com/2015/01/08/du-fanatisme/. The maxim attributed to Voltaire is believed to be the creation of his early twentieth-century English biographer Evelyne Beatrice Hall.

3. Cédric Pietralunga, Bastien Bonnefous, and Solenn de Royer, "Emmanuel Macron triomphe et doit réconcilier un pays divisé," *Le Monde*, May 8, 2017. A video of Macron's victory speech, in French, is linked online as part of Robin Korda, "Emmanuel Macron au Louvre: les cinq symboles d'une séquence historique," *Le Parisien*, May 8, 2017, https://www.leparisien.fr/elections/presidentielle/emmanuel-macron-au-louvre-les-cinq-symboles-d-une-sequence-historique-08-05-2017-6928899.php.

4. David Brooks, "The Enlightenment Project," *New York Times*, February 28, 2017.

5. Steven Pinker, *Enlightenment Now: The Case for Reason, Science, Humanism, and Progress* (New York: Penguin, 2018).

6. The movement to pluralize the Lumières was launched by Roy Porter and Mikulas Teich, eds., *The Enlightenment in National Context* (Cambridge: Cambridge University Press, 1981). See also, in the same vein, Charles Withers, *Placing the Enlightenment: Thinking Geographically about the Age of Reason* (Chicago: University of Chicago Press, 2008); Richard Butterwick, Simon Davies, and Gabriel Sánchez Espinosa, eds., *Peripheries of the Enlightenment* (Oxford: Voltaire Foundation, 2008); Jesús Astigarraga, ed., *The Spanish Enlightenment Revisited* (Oxford: Voltaire Foundation, 2015); Steffen Martus, *Aufklärung: Das deutsche 18: Jahrhundert: Ein Epochenbild* (Berlin: Rowohlt, 2015); Caroline Winterer, *American Enlightenments: Pursuing Happiness in the Age of Reason* (New Haven, CT: Yale University Press, 2016).

7. The most eloquent formulation of the argument that sees the Lumières as irreducibly plural was made by J. G. A. Pocock, *Barbarism and Religion*, vol. 1, *The Enlightenments of Edward Gibbon* (Cambridge: Cambridge University Press, 1999).

8. Mario Rosa, "Le contraddizioni della modernità: Apologetica cattolica e Lumi nel settecento," *Rivista di storia e letteratura religiosa* 44 (2008): 73–114; David Sorkin, *The Religious Enlightenment: Protestants, Jews, and Catholics from London to Vienna* (Princeton, NJ: Princeton University Press, 2011); Jonathan Sheehan, "Enlightenment, Religion, and the Enigma of Secularization: A Review Essay," *American Historical Review* 108, no. 4 (2003): 1061–80; Ulrich Lehner, *The Catholic Enlightenment: The Forgotten History of a Global Movement* (Oxford: Oxford University Press, 2016).

9. Jessica Riskin, *Science in the Age of Sensibility: The Sentimental Empiricists of the French Enlightenment* (Chicago: University of Chicago Press, 2002); Robert Darnton, *Mesmerism and the End of the Enlightenment in France* (Cambridge, MA: Harvard University Press, 1968); Dan Edelstein, ed., *The Super-Enlightenment: Daring to Know Too Much* (Oxford: Voltaire Foundation, 2010).

10. Charles Walton, *Policing Public Opinion in the French Revolution: The Culture of Calumny and the Problem of Free Speech* (New York: Oxford University Press, 2009); Edoardo Tortarolo, *L'Invenzione della libertà di stampa: Censura e scrittori nel Settecento* (Rome: Carocci, 2011).

11. Barbara Taylor and Sarah Knott, eds., *Women, Gender, and Enlightenment* (New York: Palgrave Macmillan, 2005); Silvia Sebastiani, *The Scottish Enlightenment: Race, Gender, and the Limits of Progress* (New York: Palgrave Macmillan, 2013); Florence Lotterie, *Le Genre des Lumières: Femme et philosophe au XVIIIe siècle* (Paris: Classiques Garnier, 2013).

12. Linda Colley, *Britons: Forging the Nation, 1707–1837* (New Haven, CT: Yale University Press, 1992); David A. Bell, *The Cult of the Nation in France: Inventing Nationalism, 1680–1800* (Cambridge, MA: Harvard University Press, 2009).

13. Bronisław Baczko, *Job, mon ami: Promesses du bonheur et fatalité du mal* (Paris: Gallimard, 1997).

14. Lynn Hunt, Margaret C. Jacob, and Wijnand Mijnhardt, *The Book That Changed Europe: Picart and Bernard's Religious Ceremonies of the World* (Cambridge, MA: Harvard University Press, 2010).

15. Carla Hesse, *The Other Enlightenment: How French Women Became Modern* (Princeton, NJ: Princeton University Press, 2001); Élisabeth Badinter, *Émilie, Émilie: L'ambition féminine au XVIIIe siècle* (Paris: Flammarion, 1983); Paula Findlen, "Science as a Career in Enlightenment Italy: The Strategies of Laura Bassi," *Isis* 84, no. 3 (1993): 441–69; Huguette Krief and Valérie André, eds., *Dictionnaire des femmes des Lumières*, 2 vols. (Paris: Honoré Champion, 2015, 2 volumes).

16. Anthony J. La Vopa, *The Labor of the Mind: Intellect and Gender in Enlightenment Culture* (Philadelphia: University of Pennsylvania Press, 2017).

17. Jorge Cañizares-Esguerra, "Whose Enlightenment Was It Anyway?" in *How to Write the History of the New World: Histories, Epistemologies, and Identities in the Eighteenth-Century Atlantic World* (Stanford, CA: Stanford University Press, 2001): 266–345.

18. Anthony Pagden, *The Enlightenment and Why It Still Matters* (Oxford: Oxford University Press, 2015); John Robertson, *The Case for the Enlightenment, Scotland, and*

Naples, 1680–1760 (Cambridge: Cambridge University Press, 2005); Jonathan Israel, *Radical Enlightenment: Philosophy and the Making of Modernity, 1650–1750* (Oxford: Oxford University Press, 2001); Margaret Jacob, *The Enlightenment: A Brief History with Documents* (New York: St. Martin's Press, 2001); Vincenzo Ferrone, *Lezioni Illuministiche* (Rome: Laterza, 2010).

19. Dorinda Outram, *The Enlightenment* (Cambridge: Cambridge University Press, 1995); Thomas Munck, *The Enlightenment: A Comparative Social History, 1721–1794* (New York: Oxford University Press, 2000); Daniel Roche, *France in the Enlightenment*, trans. Arthur Goldhammer (Cambridge, MA: Harvard University Press, 2000); John Brewer, *The Pleasures of the Imagination: English Culture in the Eighteenth-Century* (London: Harper Collins, 1997); Roger Chartier, *The Cultural Origins of the French Revolution*, trans. Lydia G. Cochrane (Durham, NC: Duke University Press, 1991); Pierre-Yves Beaurepaire, *L'Europe des Lumières* (Paris: Presses Universitaires de France, 2004); Arlette Farge, *Subversive Words: Public Opinion in Eighteenth-Century France*, trans. Rosemary Morris (University Park: Pennsylvania State University Press, 1995); Antoine Lilti, *The World of the Salons: Sociability and Worldliness in Eighteenth-Century Paris* (Oxford: Oxford University Press, 2015); Stéphane Van Damme, *À toutes voiles vers la vérité: Une autre histoire de la philosophie au temps des Lumières* (Paris: Seuil, 2014).

20. Daniel Roche, "Histoire de la France des Lumières," Collège de France inaugural lecture, 1999, available online at https://www.college-de-france.fr/sites/default/files/media/document/2023-02/1999-2000_roche.pdf; Robert Darnton, "George Washington's False Teeth, *New York Review of Books*, March 27, 1997: 34–38, Robert Darnton, *Pour les Lumières: Défense, illustration, méthode*, trans. Jean-François Baillon (Bordeaux: Presses Universitaires de Bordeaux, 2002).

21. Leo Strauss, *Philosophy and Law: Contributions to the Understanding of Maimonides and His Predecessors*, trans. Eve Adler (Albany, NY: SUNY Press, 1995); Kenneth Hart Green, ed., *Leo Strauss on Maimonides: The Complete Writings* (Chicago: Chicago University Press, 2013); Pierre Bouretz, *Lumières du Moyen Âge: Maïmonide philosophe* (Paris: Gallimard, 2015); Vera Schwarcz, *The Chinese Enlightenment: Intellectuals and the Legacy of the May Fourth Movement of 1919* (Berkeley: University of California Press, 1986); Malek Chebel, *Manifeste pour un Islam des Lumières* (Paris: Fayard, 2004).

22. Ernst Cassirer, *The Philosophy of the Enlightenment*, updated edition with a new foreword by Peter Gay (Princeton, NJ: Princeton University Press, 2009 [1932]).

23. Alphonse Dupront, *Qu'est-ce que les Lumières?* (Paris: Gallimard, 1996 [1962]).

24. Tzvetan Todorov, *In Defense of the Enlightenment*, trans. Gila Walker (London: Atlantic Books, 2009).

25. Pagden, *Enlightenment and Why It Still Matters*, vii.

26. Yann Fauchois, Thierry Grillet, and Tzvetan Todorov, eds., *Lumières! Un héritage pour demain* (Paris: Bibliothèque Nationale de France, 2006). The quotations appear on the back cover and come from the preface by Jean-Noël Jeanneney.

27. Darrin McMahon, *Enemies of the Enlightenment: The French Counter-Enlightenment and the Making of Modernity* (New York: Oxford University Press, 2001).

28. Peter Gordon, *Continental Divide: Cassirer, Heidegger, Davos* (Cambridge, MA: Harvard University Press, 2012); Adriano Viarengo, *Franco Venturi: Politica e Storia nel*

Novecento (Rome: Carocci, 2014); Theodor W. Adorno and Max Horkheimer, *Dialectic of Enlightenment: Philosophical Fragments*, ed. Gunzelin Schmid Noerr, trans. Edmund Jephcott (Stanford, CA: Stanford University Press, 2007 [1944]).

29. We have no true history of the notion with its linguistic variations (*Aufklärung, Enlightenment, Iluminismo, Illustracion, Lumières*). However, important work has been done by James Schmidt; see his "Inventing the Enlightenment: Anti-Jacobins, British Hegelians, and the Oxford English Dictionary," *Journal of the History of Ideas* 64, no. 3 (2003): 421–43; Daniel Roche and Vincenzo Ferrone, eds., *Le Monde des Lumières* (Paris: Fayard, 1999): 495–569; Giuseppe Ricuperati, ed., *Historiographie et usages des Lumières* (Berlin: Berlin Verlag, 2002); Keith Michael Baker and Peter Hans Reill, eds., *What's Left of Enlightenment? A Postmodern Question* (Stanford, CA: Stanford University Press, 2003).

30. George Benrekassa, *Le Concentrique et l'Excentrique: Marges des Lumières* (Paris: Payot, 1980): 13.

31. Antoine Lilti, "Rabelais est-il notre contemporain ? Histoire intellectuelle et herméneutique critique," *Revue d'histoire moderne et contemporaine* 5 (2012): 65–84.

32. On ecological reflexivity, see Fredrik Albritton Jonsson, *Enlightenment's Frontier: The Scottish Highlands and the Origins of Environmentalism* (New Haven, CT: Yale University Press, 2013); Richard Grove, *Green Imperialism: Colonial Expansion, Tropical Islands Edens and the Origins of Environmentalism, 1600–1860* (Cambridge: Cambridge University Press, 1996); and Grégory Quenet, "Protéger le jardin d'Éden," in Richard H. Grove, *Les Îles du Paradis: L'invention de l'écologie aux colonies, 1660–1854*, trans. Mathias Lefèvre (Paris: La Découverte, 2013): 77–120. On the debates over political economy: Jean-Claude Perrot, *Une histoire intellectuelle de l'économie politique, XVII–XVIIIe siècles* (Paris: Éditions de l'EHESS, 1992); Catherine Larrère, *L'Invention de l'économie au XVIIIe siècle* (Paris: Presses Universitaires de France, 1992); Steven L. Kaplan, *Raisonner sur les blés: Essais sur les Lumières économiques* (Paris: Fayard, 2017).

33. Dan Edelstein, *The Enlightenment: A Genealogy* (Chicago: University of Chicago Press, 2010); Céline Spector, "Les Lumières avant les Lumières: tribunal de la raison et opinion publique," in *Les Lumières, un héritage et une mission: Hommage à Jean Mondot* (Bordeaux: Presses Universitaires de Bordeaux, 2012): 53–66; Dan Brewer, *The Enlightenment Past: Reconstructing Eighteenth-Century French Thought* (Cambridge: Cambridge University Press, 2008).

34. Hans Blumenberg, "Licht als Metaphor der Wahrheit" [1957], published as "Light as a Metaphor for Truth" in *History, Metaphors, Fables: A Hans Blumenberg Reader*, ed. and trans. by Hannes Bajohr, Florian Fuchs, and Joe Paul Kroll (Ithaca, NY: Cornell University Press, 2020); Roland Mortier, "'Lumière' et 'Lumières' au XVIIe et au XVIIIe siècle," in *Clartés et ombres du siècle des Lumières* (Geneva: Droz, 1969): 13–59.

35. Jean-Marie Goulemot and Éric Walter, "Les centenaires de Voltaire et de Rousseau: Les deux lampions des Lumières," in *Les Lieux de mémoire*, vol. 1, *La République*, ed. Pierre Nora (Paris: Gallimard, 1984): 381–420; J.-M. Goulemot, *Adieu les philosophes: Que reste-t-il des Lumières?* (Paris: Seuil, 2001): 76–85.

36. Voltaire, *Remarques sur l'histoire* [1742], in *Œuvres historiques* (Paris: Gallimard, 1957): 44.

37. *Remarques sur l'histoire*, 44.

38. "Remarques pour servir de Supplément à *l'Essai sur les moeurs*," *Essai sur les*

mœurs et l'espirit des nations et sur les principaux faits de l'histoire, depuis Charlamagne jusqu'à la mort de Louis XIII [1756], vol. 2: 903.

39. Urs App, *The Birth of Orientalism* (Philadelphia: University of Pennsylvania Press, 2010): 15–76.

40. Voltaire, *Essai sur les mœurs et l'esprit des nations et sur les principaux faits de l'histoire depuis Charlemagne jusqu'à Louis XIII* [1756], vol. 1 (Paris: Classiques Garnier, 1963): 330.

41. Voltaire, *Essai sur les mœurs*, 332.

42. Voltaire, "Des conspirations contre les peuples, ou des proscriptions" [1766]. He will return to this theme in 1772 in *Questions sur l'Encyclopédie* (see *Œuvres complètes*, vol. 40 [Oxford, Voltaire Foundation, 2009]: 216).

43. Voltaire, *Candide, or Optimism* [1759], trans. Burton Raffel (New Haven, CT: Yale University Press, 2005): 68.

44. Claude-Adrien Helvétius, *De l'Esprit* (Paris: Durand, 1758): 25.

45. Voltaire, *Candide*, 69.

46. For a measured approach to Voltaire's positions that takes into account their evolution, see Carlo Ginzburg, "Tolerance and Commerce: Auerbach Reads Voltaire," in *Threads and Traces: True False Fictive* (Berkeley: University of California Press, 2012): 96–114.

47. Jean Starobinski, "Voltaire's Double-Barreled Musket," in *Blessings in Disguise; or, The Morality of Evil*, trans. Arthur Goldhammer (Cambridge, MA: Harvard University Press, 1993): 84–117.

48. Kate Soper, "Feminism and Enlightenment Legacies" in *Women, Gender, and Enlightenment*, eds. Knott and Taylor, 705–15; Olaudah Equiano, *The Interesting Narrative of the Life of Olaudah Equiano, or Gustavus Vassa the African, Written by Himself* (London: n.p., 1789); Srinivas Aravamudan, *Tropicopolitans: Colonialism and Agency, 1688–1804* (Durham, NC: Duke University Press, 1999): 233–88.

PART I: UNIVERSALISM

1. Sophia Rosenfeld, "L'Europe des cosmopolites. Quand le XVIIIe siècle rencontre le XXIe," in *Penser l'Europe au XVIIIe siècle: Commerce, Civilisation, Empire*, eds. Antoine Lilti and Céline Spector (Oxford: Oxford University Press, 2014).

2. Jacques Le Goff, *The Birth of Europe*, trans. Janet Lloyd (Malden: Blackwell, 2005).

3. Antonella Romano, *Impressions de Chine: L'Europe et l'englobement du monde, XVIe–XVIIe siècles* (Paris: Fayard, 2016); Patrick Boucheron, ed., *Histoire du monde au XVe siècle* (Paris: Fayard, 2009); Serge Gruzinski, *Les Quatre Parties du monde: Histoire d'une mondialisation* (Paris: La Martinière, 2004).

4. Pierre-Yves Beaurepaire, *Les Lumières et le monde: Voyager, explorer, collectionner* (Paris: Belin, 2019).

5. Nicolas Lenglet-Dufresnoy, *Méthode pour étudier la géographie*, vol. 1 (Paris: Rollin fils, 1742): 397. On the discovery of Asia in the eighteenth century, see Jürgen Osterhammel, *Unfabling the East: The Enlightenment's Encounter with Asia* (Princeton, NJ: Princeton University Press, 2008).

6. Michèle Duchet, *Anthropologie et histoire au siècle des Lumières* (Paris: Albin Michel, 1995 [1971]).

7. Antoine Lilti, "'Et la civilisation deviendra générale': L'Europe de Volney ou l'orientalisme à l'épreuve de la Révolution," *La Révolution française* 4 (2011), http://journals.openedition.org/lrf/290.

8. Maurice Merleau-Ponty, *Signes* [1960], trans. Richard C. McCleary (Evanston, IL: Northwestern University Press, 1964). See the commentaries by Souleymane Bachir Diagne, "Universel et universalisme," in Souleymane Bachir Diagne and Jean-Loup Amselle, *En quête d'Afrique(s): Universalisme et pensée décoloniale* (Paris: Albin Michel, 2018): 65–85.

CHAPTER 1

1. Edward W. Said, *Orientalism* (New York: Pantheon, 1978).

2. Homi K. Bhabha, *The Location of Culture* (London: Routledge, 1994).

3. Dipesh Chakrabarty, *Provincializing Europe: Postcolonial Thought and Historical Difference* (Princeton, NJ: Princeton University Press, 2007).

4. Jacques Pouchepadass, "Les Subaltern Studies ou la critique postcoloniale de la modernité," *L'Homme* 156 (2000): 161–85.

5. Jean-François Bayart, *Les Études postcoloniales: Un carnaval académique* (Paris: Karthala, 2010).

6. Edward Said's own trajectory is evidence of this evolution, or polarity one should say, since his texts alternate between anti-Western militancy and a refusal to essentialize identities. The major problem encountered by most postcolonial authors is how to avoid having the critique of Western universalism result in a glorification of the autonomy of each culture or collapse into epistemological and moral relativism. For a critique of the culturalist excesses of postcolonial approaches, see Jean-Loup Amsell, *L'Occident décroché: Enquête sur les postcolonialismes* (Paris: Stock, 2008).

7. Achille Mbembe, *On the Postcolony* (Berkeley: University of California Press, 2001); Walter Mignolo, *The Darker Side of Western Modernity: Global Futures, Decolonial Options* (Durham, NC: Duke University Press, 2011); Thomas Brisson, *Décentrer l'Occident: Les intellectuels postcoloniaux chinois, arabes et indiens et la critique de la modernité* (Paris: La Découverte, 2018).

8. Daniel Carey and Lynn Festa, eds., *Postcolonial Enlightenment: Eighteenth-Century Colonialism and Postcolonial Theory* (Oxford: Oxford University Press, 2009): 10: "simultaneously ubiquitous and elusive."

9. Said, *Orientalism*, 3.

10. See the lucid presentation by Daniel Carey and Lynn Festa in "Some Answers to the Question 'What is Postcolonial Enlightenment?'" in *Postcolonial Enlightenment*, 1–33.

11. Srinivas Aravamudan, *Enlightenment Orientalism: Resisting the Rise of the Novel* (Chicago: University of Chicago Press, 2011).

12. See the call of Louis Sala-Molins to read Enlightenment authors and the *code noir* side by side—"lire les Lumières le code noir sous la main," in *Les Misères des Lumières: Sous la raison, l'outrage* (Paris: Homnisphères, 2008 [1992]): 24.

13. Achille Mbembe, *Critique of Black Reason*, trans. Laurent Dubois (Durham, NC: Duke University Press, 2017): 16–17.

14. Jean Ehrard, *Lumières et esclavage: L'esclavage et l'opinion publique en France au XIIIe siècle* (Brussels: André Versaille, 2008).

15. Gaetano Filangieri, *La Science de la législation* (Paris: Dufart, 1799 [1784]): 75. See Alessandro Tuccillo, *Il commercio infame: Antischiavismo e diritti dell'uomo nel Settecento italiano* (Naples: Clio Press, 2013); and Alessandro Tuccillo, "Antiesclavagisme sans colonies: *Illuminismo* et esclavage colonial," *Dix-huitième siècle* 45 (2013): 629–49. On Filangieri, see also Vincenzo Ferrone, *La Politique des Lumières: Constitutionnalisme, républicanisme, droits de l'homme, le cas Filangieri*, trans. Sylvie Pipari and Thierry Ménissier (Paris: L'Harmattan, 2009).

16. Ferdinando Galiani, *De la monnaie: Della moneta*, trans. Anne Machet (Paris: Economica, 2005 [1751]): 51, cited in Alessandro Tuccillo, "L'esprit de commerce à l'épreuve de la colonisation dans le traité *Della moneta*," in *Ferdinando Galiani, économie et politique*, eds. André Tiran and Cecilia Carnino (Paris: Classiques Garnier, 2018): 485–505.

17. Sankar Muthu, *Enlightenment against Empire* (Princeton, NJ: Princeton University Press, 2009).

18. David Allen Harvey, *The French Enlightenment and Its Others: The Mandarin, the Savage, and the Invention of the Human Sciences* (New York: Palgrave Macmillan, 2012).

19. François Bernier, *Un libertin dans l'Inde moghole: Les voyages de François Bernier (1656–1669)*, ed. Frédéric Tinguely (Paris: Chandeigne, 2008); Nicholas Dew, *Orientalism in Louis XIV's France* (Oxford: Oxford University Press, 2009); Joan-Pau Rubiés, "From Antiquarianism to Philosophical History: India, China and the World History of Religion in European Thought (1600–1770)," in *Antiquarianism and Intellectual Life in Europe and China, 1500–1800*, eds. Peter N. Miller and François Louis (Ann Arbor: University of Michigan Press, 2012): 313–67; Stéphane Van Damme, "La mappemonde sceptique: une géographie des 'libertins érudits,'" *Littératures classiques*, 1, no. 92 (2017): 77–112; App, *Birth of Orientalism*; Alexander Bevilacqua, *The Republic of Arabic Letters: Islam and the European Enlightenment* (Cambridge, MA: Harvard University Press, 2018); Osterhammel, *Unfabling the East.*

20. Greg Dening, *Mr. Bligh's Bad Language: Passion, Power, and Theater on the Bounty* (Cambridge: Cambridge University Press, 1992): 372.

21. Grove, *Green Imperialism.*

22. Jonathan Swift, *Gulliver's Travels*, ed. and with notes and an introduction by Robert DeMaria Jr., Penguin Classics (New York: Penguin, 2001 [1726]): 269.

23. Tzvetan Todorov, *Nous et les autres: La réflexion française sur la diversité humaine* (Paris: Seuil, 1989); Larry Wolff, "Discovering Cultural Perspective. The Intellectual History of Anthropological Thought in the Age of Enlightenment," in *The Anthropology of the Enlightenment*, eds. Larry Wolff and Marco Cipolloni (Stanford, CA: Stanford University Press, 2007): 3–32.

24. Baron de Lahontan, *Dialogues de M. le baron de Lahontan et d'un sauvage dans l'Amérique* (Paris: Découverte, 2007 [1703]): 61. English translation cited from Baron de Lahontan, *New Voyages to North America*, trans. Reuben Gold Thwaites (Chicago: A. C. McClurg, 1905): 553.

25. Denis Diderot, *Supplément au Voyage de Bougainville*, ed. Michel Delon (Paris: Gallimard, 2002 [1796]): 94, English translation quoted from Diderot, *Political Writ-*

ings, eds. and trans. John Hope Mason and Robert Wokler (Cambridge: Cambridge University Press, 1992): 74.

26. Montesquieu, *De l'Esprit des lois*, ed. Robert Derathé (Paris: Garnier, 1973): vol. 2, book 21 [Montesquieu, *The Spirit of the Laws*, eds. and trans. Anne M. Cohler, Basia C. Miller, and Harold S. Stone (Cambridge: Cambridge University Press, 1989)]; Céline Spector, "Civilisation et empire: la dialectique négative de l'Europe au siècle des Lumières," in Lilti and Spector, eds., *Penser l'Europe au XVIIIe siècle.*

27. "The speech seems fierce to me, but in spite of what I find abrupt and primitive, I detect ideas and turns of phrase which appear European" (Diderot, *Political Writings*, 46).

28. Simon Schaffer, "The Asiatic Enlightenments of British Astronomy," in *The Brokered World: Go-Betweens and Global Intelligence, 1770–1820*, eds. Simon Schaffer, Lissa Roberts, Kapil Raj, and James Delbourgo (Sagamore Beach, MA: Science History Publications, 2009): 59–104.

29. Withers, *Placing the Enlightenment.*

30. A striking example is given by Neil Safier, *Measuring the New World: Enlightenment Science and South America* (Chicago: University of Chicago Press, 2008). For a general presentation of the stakes, see Stéphane Van Damme, "Un ancien Régime des sciences et des savoirs," in *Histoire des sciences et des savoirs*, vol. 1, *De la Renaissance aux Lumières* (Paris: Seuil, 2015): 19–40.

31. See the remarks along these lines by Antonella Romano in "*Fabriquer l'histoire des sciences modernes: Réflexions sur une discipline à l'ère de la mondialisation*," *Annales HSS* 70, no. 2 (2015): 381–408.

32. Cañizares-Esguerra, *How to Write the History of the New World.*

33. C. L. R. James, *The Black Jacobins: Toussaint L'Ouverture and the San Domingo Revolution* [1963], with a new introduction by David Scott (New York: Penguin, 2023); Laurent Dubois, "An Enslaved Enlightenment. Rethinking the Intellectual History of the French Atlantic," *Social History* 31, no. 1 (2006): 1–14; Laurent Dubois, *Avengers of the New World: The Story of the Haitian Revolution* (Cambridge, MA: Harvard University Press, 2004).

34. Sebastian Conrad, "Enlightenment in Global History: A Historiographical Critique," *American Historical Review* 117, no. 4 (2012): 999–1027.

35. Edward W. Said, *Culture and Imperialism* (New York: Knopf, 1993).

36. Bhabha, *Location of Culture*, 248 and 245, respectively.

37. Chakrabarty, *Provincializing Europe*, 16.

38. See the assessment by Cecil Courtney and Jenny Mander, "Introduction," in their *Raynal's Histoire des Deux Indes: Colonialism, Networks and Global Exchanges* (Oxford: Voltaire Foundation, 2015).

39. Abbé Raynal, *L'Anticolonialisme au XVIIIe siècle: L'histoire philosophique et politique des établissements et du commerce des Européens dans les deux Indes*, ed. Gabriel Esquer (Paris: Presses Universitaires de France, 1951). A short review by Marcel Émerit in the journal *Annales* opens with this remark: "No one any longer has the courage to read the enormous volumes of Abbé Raynal. A compiler with a fluid pen, he was once quite the celebrity, but is now hardly more than a name cited in books on the origins of the French revolution." *Annales ESC* 7, no. 3 (1952): 424.

40. See Hans-Jürgen Lüsebrink and Manfred Tietz, *Lectures de Raynal: L'Histoire*

des deux Indes en Europe et en Amérique au XVIIIe siècle (Oxford: Voltaire Foundation, 1991). This study marks the beginning of the new wave of interest in Raynal.

41. Gianluigi Goggi, "La collaboration de Diderot à l'*Histoire des deux Indes*: l'édition de ses contributions," *Diderot Studies* 33 (2013): 167–212.

42. Abbé Raynal, *Histoire philosophique et politique des établissements et du commerce des Européens dans les deux Indes* [*Histoire philosophique des deux Indes*] (Geneva: Pellet, 1780): vol. 1, 175. The English translation is from Peter Jimack, ed., *A History of the Two Indies: A Translated Selection of Writings from Raynal's Histoire philosophique et politique des établissements des Européens dans les Deux Indes* (London: Routledge, 2017).

43. Raynal, *Histoire philosophique des deux Indes*, vol. 1, 258. English translation from Jimack edition of selections from Raynal's text.

44. On this passage, the written and oral sources of Diderot, and the more general context of the image of the Hottentot in the eighteenth century, see François-Xavier Fauvelle-Aymar, *L'Invention du Hottentot, Histoire du regard occidental sur les Khoisan (XVe–XIXe siècle)* (Paris: Publications de la Sorbonne, 2002): 249–303, especially 294–303. See also Fauvelle-Aymar, *À la recherche du sauvage idéal* (Paris: Seuil, 2017).

45. Yves Benot, "Diderot, Pechmja, Raynal et l'anticolonialisme" [1963], in *Les Lumières, l'esclavage, la colonisation*, eds. Roland Desné and Marcel Dorigny (Paris: La Découverte, 2005): 107–23, especially 112.

46. Upon close inspection of the text, one may note that the paragraphs added by Diderot clash glaringly with what precedes and follows. The long, virulent passage calling on the Hottentots to exterminate the Dutch is immediately followed by a serene evaluation of the successes of the Cape Town colony that allow one to say that it is truly "the most beautiful settlement in the world," as most voyagers affirmed. The 1770 edition was more coherent on this point because it presented the pacification of the Hottentots in the form of a rather satisfying commercial transaction.

47. Bell, *Cult of the Nation in France*.

48. Duchet, *Anthropologie et histoire au siècle des Lumières*.

49. Kenta Ohji, "Civilisation et naissance de l'histoire mondiale dans *l'Histoire des deux Indes* de Raynal," *Revue de synthèse* 129, no. 1 (2008): 57–83; Ohji, "La fin de l'Ancien Régime en Europe selon *l'Histoire des deux Indes*," in Lilti and Spector, eds., *Penser l'Europe au XVIIIe siècle*.

50. Anoush Terjanian, *Commerce and Its Discontents in Eighteenth-Century French Political Thought* (Cambridge: Cambridge University Press, 2013).

51. Raynal, *Histoire philosophique des deux Indes*, vol. 1, 4. English translation from *A Philosophical and Political History of the Settlements and Trade of the Europeans in the East and West Indies*, 2nd ed., trans. J. O. Justamond (London: W. Strahan and T. Cadell, 1798): vol. 1, 3–4.

52. Yves Benot, *Diderot, de l'athéisme à l'anticolonialisme* (Paris: Maspero, 1970).

53. Raynal, *Histoire philosophique des deux Indes*, vol. 1, 206. English translation from Jimack edition of selections from Raynal's text.

54. Raynal, *Histoire philosophique des deux Indes*, vol. 1, 545. English translation from Justamond, trans., *Philosophical and Political History*, vol. 2, 167.

55. English translation from Justamond, trans., *Philosophical and Political History*, vol. 2, 169.

56. English translation from Justamond, *Philosophical and Political History*, vol. 2, 167–68.

57. English translation from Justamond, trans., *Philosophical and Political History*, vol. 2, 167.

58. Sunil Agnani, "Doux commerce, douce colonisation," in Wolff and Cipolloni, eds., *Anthropology of the Enlightenment*, 65–84.

59. "*À quoi bon vous opposer à une révolution éloignée, sans doute, mais qui s'exécutera malgré vos efforts? Il faut que le monde que vous avez envahi s'affranchisse de celui que vous habitez. Alors, les mers ne sépareront plus que deux amis, que deux frères. Quel si grand malheur voyez-vous à cela, injustes, cruels, inflexibles tyrans*" (Raynal, *Histoire philosophique des deux Indes*, vol. 1, 547). "To what purpose is it that ye oppose a revolution, which, though distant, will certainly be accomplished, notwithstanding all your efforts to prevent it? The world that you have invaded must free itself from that which you inhabit. Then the seas will only separate friends and brothers. What great calamity do ye see in this, ye unjust, cruel, and inflexible tyrants?" English translation from Justamond, trans., *Philosophical and Political History*, vol. 2, 170.

60. Raynal, *Histoire philosophique des deux Indes*, vol. 1, 205. English translation from Justamond, trans., *Philosophical and Political History*, vol. 1, 233.

61. Raynal, *Histoire philosophique des deux Indes*, vol. 1, 1–2. English translation from Justamond, trans., *Philosophical and Political History*, vol. 1, 3–4.

62. Paul Cheney, *Revolutionary Commerce: Globalization and the French Monarchy* (Cambridge, MA: Harvard University Press, 2010).

63. Hans-Jürgen Lüsebrink, "L'*Histoire des deux Indes* et ses 'extraits': Un mode de dispersion textuelle au XVIIIe siècle," *Littérature* 69 (1988): 28–41.

64. Raynal, *Histoire philosophique des deux Indes*, vol. 3, 204. English translation from Justamond, trans., *Philosophical and Political History*, vol. 4, 128–29. This famous text—which concludes with an evocation of revolutionary violence ("American fields will become drunk on the blood they had expected for a long time") and the glory of the liberator ("the old world will add its applause to the new")—marks a passage in Louis-Sébastien Mercier's *L'An 2440, rêve s'il en fut jamais*, ed. Alain Pons (Paris: France Adel, 1977 [1770]). In the Mercier passage, the narrator discovers the statue of the avenger of the new world, "this immortal man who must deliver the world from the most atrocious, longest, and most insulting tyranny."

65. James, *Black Jacobins*, 116.

66. James, *Black Jacobins*, 91.

67. C. L. R. James, in an interview quoted by Edward Said in *Culture and Imperialism*, 248. See also Matthieu Renault, *C.L.R. James: La vie révolutionnaire d'un "Platon noir"* (Paris: La Découverte, 2015).

68. James, *Black Jacobins*, 198.

69. Said, *Culture and Imperialism*, 281.

70. Michel Foucault, "What Is Enlightenment?" in *The Foucault Reader*, ed. Paul Rabinow (New York: Pantheon, 1984): 42.

71. Sunil Agnani, *Hating Empire Properly: The Two Indies and the Limits of Enlightenment Anticolonialism* (New York: Fordham University Press, 2013).

72. Theodor W. Adorno, *Minima Moralia: Reflections on a Damaged Life* [1951] (London: Verso, 2005).

73. Sebastiani, *Scottish Enlightenment.*

74. Larry Wolff, *Inventing Eastern Europe: The Map of Civilization on the Mind of the Enlightenment* (Stanford, CA: Stanford University Press, 1994); Michael Broers, *The Napoleonic Empire in Italy, 1796–1814: Cultural Imperialism in a European Context?* (New York: Palgrave MacMillan, 2005); Rahul Markovits, *Civiliser l'Europe: Politiques du théâtre français en Europe au XVIIIe siècle* (Paris: Fayard, 2014).

75. Étienne Balibar, *On Universals: Constructing and Deconstructing Community,* trans. Joshua David Jordan (New York: Fordham University Press, 2020).

76. Michel de Certeau, "Ethno-graphy: *Speech, or the Space of the Other,* by Jean de Léry," in *The Writing of History,* trans. Tom Conley (New York: Columbia University Press, 1992); Anthony Pagden, *The Fall of Natural Man: The American Indian and the Origins of Comparative Ethnology* (Cambridge: Cambridge University Press, 1982).

77. Jean-Jacques Rousseau, *Discours sur l'origine et les fondements de l'inégalité parmi les hommes,* ed. J. Starobinski, in *Œuvres complètes,* vol. 3 (Paris: Gallimard, 1964): 212. The English translation is from Rousseau, *The Discourses and Other Early Political Writings,* 2nd ed., ed. and trans. Victor Gourevitch (Cambridge: Cambridge University Press, 2019 [1997]): 215.

78. Jean Copans and Jean Jamin, eds., *Aux origines de l'anthropologie française: Les mémoires de la Société des observateurs de l'Homme en l'an VIII* (Paris: Jean Michel Place, 1994 [1978]); Sergio Moravia, *La Scienza dell'uomo nel Settecento* (Rome-Bari: Laterza, 1978); Jean-Luc Chappey, *La Société des observateurs de l'homme (1799–1804): Des anthropologues au temps de Bonaparte* (Paris: Société des études robespierristes, 2002).

79. Georg Forster, *A Voyage round the World,* eds. Nicholas Thomas and Olivier Berghof (Honolulu: Hawaii University Press, 1999–2000); Nicholas Thomas, *The Extraordinary Voyages of Captain James Cook* (New York: Walker and Company, 2004).

80. Han F. Vermeulen, *Before Boas: The Genesis of Ethnography and Ethnology in the German Enlightenment* (Lincoln: University of Nebraska Press, 2015).

81. Edmund Burke to William Robertson, June 9, 1777, in *The Correspondence of Edmund Burke* (Cambridge: Cambridge University Press, 1961): vol. 3, 350–51; see Peter James Marshall and Glyndwr Williams, *The Great Map of Mankind: British Perceptions of the World in the Age of Enlightenment* (London: Dent, 1982).

82. Bernard Picart, *Cérémonies et coutumes religieuses des peuples du monde* (Amsterdam: J. F. Bernard, 1723–1737); Hunt, Jacob, and Mijnhardt, *Book That Changed Europe.* On Enlightenment uses of comparison, see Jacques Revel, "The Uses of Comparison: Religions in the Early Eighteenth Century," in Lynn Hunt, Margaret Jacob, and Wijnand Mijnhardt, eds., *Bernard Picart and the First Global Vision of Religion* (Los Angeles, CA: Getty Research Institute, 2010): 331–47. See also Daniel Roche, "Lumières, tolérance et radicalité: histoire intellectuelle et débat religieux au XVIIIe siècle," *Revue d'histoire moderne et contemporaine* 65, no. 2 (2018): 151–59.

83. Talal Asad, ed., *Anthropology and the Colonial Encounter* (London: Ithaca Press, 1973); Johannes Fabian, *Time and the Other: How Anthropology Makes Its Object, with a New Postscript by the Author* (New York: Columbia University Press, 2014); James Clifford and George Marcus, eds., *Writing Culture: The Poetics and Politics of Ethnography* (Berkeley: University of California Press, 1986).

84. Antoine Lilti, "1779: mourir à Hawaï: La fin tragique du capitaine Cook," in

L'Exploration du monde: Une autre histoire des Grandes Découvertes, ed. Romain Bertrand (Paris: Seuil, 2019).

85. Marshall Sahlins, *Islands of History* (Chicago: University of Chicago Press, 1987).

86. Gananath Obeyesekere, *The Apotheosis of Captain Cook: European Mythmaking in the Pacific* (Princeton, NJ: Princeton University Press, 1997 [1992]): 3.

87. On the anthropological side of the controversy, see the following two presentations, which mostly favor Sahlins: Robert Borofski, "Cook, Lono, Obeyesekere and Sahlins," *Current Anthropology* 38, no. 2 (1997): 255–82; Francis Zimmerman, "Sahlins, Obeyesekere et la mort du Capitaine Cook," *L'Homme* 38 (1998): 191–205.

88. Marshall Sahlins, *How "Natives" Think: About Captain Cook, for Example* (Chicago: University of Chicago Press, 2005): 116.

89. Marshall Sahlins, "What Is Anthropological Enlightenment? Some Lessons of the Twentieth Century," *Annual Review of Anthropology* 28, no. 1 (1999): i–xxiii, at ii.

90. Avant-propos, *La découverte du vrai Sauvage et autres essais* (Gallimard, 2007), p. 13.

91. John H. Zammito, *Kant, Herder, and the Birth of Anthropology* (Chicago: University of Chicago Press, 2002); David Denby, "Herder: Culture, Anthropology and the Enlightenment," *History of Human Sciences* 18, no. 1 (2005): 55–76; Reto Speck, "Johann Gottfried Herder and Enlightenment Political Thought: From the Reform of Russia to the Anthropology of *Bildung*," *Modern Intellectual History* 11, no. 1 (2014): 31–58.

92. Muthu, *Enlightenment against Empire*.

93. Claude Lévi-Strauss, "Jean-Jacques Rousseau, Founder of the Sciences of Man," in *Structural Anthropology*, vol. 2, trans. Monique Layton (Chicago: University of Chicago Press, 1976): ch. 2.

94. Lévi-Strauss's insistence on Rousseau's experiment with the dissolution of the subject may seem to contradict readings that see in Rousseau the prophet of the romantic I and a morality of authenticity. Here, Lévi-Strauss's horizon is the rejection of Western philosophical modernity, especially the cogito and the dualism of nature/culture. He credits Rousseau as having contributed to dissolving the epistemological and ontological privilege of the human, and thereby to the development of contemporary human sciences marked by structuralism and the "death of man."

95. Mark Hulliung, *The Autocritique of Enlightenment: Rousseau and the Philosophes* (Cambridge, MA: Harvard University Press, 1994).

96. Maurice Merleau-Ponty, "From Mauss to Lévi-Strauss," in *Signs*, trans. Richard C. McCleary (Evanston, IL: Northwestern University Press, 1964).

97. Lynn Hunt, *Writing History in the Global Era* (New York: W. W. Norton, 2014).

CHAPTER 2

1. Paul Hazard, *The Crisis of the European Mind, 1680–1715* [1935], trans. J. Lewis May (New York: New York Review Books, 2013).

2. Bertrand Binoche, ed., *Les Équivoques de la civilisation* (Seyssel: Champ Vallon, 2005).

3. Leading publications within a sizeable bibliography include: Norbert Elias, *The Civilizing Process* [1939] (Oxford: Blackwell, 1994); Jean Starobinski, "The Word *Civilization*," in *Blessings in Disguise*; Joachim Moras, *Ursprung und Entwicklung des Begriffs*

der Zivilisation in Frankreich (1756–1830) (Hamburg: Hans Christians Druckerei und Verlag, 1930); Victor Goldschmidt, "Le problème de la civilisation chez Rousseau (et la réponse de d'Alembert)," *Écrits*, vol. 2, *Études de philosophie moderne* (Paris: Vrin, 1984): 81–128.

4. See Wolff and Cipolloni, eds., *Anthropology of the Enlightenment.*

5. Jack Goody, *The Theft of History* (Cambridge: Cambridge University Press, 2006).

6. For a presentation of many attempts across several centuries to write a history of Europe, see Marcello Verga, *Storie d'Europa* (Rome: Carocci, 2004).

7. Jean-Frédéric Schaub, *Oroonoko, prince et esclave: Roman colonial de l'incertitude* (Paris: Seuil, 2008).

8. Franck Lestringant, *Le Huguenot et le sauvage: L'Amérique et la controverse coloniale, en France, au temps des guerres de religion (1555–1589)* (Paris: Klincksieck, 1999 [1990]) and *L'Atelier du cosmographe ou l'image du monde à la Renaissance* (Paris: Albin Michel, 1991). See also, more generally, François Hartog, *Anciens, modernes, sauvages* (Paris: Seuil, 2008 [2005]).

9. The bibliography is extensive on the English-speaking world. On the case of French parts of America, see Gilles Havard, "Le rire des jésuites: Une archéologie du mimétisme dans la rencontre franco-amérindienne, XVIIe–XVIIIe siècle," *Annales HSS* 62, no. 3 (2007): 539–574.

10. This tradition would remain important in the discourse of German cameralism, which conceives of European political space as an ensemble of states each with a parallel description. See Hans Erich Bödeker, "'Europe' in the Discourse of the Sciences of State in Eighteenth-Century Germany," *Cromohs* 8 (2003): 1–14.

11. Wolff, *Inventing Eastern Europe.*

12. Reinhart Koselleck, *Futures Past: On the Semantics of Historical Time*, trans. Keith Tribe (New York: Columbia University Press, 2004); Hans Blumenberg, *The Legitimacy of the Modern Age*, trans. Robert M. Wallace (Cambridge, MA: MIT Press, 1985).

13. Karen O'Brien, *Narratives of Enlightenment: Cosmopolitan History from Voltaire to Gibbon* (New York: Cambridge University Press, 1997); J. G. A. Pocock, *Barbarism and Religion*, vol. 2, *Narratives of Civil Government* (Cambridge: Cambridge University Press, 1999).

14. Voltaire begins working on his "general history" in 1741, publishes an outline in 1745, and then publishes a first edition in 1756, in reaction to an error-filled pirated edition published in 1753. New expanded and corrected editions are published in 1768 and 1775 under the title *Essai sur les mœurs et l'esprit des nations.* The posthumous edition of 1785 includes Voltaire's last additions. On the history of the text, see the preface by René Pomeau in Voltaire, *Essai sur les mœurs et l'esprit des nations et sur les principaux faits de l'histoire depuis Charlemagne jusqu'à Louis XIII*, 2 vols. (Paris: Garnier, 1963), which is the edition used here. See also the new critical edition in nine volumes: Voltaire, *Œuvres complètes* (Oxford: Voltaire Foundation, 2009).

15. The Italian historiography, however, recognized early on the importance of the *Essai sur les mœurs et l'esprit des nations.* See Furio Diaz, *Voltaire storico* (Turin: Giulio Einaudi, 1958); and Federico Chabod, *Storia dell' idea di Europa* (Bari: Laterza, 1961).

16. Voltaire, *Essai sur les mœurs et l'esprit des nations*, vol. 1, 310.

17. Voltaire, *Essai sur les mœurs et l'esprit des nations*, vol. 1, 632.

18. Voltaire, *Essai sur les mœurs et l'esprit des nations*, vol. 2, 811.

19. Voltaire, *Essai sur les mœurs et l'esprit des nations*, vol. 2, 904.

20. Voltaire, *Le Siècle de Louis XIV*, in *Œuvres historiques*, 616.

21. On the writings of William Robertson, see Richard B. Sher, *Church and University in the Scottish Enlightenment: The Moderate Literati of Edinburgh* (Princeton, NJ: Princeton University Press, 1985); and Stewart Brown, ed., *William Robertson and the Expansion of Empire* (Cambridge: Cambridge University Press, 1997). On Robertson as a European historian, see Karen O'Brien, *Narratives of Enlightenment*, ch. 4–5; Pocock, *Barbarism and Religion*, vol. 2, 258–308; Colin Kidd, *Subverting Scotland's Past: Scottish Whig Historians and the Creation of an Anglo-British Identity, 1680–c.1830* (Cambridge: Cambridge University Press, 1993). On the dialogue between the history of America and the history of Europe, see Sebastiani, *Scottish Enlightenment*.

22. William Russell, *The History of Modern Europe with an Account of the Decline and Fall of the Roman Empire and a View of the Progress of Society from the Rise of the Modern Kingdoms to the Peace of Paris in 1763* (Dublin: S. Price, 1779). This book was republished many times and was even extended in time up to 1811 to include the 1802 Treaty of Amiens.

23. One must also add works of national history that are part of this narrative frame, such as David Hume's important *The History of England* (1754–1761), a work written in installments that inscribes British history squarely within a European context. See Duncan Forbes, "The European, or Cosmopolitan, Dimension in Hume's Science of Politics," *British Journal for Eighteenth-Century Studies* 1 (1978): 57–60.

24. Voltaire, *Remarques sur l'histoire*, in *Œuvres historiques*, 44.

25. Nicolas de Bonneville, *Histoire de l'Europe moderne, depuis l'irruption des peuples du Nord dans l'Empire romain jusqu'à la paix de 1783*, vol. 1 (Geneva: n.p., 1789): 2.

26. David Hume, "Of the Rise and Progress of the Arts and Science," in *Selected Essays*, ed. Stephen Copley and Andrew Edgar (Oxford: Oxford University Press, 1998): 63.

27. William Robertson, *The History of the Reign of the Emperor Charles V, with a View of the Progress of Society, from the Subversion of the Roman Empire to the Beginning of the Sixteenth Century*, vol. 1 (London: W. Sharpe and Son, 1820 [1769]): 489.

28. Isaac Iselin, *Uber die Geschichte der Menschheit* (Bâle: Johannes Schweighauser, 1779). See Bertrand Binoche, *Les Trois Sources des philosophies de l'histoire (1764–1798)* (Paris: Presses Universitaires de France, 1994).

29. J. G. A. Pocock, "Classical and Civil History: The Transformation of Humanism," *Cromohs* 1 (1996): 1–34; *Barbarism and Religion*, vol. 2.

30. *De l'Esprit des lois* is a constant reference. Montesquieu was probably the first to insist so strongly on the link between commerce and mores, and also to propose a history of trade as establishing the specificity of modern Europe and its domination.

31. O'Brien, *Narratives of Enlightenment*, 99–100.

32. László Kontler, *Translations, Histories, Enlightenments: William Robertson in Germany, 1760–1795* (New York: Palgrave MacMillan, 2014); Franco Venturi, "Scottish Echoes in Eighteenth-Century Italy," in *Wealth and Virtue: The Shaping of Political Economy in the Scottish Enlightenment*, eds. Istvan Hont and Michael Ignatieff (Cambridge: Cambridge University Press, 1985); Cañizares-Esguerra, *How to Write the History of the New World*, 171.

33. See the correspondence between Suard and Robertson quoted in John Renwick, "Robertson's Reception in Eighteenth-Century France," in Brown, ed., *William Robertson and the Expansion of Empire*, 145–63; and David Hume, *The Letters of David Hume* (Oxford: Clarendon Press, 1932): 193–96.

34. Antonello Gerbi, *The Dispute of the New World: The History of a Polemic, 1750–1900* (Pittsburgh, PA: University of Pittsburgh Press, 1973).

35. William Robertson, preface, *History of America*, in *The Works of William Robertson, D.D. to which Is Prefixed, an Account of the Life and Writings of the Author, by Dugald Stewart: In Eight Volumes* [London: T. Cadell, 1840]: vol. 3, book 1 (Dublin: n.p., 1778).

36. The last publication of William Robertson enlarged the horizon even more with a history of the relations between Europe and India: *A Historical Disquisition Concerning the Knowledge which the Ancients Had of India* (London: A. Strahan and T. Cadell, 1791). See Stewart J. Brown, "William Robertson: Early Orientalism and the Historical Disquisition on India of 1791," *Scottish Historical Review* 88, no. 2 (2009): 289–312; Silvia Sebastiani, "William Robertson, entre l'Amérique et l'Inde: D'un nouveau monde sans histoire au berceau de la culture et du commerce," *Purusārtha* 31, *L'Inde des Lumières: Discours, histoire, savoirs (XVIIe–XIXe siècles)* (2013): 41–71.

37. Joseph François Lafitau, *Mœurs des sauvages américains comparées aux mœurs des premiers temps* (Paris: Saugrain, 1724); Voltaire, *Essai sur les mœurs et l'esprit des nations*, 29–30, and, to a lesser degree, Robertson, *History of America*, book 1, 484: "Lafitau's *Mœurs des Sauvages* extends to 347 tedious pages in quarto."

38. Bruce Lenman, "From Savage to Scot via the French and the Spaniards: Principal Robertson's Spanish Sources," in Brown, ed., *William Robertson and the Expansion of Empire*, 196–209; Cañizares-Esguerra, *How to Write the History of the New World*. This effort is judged insufficient by the Spanish and especially by Creole Americans. On the Atlantic dimension of the controversy and the importance of the racial stakes, see Silvia Sebastiani, "L'Amérique des Lumières et la hiérarchie des races," *Annales. Histoire, Sciences Sociales* 67, no. 2 (2012): 327–61.

39. Robertson, *History of America*, book 4, 294. One finds the same nuance, or the same burden, when it comes to the question of their artistic productions. After having announced that "the progress of the Mexicans in various arts is considered as the most decisive proof of their superior refinement," Robertson modifies the opinion of Cortes, who considered Mexican artists to be superior, even, to Europeans (*History of America*, book 7, 270, in *The Works of William Robertson, D.D. to which is Prefixed, an Account of the Life and Writings of the Author, by Dugald Stewart: In Eight Volumes* [London: T. Cadell, 1840]: vol. 7, "*The History of America*," books 5–8).

40. Voltaire, *De la gloire: Entretien avec un Chinois*, in *Œuvres complètes*, vol. 18-A (Oxford, Voltaire Foundation, 2007).

41. Voltaire, *Supplément à l'Essai sur les mœurs et l'esprit des nations*, 903.

42. During the same period (1759 and 1763), Voltaire writes his *Histoire de la Russie*, which poses the question of the enterprise of civilization and therefore of the Europeanization of Russia. In 1773, he will publish *Fragments historiques sur l'Inde*.

43. Voltaire made intensive use of travel narratives, but also those of relations between Jesuits, as well as numerous works by antiquarians and scholarly orientalists. He attempted to integrate them within a new grand narrative about the ruins of Christian

universalism, which had been teetering since the end of the seventeenth century. See Rubiés, "From Antiquarianism to Philosophical History."

44. Voltaire, *Essai sur les mœurs et l'esprit des nations*, 55.

45. Voltaire, *Essai sur les mœurs et l'esprit des nations*, 196–197.

46. Voltaire, *Essai sur les mœurs et l'esprit des nations*, 807.

47. Voltaire, *Essai sur les mœurs et l'esprit des nations*, 808.

48. See in particular the second chapter of *Essai sur les mœurs et l'esprit des nations*, "Des différentes races d'hommes." Voltaire's insistence on the diversity of human races has provoked much commentary on account of remarks about the physical and intellectual inferiority of Blacks. Without minimizing the troubling nature of those pages, it is worth noting that for Voltaire the diversity of human races is above all a political tool used against the biblical narrative and belongs within the tradition of libertine thinking of the seventeenth century. Also, it is not incompatible with an affirmation of the unity of human nature.

49. It is this resolutely "presentist" option that allows Voltaire to criticize mores of the past in the name of the superior principles which are his as a modern European. On this point, see Pierre Force, "Voltaire and the Necessity of Modern History," *Modern Intellectual History* 6, no. 3 (2009): 457–84. Inversely, the onlooker principle, outside of history, is symbolized by the figure of the extraterrestrial; for example, the one who discovers Africa in the *Traité de métaphysique* (1734) and of course in the tale *Micromégas* (1752). For a lengthier discussion of these questions, see the special issue edited by John Brewer and Silvia Sebastiani, *Modern Intellectual History* 11, no. 3 (2014).

50. Gérard Laudin, "La cohérence de l'histoire: Aspects de la réception de Voltaire dans l'Allemagne des années 1760–1770," in *Voltaire et ses combats*, eds. Ulla Kölving and Christiane Mervaud (Oxford: Voltaire Foundation, 1997): vol. 2, 1435; and Gérard Laudin, "L'histoire comme science de l'homme chez Gatterer et Schlozer," in *Göttingen vers 1800, l'Europe des sciences de l'homme*, eds. Hans Erich Bödeker, Philippe Büttgen, and Michel Espagne (Paris: Éditions du Cerf, 2010): 483–514. See also Alexandre Escudier, "Histoire universelle et comparaison en Allemagne à la fin du XVIIIe siècle," *Eurostudia* 4, no. 2 (2008).

51. Far from constructing the Orient as a radical alterity, Voltaire always sought to bring closer together the characteristic traits of distant societies. He vigorously criticized the theme of Asiatic despotism. Unlike Montesquieu, he saw no systematic differences between the uses of power in the Orient and the Occident. Similarly, he refused to make feudalism a specificity of European history but saw it rather as a social form that one found also among the "*Tartares occidentaux*"—in other words, the Mongols—since Genghis Khan. See Rolando Minuti, *Oriente barbarico e storiografia settecentesca: Rappresentazioni della storia dei Tartari nella cultura francese del XVIII secolo* (Venice: Marsilio, 1994): 95–139. And when Voltaire evoked Japan, he did so in order to compare the seizure of power by the Tokugawa with certain episodes in German history.

52. Sebastiani, *Scottish Enlightenment*; Taylor and Knott, eds., *Women, Gender, and Enlightenment*.

53. Karen O'Brien notes that the last editions (of 1769, and especially the posthumous edition of 1785, which integrates Voltaire's handwritten corrections and additions to the manuscript) are more ironic and skeptical, and that they often pushed literary historians to see in *Essai sur les mœurs et l'esprit des nations* a denunciation of human

folly and an incoherent narrative, whereas the original edition was much more of a coherent narrative of the birth of modern Europe. See O'Brien, *Narratives of Enlightenment*, 47–48. Her conclusion is that this coherence is central to the Enlightenment narrative. But one may also insist on the instability of the enterprise which became more and more flagrant as Voltaire advanced further into it.

54. Voltaire, *Essai sur les mœurs et l'esprit des nations*, vol. 2, 798.

55. Ohji, "Civilisation et naissance de l'histoire mondiale dans *l'Histoire des deux Indes* de Raynal."

56. Friedrich Schiller, "What Is, and to What End Do We Study, Universal History?" trans. Caroline Stephan and Robert Trout, 262. The lecture was delivered on May 26–27, 1789, at Jena University in Jena, Germany. It is available online here via the Schiller Institute, 1988: https://archive.schillerinstitute.com/transl/Schiller_essays/universal_history.pdf.

57. Koselleck, *Futures Past*; François Hartog, *Régimes of Historicity: Presentism and Experiences of Time*, trans. Saskia Brown (New York: Columbia University Press, 2016).

58. Condorcet, *Tableau historique des progrès de l'esprit humain: Projets, esquisse, fragments et notes (1772–1794)*, ed. Jean-Pierre Schandeler, Pierre Crépel, and le Groupe Condorcet (Paris: Ined, 2004): 429. On Condorcet's philosophy of history and its articulation with a project of social art, see Keith M. Baker, *Condorcet: From Natural Philosophy to Social Mathematics* (Chicago: University of Chicago Press, 1975).

59. Condorcet, *Tableau historique des progrès de l'esprit humain*, 430.

60. Condorcet, *Tableau historique des progrès de l'esprit humain*, 430.

61. Constantin-François Volney, *Les Ruines, ou méditation sur les révolutions des empires* [1791] *Œuvres*, vol. 1, eds. Anne and Henry Deneys (Paris: Fayard, 1990): 166–440.

CHAPTER 3

1. Lucien Febvre, "Sur une nouvelle collection d'histoire," *Annales ESC* 9, no. 1 (1954): 1–6.

2. Febvre, "Sur une nouvelle collection d'histoire," 6.

3. Sanjay Subrahmanyam, "Connected Histories: Notes towards a Reconfiguration of Early Modern Eurasia," *Modern Asian Studies* 31, no. 3 (1997): 735–62; Serge Gruzinski, *La Pensée métisse* (Paris: Fayard, 1999).

4. Jacques Revel, "Le récit du monde," *La Vie des idées*, April 26, 2011, https://www.laviedesidees.fr/Le-recit-du-monde.html.

5. Sylvain Gouguenheim, *Aristote au Mont Saint-Michel: Les racines grecques de l'Europe chrétienne* (Paris: Seuil, 2008).

6. Étienne Anheim, *Le Travail de l'histoire* (Paris: Publications de la Sorbonne, 2018): 182–91.

7. See Blaise Dufal, "Faire et défaire l'histoire des civilisations," in Philippe Büttgen *et al.* (eds.), *Les Grecs, les Arabes et nous: Enquête sur l'islamophobie savante*, eds. Philippe Büttgen, Alain de Libera, Marwan Rashed, and Irène Rosier-Catach (Paris: Fayard, 2009): 317–58. I borrow certain elements from this article but do not share its conclusions.

8. Fernand Braudel, *Grammaire des civilisations* (Paris: Flammarion, 1987); *A History of Civilizations*, trans. Richard Mayne (New York: Penguin, 1995).

9. Dufal, "Faire et défaire l'histoire des civilisations." See also Paul-André Rosental, "Métaphore et stratégie épistémologique: *La Méditerranée* de Fernand Braudel," in Alain Boureau and Daniel Milo, *Alter histoire: Essais d'histoire expérimentale* (Paris: Les Belles Lettres, 1991): 109–26.

10. Fernand Braudel, *On History*, trans. Sarah Matthews (Chicago: University of Chicago Press, 1980): 200.

11. See in particular, starting in 1959, an article entitled, "Histoire des civilisations: Le passé explique le présent," in *Encyclopédie française*, vol. 5, republished in Fernand Braudel, *Écrits sur l'histoire* (Paris: Flammarion, 1969). See "The History of Civilizations: The Past Explains the Present," in Braudel, *On History*, trans. Matthews.

12. However, he adds lucidly, "I would willingly agree with Pirenne. But let us use words as they fall to us, in their living, their provisionally living meaning. But let us also be aware of the other possibilities which they suggest and have suggested, and of the traps which they can lay for the unwary" (Braudel, "History of Civilizations," 183).

13. For example, see Étienne Anheim, Jean-Yves Grenier, and Antoine Lilti, "Repenser les statuts sociaux," *Annales HSS* 68, no. 4 (2013): 949–53. On the level of metahistorical concepts, this ambition was central to the project of *Begriffsgeschichte*. See Koselleck, "*Begriffsgeschichte* and Social History," in *Futures Past*, 75–92.

14. Braudel, "History of Civilizations."

15. Lucien Febvre, "*Civilization*: Evolution of a Word and a Group of Ideas" [1930] in *A New Kind of History: From the Writings of Febvre*, ed. Peter Burke, trans. K. Folca (London: Routledge and Kegan Paul, 1973). At the same time, in a very different intellectual context, Norbert Elias was initiating his study of the civilization of mores, and Joachim Moras was writing his thesis. On this episode, see the presentation by Éric Brian and Marie Jaisson, *Revue de synthèse* 129, no. 1 (2008): 147–57.

16. In the meantime, Lucien Febvre was elected in 1932 to the Collège de France and the chair of "Histoire de la civilisation moderne."

17. The 1994 editorial in *Annales* announcing the abandonment of the title speaks of a "division tripartite" that is no longer adapted to the organization of the levels of analysis ["l'agencement des niveaux d'analyse"].

18. Lucien Febvre, "Face au vent: Manifeste des *Annales* nouvelles," *Annales ESC* 1, no. 1 (1946), republished in *Vivre l'histoire*, ed. Brigitte Mazon (Paris: Robert Laffont, 2019), 35–43.

19. Lucien Febvre, *L'Europe: Genèse d'une civilisation: Cours au Collège de France 1944–1945* (Paris: Perrin, 1999).

20. Febvre, *L'Europe: Genèse d'une civilisation*, 103.

21. Febvre, *L'Europe: Genèse d'une civilisation*, 305, 315.

22. Febvre, *L'Europe: Genèse d'une civilisation*, 67.

23. Marcel Mauss, "Les civilisations: Éléments et formes," *Œuvres*, vol. 2, *Représentations collectives et diversité des civilisations* (Paris: Minuit, 1969 [1929]); "Civilizations: Their Elements and Forms," *Techniques, Technology, and Civilization*, ed. Nathan Schlanger (Oxford: Berghahn Books, 2006). This is the lecture Mauss gave during the week of synthesis. Mauss had already developed with Durkheim a first definition of civilization. See Émile Durkheim and Marcel Mauss, "Note sur la notion de civilisation," *L'année sociologique* 12 (1913): 45–60, republished in Mauss, *Œuvres*, vol. 2; "Note on the Notion of Civilization," *Social Research* 38, no. 4 (1971): 808–13. See

Jean-François Bert, "Marcel Mauss et la notion de 'civilisation,'" *Cahiers de recherche sociologique* 47 (2009): 123–42.

24. The course follows that of 1945–1946 on the national sentiment in France. See Lucien Febvre, *Honneur et patrie: Une enquête sur le sentiment d'honneur et l'attachement à la patrie*, eds. Thérèse Charmasson and Brigitte Mazon (Paris: Perrin, 1996). The ideal of global history does not substitute for national history; it accompanies a critical history of the fact of the nation. Febvre attempted to articulate the two histories in a book project with François Crouzet. See *Nous sommes des sang-mêlés: Manuel d'histoire de la civilisation française*, eds. Denis and Élisabeth Crouzet (Paris: Albin Michel, 2012).

25. Gabriela Goldin and Rahul Markovits, "The First Journal of World History: Re-Problematizing Global History from Inside the Kitchen," *Journal of Global History* 14, no. 2 (2019): 157–78.

26. The impossibility for the historian to escape his own historicity and the effects of history is the great lesson of part 2 of Hans-Georg Gadamer's *Truth and Method*, trans. Joel Weinsheimer and Donald G. Marshall (London: Bloomsbury, 2013).

27. Lucien Febvre, "*De la* Revue de Synthèse *aux* Annales," in *Lettres à Henri Berr, 1911–1954*, eds. Gilles Candar and Jacqueline Pluet-Despatin (Paris: Fayard, 1997): 357.

28. Febvre, *L'Europe: Genèse d'une civilisation*, 128. See also this formulation, which is presented in the negative but changes nothing about the connotation of the term: "*D'autant que* [*dire en*] *1945, nous les civilisés! nous les civilisateurs! Non! c'est impensable*" (67). [All the more in 1945, we the civilized! We the civilizers! No! It's unthinkable.]

29. Such privileging of homogeneity is evident in *Le Monde actuel*, for pedagogical reasons. The tension is already present in Febvre because the point is to account for a coherent entity by a history of its borrowings.

30. Foucault, "What Is Enlightenment?" On the different versions of this text, see note 1 in the last chapter.

31. Febvre, in Burke, ed., "New Kind of History."

PART II: MODERNITY

1. Kenneth Pomeranz, *The Great Divergence: China, Europe, and the Making of the Modern World Economy* (Princeton, NJ: Princeton University Press, 2021 [2000]).

2. Joel Mokyr, *A Culture of Growth: The Origins of the Modern Economy* (Princeton, NJ: Princeton University Press, 2017).

3. "AHR Roundtable: Historians and the Question of 'Modernity,'" *American Historical Review* 116, no. 3 (2011): 631–751. The participants are Zvi Ben-Dor Benite, Gurminder K. Bhambra, Carol Gluck, Mark Roseman, Dorothy Ross, Carol Symes, Lynn M. Thomas, and Richard Wolin.

4. Roger Chartier, *The Cultural Origins of the French Revolution*, trans. Lydia G. Cochrane (Durham, NC: Duke University Press, 1991).

CHAPTER 4

1. Bernard Lepetit, ed., *Les Formes de l'expérience: Une autre histoire sociale* (Paris: Albin Michel, 1995).

2. Philippe Ariès and Georges Duby, general eds., *A History of Private Life*, vol.

3, *Passions of the Renaissance,* ed. Roger Chartier, trans. Arthur Goldhammer (Cambridge, MA: Harvard University Press, 1987).

3. Annick Pardailhé-Galabrun, *La Naissance de l'intime: 3000 foyers parisiens, XVIIe–XVIIIe siècles* (Paris: Presses Universitaires de France, 1988).

4. Michel Delon, *L'Invention du boudoir* (Cadeilhan: Zulma, 1999).

5. Arlette Farge, *Vivre dans la rue à Paris au XVIIIe siècle* (Paris: Gallimard-Julliard, 1979); Daniel Roche, *The People of Paris: An Essay in Popular Culture in the Eighteenth Century,* trans. Marie Evans with Gwynne Lewis (Berkeley: University of California Press, 1987).

6. Daniel Roche, *A History of Everyday Things: The Birth of Consumption in France, 1600–1800* (Cambridge: Cambridge University Press, 2000); Joël Cornette, "La révolution des objets: Le Paris des inventaires après-décès (XVIIe–XVIIIe siècle)," *Revue d'histoire moderne et contemporaine* 36, no. 3 (1989): 476–86.

7. Roger Chartier, *Lectures et lecteurs dans la France d'Ancien Régime* (Paris: Seuil, 1987).

8. Roger Chartier, *Effacer et inscrire: Culture écrite et littérature (XIe–XVIIIe siècle)* (Paris: Éditions de l'EHESS-Gallimard-Seuil, 2005): 155–75; Robert Darnton, *The Great Cat Massacre and Other Episodes in French Cultural History* (New York: Basic Books, 1984).

9. Meghan K. Roberts, *Sentimental Savants: Philosophical Families in Enlightenment France* (Chicago: University of Chicago Press, 2016).

10. Richard Rand, ed., *Intimate Encounters: Love and Domesticity in Eighteenth-Century France* (Princeton, NJ: Princeton University Press, 2007); Mark Ledbury, "Embracing and Escaping the Material: Genre Painting, Objets and Private Life in Eighteenth-Century France," in *Representing Private Lives of the Enlightenment,* ed. Andrew Kahn (Oxford: Voltaire Foundation, 2010): 187–217; Emma Barker, *Greuze and the Painting of Sentiment* (New York: Cambridge University Press, 2005).

11. Maurice Agulhon, *Pénitents et francs-maçons de l'ancienne Provence: Essai sur la sociabilité méridionale* (Paris: Fayard, 1968).

12. Daniel Roche, *Le Siècle des Lumières en province: Académie et académiciens provinciaux (1680–1789)* (Paris-La Haye: EHESS-Mouton, 1978).

13. Daniel Roche, *Les Républicains des lettres: Gens de culture et Lumières au XVIIIe siècle* (Paris: Fayard, 1988): 14–16. On Tocqueville's point of view, see Alexis de Tocqueville, *L'Ancien Régime et la Révolution* (Paris: Gallimard, 1967): 239–240.

14. Roche, *Les Républicains des lettres,* 15.

15. James McClellan, "L'Europe des académies," *Dix-huitième siècle* 25 (1993): 153–65.

16. Roche, *Les Républicains des lettres,* 15. See also Roche, *Le Siècle des Lumières en province.*

17. Jeremy Caradonna, *The Enlightenment in Practice: Academic Prize Contests and Intellectual Culture in France, 1670–1794* (Ithaca, NY: Cornell University Press, 2012).

18. Alain Viala, *La France galante: Essai historique sur une catégorie culturelle, de ses origines jusqu'à la Révolution* (Paris: Presses Universitaires de France, 2008); Jolanta T. Pekacz, *Conservative Tradition in Pre-Revolutionary France: Parisian Salon Women* (New York: Peter Lang, 1999).

19. Mélinda Caron, *Écriture et vie de société: Les correspondances littéraires de Louise*

d'Épinay (1755–1783) (Montréal: Presses de l'Université de Montréal, 2017); La Vopa, *The Labor of the Mind.*

20. Anne C. Vila, *Suffering Scholars: Pathologies of the Intellectual in Enlightenment France* (Philadelphia: Pennsylvania University Press, 2018).

21. Antoine Lilti, *The World of the Salons: Sociability and Worldliness in Eighteenth-Century Paris* (Oxford: Oxford University Press, 2015).

22. Stéphane Van Damme, *Paris, capitale philosophique: De la Fronde à la Révolution* (Paris: Odile Jacob, 2005).

23. Charlotte Guichard, "Taste Communities: The Rise of the 'Amateur' in Eighteenth-Century Paris," *Eighteenth-Century Studies* 45, no. 4 (2012): 519–47.

24. Pierre-Yves Beaurepaire, *L'Espace des francs-maçons: Une sociabilité européenne au XVIIIe siècle* (Rennes: Presses Universitaires de Rennes, 2003).

25. Augustin Cochin, *Les Sociétés de pensée et la démocratie modern: Études d'histoire révolutionnaire* (Paris: Plon, 1921); François Furet, *Interpreting the French Revolution*, trans. Elborg Forster (Cambridge: Cambridge University Press, 1981); Reinhart Koselleck, *Critique and Crisis: Enlightenment and the Pathogenesis of Modern Society* (Cambridge, MA: MIT Press, 1988).

26. Daniel Gordon, *Citizens without Sovereignty: Equality and Sociability in French Thought, 1670–1789* (Princeton, NJ Princeton University Press, 1994).

27. Jürgen Habermas, *The Structural Transformation of the Public Sphere: An Inquiry into a Category of Bourgeois Society* [1962], trans. Thomas Burger with Frederick Lawrence (Cambridge, MA: MIT Press, 1991).

28. Sara Maza, "Historians and Eighteenth-Century Private Life: An Overview," in Kahn, ed., *Representing Private Lives*, 21–33.

29. Keith M. Baker, *Inventing the French Revolution: Essays on French Political Culture in the Eighteenth Century* (Cambridge: Cambridge University Press, 1990); Mona Ozouf, "L'opinion publique," in *The French Revolution and the Creation of Modern Political Culture*, vol. 1, *The Political Culture of Old Regime*, ed. Keith M. Baker (Oxford: Pergamon Press, 1987): 419–34; Bertrand Binoche and Alain J. Lemaître, eds., *L'Opinion publique dans l'Europe des Lumières* (Paris: Armand Colin, 2013).

30. On salons, see Dena Goodman, *The Republic of Letters: A Cultural History of the French Enlightenment* (Ithaca, NY: Cornell University Press, 1994); Gordon, *Citizens without Sovereignty.*

31. For an assessment of these criticisms, see Stéphane Van Damme, "Farewell Habermas? Deux décennies d'études sur l'espace public," in *L'Espace public au Moyen Âge: Débats autour de Jürgen Habermas*, eds. Patrick Boucheron and Nicolas Offenstadt (Paris: Presses Universitaires de France, 2011): 43–71; Massimo Rospocher, "Beyond the Public Sphere: A Historiographical Transition," in *Beyond the Public Sphere: Opinions, Publics, Spaces in Early Modern Europe*, ed. Massimo Rospocher (Bologna-Berlin: Il Mulino-Duncker and Humbolt, 2012).

32. Madame Roland, *Mémoires de Madame Roland*, ed. Paul de Roux (Paris: Gallimard, 1986): 466–67.

33. Hesse, *Other Enlightenment.*

34. Arlette Farge, *Dire et mal dire: L'opinion publique au XVIIIe siècle* (Paris: Seuil, 1992); Arlette Farge and Jacques Revel, *The Vanishing Children of Paris: Rumor and*

Politics before the French Revolution, trans. Claudia Mieville (Cambridge, MA: Harvard University Press, 1993); Robert Darnton, *Poetry and the Police: Communication Networks in Eighteenth-Century Paris* (Cambridge, MA: Harvard University Press, 2012). From a more theoretical perspective, a critique of an elitist and homogeneous public sphere was carried out by Nancy Fraser, "Rethinking the Public Sphere: A Contribution to a Critique of Actually Existing Democracy," in *Habermas and the Public Sphere*, ed. Craig Calhoun (Cambridge: MIT Press, 1992): 109–42.

35. Steven L. Kaplan, *The Famine Plot Persuasion in Eighteenth-Century France* (Philadelphia, PA: American Philosophical Society, 1982); Edward P. Thompson, "The Moral Economy of the English Crowd," *Past and Present* 50 (1971): 73–136.

36. Antoine Lilti, *The World of Salons: Sociability and Worldliness in Eighteenth-Century Paris* (Oxford: Oxford University Press, 2015); Brian Cowan, *The Social Life of Coffee: The Emergence of the British Coffeehouse* (New Haven, CT: Yale University Press, 2005); Pierre-Yves Beaurepaire, *L'Autre et le frère: L'étranger et la franc-maçonnerie en France au XVIIIe siècle* (Paris: Honoré Champion, 1998).

37. Dan Edelstein, Paula Findlen, Giovanna Ceserani, Caroline Winterer, and Nicole Coleman, "Historical Research in a Digital Age: Reflections from the Mapping Republic of Letters Project," *American Historical Review* 122, no. 2 (2017): 400–24; Maria Teodora Comsa, Melanie Conroy, Dan Edelstein, Chloe Summers Edmondson, and Dan Willan, "The French Enlightenment Network," *Journal of Modern History* 88, no. 3 (2016): 495–534; Pierre-Yves Beaurepaire, ed., *La Communication en Europe, de l'âge classique au siècle des Lumières* (Paris: Belin, 2014).

38. Françoise Waquet and Hans Bost, eds., *Commercium litterarium: La communication dans la République des Lettres, 1600–1750* (Amsterdam-Maarsen: Apa-Holland University Press, 1994); Anne Goldgar, *Impolite Learning: Conduct and Community in the Republic of Letters, 1680–1730* (New Haven, CT: Yale University Press, 1995); Marc Fumaroli, *The Republic of Letters*, trans. Lara Vergnaud (New Haven, CT: Yale University Press, 2018).

39. Masano Yamashita, *Jean-Jacques Rousseau face au public: Problèmes d'identité* (Oxford: Voltaire Foundation, 2017).

40. John B. Thompson, *The Media and Modernity: A Social Theory of the Media* (Cambridge: Polity Press, 1995).

41. Gabriel Tarde, *L'Opinion et la foule* (Paris: Presses Universitaires de France, 1989 [1901]).

42. With the notable exception of Clifford Siskin and William Warner, eds., *This Is Enlightenment* (Chicago: University of Chicago Press, 2010).

43. Morellet to Shelburne, July 17–18, in *Lettres d'André Morellet*, ed. Dorothy Medlin, Jean-Claude David, and Paul Leclerc (Oxford: Voltaire Foundation, 1991–1996): vol. 1, 570.

44. Charlotte Guichard, *Les Amateurs d'art au XVIIIe siècle* (Seyssel: Champ Vallon, 2008); Thomas Crow, *Painters and Public Life in Eighteenth-Century Paris* (New Haven, CT: Yale University Press, 1985).

45. Louis-Sébastien Mercier, *Tableau de Paris* [1781–1788] (Amsterdam, 1783): vol. 5, 278.

46. Steven Shapin, *A Social History of Truth: Civility and Science in Seventeenth-Century England* (Chicago: University of Chicago Press, 1994); Simon Schaffer,

La Fabrique des sciences modernes, trans. Frédérique Aït-Touati, Loïc Marcou, and Stéphane Van Damme (Paris: Seuil, 2014).

47. Norbert Elias and John L. Scotson, *The Established and the Outsiders* [1965], 2nd ed. (London: Sage Publications, 1994).

48. Antoine Lilti, *The Invention of Celebrity*, trans. Lynn Jeffress (Cambridge: Polity Press, 2017). On scholarly mobility and the importance of visits in traditional practices within the Republic of Letters, see Goldgar, *Impolite Learning*; and Daniel Roche, *Humeurs vagabondes: De la circulation des hommes et de l'utilité des voyages* (Paris: Fayard, 2003).

49. Jean-Jacques Rousseau, *Les Confessions*, in *Œuvres complètes* (Paris: Gallimard, 1959): vol. 1, 611.

50. Thomas Medwin, *Conversations of Lord Byron: Noted during a Residence with his Lordship at Pisa, in the Years 1821 and 1822* (London: H. Colburn, 1824): 11.

51. Arit Adut, *Reign of Appearances: The Misery and Splendor of the Public Sphere* (Cambridge: Cambridge University Press, 2018).

52. Germaine de Staël, "Des femmes qui cultivent les lettres," in *De la littérature considérée dans ses rapports avec les institutions sociales* (Paris: Classiques Garnier, 1998 [1800]): 323–34. The English translation is cited from *An Extraordinary Woman: Selected Writings of Germaine de Staël*, trans. Vivian Folkenflik (New York: Columbia University Press, 1987): 22.

53. Germaine de Staël, *De l'influence des passions sur le bonheur des individus et des nations* (Lausanne: Jean Mourer, 1796): 3.

54. Germaine de Staël, *Des circonstances actuelles qui peuvent terminer la Révolution et des principes qui doivent fonder la Révolution en France*, ed. Lucia Omacini (Paris-Genève, Droz, 1979): 117.

55. Bronislaw Baczko, "Utopie salonnière et réalisme politique," in *Politiques de la Révolution française* (Paris: Gallimard, 2008): 341–491.

56. Daniel Dayan and Elihu Katz, *La Télévision cérémonielle: Anthropologie et histoire en direct* (Paris: Presses Universitaires de France, 1996). Gabriel Tarde was the first to theorize the conversation as a mode of socialization of the information produced by mass media. See Gabriel Tarde, "La conversation et l'opinion," in *L'Opinion et la foule*.

57. On nervousness about the amount of print matter at the end of the eighteenth century, see Elizabeth Eisenstein, *Divine Art, Infernal Machine: The Reception of Printing in the West from First Impressions to the Sense of an Ending* (Philadelphia: Pennsylvania University Press, 2011): 98–152; and Lucien Nouis, *De l'infini des bibliothèques au livre unique: L'archive épurée au XVIIIe siècle* (Paris: Classiques Garnier, 2013).

58. Habermas, *Structural Transformation of the Public Sphere*, 49.

59. David Denby, *Sentimental Narrative and the Social Order in France, 1760–1820* (Cambridge: Cambridge University Press, 1994); William M. Reddy, *The Navigation of Feeling: A Framework for the History of Emotions* (Cambridge: Cambridge University Press, 2001); Lynn Hunt, *Inventing Human Rights: A History* (New York: W. W. Norton, 2007).

60. Adam Smith, *The Theory of Moral Sentiments* [1759], ed. Ryan Patrick Hanley, with an introduction by Amartya Sen (New York: Penguin Classics, 2009): part 1: On the Propriety of Action; section 1: On the Sense of Propriety; chapter 1: Of Sympathy.

61. Luc Boltanski, *Distant Suffering: Morality, Media, and Politics*, trans. Graham D. Burchell (Cambridge: Cambridge University Press, 1999).

62. Niklas Luhmann, *The Reality of the Mass Media*, trans. Kathleen Cross (Stanford, CA: Stanford University Press, 2000).

63. Brewer, *Pleasures of the Imagination*.

64. Robert Darnton, *The Business of Enlightenment: A Publishing History of the "Encyclopédie," 1775–1800* (Cambridge, MA: Harvard University Press, 1979).

65. Nicole Castan, "The Public and the Private," in Chartier, ed., *History of Private Life*, vol. 3.

66. Jean-Louis Halpérin, "Protection de la vie privée et *privacy*: deux traditions juridiques différentes?" *Les Nouveaux Cahiers du Conseil constitutionnel* 48, no. 3 (2015): 59–68.

67. Jean-Jacques Rousseau, *Rousseau, juge de Jean-Jacques: Dialogues*, in *Œuvres complètes*, vol. 1, 985; *Rousseau, Judge of Jean-Jacques: Dialogues*, eds. Roger D. Masters and Christopher Kelly, trans. Judith Bush, Christopher Kelly, and Roger D. Masters (Hanover, NH: University Press of New England, 1990): 252. See also Barbara Carnevali, *Romantisme et reconnaissance: Figures de la conscience chez Rousseau*, trans. Philippe Audegean (Geneva: Droz, 2011).

68. Chantal Thomas, *La Reine scélérate: Marie-Antoinette dans les pamphlets* (Paris: Seuil, 1989); Simon Burrows, *Blackmail, Scandal, and Revolution: London's French Libellistes, 1758–1792* (Manchester: Manchester University Press, 2006); Robert Darnton, *The Devil in the Holy Water, or The Art of Slander from Louis XIV to Napoleon* (Philadelphia: University of Pennsylvania Press, 2010); Lilti, *Invention of Celebrity*, 164–76.

69. Philippe Lejeune, *Le Pacte autobiographique* (Paris: Seuil, 1975); Pierre Pachet, *Les Baromètres de l'âme: Naissance du journal intime* (Paris: Hatier, 1990).

70. Jean-Marie Goulemot, "Literary Practices: Publicizing the Private," in Chartier, ed., *History of Private Life*, vol. 3; Antoine Lilti, "The Writing of Paranoia: Jean-Jacques Rousseau and the Paradoxes of Celebrity," *Representations* 103, no. 1 (2008): 53–83.

71. Sarah Maza, *Private Lives and Public Affairs: The Causes Célèbres of Prerevolutionary France* (Berkeley: University of California Press, 1993).

72. Olivier Ferret, Anne Marie Mercier-Faivre, and Chantal Thomas, eds., *Dictionnaire des vies privées (1722–1842)* (Oxford: Voltaire Foundation, 2011).

73. [Giovanni Barberi], *Vie de Joseph Balsamo, connu sous le nom de comte Cagliostro* (Paris: Onfroy, 1791): iii.

CHAPTER 5

1. Margaret Jacob, *The Radical Enlightenment: Pantheists, Freemasons, and Republicans* (Lafayette, IN: Cornerstone Book Publishers, 2006 [1981]).

2. Jonathan I. Israel, *Radical Enlightenment: Philosophy and the Making of Modernity, 1650–1750* (Oxford: Oxford University Press, 2001). The French translation was published in 2005: *Les Lumières radicales: La philosophie, Spinoza et la naissance de la modernité (1650–1750)*, trans. Pauline Hugues, Charlotte Nordmann, and Jérôme Rosanvallon (Paris: Éditions Amsterdam, 2005).

3. Jonathan I. Israel, *Enlightenment Contested: Philosophy, Modernity, and the Emancipation of Man, 1670–1752* (Oxford: Oxford University Press, 2006); *Democratic*

Enlightenment: Philosophy, Revolution, and Human Rights, 1750–1790 (Oxford: Oxford University Press, 2013); *Revolutionary Ideas: An Intellectual History of the French Revolution from the Rights of Man to Robespierre* (Princeton, NJ: Princeton University Press, 2014); *How the American Revolution Ignited the World, 1775–1848* (Princeton, NJ: Princeton University Press, 2017).

4. Among the most incisive commentaries, see Anthony J. La Vopa, "A New Intellectual History? Jonathan Israel's Enlightenment," *Historical Journal* 52, no. 3 (2009): 717–38; Samuel Moyn, "Mind the Enlightenment," *Nation*, May 12, 2010; David A. Bell, "Where Do We Come From?" *New Republic*, February 8, 2012; Anaïs De Dijn, "The Politics of Enlightenment: From Peter Gay to Jonathan Israel," *Historical Journal* 55, no. 3 (2012): 785–805; Margaret Jacob, "Spinoza Got It," *London Review of Books* 34, no. 21 (2012); Jean-Fabien Spitz, "Jonathan Israel et les origines de la Republique moderne," *Raison Publique*, September 28, 2023, https://www.raisonpublique.fr. See also texts by Keith Baker and Johnson Kent Wright published at h-france.net in 2014: https://h-france.net/h-france-forum-volume-9-2014/.

5. As one example, in a fifty-page reply to a first draft of the present chapter, Israel takes issue with the cultural history of the Enlightenment incarnated in his view by "Roger Chartier, Robert Darnton, and François Furet" (*sic*) and their disciples—scholars whose propositions he judges "inept," "poor," and dangerous because they "introduce confusion in the minds of students." He then repeats peremptorily the theses of his book without the slightest concession to me or any of his critics (Jonathan Israel, "L'histoire intellectuelle des Lumières et de la Révolution: Une incursion critique," *La Lettre clandestine* 19 [2011]: 173–225). Similar exchanges of many words but of slight instructive value occurred with other Enlightenment historians who dared raise questions about his theses.

6. Jonathan I. Israel, *A Revolution of the Mind: Radical Enlightenment and the Intellectual Origins of Modern Democracy* (Princeton, NJ: Princeton University Press, 2010). The French translation was published in 2017: *Une révolution des esprits: Les Lumières radicales et les origines intellectuelles de la démocratie moderne*, trans. Matthieu Dumont and Jean-Jacques Rosat (Marseille: Agone, 2017).

7. See Israel, *Enlightenment Contested*, 60 and 869.

8. Israel, *Enlightenment Contested*, 58.

9. For an alternative view, see Timothy Tackett's research, which insists on the properly political dynamic of the Revolution, both among deputies and ordinary participants. Timothy Tackett, *Par la volonté du people: Comment les députés de 1789 sont devenus révolutionnaires*, trans. Alain Spiess (Paris: Albin Michel, 1997); and *The Coming of the Terror in the French Revolution* (Cambridge, MA: Harvard University Press, 2015).

10. This point, which I will not develop in these pages because it is among the least convincing, has generally been refuted by historians of the Revolution. See David A. Bell, "A Very Different French Revolution," *New York Review of Books*, July 10, 2014; Jeremy Popkin, "Review [of Jonathan Israel's *Revolutionary Ideas*]," *H-France* 15, no. 66 (2015). On the errors that lead to linking the *Declaration of the Rights of Man and the Citizen* to Spinozism, see Dan Edelstein, "A Response to Jonathan Israel," in *Self-Evident Truths? Human Rights and the Enlightenment*, ed. Kate Tunstall (London: Bloomsbury, 2012): 127–136.

11. Darrin M. McMahon, "What are Enlightenments?" *Modern Intellectual History* 4, no. 3 (2007): 601–16, at 609.

12. Spinoza's thinking started to be known within a small Dutch circle in the early 1660s, and within certain networks of the Republic of Letters, notably through Harry Oldenburg, who had visited Spinoza in Amsterdam in 1661 and maintained afterwards an extensive correspondence. But it was especially the publication in 1670 of the *Tractatus theologico-politicus*, the scandal it provoked, and its wide European circulation that established Spinoza's fame. In contrast, the *Ethics* only appeared after his death in 1677 as part of the *Opera posthuma* (published clandestinely in the winter of 1677–1678), which also contained uncompleted treatises and letters. The work was immediately condemned by civil and religious authorities. See Israel, *Radical Enlightenment*.

13. Israel, *Radical Enlightenment*, 7.

14. Wiep van Bunge, ed., *The Early Enlightenment in the Dutch Republic, 1650–1750* (Leiden: Brill, 2003).

15. This return to Spinoza probably originates in part from the rereadings inspired by the Marxist thinking of Louis Althusser and then Pierre Macherey and Étienne Balibar, and in part from the work of Gilles Deleuze, whose writings on Spinoza are probably the decisive reference among the many recent studies that could be characterized as neo-Spinozism. More recently, references to Spinoza are explicit and numerous in the work of Antonio Negri, Michael Hardt, Frédéric Lordon, and Christian Lazzeri. See Toni Negri, *Spinoza et nous* (Paris: Galilée, 2010). For an assessment, see Yves Citton and Frédéric Lordon, eds., *Spinoza et les sciences sociales: De la puissance de la multitude à l'économie des affects* (Paris: Éditions Amsterdam, 2008); and Céline Spector, "Le spinozisme politique aujourd'hui: Toni Negri, Étienne Balibar . . . ," *Esprit* 5 (2007): 27–45. Turning to Spinoza is today one of the main features in the theoretical arsenal of the altermondialist and anti-capitalist intellectual Left that may fairly be called "radical." See Frédéric Lordon, *La Société des affects: Pour un structuralisme des passions* (Paris: Seuil, 2013); Matthieu Renault and Guillaume Sibertin-Blanc, "Se réapproprier Spinoza: Usages et mésusages d'un philosophe à la mode," *Revue du Crieur* 10 (2018): 122 passim.

16. Israel, *Revolution of the Mind*.

17. Gilles Deleuze, *Spinoza: Practical Philosophy*, trans. Robert Hurley (San Francisco, CA: City Lights, 1988); Antonio Negri, *Savage Anomaly: The Power of Spinoza's Metaphysics and Politics*, trans. Michael Hardt (Minneapolis: University of Minnesota Press, 1991); Michael Hardt and Antonio Negri, *Multitude: War and Democracy in the Age of Empire* (New York: Penguin, 2004).

18. Antonio Negri, "Spinoza's Anti-Modernity," in *Subversive Spinoza: (Un)Contemporary Variations*, ed. Timothy S. Murphy, trans. Timothy S. Murphy, Michael Hardt, Ted Stolze, and Charles T. Wolfe (Manchester: Manchester University Press, 2004): 79–93; Yves Citton and Frédéric Lordon, "Un devenir spinoziste des sciences sociales," in Citton and Lordon, eds., *Spinoza et les sciences sociales*, 15–44, at 19.

19. See Jonathan I. Israel, *Race, Class, and Politics in Colonial Mexico, 1610–1670* (London: Oxford University Press, 1975); *Empires and Entrepots: The Dutch, the Spanish Monarchy, and the Jews, 1585–1713* (London: Hambledon Press, 1990); *The Dutch Republic: Its Rise, Greatness, and Fall, 1477–1806* (Oxford: Clarendon Press, 1995); *Di-*

asporas within a Diaspora: Jews, Crypto-Jews and the World Maritime Empires (1540–1740) (Leiden: Brill, 2002).

20. Israel, *Enlightenment Contested,* 865.

21. Israel, *Enlightenment Contested,* 15–26.

22. Israel, "L'histoire intellectuelle des Lumières et de la Révolution," 195.

23. Dominick LaCapra, *Rethinking Intellectual History: Texts, Contexts, Language* (Ithaca, NY: Cornell University Press, 1983); *History and Reading: Tocqueville, Foucault, French Studies* (Toronto: University of Toronto Press, 2000): especially p. 21–72 for valuable remarks on method.

24. James Swenson, *On Jean-Jacques Rousseau, Considered as One of the First Authors of the Revolution* (Stanford, CA: Stanford University Press, 2000); Carla Hesse, "Lire Rousseau pendant la Révolution française," *Lumières* 15 (2011): 17–32; Céline Spector, *Au prisme de Rousseau: Usages politiques contemporains* (Oxford: Voltaire Foundation, 2011).

25. In a 2018 interview in which he mentions criticisms I made about his work, Israel identifies me as "a leading proponent of postmodernist deconstruction"; for good measure, he derides the work of Daniel Roche in similar fashion. See Jonathan I. Israel, "Radicalising the Enlightenment," *Spiked,* May 4, 2018, https://www.spiked-online.com/2018/05/04/radicalising-the-enlightenment/#.WvQoWa3MxdA.

26. This ambiguity is particularly evident in the conclusion to the second volume, which plays on the meaning of the term *importance* in both the historical and philosophical senses. See Israel, *Enlightenment Contested,* 865–66.

27. One may take the case of Henri, compte de Boulainvilliers, since Israel devotes a chapter and many commentaries to him. Although Boulainvilliers's writings on the history of political institutions and the nobility, in which he defends nobles' interests, were published and republished in his lifetime with great success, his writings of deist and Spinozist inspiration remained much less well known. His *Abrégé d'histoire universelle* only circulated among a few close friends and was never published. His *Essai de métaphysique* was only published, and only clandestinely, after his death. Finally, his translation of Spinoza's *Ethics* remained largely unknown until the nineteenth century, and whether he actually wrote it is still an open question. On the publication and reception of radical works, see the comments of Harvey Chisick, "Interpreting the Enlightenment," *European Legacy* 13, no. 1 (2008): 35–57.

28. The "package" contains eight points: reason as the unique criteria of truth, the rejection of supernatural explanations, racial and sexual equality, a universal and secular ethics, tolerance and freedom of thought, acceptance of freedom of sexual behavior, freedom of public expression, and democratic republicanism (Israel, *Enlightenment Contested,* 866).

29. Paul Vernière, *Spinoza et la pensée française avant la Révolution* (Paris: Presses Universitaires de France, 1954); Wiep van Bunge and Wim Klever, eds., *Disguised and Overt Spinozism around 1700* (Leiden: Brill, 1996); Olivier Bloch, ed., *Spinoza au XVIIIe siècle* (Paris: Méridiens Klincksieck, 1990); Sylvain Zac, *Spinoza en Allemagne: Mendelssohn, Lessing et Jacobi* (Paris: Méridiens Klincksieck, 1989); David Bell, *Spinoza in Germany from 1670 to the Age of Goethe* (London: Institute of Germanic Studies, 1984); Winfried Schröder, *Spinoza in der deutschen Frühaufklärung* (Würzburg: Königshausen-Neumann, 1987).

30. Silvia Berti, "At the Roots of Unbelief," *Journal of the History of Ideas* 56, no. 4 (1995): 555–75.

31. Laurent Jaffro, Benoît Frydman, Emmanuel Cattin, and Alain Petit, eds., *Léo Strauss: art d'écrire, politique, philosophie: La persécution et l'art d'écrire* (Paris: Vrin, 2001).

32. Gianluca Mori, *Bayle philosophe* (Paris: Honoré Champion, 1999): 181. For a careful presentation of the current debates around Pierre Bayle, see also Antony McKenna and Gianni Paganini, eds., *Pierre Bayle dans la République des Lettres: Philosophie, religion, critique* (Paris: Honoré Champion, 2004).

33. Richard Popkin, *The History of Skepticism: From Savonarola to Bayle*, revised and expanded ed. (Oxford: Oxford University Press, 2003); Frédéric Brahami, *Le Travail du scepticisme: Montaigne, Bayle, Hume* (Paris: Presses Universitaires de France, 2001); Anton Matytsin, *The Specter of Skepticism in the Age of Enlightenment* (Baltimore, MD: Johns Hopkins University Press, 2016): 53–69.

34. Robertson, *The Case for the Enlightenment*; Giuseppe Ricuperati, "In margine al *Radical Enlightenment* di Jonathan I. Israel," *Rivista storica italiana* 115, no. 1 (2003): 285–329.

35. Gustave Lanson, "Questions diverses sur l'histoire de l'esprit philosophique en France avant 1750," *Revue d'histoire littéraire de la France* 19, no. 1 (1912): 1–29; Ira O. Wade, *The Clandestine Organisation and Diffusion of Philosophic Ideas in France from 1700 to 1750* (Princeton, NJ: Princeton University Press, 1938).

36. Olivier Bloch, ed., *Le Matérialisme du XVIIIe siècle et la littérature clandestine* (Paris: Vrin, 1982); Miguel Benítez, *La Face cachée des Lumières: Recherches sur les manuscrits philosophiques clandestins de l'âge classique* (Paris-Oxford: Universitas-Voltaire Foundation, 1996); Geneviève Artigas-Menant, *Du secret des clandestins à la propagande voltairienne* (Paris: Honoré Champion, 2001); Alan C. Kors, *Atheism in France, 1650–1729*, vol. 1, *The Orthodox Sources of Disbelief* (Princeton, NJ: Princeton University Press, 1990); Gianni Paganini, Miguel Benítez, and James Dybikowski, eds., *Scepticisme, clandestinité et libre-pensée* (Paris: Honoré Champion, 2002).

37. Israel, *Radical Enlightenment*, 694.

38. G. Paganini, "Avant la promenade du sceptique: Pyrrhonisme et clandestinité de Bayle à Diderot," in Paganini, Benítez, and Dybikowski, eds., *Scepticisme, clandestinité et libre-pensée*, 17–46.

39. See Tristan Dagron, "Néo-spinozisme ou antispinozisme: le cas Toland," in *Qu'est-ce que les Lumières radicales? Libertinage, athéisme et spinozisme dans le tournant philosophique de l'âge classique*, eds. Catherine Secrétan, Tristan Dagron, and Laurent Bove (Paris: Éditions Amsterdam, 2007): 325–341.

40. Ann Thomson, *Bodies of Thought: Science, Religion, and the Soul in the Early Enlightenment* (Oxford: Oxford University Press, 2008).

41. Martin Mulsow, *Enlightenment Underground: Radical Germany (1680–1720)* (Charlottesville: Virginia University Press, 2015).

42. See Silvia Berti, Françoise Charles-Daubert, and Richard Popkin, eds., *Heterodoxy, Spinozism, and Free Thought in Early Eighteenth-Century Europe: Studies on the* Traité des trois imposteurs (Dordrecht-Boston: Kluwer Academic Publishers, 1996); Françoise Charles-Daubert, ed., *Le* Traité des trois imposteurs *et* L'Esprit *de Spinoza: Philosophie clandestine entre 1678 et 1768* (Oxford: Voltaire Foundation, 1999).

43. Margaret Jacob made the discovery of these "Chevaliers de la jubilation." See Jacob, *Radical Enlightenment*. The nature and function of their meetings is still debated.

For an adverse opinion, see Christiane Berkvens-Stevelinck, "Les Chevaliers de la Jubilation: maçonnerie ou libertinage? À propos de quelques publications de Margaret C. Jacob," *Quaerendo* 13, no. 1 (1983): 50–73 and 13, no. 2 (1983): 124–48.

44. Jacob, *Radical Enlightenment*, esp. 215–33.

45. Israel, *Radical Enlightenment*, 695.

46. Similarly, the treatment of Abbé Jean Meslier's famous "Mémoire des pensées et sentiments," which had a considerable impact on the Enlightenment's anti-religious thinking, is rather odd. Although his text is ranked fourth in the table of the most widely circulated clandestine philosophical manuscripts (Israel, *Radical Enlightenment*, 690), Israel devotes no commentary to him whatsoever. It is true that Meslier had not read Spinoza, whom he only knew of through the refutation by Father Tournemine. And yet, in Israel's second volume Meslier is judged to be the "most systematic" radical thinker (Israel, *Enlightenment Contested*, 456, 716, 724) based on his atheism, even though his relation to Spinoza is hardly clear. What's more, it is known that Voltaire was the first to publish Meslier's text in a clearly expurgated version. The intellectual and editorial genealogies are thus infinitely more complex than what is suggested by the binary opposition between radicals and moderates.

47. Martin Mulsow, "Freethinking in Early Eighteenth-Century Germany," in Berti, Charles-Daubert, and Popkin, eds., *Heterodoxy, Spinozism, and Free Thought*, 193–237. It should be noted that Peter Friedrich Arpe highly praised Jean Bodin's *Colloquium* and possessed a copy of it.

48. Mulsow, *Enlightenment Underground*, ch. 4.

49. Martin Mulsow, "The Radical Enlightenment: Problems and Perspectives," *Izea: Kleine Schriften* 5 ("Concepts of (Radical) Enlightenment") (2014): 81–94.

50. Pierre-François Moreau, "Spinoza était-il spinoziste?" in Secrétan, Dagron, and Bove, *Qu'est-ce que les Lumières radicales?* 289–97.

51. Wiep van Bunge, *From Stevin to Spinoza: An Essay on Philosophy in the Seventeenth-Century Dutch Republic* (Leiden: Brill, 2001).

52. See Pierre-Henri Tavoillot, *Le Crépuscule des Lumières: Les documents de la "querelle du Panthéisme" (1780–1789)* (Paris: Éditions du Cerf, 1995).

53. Pierre Macherey, *Avec Spinoza: Études sur la doctrine et l'histoire du spinozisme* (Paris: Presses Universitaires de France, 1992): 7.

54. Israel, *Radical Enlightenment*, 298.

55. Jean-Louis Fabiani, "Controverses scientifiques, controverses philosophiques: Figures, positions, trajets," *Enquête* 5 (1997): 11–34; Christophe Prochasson and Anne Rasmussen, eds., "Comment on se dispute: Les formes de la controverse," *Mil neuf cent, revue d'histoire intellectuelle* 25 (2007).

56. Israel, *Enlightenment Contested*.

57. See Stéphane Van Damme, *L'Épreuve libertine: Morale, soupçon et pouvoirs dans la France baroque* (Paris: CNRS Éditions, 2008). For a more transversal approach and one very attentive to the intellectual effects of controversies and the way categories get constructed, see McMahon, *Enemies of the Enlightenment*.

58. See the refutation written by Father Tournemine and published as a preface to Fénelon's *Démonstration de l'existence de Dieu* in 1713; see also Christopher Wittich's *Anti-Spinoza*, published in Amsterdam in 1690.

59. Israel, *Radical Enlightenment*, 159.

60. Vernière, *Spinoza et la pensée française avant la Révolution*, 528–611. About Diderot, Vernière claims that it is a fool's errand to try and establish a univocal interpretation of this "rhetorician capable of making a shiny display of every thesis"—"rhéteur apte à faire miroiter toutes les theses," 555.

61. "Modern Spinozists" can be found in the *Encyclopédie* entry for "Spinozist," which distinguishes between modern Spinozists and older ones. The original entry is "Spinosiste."

62. Yves Citton, *L'Envers de la liberté: L'invention d'un imaginaire spinoziste dans la France des Lumières* (Paris: Éditions Amsterdam, 2006): 27.

63. A formulation attributed to Father Tournemine and quoted in Yves Citton, *L'Envers de la liberté*, 46.

64. Johannes Colerus, *La Vie de B. Spinoza, tirée des écrits de ce fameux Philosophe et du témoignage de plusieurs personnes qui l'ont connu particulièrement* (The Hague: T. Johnson, 1706); Israel, *Radical Enlightenment*, 301. On the importance of biographical writing for the history of philosophy during the Enlightenment, see Dinah Ribard, *Raconter, vivre, penser: Histoires de philosophies, 1650–1766* (Paris: Vrin-Éditions de l'EHESS, 2002): esp. 127–32 on anecdotes about Spinoza.

65. Macherey, *Avec Spinoza*, 19.

66. Moreau, "Spinoza était-il spinoziste?" The *Tractatus Theologico-Politicus* and the *Tractatus Politicus* (which contains no chapter on democracy) may be interpreted in divergent ways. It is perfectly possible, against the grain of analyses of Spinoza as the subversive prophet of multitudes and radical democracy, to insist on the aporias in his theory of democracy marked by a "fear of the masses" and by the tensions of democratic institutionalization. See Étienne Balibar, *Spinoza and Politics*, trans. Peter Snowdon (London: Verso, 2008 [1998]) and *Masses, Classes, Ideas: Studies on Politics and Philosophy before and after Marx*, trans. James Swenson (London: Routledge, 1994). For a summary presentation of the contemporary stakes of these debates, see Spector, "Le spinozisme politique aujourd'hui."

67. François Furet, "Deux légitimations historiques de la société française au XVIIIe siècle: Mably et Boulainvilliers," in *L'Atelier de l'histoire* (Paris: Flammarion, 1982): 165–83; Diego Venturino, *Le Ragioni della tradizione: nobiltà e mondo moderno in Boulainvilliers, 1658–1722* (Florence: Le Lettere, 1993); Michel Foucault, *Society Must Be Defended: Lectures at the Collège de France, 1975–1976*, eds. Mauro Bertani and Alessandro Fontana, trans. David Macey (New York: Picador, 2003).

68. Pim den Boer, "Le dictionnaire libertin d'Adrien Koerbagh," in Secrétan, Dagron, and Bove, eds., *Qu'est-ce que les Lumières radicales?* 104–30.

69. Jean-Pierre Cavaillé, "Libertinage ou Lumières radicales," in Secrétan, Dagron, and Bove, eds., *Qu'est-ce que les Lumières radicales?* 61–74.

70. This matter is delicate. A mixture of prudence and elitism led Spinoza to make reserved use of his writings and to sometimes use a double language that some authors have associated with the Marrano tradition (Yirmiyahu Yovel, *Spinoza and Other Heretics: The Marrano of Reason* [Princeton, NJ: Princeton University Press, 1989]). But one should not neglect the fact that Spinoza did not hesitate to publicly affirm his break with Mosaic Law, an act that led to his exclusion from Amsterdam's Jewish community in 1656; and that he published the *Tractatus Theologico-Politicus*, which among other

traits is a manifesto for freedom of expression; and that he had at one time taken steps for the publication of his *Ethics*.

71. And not always implicitly. Jonathan Israel states that the radical authors rebel "one might say from the left" (*Enlightenment Contested*, 43).

72. Israel, *Enlightenment Contested*, 12.

73. Michel Foucault, *The Government of the Self and Others I: Lectures at the Collège de France, 1983–1984*, ed. Frédéric Gros, trans. Graham Burchell (New York: Palgrave Macmillan, 2010).

74. Jonathan Israel is particularly severe with Voltaire, whom he presents as a moderate deist providentialist, or even as conservative. That Voltaire on many counts, socially and politically for example, is not a revolutionary may be granted; but on the religious plane, his critique of miracles and holy scripture made him someone that ecclesiastical authorities found difficult to accept. Also, as Margaret Jacob noted, Newtonian thinking as it circulated in France and across Europe was largely de-Christianized compared to its English version.

75. Israel, *Radical Enlightenment*.

76. Israel, *Enlightenment Contested*, 11; Graeme Garrard, *Rousseau's Counter-Enlightenment: A Republican Critique of the Philosophes* (Albany: State University of New York Press, 2003).

77. Jean-Pierre Cavaillé, *Dis/simulations: Jules-César Vanini, François La Mothe Le Vayer, Gabriel Naudé, Louis Machon et Torquato Accetto: Religion, morale et politique au XVIIe siècle* (Paris: Honoré Champion, 2002); Sophie Gouverneur, *Prudence et subversion libertines: La critique de la raison d'État chez François de la Mothe Le Vayer, Gabriel Naudé et Samuel Sorbière* (Paris: Honoré Champion, 2005).

78. Alain Sandrier, *Le Style philosophique du baron d'Holbach: Conditions et contraintes du prosélytisme athée en France dans la seconde moitié du XVIIIe siècle* (Paris: Honoré Champion, 2004).

79. Christopher Kelly, *Rousseau as Author: Consecrating One's Life to the Truth* (Chicago: University of Chicago Press, 2003).

80. Jean-Jacques Rousseau, *Lettres écrites de la Montagne*, in *Œuvres complètes*, vol. 3 (Paris: Gallimard, 1964): 791–92.

81. Lilti, "The Writing of Paranoia."

82. When Rousseau wishes to denounce the persecution that he feels he has suffered on account of his publications, he contrasts it with the consideration he enjoyed at earlier moments in his life and with "the atheist Spinoza [who] taught peacefully his doctrine" and "lived and died tranquilly, and even well considered" (*Lettre à Christophe de Beaumont*, in *Oeuvres completes*, vol. 4, 931).

83. Israel, *Enlightenment Contested*, 866.

84. Israel, "L'histoire intellectuelle des Lumières et de la Révolution."

85. Perrot, *Une histoire intellectuelle de l'économie politique*; Robertson, *Case for the Enlightenment*.

86. J. G. A. Pocock, "Historiography and Enlightenment: A View of their History," *Modern Intellectual History* 5, no. 1 (2008): 83–96.

87. For a recent presentation, see Anton M. Matytsin and Dan Edelstein, eds., *Let There Be Enlightenment: The Religious and Mystical Sources of Rationality* (Baltimore, MD: Johns Hopkins University Press, 2018).

PART III: POLITICS

1. Voltaire to Helvétius, October 1760, in *Correspondance*, 13 vols. (Paris: Gallimard, 1985): vol. 6, 49.

2. Denis Diderot, "Avertissement" [1765], in *Encyclopédie ou Dictionnaire raisonné des sciences, des arts et des métiers* (Paris: Briasson-David-Le Breton-Durand, 1751–1772): vol. 8 (1765), http://enccre.academie-sciences.fr/encyclopedie.

3. Benjamin Franklin, *The Papers of Benjamin Franklin*, vol. 37, *March 16 through August 15, 1782*, ed. Ellen R. Cohn (New Haven, CT: Yale University Press, 2003): 472–73, https://founders.archives.gov/documents/Franklin/01-37-02-0299.

4. de Staël, *Des circonstances actuelles qui peuvent terminer la Révolution*, 270. Written in 1798, this important political text would remain in manuscript form. Her *De la littérature*, published in 1800, aimed to study the sociopolitical conditions for the "future progress" of the Enlightenment.

5. Pierre-Louis Roederer, *Opuscules*, vol. 2 (Paris: Imprimerie du Journal de Paris, [1802]): 6.

6. Christoph Streb, "La posture d'auteur du publiciste et la médiatisation de la communication politique, 1760–1800," PhD diss., EHESS/University of Heidelberg, 2020.

7. Victor Hugo, "Centenaire de Voltaire" [1878], *Actes et paroles IV: Depuis l'exil, 1876–1885*, in *Œuvres complètes: Politique* (Paris: Robert Laffont, 1985): 984–991, at 987.

8. Jean-Paul Sartre, *"What Is Literature?" and Other Essays* (Cambridge, MA: Harvard University Press, 1988): 83 and 103.

CHAPTER 6

1. François de La Mothe Le Vayer, *Cinq dialogues faits à l'imitation des anciens* (Mons: Paul de la Flèche, 1673): 328. See also the critical edition of the same title, ed. Bruno Roche (Paris: Honoré Champion, 2015). On the practices and strategies of libertines, see the work of Jean-Pierre Cavaillé, especially *Dis/simulations: Jules-César Vanini, François La Mothe Le Vayer, Gabriel Naudé, Louis Machon et Torquato Accetto, Religion, morale et politique au XVIIe siècle* (Paris: Honoré Champion, 2002); and *Postures libertines (la culture des esprits forts)* (Toulouse: Anarcharsis, 2011). See also Isabelle Moreau, *"Guérir du sot": Les stratégies d'écriture des libertins à l'âge classique* (Paris: Honoré Champion, 2007).

2. Nevertheless, an esoteric current reemerges at the end of the century, in the context of Freemasonry and debates about the Egyptian "double religion"; however, that current is difficult to measure, it is engaged in most likely by only a small minority, and its secret is considered provisional. See Jan Assmann, *Religio Duplex: How the Enlightenment Reinvented Egyptian Religion*, trans. Robert Savage (Cambridge: Polity Press, 2014).

3. Roland Mortier, "Ésotérisme et Lumières: Un dilemme de la pensée au XVIIIe siècle," in *Clartés et ombres du siècle des Lumières*, (Geneva: Droz, 1969): 60–103.

4. Deborah Cohen, *La Nature du peuple: Les formes de l'imaginaire social (XVIIIe–XXIe siècles)* (Seyssel: Champ Vallon, 2010).

5. Robert Darnton, *Censors at Work: How States Shaped Literature* (New York: W. W. Norton, 2014); Raymond Birn, *La Censure royale des livres dans la France des*

Lumières (Paris: Odile Jacob, 2007); Barbara de Negroni, *Lectures interdites: Le travail des censeurs au XVIIIe siècle, 1723–1774* (Paris: Albin Michel, 1995); Edoardo Tortarolo, *Invenzione della libertà di stampa* (Rome: Carocci, 2011).

6. Voltaire, article on "Blé" [Wheat], *Questions sur l'Encyclopédie*, in *Œuvres complètes* (Genève: Cramer, 1768–1777): vol. 26 (1775), 296.

7. Voltaire, quoted in Mortier, *Clartés et ombres du siècle des Lumières*, 76.

8. Voltaire to the Marquis de Villevielle, December 20, 1768, in *Correspondance*, vol. 9, 710.

9. Voltaire, "FRAUDE—S'il faut user de fraudes pieuses avec le peuple?" [FRAUD: If pious fraud must be used on the people?], in *Dictionnaire philosophique*, ed. Béatrice Didier (Paris: Imprimerie nationale, 1994): 265–69, at 268.

10. See, for example, the use made by La Mettrie of the term "the people" in the "Discours préliminaire" to *L'Homme machine* (Julien Offray de La Mettrie, *Man a Machine and Man a Plant* [1748], trans. Richard A. Watson and Maya Rybalka, with introduction and notes by Justin Leiber [Indianapolis/Cambridge: Hackett Publishing, 1994]), and the commentary on La Mettrie in Van Damme, *À toutes voiles vers la vérité*, 69–70.

11. Voltaire to Helvétius, October 27, 1760, in *Correspondance*, vol 6, 49.

12. Lilti, *World of the Salons*. On the role of academies and provincial elites, see Roche, *Le Siècle des Lumières en province*.

13. Harvey Chisick, *The Limits of Reform in the Enlightenment: Attitudes toward the Education of the Lower Classes in Eighteenth-Century France* (Princeton, NJ: Princeton University Press, 1981).

14. Condorcet, "Dissertation sur cette question: S'il est utile aux hommes d'être trompé," in *Œuvres complètes*, vol. 5, ed. François Arago (Paris: Firmin, 1847): 361–62. Written in 1779, the text was not published until 1791 during the Revolution—but it was published with no modifications, states Condorcet.

15. Diderot, "Avertissement," ii.

16. D'Holbach, *Système de la Nature* (London, 1770): vol. 2, 383, quoted in Mortier, *Clartés et ombres du siècle des Lumières*, 93.

17. Sophia Rosenfeld, *Common Sense: A Political History* (Cambridge, MA: Harvard University Press, 2011). This work reviews the parallel history of "common sense" in the Scottish epistemology context (Thomas Reid, James Beattie) and the radical context of "good sense"; it then examines the populist synthesis carried out by Thomas Paine in Philadelphia in 1776.

18. D'Holbach, *Le Bon Sens* (London, 1772), section 195, quoted in Rosenfeld, *Common Sense*, 119.

19. Bronislaw Baczko, *Une éducation pour la démocratie: Textes et projets de l'époque révolutionnaire* (Paris: Garnier, 1982); Dominique Julia, *La Révolution: Les Trois couleurs du tableau noir* (Paris: Belin, 1981).

20. Condorcet, *Cinq mémoires sur l'instruction publique* [1791], eds. Charles Coutel and Catherine Kintzler (Paris: Garnier-Flammarion, 1994).

21. Condorcet, *Esquisse d'un tableau historique de l'esprit humain*, ed. Alain Pons (Paris: Flammarion, 1988): 274–75. The English translation is from Condorcet, *Outlines of an Historical View of the Progress of the Human Mind* (London: J. Johnson, 1795): 333–34.

22. Catherine Kintzler, *Condorcet: L'instruction publique et la naissance du citoyen* (Paris: Minerve, 1984).

23. Keith M. Baker, *Condorcet*, 285–303.

24. Françoise Waquet, "La Bastille académique," in *La Carmagnole des Muses: L'homme de lettres et l'artiste sous la Révolution*, ed. Jean-Claude Bonnet (Paris: Armand Colin, 1988): 19–36.

25. Condorcet, "Fragment sur l'Atlantide," in *Esquisse d'un tableau historique de l'esprit humain*, 299–348, at 299 and 301.

26. Condorcet, "Fragment sur l'Atlantide," 303.

27. Condorcet, "Fragment sur l'Atlantide," 301.

28. Chartier, *Lectures et lecteurs dans la France d'Ancien Régime.*

29. Chrétien-Guillaume Lamoignon de Malesherbes, "Discours prononcé dans l'Académie française" [1775], in *Œuvres inédites* (Paris: Hénée-Buisson-Michaud, 1808): 151. See Franck Salaün, "Les livres nécessaires et l'opinion publique selon Malesherbes," in Binoche and Lemaître, eds., *L'Opinion publique dans l'Europe des Lumières*, 61–86.

30. Alexandre Deleyre and Abbé Raynal, *Tableau de l'Europe pour servir de suite à l'histoire philosophique et politique des établissements et du commerce des Européens dans les deux Indes* (Maastricht: Jean Edme Dufour, 1774): 149.

31. The English translation is from Condorcet, *Outlines of an Historical View of the Progress of the Human Mind*, 179.

32. Nouis, *De l'infini des bibliothèques au livre unique*. See also Jennifer Tsien, *The Bad Taste of Others: Judging Literary Value in Eighteenth-Century France* (Philadelphia: University of Pennsylvania Press, 2012).

33. Voltaire to Diderot, September 8, 1776, in *Correspondance*, vol. 12, 707.

34. "Encyclopédie," *Encyclopédie*, vol. 5, 1755.

35. de Staël, *Des circonstances actuelles qui peuvent terminer la Révolution*, 117.

36. de Staël, *Des circonstances actuelles qui peuvent terminer la Révolution*, 113–14.

37. Éléonore Reverzy, *Portrait de l'artiste en fille de joie: La littérature publique* (Paris: CNRS Éditions, 2016).

38. Geoffrey Turnovsky, *The Literary Market: Authorship and Modernity in the Old Regime* (Philadelphia: University of Pennsylvania Press, 2010).

39. Raynal, *Histoire philosophique des Deux Indes*, vol. 3, 61. See Sandro Landi, "'Laissez écrire': The Call for a Free Trade of Ideas in Raynal's *Histoire des deux Indes*: A Long Enlightenment's Belief," *Storia della storiografia* 71, no. 1 (2017): 77–88.

40. Mercier, *L'An 2440*, chapter 23. See also the commentary in Nouis, *De l'infini des bibliothèques au livre unique*.

41. Louis-Sébastien Mercier, "Triomphe de Voltaire: Janot," in *Tableau de Paris*, 264–69. See Lilti, *Invention of Celebrity*, 20–23.

42. Louis-Sébastien Mercier, *Tableau de Paris.*

43. Jean-Jacques Rousseau, *Rousseau juge de Jean-Jacques*, in *Œuvres complètes*, vol. 1, 940; English translation from *Rousseau: Judge of Jean-Jacques: Dialogues*, eds. Roger D. Masters and Christopher Kelly, trans. Judith R. Bush, Christopher Kelly, and Roger D. Masters (Hanover, NH: University Press of New England, 1990): 217.

44. On the denunciation of the fabrication of opinion, see Yves Citton, "Fabrique de

l'opinion et folie de la dissidence: le 'complot' dans *Rousseau juge de Jean-Jacques,*" in *Rousseau juge de Jean-Jacques: Études sur les dialogues* (Ottawa: University of Ottawa Press, 1998): 101–14. On the relations Rousseau maintained with the mechanisms of celebrity status, see Lilti, *Invention of Celebrity*, 109–59.

45. Yamashita, *Jean-Jacques Rousseau face au public*, 23.

46. Diderot, "Multitude," in *Encyclopédie*, vol. 10, 860.

47. Colas Duflo, *Diderot philosophe* (Paris: Honoré Champion, 2013 [2003]): 13–20.

48. See chapter 7 on Diderot in the present volume.

49. Dorothea E. von Mücke, *The Practices of The Enlightenment: Aesthetics, Authorship, and the Public* (New York: Columbia University Press, 2015); Martus, *Aufklärung*.

50. Immanuel Kant, "An Answer to the Question: 'What Is Enlightenment?'" in *Perpetual Peace and Other Essays*, trans. Ted Humphrey (Indianapolis, IN: Hackett, 1992).

51. Günter Birtsch, "The Berlin Wednesday Society," in *What Is Enlightenment? Eighteenth-Century Answers and Twentieth-Century Questions*, ed. James Schmidt (Berkeley: California University Press, 1996): 235–69.

52. Johann Karl Möhsen, "What Is to Be Done towards the Enlightenment of the Citizenry?" in Schmidt, ed., *What Is Enlightenment?* 49–52.

53. James Schmidt, "What Is Enlightenment? A Question, Its Context, and Some Consequences," in *What Is Enlightenment?* 1–44. See also Jean Mondot, ed. and trans., *Qu'est-ce que les Lumières?* (Pessac: Presses Universitaires de Bordeaux, 2007).

54. Terence James Reed, *Light in Germany: Scenes from an Unknown Enlightenment* (Chicago: University of Chicago Press, 2015): 9–29.

55. Kant, "An Answer to the Question: 'What Is Enlightenment?'"

56. Kant, "An Answer to the Question: 'What Is Enlightenment?'"

57. Kant, "An Answer to the Question: 'What Is Enlightenment?'"

58. Immanuel Kant, *Critique of the Power of Judgment.*

59. Immanuel Kant, *The Conflict of the Faculties*, trans. Mary J. Gregor (Lincoln: University of Nebraska Press, 1992): 162.

60. Christoph Martin Wieland, "Sechs Antworten auf Sechs Fragen," *Teutscher Merkur* (April 1789), reprinted in Mondot, ed., *Qu'est-ce que les Lumières?*, 123–27, at 126.

61. Blumenberg, *Legitimacy of the Modern Age*, 429–31.

62. Bertrand Binoche, *"Écrasez l'infâme!" Philosopher à l'âge des Lumières* (Paris: La Fabrique, 2018): 30–43.

63. Sophia Rosenfeld, *Democracy and Truth: A Short History* (Philadelphia: University of Pennsylvania Press, 2019).

64. Jean-Paul Sartre, *Situations*, vol. 10, *Politique et autobiographie* (Paris: Gallimard, 1976): 86.

65. Jacques Rancière, *The Ignorant Schoolmaster: Five Lessons in Intellectual Emancipation*, trans. Kristin Ross (Stanford, CA: Stanford University Press, 1991): 7.

66. Jean-Claude Milner, *De l'école* (Paris: Seuil, 1984): 108.

67. See chapter 8 on Michel Foucault in the present volume.

CHAPTER 7

1. The origin of this declaration, which may not be authentic, is hard to identify. It is generally thought to have happened at the time of the Algerian War but sometimes, less convincingly, during the events of May 1968.

2. *Le Monde*, April 2, 1966, quoted in Jeanne Favret-Saada, *Les Sensibilités religieuses blessées: Christianismes, blasphèmes et cinéma, 1965–1988* (Paris: Fayard, 2017): 106. Many left-leaning journalists defended the idea of exercising censorship against Diderot and Rivette's movie: "Diderot encore sous la censure," was the headline in the communist newspaper *Humanité*; "Diderot à l'Index," was the choice of the magazine *l'Express* (71).

3. See the remarks by Georges May in his preface to Denis Diderot, *La Religieuse*, in *Œuvres complètes*, vol. 11 (Paris: Hermann, 1975). The English edition is *The Nun*, trans. Russell Gouldbourne (Oxford: Oxford University Press, 2005).

4. Robert Darnton, *Bohème littéraire et Révolution: Le monde des livres au XVIIIe siècle* (Paris: Éditions de l'EHESS-Gallimard-Seuil, 1983); Darnton, *Édition et sedition: L'univers de la littérature clandestine au XVIIIe siècle* (Paris: Gallimard, 1991).

5. On the life of Diderot, the authoritative biography remains that of Arthur M. Wilson, published in two volumes as *Diderot: The Testing Years, 1713–1759* and *Diderot: The Appeal to Posterity, 1759–1784* (Oxford: Oxford University Press, 1957 and 1972).

6. Denis Diderot, *Lettre sur le commerce de la librairie* [1763], in *Œuvres*, vol. 3, *Politique*, ed. Laurent Versini (Paris: Robert Laffont, 1995): 108. On this text, written at the request of Paris booksellers, see Roger Chartier, "Diderot et ses corsaires," *Inscrire et effacer: Culture écrite et littérature (Xie--XVIIIe siècle)* (Paris: Seuil/Gallimard, 2005), 177–92.

7. Jules Michelet, *Histoire de France*, vol. 15, *Louis XV* (Paris: Flammarion, 1893): 399.

8. Emmanuel Boussuge and Alain Mothu, "Autour de Diderot: Archives policières de la Bastille, 1748–1749," *La Lettre clandestine* 19 (2011): 317–64.

9. Michel Delon, "Vincennes," in *Diderot, cul par-dessus tête* (Paris: Albin Michel, 2013).

10. Denis Diderot, "Socratique," in *Encyclopédie*, vol. 15: 262–65. Quote on p. 262.

11. Olivier Ferret, "*Vade mecum, vade retro*: Le recours au pseudonyme dans la démarche pamphlétaire voltairienne," *La Lettre clandestine* 8 (1999): 65–82; Georges Benrekassa, "L'interlocuteur voltairien: le masque et la plume," in *Le Siècle de Voltaire: Hommage à R. Pomeau*, eds. Christiane Mervaud and Sylvain Menant (Oxford: Voltaire Foundation, 1987): vol. 1, 89–97.

12. Geneviève Lloyd, *Enlightenment Shadows* (Oxford: Oxford University Press, 2013), 45–48.

13. Rousseau, *Lettres écrites de la montagne*.

14. Michel Foucault, *The Government of Self and Others: Lectures at the Collège de France, 1982–1983*, ed. Frédéric Gros, trans. Graham Burchell (New York: Palgrave Macmillan, 2010).

15. Antoine Lilti, "Reconnaissance et célébrité: Jean-Jacques Rousseau et la politique du nom propre," *Orages, Littérature et culture* 9 (2010): 77–94.

16. Sandrier, *Le Style philosophique du baron d'Holbach*; Mark Curran, *Atheism,*

Religion and Enlightenment in Pre-Revolutionary Europe (London: Royal Historical Society, 2012).

17. Denis Diderot, *Correspondance*, vol. 6, *janvier 1766-décembre 1766*, ed. Georges Roth (Paris: Minuit, 1961): 334.

18. Denis Diderot, *Essai sur les règnes de Claude et Néron*, in *Œuvres*, vol. 1, *Philosophie*, ed. Laurent Versini (Paris: Robert Laffont, 1994): 1120.

19. Jean-Claude Bonnet, *Naissance du Panthéon: Essai sur le culte des grands hommes* (Paris: Fayard, 1998): 157–98.

20. Denis Diderot, *Mélanges pour Catherine II*, in *Œuvres*, vol. 3, 348.

21. Pascale Pellerin, "Naigeon: une certaine image de Diderot sous la Révolution," *Recherches sur Diderot et sur l'Encyclopédie* 29 (2000): 25–44. See also Pascale Pellerin, "Diderot et l'appel à la postérité: une certaine relation à l'œuvre," *Recherches sur Diderot et sur l'Encyclopédie* 35 (2003): 25–40.

22. Denis Diderot to Falconet, August 1766, in *Œuvres*, vol. 5, *Correspondance*, ed. Laurent Versini (Paris: Robert Laffont, 1997): 664 and 680; Denis Diderot, *Essai sur les règnes de Claude et de Néron.*

23. Gianluigi Goggi, *De l'Encyclopédie à l'éloquence républicaine: Étude sur Diderot et autour de Diderot* (Paris: Honoré Champion, 2013).

24. Jacques Proust, *Diderot et l'Encyclopédie* (Paris: Armand Colin, 1966): 81–116.

25. Paulin Ismard, *L'Événement Socrate* (Paris: Flammarion, 2013).

26. Denis Diderot, *Entretien d'un philosophe avec la Maréchale de* ***, *Œuvres*, vol. 1, 943.

27. Denis Diderot, "Encyclopédie," in *Encyclopédie*, vol. 5, 635–48, quote p. 643.

28. Denis Diderot, "Multitude," in *Encyclopédie*, vol. 10, 860.

29. Denis Diderot to Falconet, September 1766, in *Œuvres*, vol. 5, 679.

30. Denis Diderot to Falconet, February 1766, in *Œuvres*, vol. 5, 616: "En quoi donc, et quand est-ce que la multitude a raison? En tout; mais au bout d'un très-longtem[p]s, parce qu'alors c'est un écho qui répète le jugement d'un petit nombre d'hommes sensés qui forment d'avance celui de la postérité" ("Multitudes," art. cit.), "le peuple, mon ami, n'est à la longue que l'écho de quelques hommes de goût." From the entry for "Multitude": "About what and when is the crowd [*multitude*] right? About everything; but only at the end of a long lapse of time, because then their pronouncement has become an echo that repeats the judgment of a small number of sensible men who shape in advance the judgment of posterity [. . .] The people, my friend, are in the end but the echo of a few men of good taste."

31. Denis Diderot, *Promenades du sceptique*, in *Œuvres*, vol. 1, 74.

32. Diderot, *Mélanges pour Catherine II*, 265.

33. Denis Diderot, *Addition aux pensées philosophiques*, in *Œuvres*, vol. 1, 48: "Satis triumphat veritas si apud paucos eosque bonos accepta sit; nec ejus indoles placere multis." See Delon, *Diderot.*

34. Bertrand Binoche, *Nommer l'histoire: Parcours philosophiques* (Paris: Éditions de l'EHESS, 2018): 163–64.

35. Ariane Revel, "'Si j'étais prince ou législateur, je ne perdrai pas mon temps à dire ce qu'il faut faire . . . ,' Écriture philosophique et transformation politique en France, 1750–1780," PhD diss., Université Paris-Est Créteil, 2017.

36. Denis Diderot to Madame de Meaux, *Correspondance*, vol. 9, 112.

37. Denis Diderot, *Lettre apologétique de l'abbé Raynal à Mr Grimm*. The letter is dated March 25, 1781, with a postscript dated May 25. It was kept among the manuscripts bequeathed to Diderot's daughter and discovered by Herbert Dieckmann in the Vandeul collection. The original is at the Bibliothèque Nationale de France (Mss NAF 24932, 3–12). The text was published by Dieckmann in *Inventaire du fonds Vandeul* (Geneva: Droz, 1951), 238–53, and reprinted by Georges Roth in his edition of Diderot's *Correspondance*, vol. 15, 210–27.

38. Georges Benrekassa, "Scène politique, scène philosophique, scène privée: à propos de la *Lettre apologétique de l'abbé Raynal à Monsieur Grimm*," in *Interpréter Diderot aujourd'hui: Actes du colloque de Cerisy* (Paris: Le Sycomore, 1983): 181.

39. Stéphane Lojkine, "Diderot, l'engagement sans le nom," *Littérature classique* 80 (2013).

40. Diderot, *Lettre apologétique de l'abbé Raynal à Mr Grimm*. The same formulation, "Philosophize first and live afterwards," appeared earlier, in a 1775 letter to Necker, where Diderot reflects on the role of philosophers, and it appeared again in 1778 in the *Essai sur les règnes de Claude et de Néron*—this time with the reference to Socrates added to it.

41. This effacement corresponds to an anti-individualist tendency at work in Enlightenment thinking. See Charly Coleman, *The Virtues of Abandon: An Anti-Individualist History of the French Enlightenment* (Stanford, CA: Stanford University Press, 2014).

42. Didier Masseau, *L'Invention de l'intellectuel dans l'Europe du XVIIIe siècle* (Paris: Presses Universitaires de France, 1994).

43. Jean Starobinski, *Diderot, un diable de ramage* (Paris: Gallimard, 2012): 82.

CHAPTER 8

1. Michel Foucault, "Qu'est-ce que les Lumières?" [from the January 5, 1983, course at the Collège de France], *Magazine littéraire* 207 (1984), reprinted in *Dits et Écrits*, vol. 4, 679–88; Foucault, "What Is Enlightenment?" reprinted in a French translation and entitled "Qu'est ce que les Lumières? [What Is Enlightenment ?]," in Michel Foucault, *Dits et Écrits*, vol. 4, 562–78.

2. Foucault, *Government of the Self and Others*, 000.

3. "Comment est-il possible que ce type de compréhension affirmée d'un philosophe moderne, constamment dirigé vers notre actualité, et inscrit dans le temps présent, cadre avec la critique inflexible que Foucault fait de la modernité ? Comment peut-on faire cohabiter le fait que Foucault se comprenne comme un penseur de la tradition de l'*Aufklarüng* avec la critique indiscutable qu'il produit à l'encontre de cette forme de savoir de la modernité ?" asks Habermas in "Une flèche au cœur du temps présent" [An Arrow at the Heart of the Present Time], *Critique* 471–72 (1986): 794–99, at 797. "How can this type of affirmative understanding of a modern philosopher, as one constantly directed at our current affairs and inscribed in the present time, be compatible with the inflexible critique that Foucault levels against modernity? How can one reconcile the fact that Foucault regards himself as a thinker indebted to the Aufklärung tradition with the intransigent critique he directed at this form of knowledge about modernity?" asks Habermas in his essay, "An Arrow at the Heart of the Present Time." Habermas's text

was first published in July 1984 in the journal *Taz*—in other words, two months before Foucault's previously unknown text appeared in *Le Magazine Littéraire*.

4. Michel Foucault, *Discipline and Punish: The Birth of the Prison*, trans. Alan Sheridan (New York: Vintage Books, 1995): 222.

5. Maurice Agulhon, "Postface," in *L'Impossible Prison*, ed. Michelle Perrot (Paris: Seuil, 1980): 313–16.

6. Michel Foucault, "Postface" [1980], in Perrot, ed., *L'Impossible Prison*, 316–18, reprinted in *Dits et Écrits*, vol. 4, 35–37.

7. Michel Foucault, "Qu'est-ce que la critique?" *Bulletin de la Société française de philosophie* 84, no. 2 (1990): 35–63. A critical edition is now available: Michel Foucault, *"Qu'est-ce que la critique," suivi de "La culture de soi,"* eds. Henri-Paul Fruchaud, Daniele Lorenzini, and Arnold Davidson (Paris: Vrin, 2015). French page references are to the 1990 edition. The English-language edition is *"What Is Critique?" and "The Culture of the Self,"* eds. Henri-Paul Fruchaud, Daniele Lorenzini, and Arnold I. Davidson, trans. Clare O'Farrell (Chicago: University of Chicago Press, 2024).

8. Michel Foucault, "What Is Critique?" in *"What Is Critique?" and "The Culture of the Self,"* 36.

9. Michel Foucault, "Introduction par Michel Foucault" [1978], in *Dits et Écrits*, vol. 3, *1976–1979* (Paris: Gallimard, 1994): 429–42.

10. Bibliothèque nationale de France, NAF 28730, box 60, folder 1.

11. Foucault, "What Is Enlightenment?" 38.

12. Foucault, "What Is Enlightenment?" 42 and 45.

13. Foucault, "What Is Enlightenment?" 42.

14. Jean-François Lyotard, *La Condition postmoderne: Rapport sur le savoir* (Paris: Minuit, 1979), published in English as *The Postmodern Condition: A Report on Knowledge*, trans. Geoffrey Bennington and Brian Massumi (Minneapolis: University of Minnesota Press, 1984).

15. See, for example, Foucault's interview with Georges Raulet, "Structuralisme et poststructuralisme" [1983], in *Dits et Écrits*, vol. 4, 431–57.

16. Jürgen Habermas, "La modernité: un projet inachevé," trans. Georges Raulet, *Critique* 413 (1981): 950–67, delivered in English as "Modernity: An Incomplete Project" in 1981 and then published as "Modernity versus Postmodernity" in *New German Critique* 22 (Winter 1981) and reprinted thereafter.

17. Jürgen Habermas, *The Philosophical Discourse of Modernity*, trans. Frederick G. Lawrence (Cambridge, MA: MIT Press, 1990).

18. When the two men met in Paris for the first and only time in March 1983, Foucault proposed to Habermas the organization of a seminar on Kant's text for the following year that would include American colleagues (Jürgen Habermas, "Une flèche dans le cœur du temps present," *Critique* 471–472 [1986]: 794).

19. Céline Spector, "Des Lumières aux anti-Lumières ou l'éclipse de la Révolution: Foucault, Kant, Baudelaire," *Diderot Studies*, forthcoming.

20. Foucault, "What Is Enlightenment?" in *The Foucault Reader*, ed. Paul Rabinow (New York: Pantheon, 1984), 45.

21. Foucault, "What Is Critique?"

22. This criticism was addressed to him early on by Pierre Hadot, *Exercices spirituels et philosophie antique*, (Paris, Albin Michel, 2002), 323–32.

23. Foucault, "What Is Enlightenment?" 42.

24. Michel Foucault, *Subjectivity and Truth: Lectures at the College de France, 1980–1981*, ed. Frédéric Gros, trans. Graham Burchell (London: Palgrave Macmillan, 2017).

25. Bruno Karsenti, "Foucault et la parole de vérité des modernes," in *Usages de Foucault*, ed. Hervé Oulc'hen (Paris: Presses Universitaires de France, 2014): 319–35.

26. Pascal Engel, "Michel Foucault: connaissance, vérité et éthique," *Cahier de l'Herne* 95, *Michel Foucault* (2011): 319–26.

27. Jean Terrel, *Politiques de Foucault* (Paris: Presses Universitaires de France, 2010): 137–49.

28. Michel Foucault, "Michel Foucault: An Interview by Stephen Riggins," in *Essential Works of Foucault, 1954–1984*, vol. 1, *Ethics, Subjectivity, and Truth*, ed. Paul Rabinow (New York: The New Press, 1997), 130–31.

29. Michel Foucault, "Une interview de Michel Foucault par Stephen Riggins" [1983], *Dits et Écrits*, vol. 4, 525–38, here 535. "Pour moi, le travail intellectuel est lié à ce que vous définiriez comme une forme d'esthétisme—par cela, j'entends la transformation de soi." English translation: "For me, intellectual work is related to what you could call 'aestheticism,' meaning transforming yourself" (*Essential Works*, vol. 1, 130).

30. Foucault, "Une interview de Michel Foucault," 536: "Je ne me soucie aucunement du statut universitaire de ce que je fais, parce que mon problème est ma propre transformation. Cette transformation de soi par son propre savoir est, je crois, quelque chose d'assez proche de l'expérience esthétique. Pourquoi un peintre travaillerait-il s'il n'est pas transformé par sa peinture?" English translation: "I am not interested in the academic status of what I am doing, because my problem is my own transformation. [. . .] This transformation of one's self by one's own knowledge is, I think, something rather close to the aesthetic experience. Why should a painter work if he is not transformed by his own painting?" (*Essential Works*, vol. 1, 131).

31. Michel Foucault, *La Grande Étrangère: À propos de littérature*, eds. Philippe Artières, Jean-François Bert, Matthieu Potte-Bonneville, and Judith Revel (Paris: Éditions de l'EHESS, 2013).

32. Philippe Artières, ed., *Le Beau Danger: Entretien avec Claude Bonnefoy* (Paris: Éditions de l'EHESS, 2011): 40.

33. Michel Foucault, "Nietzsche, Genealogy, History," in *Language, Counter-Memory, Practice: Selected Essays and Interviews*, ed. D. F. Bouchard (Ithaca, NY: Cornell University Press, 1977); also in Rabinow, ed., *Foucault Reader*.

34. James Schmidt, "Misunderstanding the Question 'What Is Enlightenment?': Venturi, Habermas, and Foucault," *History of European Ideas*, 37 (2011): 43–52.

35. Franck Fischbach, "Aufklärung et modernité philosophique: Foucault entre Kant et Hegel," in *Lectures de Michel Foucault*, vol. 2, *Foucault et la philosophie*, ed. Emmanuel da Silva (Lyon: ENS Éditions, 2003): 115–34.

36. On the diagnosis of the present as an act of writing but also a physical commitment, see Philippe Artières, "Dire l'actualité: Le travail de diagnostic chez Michel Foucault," in *Foucault: Le courage de la verité*, ed. Frédéric Gros (Paris: Presses Universitaires de France, 2002): 11–34.

37. This question is one of the big objections addressed to Foucault by Axel Honneth, who contrasts him with Jürgen Habermas on this point. Honneth articulated these objections in his doctoral dissertation, completed in 1982 and published in Ger-

man in 1985: *Critique du pouvoir: Michel Foucault et l'École de Francfort, élaborations d'une théorie critique de la société*, trans. Marianne Dautrey and Olivier Voirol (Paris: La Découverte, 2016). The English edition is *The Critique of Power: Reflective Stages in a Critical Social Theory*, trans. Kenneth Baynes (Cambridge, MA: MIT Press, 1991).

38. Foucault, "What Is Enlightenment?" 46.

39. Jacques Revel, *Foucault avec Merleau-Ponty: Ontologie politique, présentisme et histoire* (Paris: Vrin, 2015).

40. Hervé Oulc'hen, "La politique de la vérité de l'intellectuel. Entre Foucault et Sartre," in Oulc'hen, ed., *Usages de Foucault*, 293–318; Gérard Noiriel, "Michel Foucault: les trois figures de l'intellectuel engagé," in *Penser avec, penser contre*: *Itinéraire d'un historien* (Paris: Belin, 2003): 229–248.

41. Behrooz Ghamari-Tabrizi, *Foucault in Iran: Islamic Revolution After the Enlightenment* (Minneapolis: University of Minnesota Press, 2016).

42. Michel Foucault, "Inutile de se soulever?" [1979], in *Dits et Écrits*, vol. 3, 790–94.

43. See Frédéric Gros, "Foucault et la leçon kantienne des Lumières," *Lumières* 8 (2007): 159–67.

44. Didier Eribon, *Michel Foucault*, new and expanded edition (Paris: Flammarion, 2011): 407–16, 476–98. The work was first published in 1989 by Gallimard and translated into English as *Michel Foucault*, trans. Betsy Wing (Cambridge, MA: Harvard University Press, 1991).

45. Translator's note: This falling out of love with communism was belated in France—compared to the US of course where Hannah Arendt's takedown of totalitarianism had fueled anticommunism since the 1950s—because the PCF (Parti communiste français) retained a lot of power (due to union labor support in the workplace and at the polls) until the mid-80s.

46. Michel Foucault, *Le Gouvernement de soi et des autres*, vol. 2, *Le Courage de la verité: Cours au Collège de France 1983–1984* (Paris: Éditions de l'EHESS-Gallimard-Seuil, 2009): 166; *The Courage of Truth*: *The Government of Self and Others II; Lectures at the Collège de France, 1983–1984*, ed. Frédéric Gros, trans. Graham Burchell (New York: Palgrave Macmillan, 2012).

47. Michel Foucault, *Le Gouvernement de soi et des autres*, vol. 1, *Cours au Collège de France 1982–1983* (Paris: Éditions de l'EHESS-Gallimard-Seuil, 2008), 322: "En tout cas, si j'ai commencé le cours de cette année par Kant, c'est dans la mesure où il me semble que ce texte sur l'*Aufklärung* écrit par Kant est une certaine manière, pour la philosophie, de prendre conscience, à travers la critique de l'*Aufklärung*, des problèmes qui étaient traditionnellement dans l'Antiquité ceux de la *parrêsia*, et qui vont réémerger ainsi au cours du XVIe et [du] XVIIe siècle, et qui ont pris conscience d'eux-mêmes dans l'*Aufklärung*, et particulièrement dans ce texte de Kant." [In any case, if I began this year's course with Kant, it is because I feel that the text on *Aufklärung* written by Kant is a way for philosophy to become aware—through a critique of *Aufklärung*—of problems that were traditionally, in antiquity, those of *parrêsia*, and that reemerged in the sixteenth and seventeenth century and became openly recognized during the Aufklärung, and in particular in Kant's text.] *Government of the Self and Others*, 350.

48. Michel Foucault, *Le Gouvernement de soi et des autres*, vol. 2, 262; *Courage of Truth*, 285.

49. Michel Foucault, "Le souci de verité" [1984], in *Dits et Écrits*, vol. 4, 668–78, at 675.

50. See the testimony of Paul Veyne, *Foucault: His Thought, His Character* (Cambridge: Polity Press, 2010).

51. Foucault, "What Is Enlightenment?" 35.

52. Foucault, "What Is Enlightenment?" 41.

53. Étienne Balibar, "Dire, contredire: sur les formes de la *parrêsia* selon Foucault," in *Libre parole* (Paris: Galilée, 2018): 81–120, especially 117–19.

54. Foucault, *Le Gouvernement de soi et des autres*, vol. 2, 67–143.

55. Louise Shea, *The Cynic Enlightenment: Diogenes in the Salon* (Baltimore, MD: Johns Hopkins University Press, 2010). On the case of Rousseau, a new Diogenes confronting the mediatization of the philosophical life, see Lilti, *Invention of Celebrity*, especially 157–58.

56. See, for example, his anonymous interview, "le philosophe masqué," published in *Le Monde* on April 6, 1980. See also Franck Olivar, "PHILO—Michel Foucault tombe le masque (ou presque)," May 15, 2020, *Radio France*, https://www.radiofrance.fr/franceinter/philo-michel-foucault-tombe-le-masque-ou-presque-2963798.

57. In the 1983 course, Foucault expresses his incomprehension regarding what he considers to be Kant's lack of political daring when the German philosopher, after having defended *Aufklärung* as an overcoming of a state of dependency [*Unmündigkeit*] thanks to the courage to think, concludes with praise for Frederick II and recommends obedience to the ruling power with the formula, "Argue as much as you like and about whatever you like, but obey!" This dramatic final gesture appears to Foucault as a contradiction "putting into question the entire analysis," something that Kant cannot extricate himself from in 1798 except by attributing to revolutionary enthusiasm the role that obedience to Frederick II had played in 1784.

58. Vincent Descombes perfectly identified this blind spot, this absence of a sociological definition of the "we" that the Foucauldian critique addresses. See Vincent Descombes, "Une question de chronologie," *Le Raisonnement de l'ours et autres essais de philosophie pratique* (Paris: Seuil, 2007): 155–95 ; and "Quand la mauvaise critique chasse la bonne," *Tracés* 8 (2008): 45–69.

59. Michel Foucault, "Introduction par Michel Foucault" [1978], in *Dits et écrits*, vol. 3, 429–42, at 433 ; and "La vie: l'expérience et la science" [1985], in *Dits et écrits*, vol. 4, 763–76, at 768.

60. David A. Hollinger, "The Enlightenment and the Genealogy of Cultural Conflict in the United States," in Baker and Reill, eds., *What's Left of Enlightenment?* 7–18.

61. Foucault, "Postface."

62. Foucault, "Postface," 37.

INDEX